# Plug-in to After Effects

# Plug-in to After Effects
## Third Party Plug-in Mastery

Michele Yamazaki

ELSEVIER

AMSTERDAM • BOSTON • HEIDELBERG • LONDON • NEW YORK • OXFORD
PARIS • SAN DIEGO • SAN FRANCISCO • SINGAPORE • SYDNEY • TOKYO

Focal Press is an imprint of Elsevier

Focal Press is an imprint of Elsevier
225 Wyman Street, Waltham, MA 02451, USA
The Boulevard, Langford Lane, Kidlington, Oxford, OX5 1GB, UK

**Notices**
Knowledge and best practice in this field are constantly changing. As new research and experience broaden
our understanding, changes in research methods, professional practices, or medical treatment may become
necessary.

Practitioners and researchers must always rely on their own experience and knowledge in evaluating and using
any information, methods, compounds, or experiments described herein. In using such information or methods
they should be mindful of their own safety and the safety of others, including parties for whom they have a
professional responsibility.

To the fullest extent of the law, neither the Publisher nor the authors, contributors, or editors, assume any liability
for any injury and/or damage to persons or property as a matter of products liability, negligence or otherwise, or
from any use or operation of any methods, products, instructions, or ideas contained in the material herein.

**Library of Congress Cataloging-in-Publication Data**
Application submitted

**British Library Cataloguing-in-Publication Data**
A catalogue record for this book is available from the British Library.

ISBN: 978-0-240-81565-7

For information on all Focal Press publications
visit our website at *www.elsevierdirect.com*

Printed in the United States of America
11  12  13  14  15   5  4  3  2  1

*Typeset by*: diacriTech, Chennai, India

# CONTENTS

# Contributors

I'd like to thank all of the pros in the industry, that so graciously spent their time and energy helping me produce content for this book and DVD. Thank you from the bottom of my heart!

—Michele Yamazaki

(Contributor bios and headshots are on the DVD included in this book).

| | | |
|---|---|---|
| David Torno | Dustin Klein | Matt Silverman |
| Rob Birnholz | Dru Nget | Eran Stern |
| Dr. Sassi | Alicia VanHeulen | Zax Dow |
| Joe Mason | Peder Norrby/Rymden Music | Lutz Albrecht |
| Joe Mercier | Wes Plate | Jerzy Drozda, jr. |
| Jeremy Hanke | Mark Eaton | Ryan 'Presto' Snider |
| Jason James | Andrew Embury | Jason Sharp |
| Atilla Bokor | Harry Frank | |

## About the Author

Michele Yamazaki is VP marketing and Web Development Czarina for Toolfarm (*www.toolfarm .com*), a value-added reseller and distributor of visual effects software. She co-authored *Greenscreen Made Easy: Keying and Compositing Techniques for Indie Filmmakers* with Jeremy Hanke, published in 2009 by MWP, and was a contributing author to *After Effects @ Work*, edited by Richard Harrington, published by CMP in 2006.

Michele began her career at Postworks in Grand Rapids, Michigan, where she worked as a motion graphics artist for 10 years. She has previously taught After Effects and Photoshop at Kendall College of Art and Design. In 2001 she launched AEFreemart.com and in 2002 she and Matt Schirado cofounded West Michigan Animation and Effects User Group. She is past-president of Media Communications Association International Mid Michigan and a former board member of West Michigan Film and Video Alliance.

# Acknowledgments

Thank you to **Chris and Trish Meyer**, my technical editors. Your knowledge of After Effects and your willingness to share your expertise and give honest feedback really helped make this book something special.

A special thank you to my fellow **Toolfarmers, Colin, Jason and Alicia**. Thank you for the wonderful foreword, Jason, and your introductions to chapters! Thanks to **Alicia VanHeulen** for keeping things running smoothly at Toolfarm and for contributing to book content.

Thank you to **Mathew Schirado**, proofreader extraordinaire, and to Brandon Smith for help with the DVD. Lastly, thank you to my daughter **Lillian Yamazaki**, actress and model for much of the footage in the book.

# Foreword

Figure 1 Painterly effects applied to footage. Footage: Michele Yamazaki.

I used to think plug-ins were for people who could afford to buy creativity. Then I realized it was for those who had creativity, but were burdened and held back by the process, or lack of tools, for their creativity. After Effects plug-ins are not someone's project files or templates for you to copy, but rather tools for accentuating your existing talents. After Effects users are artists, the host application being their scaffolding, and plug-ins being their palette of paints. The artist, in the end, is the one that creates the masterpiece.

The world of video creation over all mediums has been a fast-evolving industry, especially in the last decade, and After Effects has been at the cutting edge of it all. From movie trailers, to music videos, commercials, and even my own wedding video, visual effects have defined the modern "look" in video. This all stems from artists expressing themselves, and never being satisfied with the current standard. This came clear to me the first time I met Michele Yamazaki. Michele was running an After Effects portal called AEFreemart, which subsequently became an affiliate partner of Toolfarm. I was just taking over Toolfarm after serving several years in the industry working on video compression for plug-in companies. She called me initially to inquire about some paperwork. Before I was able to find it, she quickly jumped into exchanges such as, "Hey, didn't you hear Trapcode came out with Starglow! How come it's not on your site?!" or, "You really need more video introductions to show off Boris Continuum Complete, you really aren't doing it justice with just text." Each time she would call, she excitedly taught me more about my own business, and the real reason After Effects users became customers of plug-ins. It was, of course, not a hard decision to ask her to join Toolfarm.

Over the last decade, as the After Effects plug-ins industry has grown, certain plug-ins have become more popular than others. Why is this? Are they more widely used across shared projects, therefore being needed to open a previous project; or just so useful, that anyone using After Effects cannot do without them? It could be argued that the popularity of a plug-in arises because certain developers have more resources to create demand, or that others have the good business sense of being able to piggyback on Adobe with OEM bundle deals, or even a smart marketing sense to advertise their use in big-budget films. In the end, it always comes down to providing a solid plug-in that gets the job done, and opens up the artist's path to creativity. After Effects users are understandably excited about the tools that allow them the freedom to express themselves. Word of mouth will always be the strongest marketing tool in the plug-in industry, which is the reason why it is not dominated by large conglomerates, but rather populated by genuine artists. Plugging into After Effects is one of the most comprehensive openings into the world of plug-in creativity.

Jason Sharp
President,
Toolfarm.com, Inc.

# INTRODUCTION TO PLUG-INS

This book focuses on the hundreds of plug-ins, filters, and effects for Adobe After Effects, a topic near and dear to my heart. The variety and sheer number of plug-ins available can be overwhelming, especially to artists new to the software. Some effects try to recreate reality, while others produce bold graphics and eye candy. Some merely exist to make workflow smoother and others to fix video predicaments. Many exist in massive bundles of 200 or more, making it difficult to single out the features of a single plug-in in the package. Others are single plug-ins created by a lone developer, and live in obscurity, even when they're extremely useful tools.

How does one navigate through this gargantuan list of choices? At Toolfarm, I helped build the Plug-in Finder, a massive database of video plug-ins for After Effects and other host apps. This database has been a great resource to the book, linking to tutorials, samples, reviews, and more. The Plug-in Finder has been marketed as "doing the legwork for you" with everything in one place. With this book my aim is to take it a step further. I show you how to use the plug-ins (with the help of several generous contributors) and give you hot tips on how to speed up your workflow with unique samples not on the developer's sites and tips not otherwise found on the web. Consider this book a tool to help you decide which plug-in is the best choice for the job, because quite often there are multiple choices for the same type of effect.

## What Is a Plug-in?

A plug-in is a mini-application that "plugs into" or expands a host application (like After Effects), allowing it to do more. When trying to explain this to a friend who does not work in postproduction, he came up with a car analogy. You can buy a basic model of a car and upgrade it with an aftermarket exhaust system with dual tailpipes, a GPS, power windows, nice rims, a higher quality sound system… even fancy wiper blades and all-weather radials. You can detail the car with pinstripes and bumper stickers and cut a sunroof in the top. Adding a remote car starter and airbrushed flames are the equivalent of adding a better keyer and a particle system to After Effects! You're making improvements and expanding the usage of an already great product.

## Why You Need Third-Party Plug-ins

Sure, you do get loads of great plug-ins with After Effects but try building an incredible lens flare like you can in **Video Copilot's Optical Flares** with the plug-ins that ship with After Effects. You cannot even come close to the speed, complexity, flexibility, and beauty that the plug-in provides. How about removing a moving element from your shot? You could roto-scope it and manually paint the background in, but how long would that take you? With **Boris Continuum Motion Key**, you can do it in minutes. How about particles? **Adobe's Particle Playground**, let's be honest, is pretty lame. It can't compare to the awesome power of **Trapcode Particular** or the ease of use of **Wondertouch particleIllusion** by **GenArts**. Your time is valuable. If you are able to save two hours with a $299 plug-in that you can use over and over on different projects, isn't it worth every penny? Plug-ins will save you time, money, and, quite often, your sanity. This book showcases the best of the best: unique, time saving, useful effects that you won't be able to work without.

The director, cinematographer, and screenwriter Anthony E. Griffin summed it up nicely "What is your personal time worth? If you think about it from that perspective, the software is not a crutch, but is a tool to get the work done in a time frame. And if you have a strong story, it can be supplemented by tools to make it more stylish."

### Criteria for Choosing What Plug-ins to Include in the Book

It wasn't always an easy choice of what to include. Some plug-ins complete the same task just as well as another, so I have comparisons sprinkled throughout the book. I chose to include the plug-ins that I consider to be the workhorses; plug-ins that I keep coming back to time and time again. I picked plug-ins for their render speed and that have more options than similar effects that ship with After Effects. I chose plug-ins that are unique—a one-of-a-kind effect that no other company has been able to recreate. I also chose to focus on plug-ins with the capability of creating a wide variety of looks, not just a one-trick pony. Lastly, I chose to include effects that I find interesting or help speed up workflow.

It should be noted that all plug-ins discussed in this book were given to me by developers of the software. I'd like to thank these vendors and Toolfarm for their generosity in helping me to obtain licenses for all of the plug-ins that I needed.

## Big Suites versus Single Plug-ins

This question comes up a lot at Toolfarm: "Should I buy a big suite of plug-ins like **Boris Continuum Complete** or **Trapcode Suite** or just buy a single plug-in?" This is not easily answered and will depend on your needs and your budget. Sometimes you may only need a single-purpose plug-in and that will be completely sufficient. Although some plug-ins come à la carte, it often makes sense to purchase a suite. If you don't own many plug-ins, you will instantly have a wide and useful variety at your fingertips. As most of the big bundles go, there will be a few standout, unique effects and many others that are similar to the plug-ins that ship with After Effects, such as blurs, noise removal, and glows. The similar effects will often be faster, offer more parameters, or make up for a shortcoming in the AE plug-ins.

If you don't own many third-party filters and would like to get started with some basics, **Boris Continuum Complete**, **GenArts Sapphire**, **Noise Industries FxFactory Pro**, **Trapcode Suite**, and **Red Giant Magic Bullet Suite** are all good places to start. All of these packages have a broad spectrum of effects, including generators, glows, blurs, titling effects, and particles that can be used over and over on multiple projects.

### Boris Continuum Complete

If you're looking for a good mix of well-designed plug-ins that help you automate a lot of the work in After Effects, look no further than **Boris Continuum Complete**, also known as

**Figure 1.1** Example of some Boris Continuum Complete plug-ins. This sample shows BCC 3D Layer Deformer, BCC 3D Extruded Text, and BCC Extruded Shatter (applied to a precomp with BCC Veined Marble, BCC Mosaic, and BCC LED). Footage: Michele Yamazaki.

BCC ($995). BCC ships with over 200 plug-ins and 2400 presets. The plug-ins use Optical Flow pixel processing, OpenGL acceleration, and offer deep color support. Many plug-ins in Continuum Complete come with a built-in motion tracker and a Pixel Chooser, which allows you to isolate certain channels, colors, or areas of video, without jumping to another tool.

A few standout plug-ins in the set are:

- **BCC Lens Flare Adv**—a robust lens flare generator
- **BCC Uprez**—upscales footage from SD to HD while maintaining high quality
- **BCC Motion Key**—quickly removes a moving element from a shot without rotoscoping
- **BCC 3D Objects**—an incredibly powerful way to create full 3D text, logos, and shapes within the After Effects interface; the BCC 3D Objects alone are worth the price of the suite

**Figure 1.2**

## GenArts Sapphire and GenArts Monsters

**GenArts Sapphire** ($1699), a suite that has been used on many major motion pictures including *X-Men Origins: Wolverine*, *The Curious Case of Benjamin Button*, *Iron Man 2*, J.J. Abram's *Star Trek*, and *Avatar*, is one of the most expensive suites on the After Effects market, and is highly coveted. Originally broken into four packages, it now combines over 220 effects. With the Sapphire v5 release, GenArts introduced new effects such as **TV Damage, Swish 3D**, and **Lens Flare Transition**.

**Figure 1.3** GenArts Monsters used on a skyline of New York City. The sky replacement is done with M_Night Sky and is enhanced with an oversized moon, created with M_Luna. M_Paint effect creates an oil painting from video or stills. Footage: Michele Yamazaki.

Sapphire supports 64-bit OS and 32-bit color support, uses full floating-point for all internal processing, and most of the plug-ins are OpenGL accelerated, so they're fast, while flexible and very stable. Sapphire's downside is that it's pricey.

**GenArts Monsters GT** ($999), acquired by GenArts from SpeedSix, includes generators, distortion and warping effects, blurs, and the usual mix of effects. What sets Monsters apart is its unusual generators. **M_Luna** renders a beautiful moon with the option to program in the exact date or moon phase. **M_Night Sky** renders a night sky with a pulldown menu of locations around the globe so that the geography of the sky is accurate. **M_Paint** generates the look of beautiful watercolor and oil paintings, pastels, and chalk pencil drawings.

In 2010 GenArts and The Foundry created a strategic alliance. GenArts acquired Tinder and Tinderbox from The Foundry and have combined the four individual Tinderboxes into a single product named **GenArts Tinder** ($2000). Tinder contains over 70 After Effects and Autodesk Combustion compatible plug-ins. At this time, GenArts says it has no plans to combine Tinder with Sapphire or Monsters.

G E N A R T S

Figure 1.4

## Noise Industries FxFactory Pro

**Noise Industries' FxFactory Pro** ($399) has over 150 GPU accelerated transitions, filters, and generators, and more plug-ins are released all of the time. FxFactory seems like it's always

**Figure 1.5** Noise Industries' FxFactory Pro example showing Cube, Dots Pattern, Advanced Blur (Box Shaped), Light Streaks, Stars, Glow Edges, and Emboss Text.
Footage: Michigan Film Reel.

Figure 1.6

being updated. Many filters have built-in masks and numerous presets.

FxFactory is an interesting product because it's not just one company's plug-ins. With FxFactory Pro, plug-ins can be created by anyone, so numerous "fourth party" plug-in developers have popped up (using the FxFactory engine) and created all sorts of interesting effects. A few that I particularly like are **idustrial revolution Volumetrix** and **SupaWipe**, and **Dashwood Stereo3D Toolbox**. FxFactory's software engine is also free so you can download and run loads of free plug-ins and try out the others.

FxFactory Pro is Mac only and a single license will work in After Effects, Apple's Final Cut Pro, and Motion on a single machine.

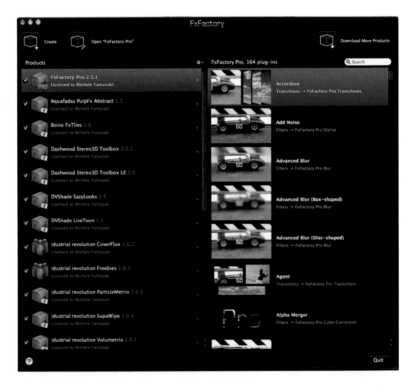

**Figure 1.7** The FxFactory app manages all plug-ins that use the FxFactory engine.
Screenshot: Michele Yamazaki.

## Trapcode Suite

**Trapcode Suite** ($899), distributed by Red Giant Software, is a favorite among After Effects artists. Trapcode plug-ins are exceedingly well-designed, and effects such as **Trapcode Particular** and **3D Stroke** are rarely matched by any other plug-ins on the market. Not only are the Trapcode products cool, they also

Figure 1.8  Trapcode Suite sample using Trapcode Form and Trapcode Starglow. Footage: Michele Yamazaki.

render fast and can be used to create thousands of different looks on a wide variety of projects.

Trapcode Suite includes all nine Trapcode plug-ins, including the highly coveted **Particular, Form, 3D Stroke, Shine, Starglow, Lux, Sound Keys, Echospace**, and **Horizon**. All plug-ins can be purchased as single products, but the full suite is worth every penny.

## Red Giant Magic Bullet Suite

**Red Giant Magic Bullet Suite** ($799) is mainly known for **Magic Bullet Looks** and **Magic Bullet Colorista II**, both developed by

Figure 1.9

Figure 1.10  Red Giant Magic Bullet Suite sample using Magic Bullet Looks and Magic Bullet Misfire. Footage: Michigan Film Reel.

Figure 1.11

"DV Rebel" Stu Maschwitz. Magic Bullet Looks allows the user to set the mood of the video with over 100 built-in presets—essentially one-touch color grading. Magic Bullet Colorista II is a 3-wheel color correction tool, unmatched for combining power and approachability. **Magic Bullet Mojo** is another color correction tool that is extremely easy to use and created for the look of action films. The suite also includes **Magic Bullet Frames**, designed for de-interlacing and high-quality conversion of 60i materials to 24p. **Magic Bullet Instant HD** is used to scale up video. Version 10 includes **Magic Bullet Denoiser**, **Magic Bullet PhotoLooks**, and **Magic Bullet Grinder**. I'll go into some of the Magic Bullet plug-ins in depth in this book.

## Digieffects Delirium

**Digieffects Delirium** ($299), the flagship product of the company, was one of the first plug-ins available for After Effects. In October 2010 Delirium v2 was released and was the first major update to the software since 1999! It contains 45 plug-ins, including natural forces (**DE Fog Factory**, **DE Fire**, **DE Snowstorm**), special effects (**DE Fairy Dust**, **DE Fireworks**, **DE Muzzle Flash**), and color and stylize filters (**DE Newsprint**, **DE Vangoughist**, **DE Solarize**). Walker Effects, acquired by Digieffects a couple of years ago, has been integrated into Delirium v2 too.

**Figure 1.12** Digieffects' Delirium v2 sample using DE VisualHarmonizer, DE MultiGradient and DE WaveDisplace. Footage: Crowd Control, clip # 00182_001_138.

Several Delirium plug-ins AutoAnimate™ too, meaning that there is no need to set keyframes for a parameter to animate. This new version has many speed optimizations, is 64-bit compatible, 32-bit per channel, and includes many new textures, presets, and project files.

Digieffects has started releasing single Delirium plug-ins à la carte for $49 each, including DE Lightwrap, DE Hyper Harmonizer, and DE Glow. The company also released several à la carte plug-ins for its other packages, **Digieffects Buena Depth Cue** and **Digieffects Damage**.

## RE:Vision Effects Effections Bundle

**RE:Vision Effects Effections Bundle** ($899, $1199 for the Plus version) contains a couple of plug-ins that no AE artist should be without: **Twixtor Pro** and **ReelSmart Motion Blur**. Twixtor Pro allows you to speed up or slow down footage and image sequences, rebuilding the in-between frames. ReelSmart Motion Blur adds realistic motion blur to video; not to the entire frame, but focusing on the action. This is great for footage shot with a high shutter speed and is great for compositing sharp, pristine 3D animation and giving it some organic-looking motion blur. Yes, After Effects can handle time remapping, frame blending, and motion blur (with a nice trick with Timewarp—see Chapter 3's Pro Tip on page 58 for more on that), but RE:Vision Effects plug-ins do it better and faster.

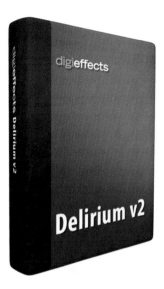

Figure 1.13

Figure 1.14 RE:Vision Effects sample showing Video Gogh. Footage: Michele Yamazaki.

Effections contains 11 plug-ins: the two mentioned above plus **Re:Map, DE:Noise, FieldsKit, RE:Fill, PV Feather, Video Gogh, RE:Flex, Shade/Shape**, and **SmoothKit**.

## Tiffen Dfx Digital Filter Suite

Tiffen is a leading manufacturer of filters, specialized lenses, and optical equipment for still and video cameras and is known for its special-effects filters. **Tiffen Dfx Filter Suite** ($599) mimics and

Figure 1.15

**Figure 1.16** Tiffen Dfx Filters sample using Three Strip, Polarizer, Bronze Gimmerglass, and Vignette. Footage: Michele Yamazaki.

simulates its camera lenses, gels, and filters. The package ships with 110 filters with thousands of presets including presets for Gobo shadows, diffusion filters, and Rosco and GamColor Gel libraries. Tiffen acquired Digital Film Tools' 55mm in 2008 and added its plug-ins to the Dfx Filter Suite.

It really makes sense for cinematographers to use plug-ins like these to treat the footage in post for added flexibility. According to reviews, the filters do not exactly match their traditional filters, but come close. The effects can be very subtle and really enhance the color and look of video with one click.

There is more on Tiffen Dfx Filters in Chapter 2, "Color Correction and Color Effects."

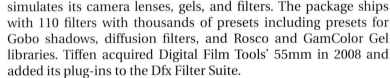

**Figure 1.17**

## CoreMelt Complete

**CoreMelt Complete** ($399) is a unique Mac-only package of plug-ins for After Effects and Final Cut Studio. One license will run in both host applications on a single machine. It includes **ImageFlow Fx**, a fantastic tool for automating photo and video montages. It's extremely fast and ships with a lot of presets

**Figure 1.18** CoreMelt Complete sample using ImageFlow Fx and C2 Shatter 3D Text Cloud. Footage: Michele Yamazaki.

and prebuilt mattes. **PolyChrome Transitions V2 TRX** and **Poly-Chrome Transitions V2 Delta V** are sets of cool transitions. There are also glow tools, editing tools, color tools, and shatter effects. All CoreMelt plug-ins are GPU accelerated and well-designed tools.

## The Foundry's Plug-ins

Although The Foundry no longer has a large bundle like Tinderbox, I didn't want to neglect to mention them as a leader in the field of After Effects plug-ins. You probably know The Foundry from its fantastic keyer, Keylight, but it also has newer GPU-accelerated plug-ins for tracking, motion blur, and more.

Figure 1.19

Figure 1.20 Text matchmoved with The Foundry CameraTracker. Footage: Michele Yamazaki.

**CameraTracker** ($280 node-locked, $420 floating) allows users to handle complicated matchmoves and 3D motion tracks within After Effects using 3D motion tracking technology developed for The Foundry's NukeX. **RollingShutter** ($500 node-locked, $740 floating) handles problems with skewed or wobbly footage from DSLR cameras. **Kronos** ($170 node-locked, $120 floating) uses Optical flow motion estimation for superior time remapping and motion blurring footage.

Figure 1.21

# Timeline of After Effects Plug-ins

January 1993 - CoSA After Effects launched
1995 - Boris Effects founded
1996 - Cycore & DigiEffects start the Plug-in Revolution
1996 - GenArts founded
May 1997 - First Windows version of After Effects launched
April 1998 - Artel Software releases Boris FX
1999 - Toolfarm.com launched in San Francisco, CA
February 2000 - Zaxwerks releases 3D Invigorator for After Effects
April 2000 - Maya Paint Effects Plug-in released For Adobe After Effects 4.1
2000 - Stu Maschwitz creates the Magic Bullet Suite
March 2001 - Pluginz.com launches
April 2001 - Creative Cow goes online
July 2000 - Boris Red announced
September 2000 - Apple releases OS X
October 2000 - AE Freemart launches
November 2000 - RE:Vision Effects Twixtor plug-in for After Effects released
April 2001 - AE 5.0 released, Atomic Power plug-ins included
July 2001 - Trapcode releases Shine
August 2001 - The Foundry ships Tinderbox for After Effects
December 2001 - Magic Bullet for After Effects ships
Jan 2002 - AE 5.5 released, Zaxwerks 3D Invigorator Classic bundled
2002 - Red Giant Software founded
May 2004 - Trapcode Particular released
June 2004 - AE 6.5 released, includes Boris Final Effects Complete, Grain Surgery & Color Finesse
July 2005 - VideoCopilot.net goes online
November 2006 - Noise Industries releases FxFactory for FCP
July 2007 - AE CS3 released, first Mac Universal Binary version of AE
Sept 2008 - AE CS4 launched, Imagineer mocha bundled
February 2009 - Toolfarm acquired the assets of Pluginz.com
January 2010 - Video Copilot releases Optical Flares
April 2010 - AE CS5 released, Synthetic Aperture Color Finesse 3, Digieffects FreeForm bundled
April 2010 - GenArts acquires Tinderbox from The Foundry
May 2011 - AE CS5.5 released

**Figure 1.22** The timeline of After Effects. Infographic: Michele Yamazaki (created using Yanobox Nodes).

## ADOBE PIXEL BENDER PLUG-INS

The Adobe Pixel Bender scripting language was introduced in CS4 and allows developers to create effects for After Effects, Flash, and Photoshop. The Pixel Bender software development toolkit is an image and video processing framework and is said to be less complicated than programming C or C++, which is what After Effects plug-ins are normally compiled in. The plug-ins use the multiple processor cores, and developers can share extensions between supported applications. The Pixel Bender Toolkit is free and runs on Mac or Windows.

**To install Pixel Bender plug-ins:** The Pixel Bender extension on a plug-in is .pbk (single-kernel effects) or .pbg (multiple-kernel effects). Place the .pbk file in the plug-ins folder for After Effects like you would other plug-ins.

- (Windows) Program Files\Adobe\Adobe After Effects CS5\Support Files
- (Mac OS) Applications/Adobe After Effects CS5

**Web Link:** Visit *www. pluginz.com/ pixelbender* for a current list of Pixel Bender plug-ins and resources for the development of the plug-ins.

**Figure 1.23** Mandelbulb (top) and Droste, Pixel Bender plug-ins. Footage: Crowd Control, clip # 00154_002_35.

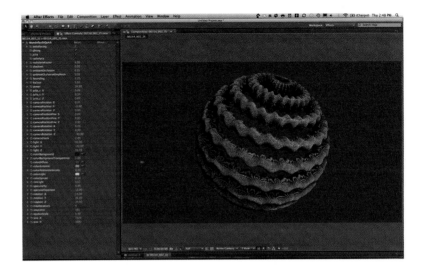

**Figure 1.24** Mandelbulb user interface. Footage: Michele Yamazaki.

## FURTHER READING: INTERESTED IN CREATING YOUR OWN PIXEL BENDER PLUG-INS?

Jerzy Drozda, who has been developing Pixel Bender plug-ins since the technology first became available, has written an in-depth tutorial on the creation of Pixel Bender plug-ins. It is included on the DVD in the back of this book.

## About the DVD

Most of the tutorials in this book have associated project files included on the accompanying DVD, including source footage, unless otherwise noted. You are encouraged to play along by creating each project from scratch with included footage and using the included project files as reference.

- **Project files** are organized in folders named by chapter number, and are mentioned in each section. Projects were created with **After Effects CS5, in 8bpc** (unless otherwise noted) and are in their finished state.
- **Copy the project files to your hard drive** instead of running them from the DVD. *You will get an error* if you save projects to your computer and change the linking structure of footage files. To realign files that have broken links, follow these instructions: http://bit.ly/AErelink
- **Most Plug-ins** used in tutorials in this book have demo versions available from the vendor's website or from Toolfarm.com. Demo versions are <u>not</u> included on the DVD, as they are updated so often. *You will get an error* when

opening a project file if you do not have a demo or licensed plug-in installed.

- **Video Format** Most projects for the book are created at HDTV 1080p 29.97 with the MP4 formatted video files. If you are on Windows and having issues with any of the video files on this DVD, try downloading CCCP Project at http://bit.ly/WinCodec. "The Combined Community Codec Pack is a simple playback pack for Windows with the goal of supporting the majority of video formats in use today."
- **Slowness** To see the detail, RAM Preview the comp at full resolution. If your computer can't handle it, export a RAM Preview by going to Composition > Save RAM Preview.
- **Fonts** Some of the fonts used are not standard (Buffied, Chinese Rocks), but can be downloaded for free from www .DaFont.com. Other fonts used in the book are standard system fonts such as Arial. If you don't have the specific font on your computer *you will get an error message*, but feel free to substitute any font that you like.
- **FAQ** The last chapter of this book is an FAQ (Frequently Asked Questions) about plug-ins and will answer many questions regarding installation, moving plug-ins, and how to contact support.
- **Support** There is a support site for the book at *www.pluginz .com*, which has updates, samples, and more.

I should also mention that the terms *effect* and *filter* are used almost interchangeably in this book, referring to plug-ins that alter the look of footage. Workflow plug-ins, for example, do not affect the look of video, so would not be called filters or effects, just plug-ins.

Also note that there are many videos and files referenced from Crowd Control that are made available on this book's DVD. It is unfortunate that Crowd Control was discontinued in March 2011, just before this book went to print, but who knows what the future will hold for Crowd Control.

**Figure 1.25** If you see the little yellow yield sign next to a plug-in in the Effect Controls panel, it means that your Depth is set to 16bpc but the plug-in only works in 8bpc. To remove the error, go to File > Project Settings. Under Color Settings, set Depth to 8bpc.

# COLOR CORRECTION AND COLOR EFFECTS

Color correction, also known as color grading, can really take your video footage to the next level. Color sets the tone, the mood, and an overall feel that gives your video the professional look to draw in your audience. The term color grading is most often used when referring to color correction using specialized equipment such as Blackmagic Designs' DaVinci at a postproduction house.

We all know color has a great impact on our perception and mood. If a red car drives by, we're quick to assume it's a fast car. A room painted blue will seem more calming that a yellow room, which will tend to seem more bright and cheery. This is the very same reason producers in TV and film lean toward specific colors to create specific moods. There's no doubt about the color themes represented in *The Matrix*, which gave a very sci-fi feel with its green tones, and *CSI:Miami* with a very red, hot tropical climate theme, as well as the movie *Twilight* showing its dark and mysterious side in its prevalent blue tones. These were all intentional choices, and all done with color correction.

Color can also be used as an effect in other ways. Adding color to an existing black and white movie, such as in the treatment applied in films such as *Pleasantville* or *Sin City*, can give a dramatic affect. Adjusting color to simulate night vision is another effect, used to great effect in movies such as *The Terminator* or *Predator*. Whatever the genre, or mood you are looking for, After Effects and the plug-ins discussed in this chapter can achieve those desired results.

This chapter begins with an interview with Eric Escobar, a man considered an expert in color grading. Then, we'll go on a tour of the 3-way color correctors for After Effects, including some tutorials that explain a few useful techniques. We take a look at one of my favorite plug-ins, Red Giant Magic Bullet Looks, useful for creating a "look" for your footage. I'll showcase a few color effects such as bleach bypass and day for night, and we conclude with a section on working with skin tones and fixing problems related to skin.

## AN INTERVIEW WITH ERIC ESCOBAR ABOUT COLOR GRADING

**By Andrew Embury**

**Figure 2.1** Eric Escobar.
Footage credit: Marc Virata.

Eric Escobar's first fiction short film, *Night Light*, was screened at the 2003 Sundance Film Festival. In 2005, Eric's short film, *One Weekend a Month* received an Honorable Mention from the Sundance Grand Jury. His feature-length screenplay, *An Army of One*, was included in the FIND 2007 Director's Lab and was selected as a finalist for the 2006 Sundance Screenwriter's Lab. In addition to making movies, Eric was part of the Final Cut Pro development team at Apple, Inc. Eric currently lives in Oakland and works in San Francisco as a commercial director at Kontent Films. Check out his blog at prepshootpost.blogspot.com.

**Andrew Embury: Can you talk a bit about color grading?**

**Eric Escobar:** Color grading is equal parts technical and artistic. It's like editing in that way. It's really a new art available to a whole new generation of practitioners on an incredibly broad scale, hence the explosion of plug-ins, self-help websites, and conflicting opinions from experts.

It's not really that difficult to understand, but can take years to master and develop a personal style. Stu Maschwitz's strategy of choosing a hero shot, applying a grade, and then building his color from there is a pretty standard, and a thoroughly logical way to start. (Stu Maschwitz is a filmmaker/director, product manager of Red Giant Magic Bullet and author of *The DV Rebel's Guide: An All-Digital Approach to Making Killer Action Movies on the Cheap.* He also cofounded the Orphanage and runs a great blog at prolost.com.)

Generally, a color grade on a shot is done in three or four steps:

1. **Primary correction:** Set white point, black point, gain level, lift level, gamma level
2. **Secondary correction:** Skin tones
3. **Further Secondary correction:** Other elements (change production design by recoloring walls, etc.)
4. **Apply a final look:** Applied to all shots in the scene

While there are objective ways to measure your skill, can you get the color temperature consistent across all shots in a scene? Can you match lift/gamma/gain, and so on? A lot of color grading is subjective and a collaborative process between the director and the colorist (and often the DP, too).

**Andrew: Do you have any tips or workflow that you generally follow? What pitfalls are there to watch out for when color grading?**

**Eric:** My best workflow tip is to stay organized, be consistent with file naming, and back up all assets in at least three separate physical locations.

Avoid postproduction tricks. Rather than trying to clean up noise in post, shoot video that is well-lit so that you're not digging into the noise bed to try and find useful information in post.

Good grading makes an excellent picture even better, so shoot great video and film. A skilled colorist can sometimes work miracles with poorly shot footage, but they never have a good time doing it, and it rarely is as good as if the mistake never happened in the first place. Make your colorist happy and don't make all those lazy mistakes in production.

**Andrew: Do you have any advice for someone who wants to get into color grading, or even filmmaking in general?**

**Eric:** The best tip for someone starting out who wants to become a professional is decide what you want to be and then do everything that you can to be that profession. Meaning if what you want to do is color movies, then color every video project for every filmmaker you know for free until you're good. But if what you want to do is direct, then do everything you can to direct as many actors in as many projects as you possibly can. Don't make the mistake of thinking you can learn a little camera, learn a little FCP, grab some plug-ins, and BOOM! You're a filmmaker. You're not. You're a hobbyist, which is a fine thing to be. Any one of the jobs in filmmaking requires years of dedicated practice to be a professional at your craft, better to decide what that is sooner rather than later.

# Three 3-Way Color Correctors in After Effects

A 3-way color corrector has three wheels, which adjust the hue, saturation, and luminance of the shadows, midtones, and highlights. At first it can seem very confusing, but it's

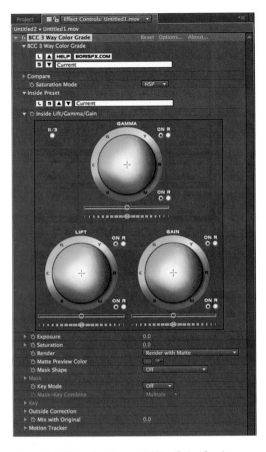

**Figure 2.2** Boris Continuum 3-Way Color Grade effect controls. Screenshot: Michele Yamazaki.

very simple once you get to know how it works. Some 3-way color correctors work in RGB color space, such as After Effects' own **Color Balance**, but others such as **Synthetic Aperture Color Finesse** work in HSL. All of the 3-way color correctors for After Effects work in the same general manner so if you learn how to use one you can easily learn another.

A 3-way color corrector is something that Final Cut Pro and Premiere Pro have included but After Effects lacks. The benefit of a 3-way color corrector is that it allows you to do all of your color correction/grading with a single plug-in. The tool lets you to fix problem colors, enhance the mood of a scene, and do special effects like isolating colors, such as seen in *Sin City* and *Pleasantville*. There are a few 3-way color correctors on the market for After Effects, and all of them are excellent tools.

I'll focus on three 3-way color correctors: Boris Continuum 3-Way Color Grade, Red Giant Magic Bullet Colorista II, and Synthetic Aperture Color Finesse.

Below is a quick comparison of the three plug-ins, with their respective pros and cons.

## Boris Continuum 3-Way Color Grade

Pros:
- Contains built-in Key and Mask tools for easy isolation of areas of the screen or to create vignettes
- BCC Motion Tracker is built in
- Compare mode allows users to see before and after

Cons:
- Users can't use different color settings for the Mask and Key

## Red Giant Magic Bullet Colorista II

Pros:
- Total control of color using Primary, Secondary, and Master controls

- Keyer for pulling mattes for Secondary color correction
- Skin Overlay for achieving correct skin tones

Cons:

- No built-in tracker
- Render times can be long with less powerful graphics cards

## Synthetic Aperture Color Finesse

Pros:

- Includes several monitoring tools including a waveform monitor, vectorscope, histogram, and correction curve displays
- Simplified interface works in the Effect Controls panel in After Effects
- Ships with After Effects, so it's not an extra expense

Cons:

- Full interface requires users to leave After Effects interface

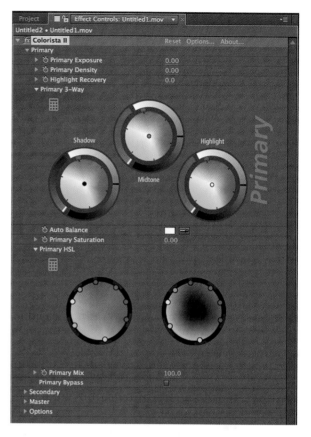

**Figure 2.3** Red Giant Magic Bullet Colorista II effect controls. Screenshot: Michele Yamazaki.

**Figure 2.4** Synthetic Aperture Color Finesse user interface, displaying the 3-way color corrector. Footage: Michigan Film Reel.

# Improving Color with Boris Continuum 3-Way Color Grade

**Figure 2.5** Before (left) and after (right) using Boris Continuum 3-Way Color Grade. Footage credit: Michele Yamazaki.

We don't all have the luxury of a high-end camera such as the RED camera on every shoot. I often use a $99 Vado HD camera, similar to a Flip HD. It is smaller than my cell phone so it's extremely portable and inconspicuous in crowds. It does a darn good job for such an inexpensive camera, and I have enhanced the colors in my footage with the **Boris Continuum 3-Way Color Grade Unit** ($99). This plug-in was first included with **Boris Continuum Complete 7** ($999), which came out in mid-2010; it's a fast and easy way to enhance the color of a shot with a single plug-in, whether your footage is consumer level or top notch.

**Figure 2.6** The Lift/Gamma/Gain color controls in Boris Continuum 3-Way Color Grade. Screenshot: Michele Yamazaki.

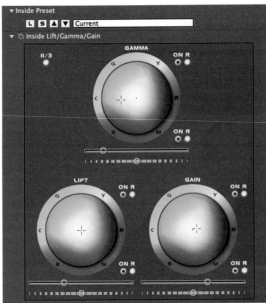

While it works similarly to other 3-way color correctors, the naming of the pots (individual color controls) is slightly different than the others. While some call them shadows, midtones, and highlights, **BCC 3-Way Color Grade** uses the terms Gamma, Lift, and Gain. BCC 3-Way Color Grade contains built-in Key and Mask tools that allow users to isolate areas of the screen or to create vignettes.

A cool feature of many BCC plug-ins is the Compare mode, which allows users to see before and after side-by-side views or split-screen. At the top of the plug-in, set the Compare mode and adjust the Wipe/Slide and Right Offset to your liking. Compare mode can also be viewed with Inside–Outside correction, which is useful for this tutorial.

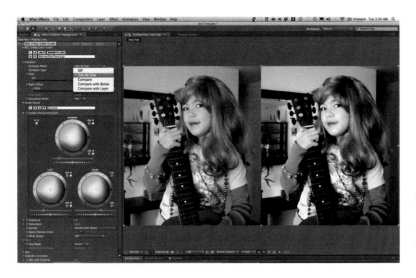

**Figure 2.7** Compare mode allows the user to see the original and the affected video in a split screen. Screenshot: Michele Yamazaki.

The project files, including the clip of a little pop star, are on the DVD in the back of this book in a folder named BCC 3-Way Color Grade – Pop Star. The object is to stylize the colors of the shot, crushing the blacks, bringing in cooler tones, but isolating her skin tones with a key to keep them warmer and give them some glow.

**Third-party plug-ins needed:**

- Boris Continuum 3-Way Color Grade or Boris Continuum Complete 7

1. Import the footage. Apply Boris Continuum 3-Way Color Grade to your shot (Effect > BCC Color Blurs > BCC 3-Way Color Grade).

2. First, we need to isolate the skin before the colors start being tweaked. Find the Key section in the Effect Controls panel. Just above it, set Key Mode to On using the pulldown menu.

3. Twirl open Key and use the Key Color eyedropper to select skin tones in the face. Under Render, which is below the Inside Lift/Gamma/Gain pots, switch to View Matte. Set Key Mode to Invert so that only the face is selected in the key. (See Figure 2.8.)

4. Back under Key, adjust Hue Threshold and Hue Softness, Sat Threshold and Sat Softness, and Lightness Threshold and Lightness Softness until you have a mostly black and white mask. Adjust the Blur Key to soften the edge slightly. (See Figure 2.9.)

5. Now that the skin tones are isolated, set Render back to Render with Matte. It may seem odd to

**Figure 2.8** Render is set to View Matte and Key Mode is set to Invert. Footage credit: Michele Yamazaki.

| ▼ Key | | |
|---|---|---|
| ○ Base Key On | | HSL ▼ |
| ○ Key Softness | | Expand Key ▼ |
| ○ Key Color | | ☐ ⊐ |
| ▶ ○ Hue Threshold | | 0.0 |
| ▶ ○ Hue Softness | | 33.7 |
| ▶ ○ Sat Threshold | | 51.0 |
| ▶ ○ Sat Softness | | 21.3 |
| ▶ ○ Lightness Threshold | | 37.0 |
| ▶ ○ Lightness Softness | | 41.7 |
| ▶ ○ Blur Key | | 8.80 |

**Figure 2.9** The Key section. Screenshot: Michele Yamazaki.

**Figure 2.10** The Key is set to isolate skin tones in the face in 3-Way Color Grade. Footage credit: Michele Yamazaki.

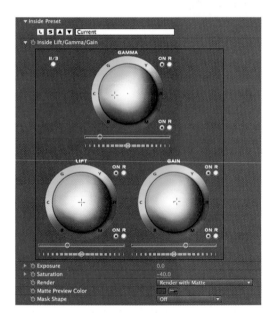

**Figure 2.11** Inside Lift/Gamma/Gain. Screenshot: Michele Yamazaki.

have the key inverted but the main shot will be adjusted with the Inside Lift/Gain/Gamma pots on top and the face will be adjusted with the Outside Lift/Gain/Gamma pots. (See Figure 2.10.)

6. Under Inside Lift/Gamma/Gain, lower the Saturation to –40 to desaturate the shot. Drag the Gamma slider (below the Gamma pot) to the left to darken the shot. In the center of the Gamma pot, drag the crosshair to the left, halfway between cyan and the center to add bluish tones to the shadows. Drag the Lift slider to the left to darken the midtones. Drag the Gain crosshair just a touch to the right to brighten the highlights in the shot. (See Figure 2.11.)

**7.** Go down to Outside Correction > Outside Lift/Gamma/Gain, to adjust the skin tones outside of the mask we set up (Key mode is inverted, remember). To add warmth and brighten the skin, drag the Lift crosshair just a bit toward the red about one-eighth of the way to the edge of the circle. Grab the Gain crosshair and move it toward the red about one-third of the way. Drag the Gain slider to the right about 60% of the way to brighten the skin tones. (See Figure 2.12.)

## Adding a Vignette with Boris Continuum 3-Way Color Grade

Boris Continuum 3-Way Color Grade will not let you use different color settings for the Mask and Key, so *we'll set up the color correction just the same as the previous tutorial, using the same project files, BCC 3-Way Color Grade – Pop Star,* except we will not isolate skin tones.

Figure 2.12 Outside Lift/Gamma/Gain. Screenshot: Michele Yamazaki.

**Third-party plug-ins needed:**

• Boris Continuum 3-Way Color Grade or Boris Continuum Complete 7

1. Apply Boris Continuum 3-Way Color Grade to the footage. Lower the Saturation to –40 Inside Lift/Gamma/Gain to desaturate the shot. Under Inside Lift/Gamma/Gain, drag the Gamma slider to the left to darken the shot. In the center of the Gamma pot, drag the crosshair to the left, halfway

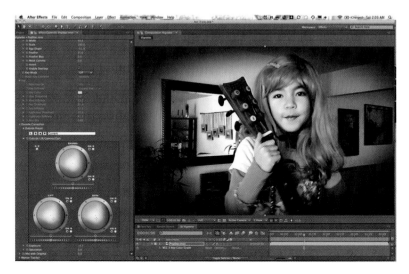

Figure 2.13 A vignette can be created at the same time as color correction using the egg-shaped Mask tool in Boris Continuum 3-Way Color Grade. Screenshot: Michele Yamazaki.

between cyan and the center to add blue to the shadows. Drag the Lift slider to the left and the Gain slider to the right just slightly. Drag the Gain crosshair just a touch to the right.

2. Make sure Enable Overlays is checked so that you can see the mask. Under Mask Shape, choose Egg Shape. Twirl down Mask Settings. Drag the points on the mask so that the oval fills most of the screen. Drag the dot on the bar in the center to adjust the shape of the egg mask. (Figure 2.14.)

3. Feather the mask so that the edges are soft, about 25.

4. Under Outside Correction > Outside Lift/Gamma/Gain, lower the Exposure until it looks like a vignette. To colorize the vignette, drag the crosshairs in the Gamma, Lift, and Gain pots until you achieve your desired color. (Figure 2.15.)

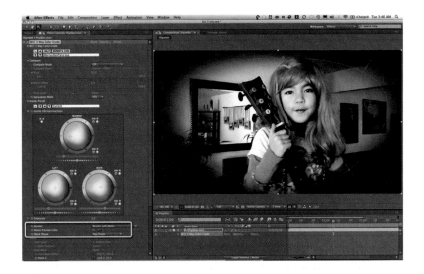

**Figure 2.14** Egg Shape Mask.
Screenshot: Michele Yamazaki.

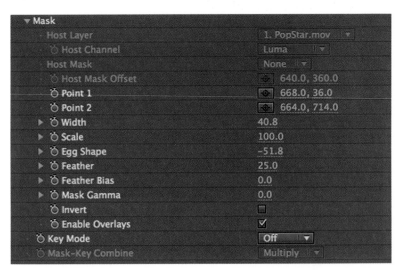

**Figure 2.15** Mask settings.
Screenshot: Michele Yamazaki.

## Isolating a Single Color with Red Giant Magic Bullet Colorista II

Red Giant Magic Bullet Colorista was a fantastic color correction tool but the new features added in **Magic Bullet Colorista II** ($299) make it essential. Colorista II is a 3-way color corrector that brings high-end color correction tools to After Effects. With the Primary, Secondary, and Master Controls, it's possible to make sweeping changes to the colors in the footage or slight tweaks to isolated colors. Like in Boris Continuum 3-Way Color Grade, users can adjust colors visually by dragging the mouse around in the color pots, and make shadow, midtone, and highlight adjustments.

Isolating a single color is easy with Colorista II. The footage I'm using is of my daughter on the deck with a picture frame. She is wearing a turquoise shirt and I'll show you how to isolate the turquoise shirt and desaturate the rest of the shot. The footage used in this tutorial was shot with a small handheld HD camera. It was a very sunny day and the shot isn't perfect with the highlights blown out. To distract the viewer from the flaw and add a stylish element, we'll isolate the turquoise shirt and desaturate the rest of the shot, while at the same time, adjusting the blown out areas of the shot.

*The clip and project files are included on the DVD included with this book in the Colorista Single Color folder.*

**Third-party plug-ins needed:**
- Red Giant Magic Bullet Colorista II
    1. Import the footage BlueShirt.mp4 into After Effects. Drag it to the Make a New Composition button at the bottom of the Project panel.
    2. Apply Magic Bullet Colorista II to the clip (Effect > Magic Bullet Colorista > Colorista II).

**Figure 2.16** Red Giant Magic Bullet Colorista II is used to isolate a color and desaturate the remaining portions of the footage. Footage credit: Michele Yamazaki.

**Figure 2.17** Primary HSL was adjusted to desaturate all colors except the turquoise and to darken the highlights in the plants. Screenshot: Michele Yamazaki.

3. In the Effect Controls panel, under Primary, slightly lower the Primary Exposure and Primary Density to lower the overall brightness of the shot.

4. Twirl down Primary HSL. Drag all of the colors on the left pot to the center except for the cyan/turquoise and blue. This will desaturate everything except the shirt. On the right pot, drag the yellow and green dots toward the center to darken the blown out areas in the green plants. Twirl Primary closed to get it out of the way. (Figure 2.17.)

5. Locate Secondary > Secondary Key > Key. Click the Edit … button under Key to open the Colorista Keyer. Select the box selection tool to grab a section of turquoise in the center of the shirt. Click the + (plus) tool and click + drag around the shirt to grab more turquoise. View the Matte to see how the mask looks. The mask needs to be reversed, so click the Invert button on the bottom right of the Colorista Keyer window. If there is an area you want to remove from the key, click the − (minus) button and then click + drag around the areas that you want to remove. Click OK to close the Colorista Keyer window. (Figure 2.18.)

6. At the top of the Secondary section, increase the Secondary Exposure and lower the Secondary Density slightly. This will only affect the shirt, since it is keyed.

7. To change the color of the shirt completely, twirl down Primary > Primary HSL. Drag the cyan/turquoise and blue dots to another area of the left pot but keep it on the outer perimeter. To increase the saturation, drag the dots outside of the pot. (Figure 2.19.)

**Final Touches:** The fence and plants on the left were showing quite a lot of artifacting due to the fact that they were blown

**Figure 2.18** Colorista Keyer with the cyan/turquoise color selected. Screenshot: Michele Yamazaki.

**Figure 2.19** Adjust cyan and blue to change the color of the shirt. Screenshot: Michele Yamazaki.

out in the original shot. If you do not start out with high-quality footage when doing major color adjustments, these changes will bring out compression artifacting. To minimize the problem areas, I applied an adjustment layer with a mask isolating the outer edges of the clip. I added a Fast Blur set to 2 and darkened these areas with Levels. This also helped to bring the focus to the child.

**Figure 2.20** An adjustment layer with masks and a levels adjustment helps with artifacting issues. Screenshot: Michele Yamazaki.

## Saving Underexposed Footage with Red Giant Magic Bullet Colorista II

Have you ever had footage that you cannot reshoot, but it's so dark it's seemingly unusable? Or you may know you're going to be shooting in low light but you're not allowed to bring in lighting equipment. What can you do?

**Red Giant Magic Bullet Colorista II** to the rescue! Magic Bullet Colorista II can pull even low-quality, under-lit footage back from the brink. This example was shot on an old Panasonic Lumix digital camera, and yes, it's extremely dark. By adjusting several parameters in Colorista II, I was able to bring up the exposure and bring out details that would otherwise be lost. If you were to try this with other tools, you would not get this good of a result.

Bringing up the levels this much does introduce more grain and compression artifacting so you may want to degrain the

**Figure 2.21** This video of Lily on Halloween was shot on a digital camera with not much lighting. Before (left) and after (right), lightened by adjusting the exposure with Colorista II. Footage credit: Michele Yamazaki.

footage after Colorista II is applied. Check out Chapter 14, "Fixing Video Problems" for more information on noise removal and degraining.

## Dazzling Black and White with Synthetic Aperture Color Finesse

**Synthetic Aperture Color Finesse** is a powerful, all-in-one color correction tool. It can work in HSL, RGB, CMY, and YCbCr color spaces, and has automatic color balancing, Auto-Color, and Auto-Exposure for one-click color correction. There is a new Highlight Recovery tool in version 3 which provides a nice way to recover blown out areas of the footage that would normally be clipped. Color Finesse also has a nice variety of gel/filter presets under the Gallery tab. The tool literally has hundreds of options for tweaking color and luminance.

Making your footage black and white is as simple as applying **Hue/Saturation** and taking the Master Saturation down to zero, but you will not get the best contrast using that method.

For much more control over luminance values try **Black & White**, which started shipping with After Effects CS5 (Effects > Color Correction > Black & White). When applied, it desaturates the footage, and has sliders to adjustment the luminance levels of areas that contain reds, yellows, greens, cyans, blues, and magentas.

If you want your video to look more like high-contrast film with a lot of detail, look no further than Synthetic Aperture Color Finesse, a plug-in that has shipped with After Effects for years.

On a side note, it's imperative that you have high-quality footage when boosting the contrast and detail because these changes will also bring out compression artifacting.

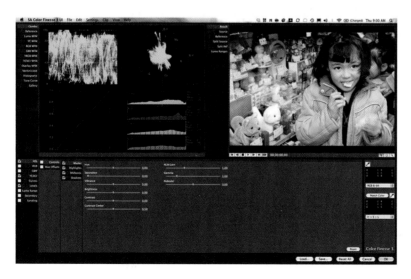

**Figure 2.22** The Color Finesse effect controls. Screenshot: Michele Yamazaki.

**Figure 2.23** The top half of the example has Black & White applied. The bottom half is the original shot, which is very colorful. Screenshot: Michele Yamazaki.

**Third-party plug-ins needed:**

- Synthetic Aperture Color Finesse
    1. Apply Color Finesse to your footage. Under Parameters, click Full Interface so that you have access to all settings. Color Finesse will launch and open in its own user interface. (Figure 2.24.)
    2. Click the checkbox for HSL > Controls > Master, then take the Saturation down to 0, which will remove all color. (Figure 2.25.)
    3. Enable HSL > Controls > Highlights, Midtones, and Shadows by checking the boxes to the left of the labels. Adjust the Brightness, Contrast, Contrast Center, Pedestal, and Gain of the Highlights, Midtones, and Shadows until you find a nice balance of light and dark with plenty of detail. (Figure 2.26.)
    4. To fine-tune it even more, go to Levels or Curves and make adjustments.

**Figure 2.24** Color Finesse 3 Effect Controls. Screenshot: Michele Yamazaki.

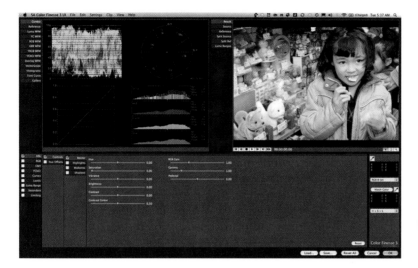

**Figure 2.25** The Combo Controls in Color Finesse. Screenshot: Michele Yamazaki.

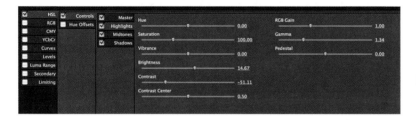

**Figure 2.26** HSL Controls in Color Finesse. Screenshot: Michele Yamazaki.

**Figure 2.27** Color footage converted to black and white using Hue/Saturation (left) and Color Finesse (right). Footage credit: Michele Yamazaki.

# Red Giant Magic Bullet Looks, Magic Bullet Quick Looks, and Magic Bullet Mojo

**Red Giant Magic Bullet Looks** ($399) is an extremely powerful and favorite tool of designers and editors everywhere, taking second place in the 2009 and fourth in the 2010 Toolfarm Plug-in Awards survey. Magic Bullet Looks can turn ho-hum into dramatic, breath-taking style with two clicks. Looks adds dramatic colorization,

**Figure 2.28** Several Magic Bullet Looks presets applied to the same footage. The original untreated clip is in the upper left corner. Eric Escobar's Remento preset is in the lower right corner. **Eric Escobar's Indie Film for Looks** ($69) is a collection of customizable presets for Magic Bullet Looks, Magic Bullet Quick Looks, or Magic Bullet PhotoLooks. Footage: Crowd Control, clip #00074_001_24.

vignettes, blurs and diffusion, highlights, anamorphic flares, and filmic effects to add mood and give footage blockbuster style.

Both **Magic Bullet Looks** and **Quick Looks** ($99) ship with a 100-preset Look Library; the main difference between the two is that presets can be modified in Looks while with Quick Looks you just have the preset library. Both Looks and Quick Looks launch a standalone application named LooksBuilder, which has its own very well-designed interface. In Looks, previewing the presets on footage in the Look Theater is fast within LooksBuilder, and the presets are interesting and well thought-out. It's extremely easy to use and a lot of fun.

There are two main problems with Looks and QuickLooks. There is no motion tracker, so highlighting a person's face, for example, only works well if the person stays in one place onscreen. The other flaw is that there are no video previews in LooksBuilder, so the frame that the playhead is on when the app is launched will be the reference frame in LooksBuilder. Looks also can't be previewed on an external monitor, but Red Giant says that it will add this feature in the next major release.

Looks also includes Misfire, which adds damaged film effects such as noise, splotches, scratches, gate weave, and flicker.

**Red Giant Magic Bullet Mojo** ($99) works on the same principle of giving footage a look of a Hollywood blockbuster or action film, with a simple user interface. Mojo is a series of sliders that tint the video warmer or cooler, crush the blacks, and isolate skin tones. It's extremely fast to render so it's a great tool when you want to give your video some sexiness but don't have a lot of time.

Figure 2.29 Magic Bullet Looks LooksBuilder with RGB Parade displayed. Footage: Michele Yamazaki.

Figure 2.30 Top left is the original shot. The other three samples have been color-treated with Red Giant Magic Bullet Mojo. Footage credit: Michigan Film Reel.

## A Tour of the Magic Bullet Looks Interface

To use Magic Bullet Looks or Quick Looks, apply the effect to your footage. In the Effect Controls panel, click the Edit button to open the custom interface, also known as LooksBuilder. The interface has drawers that tuck away on each side of the screen to keep the interface tidy.

1. At the top of the Looks interface is the Looks Theater. This is a slideshow of all of the Looks presets and previously saved Looks available, and is great if you have a client over your shoulder that doesn't quite know what he wants. The Looks

Figure 2.31 Looks Effect Controls panel. Screenshot: Michele Yamazaki.

**Figure 2.32** The Magic Bullet Looks Interface. Footage: Crowd Control, clip #00074_001_24.

Theater slideshow can be broken down into categories, so you only show the Music Video or Popular Film presets, for example.

2. The Looks presets are stored in a drawer along the left of the interface. The presets are broken into categories including Basic, Black and White, Horror, Music Video, Popular Film, Popular TV, and more. The easiest way to get started in Looks is to choose a preset that is close to the look that you are aiming for and modify from there. (If you're using Quick Looks, the presets can't be modified so after you choose a preset, click OK to go back to After Effects interface.)

   The Looks presets can either be viewed as thumbnails in the Sample view or as icons of the effects applied in the Chain view.

3. The graphs, consisting of an RGB Parade and Slice Graph, can be turned on and off by clicking the On/Off button at the top right of the interface. Use these to monitor output levels. (Figure 2.33.)

4. The Preview panel is where presets and tools are previewed as they are applied to the clip.

5. The preset name is shown just below the Looks presets. After modifying a preset, your own custom Looks can be saved by renaming the Look from "Untitled Look" to whatever you'd like to call it. Your look will appear under "Custom" in the Looks presets for future use.

Figure 2.33 The Looks RGB Parade graph. Footage: Artbeats, clip # VAN101.

6. Along the bottom of the Looks interface is the Looks Chain, which is broken down into five categories: Subject, Matte, Lens, Camera, and Post. The effect order can be modified by clicking, dragging, and dropping within their particular category. On top of each effect is a red On/Off button that will turn the effect on and off. At the top of this section is a similar red bar that will turn all of the effects on and off so that the untreated footage can be seen.

7. The Tools drawer is on the right side of the interface. Tools include controls such as Curves, Saturation, Lift-Gamma-Gain, Vignette, Crush, Star Filter, Chromatic Aberration, Edge Softness, Exposure, Spot Exposure, and many more. To apply a tool, simply double-click it. It will appear in the Looks Chain at the bottom of the interface. Apply as many as you like. To delete a tool, select it in the Looks Chain and click the delete key.

8. Click a tool in the Looks Chain and the adjustments will appear in the lower right. Clicking and dragging the value or manually entering a number modifies most effects. Others, such as Vignette and Spot Exposure are adjusted in the Preview area.

## A User Story: Shooting Video with Looks in Mind, with Anthony E. Griffin, UnSafe Film Office

Anthony E. Griffin is an award-winning writer, director, and cinematographer who has really brought Looks into his workflow by shooting specifically for the use of Magic Bullet Looks in post. He lights and shoots all of his footage as neutral as possible and effects it in post with Magic Bullet Looks, as he explains below.

**Figure 2.34** Scenes were made black and white and enhanced with Magic Bullet Looks in the independent film *Memento Mori*. Footage: Anthony E. Griffin.

As a cinematographer I've been taking more and more into account the postproduction processes and the color correction tools we can use. As artists, we may think of it as cheating, and to a degree I do agree with that, because you should still know your job. But, instead of fighting change, filmmakers should embrace it and learn these tools and use it to make the vision more clear. I shoot as quickly as possible because I am working in a no-budget economy, and then I apply those techniques in post. That may not make some of the more traditional cinematographers out there too thrilled. I read in American Cinematographer that some of these old-school guys get a little upset about digital manipulation of film, but the fact of the matter is that the way the studios do things and people who are paying for the production are always looking to cut costs. By spending the pennies up-front, Magic Bullet Looks will save me dollars on the back end. I know the tools that I have available to me in post when I go out and shoot things.

**Figure 2.35** Anthony E. Griffin. Photo: Michael McCallum.

I was able to really learn Magic Bullet Looks before a film I worked on called Memento Mori. I like to convert what I can to black and white. I prefer the aesthetic as a story device. I was able to set my camera balances based on what I needed the software to do before I even shot it. When it becomes a one-click process that can still be manipulated with careful control to create a custom look like Magic Bullet can do, I can take that and help create my vision!

## Using Red Giant Magic Bullet Looks for Compositing Greenscreen Footage

Magic Bullet Looks is the perfect tool for unifying the appearance of multiple clips, especially if they came from different sources. It's also a terrific tool for matching foreground and background plates when compositing greenscreen footage. Using more traditional methods, this can take quite a bit of time, especially if light colors are completely different or you're compositing 3D elements with greenscreen footage. An easy method of speeding up this process is to place an Adjustment Layer above all layers in your timeline and apply Magic Bullet Looks to the Adjustment Layer. Not only can you bring mood to your composite with Looks, all layers below will be brought into the same color space, and black and white levels will be more equalized.

**Figure 2.36** On the left, the original shot with no color enhancement. On the right, the same shot with Magic Bullet Looks preset Blockbuster applied. Greenscreen footage courtesy of Michigan Film Reel.

# Color Effects

Color correction tools are often used to make very specific looks, such as bleach bypass, day for night, and tinted film. Any of the effects previously mentioned in this chapter can handle the job but there are some plug-ins made specifically for a certain look.

## Bleach Bypass

According to Wikipedia, "Bleach bypass, also known as skip bleach or silver retention, is an optical effect which entails either the partial or complete skipping of the bleaching function during the processing of a color film. By doing this, the silver is retained in the emulsion along with the color dyes. The result is a black and white image over a color image. The images usually would have reduced saturation and exposure latitude, along with increased contrast and graininess. It usually is used to maximal effect in conjunction with a one-stop underexposure." Bleach bypass was used in the films *1984* and *Se7en*. See http:// en.wikipedia.org/wiki/Bleach_bypass.

**Figure 2.37** Tiffen Dfx Filter Suite Bleach Bypass filter. Footage: Michele Yamazaki.

Bleach bypass is very expensive in film because of the silver, which is normally reclaimed and sold, so doing this effect with a plug-in can save an enormous amount of expense. Luckily, it is a very popular plug-in and preset in After Effects so there are many options. **CoreMelt Pigment** color correction tool Bleach Bypass (CoreMelt Pigment is available for free) is a nice choice. **Synthetic Aperture Color Finesse** has a Bleach Bypass preset under the Galleries tab. **DVShade EasyLooks (FxFactory)**($49) has a preset called ei8ht, a takeoff on se7en. **Red Giant Magic Bullet Looks** and **Quick Looks** both have a Bleach Bypass preset, as does **Tiffen Dfx Filter Suite**($599).

## Film/Video Tinting

Color was added to many black and white films of the silent era to set the mood or establish the scene. Blue was used to represent nighttime and amber or orange to represent daylight or heat. First, dyed emulsions were used but caused problems in the audio track. Well-known examples of tinted films are *Broken Blossoms* (1919) and *The Birth of a Nation* (1915). Pretinted stocks were introduced in 1921 by Kodak.[1] More recently, Guy Maddin's *Careful* (1992), a strange and visually stunning throwback to German Expressionism, used hand-tinted color effects.

With the introduction of digital tools, tinting is now as simple as applying a filter and tweaking the settings. It's a simple effect that can have an enormous impact on the mood of a scene. You'll see tinting used today in flashbacks, dream sequences, faux old film look, horror films, music videos, and TV commercials.

[1]Source: Wikipedia entry "Film Tinting: Tinting in the silent era." http://en.wikipedia.org/wiki/Film_tinting.

**Figure 2.38** Tiffen Dfx Filter Suite Old Photo Silver Gelatin preset. Footage: Crowd Control, clip #00182_001_138.

**Tiffen Dfx Filter Suite Old Photo** filter tints shots and does everything needed to make a beautiful black and white shot or a moody tint. Don't be confused by the name Old Photo; it doesn't give a degraded look with flicker, dust, scratches, and so on. Old Photo has presets called Cyanotype, Platinum, Sepia, and Silver, or a color can be chosen with the eyedropper. Alternately, the hue, saturation, brightness, contrast, and gamma can be adjusted under the Color Correct settings.

A unique feature of this filter is that it allows the user to select the blue, green, or red channel, swapping it out for the main RGB image, in the same manner as the **Channel Combiner** plug-in that ships with After Effects. In addition to red, green, and blue, yellow and orange can be used as if they were color channels. Using the color channels to create a black-and-white shot as opposed to just desaturating allows for more variety. Quite often, a single color channel will look nicer than the combined RGB that has been desaturated. To make a black-and-white shot using Old Photo, set the Tint to black or white or any shade of gray with no saturation. Another option is Black & White, described in the earlier section "Dazzling Black and White with Synthetic Aperture Color Finesse."

There are many other options to tint footage. **Tiffen Dfx Filter Suite Mono Tint** does the same type of tinting effect but with fewer options. **Tiffen Dfx Filter Suite HFX Grads/Tints** and **Gels** tint the existing colors in a shot and use the same names as the physical gels used in lighting, which is helpful if you need to match into footage that used a certain gel in the studio. Values can be adjusted to preserve highlights and there is an exposure compensation setting to brighten a shot. Areas of the screen can be isolated with a gradient (or apply to an adjustment layer and use a mask). For a duotone effect using Gels, apply Hue/Saturation first and desaturate the shot.

**Figure 2.39** Luca's Stylizer. Footage: Crowd Control, clip #00182_001_138.

**Luca Visual FX Light Kit (FxFactory)** ($49) consists of several plug-ins which stylize video with light and color. Favorites include **Stylizer** which creates surreal tints, and **Multicolor Gradient**, which overlays gradients over footage. All filters come with multiple interesting presets.

## Day for Night

A good example of special effects with color filters is a day-for-night effect. Shooting outdoors at night can be filled with lighting challenges. Converting from day to night involves taking footage shot in the daytime and applying color filters to lower the exposure, desaturating the colors, and tinting the footage blue. **CoreMelt Pigment** color correction tool ($79) has a **Day for Night**

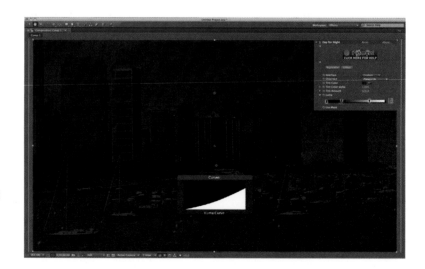

**Figure 2.40** CoreMelt Pigment color correction tool Day for Night filter with the onscreen curves graph. Screenshot: Michele Yamazaki.

**Figure 2.41** Red Giant Magic Bullet Looks interface with a modified Night Time preset applied for a day-for-night look. Screenshot: Michele Yamazaki.

filter that is very easy to use. Many of CoreMelt's tools have a nice feature: onscreen tools that pop on when dragging values. Adjust the sliders and a curves graph appears on screen in the middle of the comp. With the Day for Night filter in Pigment, the user can adjust the Tint Color, the Tint Color Alpha, the Tint Amount, and Luma Levels (a curves slider control).

**Red Giant Magic Bullet Looks** and **Quick Looks** both have presets for the day-for-night look, Days of Night and Night Time. Again, with Looks the user can modify the saturation, warm/cool, exposure, and so on. With Quick Looks, the preset settings can't be modified.

## Working with Skin Tones

Regardless of ethnicity of a person, skin tones tend to fall in the same zone on a vectorscope. This area is known as the skin tone line, flesh line, or i-line, and extends in a 45° angle from the center to the upper left. **Synthetic Aperture Color Finesse** has a built-in vectorscope. When applying plug-ins or filters that color the entire frame of video, make sure you keep an eye on the skin tones so that they don't become unnatural. Apply Color Finesse to an adjustment layer over the footage and open the full interface to see the scopes.

### Working with Skin Tones in Red Giant Magic Bullet Mojo

**Red Giant Magic Bullet Mojo** ($99) is made specifically to preserve and enhance skin tones while affecting the rest of the shot with a bleach bypass or a very saturated, poppy look. It's

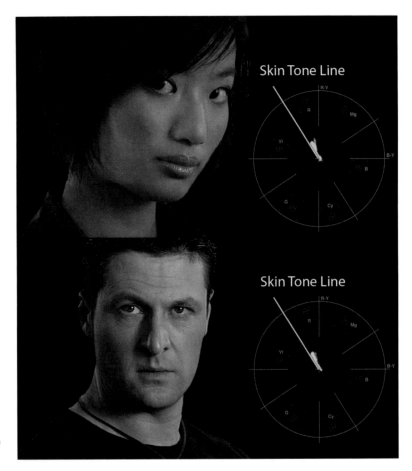

Skin Tone Line

Skin Tone Line

**Figure 2.42** Skin tones will appear in a small zone known as the skin line on a vector-scope. Footage: Crowd Control, clip # 00074_001_24 and 00126_001_93.

**Figure 2.43** Mojo with the skin overlay enabled. Footage: Crowd Control, clip # 00087_004_25.

extremely fast to learn and use; just jump in and start sliding the settings around.

Magic Bullet Mojo is a series of sliders that adjust the warm and cool tones in the shadows and highlights. To assist with skin tones, Mojo has a Skin Overlay function that lets the user isolate flesh tones, so skin tones can be adjusted separately from the rest of the shot. Colors similar to skin could be picked up by the effect but normally it is not a problem and the look does not suffer because of it.

## Using Gels to Correct or Warm Skin Tones

Have you ever forgotten to white balance your camera? Need to correct sickly, greenish skin tones shot under fluorescent lights or warm the bluish ambient light from shooting outdoors? Maybe you've shot everything neutrally to adjust in post? Apply one of the Tiffen Dfx Gels. The **Tiffen Dfx Filter Suite** ($599.95) includes Rosco and GamColor Gel libraries, which do a beautiful job of subtle and natural-looking adjustments on footage.

The **GamColor Naked Cosmetics**, named for their real-life counterparts, is specifically made to warm skin. There is also a feature for a Grad, to target the position of the gel color. The position and size can be fully controlled, allowing the gel color to blend into the original video.

**Figure 2.44** Tiffen Dfx GamColor Naked Cosmetics. *Top row from left*: Original, NCR3 Rosey Hint, NCR6 Rosey Accent, NCR9 Rosey Hi-Light. *Bottom*: NCW3 Warm Hint, NCW6 Warm Accent, NCW9 Hi-Light. Footage credit and Screenshot: Michele Yamazaki.

Color Finesse also has a nice assortment of gels and filter presets under the Gallery tab in the Full Interface. Gels can be used to warm or cool skin tones and overall footage.

**Figure 2.45** Synthetic Aperture Gels and Filters presets mimic real-life gels. Screenshot: Michele Yamazaki.

## Improving Skin Texture with Red Giant Magic Bullet Colorista II

It may seem odd to put a section about softening and adjusting skin texture in a color correction section, but many of the tools that are primarily color correction tools are also excellent tools for fixing skin. The primary focus of most shots in most films contain people, so it's an important topic. If skin colors are "off" due to lighting, the actors can look sickly or like they have a bad fake tan.

High-definition television and 52" plasma screens are not making it easy to hide skin problems. Putting a slight blur on one of the color channels, usually blue where the most noise resides in video, can often improve skin. In this section we look at a couple of methods of smoothing skin using color correction tools.

Stu Maschwitz has a fantastic series of tutorials on the Red Giant website, in particular "Skin Retouching with **Magic Bullet Colorista II**."In working through the tutorial, I was amazed at how easy it was to smooth wrinkles with the secondary color correction tools. In this sample I used a shot from Crowd Control and it's HD footage. I adjust a few settings so the skin looks smoother, freckles fade, and fine lines are diminished, and then isolate the area with a Secondary Key.

**Figure 2.46** Before (left) and after (right) adjusting the Secondary color corrections in Colorista II to smooth the skin. Footage: Crowd Control, clip # 00126_001_93.

1. Bring your footage into After Effects and apply Magic Bullet Colorista II.
2. Twirl the Primary color correction tools closed and go directly to Secondary.
3. Below the Secondary 3-Way pods is Pop. Lower the value of Pop until the skin looks smoother, but there is not a lot of skin color blooming outside of the face.
4. If other areas of the image are being affected, a Secondary Key will help isolate the face. Twirl down Secondary Key > Key. Click the Edit button to open the keying interface.
5. Use the selection box in the upper right corner of the Color-ista Keyer to select an area of skin. To add more skin, click the + (plus) button and drag around the skin in the image. To remove skin from the key, use the – (minus). Look at the Matte for reference. (Figure 2.47.)
6. Drag the cursor over the cube in the upper right of the interface or adjust saturation of the clip by clicking and dragging around the other graphs. Adjust the softness of the mask to blur the mask so you don't create hard edges with the correction. When you're happy with the key, click OK.
7. If areas outside of the face are still being affected, you can further isolate the area with a Secondary Power Mask. Choose Ellipse from the Secondary Mask pulldown menu. Click on the Center

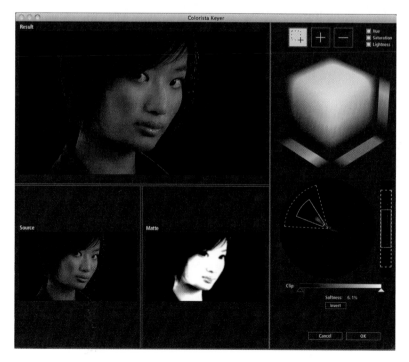

**Figure 2.47** The Colorista II Keyer. Footage: Crowd Control, clip # 00126_001_93.

crosshair then select a point near the center of the face. To see the mask, change the View mode to Show Red Overlay. Adjust the Width, Height, Rotation, and Feather size as needed to isolate the face. Set the View mode back to Apply to see the result.

8. To warm the tones or give a suntan, drag the outer ring of the Midtone pod until the skin is warmed or tanned.

## Automatic Skin Retouching with Digital Anarchy Beauty Box

**Digital Anarchy Beauty Box** ($199) gives a digital facelift to your talent. It uses face detection to analyze and smooth skin while keeping detail like eyelashes, hair, and jewelry sharp. It's very fast and easy without having to go frame by frame or rotoscoping. Says Jim Tierney, president of Digital Anarchy, "The amount of smoothing depends on the nearby details and pixel values. There's a lot more going on besides just the blur, as we attempt to keep other details sharp and keep some of the skin texture." Beauty Box works in After Effects and Final Cut Pro, and the latest update at press time includes CUDA acceleration, utilizing the computer's GPU.

**Figure 2.48** Before (left) and after (right) applying Digital Anarchy Beauty Box to smooth skin. Footage: Crowd Control, clip # 00126_001_93.

1. Apply Beauty Box to the footage (Effect > Digital Anarchy > Beauty Box).
2. Because of how the facial recognition feature works, go to a frame in the timeline with the actor facing the camera if possible. This frame will be the base, or key, frame. Click the Analyze Frame button. Beauty Box will find the correct skin colors to track. This will place keyframes for Mask parameters: Dark Color, Light Color, Hue Falloff, Saturation Falloff, and Value Falloff.
3. If the actor is moving and turning their head, or the lighting changes, you will want to analyze another frame. Find a frame with the head turned or where the lighting changes just a bit, and click Analyze Frame again. This will place another keyframe at that point in the timeline. Because the keyframes are linear, there will be a smooth transition between the points where the footage was analyzed.

If there is a scene change, go to the first frame of the scene change and Analyze Frame, but use a hold keyframe instead of a regular linear keyframe. A smooth transition could be a problem at a scene change.

4. Analyze All will analyze all frames and should only be used if you have footage with a lot of movement or lighting changes.

5. At the top of the effect controls for Beauty Box are Smoothing Amount, Skin Detail Amount, and Smoothing Radius. It is advisable to keep these values fairly low so that your actress doesn't look airbrushed and plastic; however, this could be used to a enhance a character if your actor is playing a robot or a mannequin. Due to the improved resolution, you can adjust the settings a bit higher with HD footage.

Beauty Box can also be used on other skin, such as hands, if you want to remove age spots, wrinkles, and veins. The face detection analysis will not work if there is no face in the shot so you'll need to set a mask manually. Use the eyedroppers to select the Light and Dark Colors. Under Mask, change the Mode to Foreground and Show Mask to On, then drag the mouse around the comp panel to sample areas of the skin tone that were not picked up in the mask. Skin tone areas will be represented as white in the mask.

# Hot Tip

If you have a problem with a wrinkly shirt on talent or a backdrop that could have used a hot iron, try Beauty Box! Apply Beauty Box to the shot and set the Light Colors to the colors in the backdrop or clothing then adjust the mask and smoothing settings. This works best with solid-colored fabrics. Do not attempt on paisley!

**Figure 2.49** Before (left) and after (right) using Beauty Box as a digital iron. Footage: Crowd Control, clip # 00087_004_25.

# EFFECTS

"Effects" is half of After Effects' name and it's what most people think of when considering third-party plug-ins. And, it's the reason we are here. This is the area where you create mind-boggling, eye-popping, brain-grinding, new world artistic representations of your work.

The visual effects referenced in this chapter tend to be seen more in commercials and music videos than anywhere else. Several are used to generate urgency and awareness. Effects such as motion blur can be used to make your composites look more natural. Glints can make water look more beautiful and set the mood. Other effects can turn video into a painted work of art or a comic book. Television effects can mimic a bad satellite transition or a closed circuit TV system.

There are so many effects filters for After Effects that we will barely scratch the surface, but this chapter covers some interesting effects and some of my favorites.

## Blur, Defocus, and Lens Effects

Blur is simply an area that is not in focus or is outside the depth of field. When the cameraman "pulls focus" he is bringing the shot into focus. Blurs can, of course, be done in camera, but we'll mainly discuss blurs that can be done in postproduction.

There is no shortage of blurs! After Effects ships with several blurs and every large bundle of plug-ins has several more.

### Gaussian Blur, Fast Blurs, and Box Blur

While there is little reason not to reach for the Gaussian Blur that ships with After Effects, there are a couple of third-party blurs that look great and have more options. **Boris Continuum Complete BCC Gaussian Blur** has many more variants, including the Blur Quality, the option to choose which channel to blur, Apply mode, and a Pixel Chooser to isolate areas. This plug-in, as of version 7, comes with **Beat Reactor**, which allows the user to animate to music.

Also, worth a mentioning here is **RE:Vision Effects SmoothKit** ($119.95), which contains Gaussian Blur, a true compound blur

**Figure 3.1** The sheer number of blur plug-ins for After Effects is unbelievable! Screenshot: Michele Yamazaki.

**Figure 3.2** Sample 1 is a Gaussian Blur with blurriness set to 12. Sample 2 shows Fast Blur with blurriness set to 12. Samples 3 and 4 show Box Blur, both with a blur level of 12. Sample 3 has iterations set to 1, while sample 4 has iterations set to 3. Footage: Crowd Control, clip # 00045_001_52.

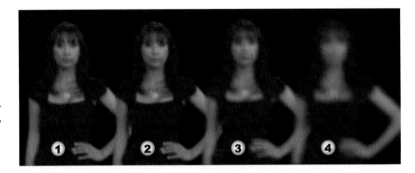

**Figure 3.3** *Left*: After Effects Gaussian Blur. *Center*: Boris Continuum Complete BCC Gaussian Blur. *Right*: RE:Vision Effects SmoothKit Gaussian Blur. Footage: Crowd Control, clip # 00045_001_52.

**Web Link:**

Gaussian Blurs, Fast Blurs, and Box Blurs are the most commonly used blurs in After Effects. Which is best? Stu Maschwitz had an interesting post on his Prolost blog, A Tale of Three Blurs (*http://bit.ly/ stublur*). Stu's favorite blur is the Box Blur with iterations set to 3 or 4 because it uses a soft, round edge.

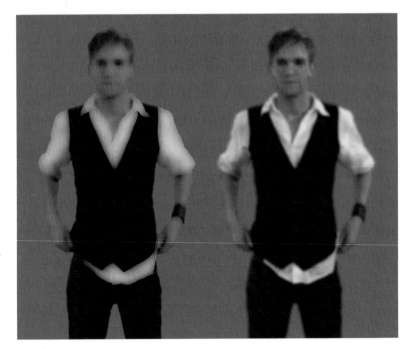

**Figure 3.4** After Effects Compound Blur with maximum blur set to 10, is on the left. RE:Vision Effects SmoothKit Gaussian Blur is on the right, with filter size set to 10. The blur was modified with a grayscale version of the image. Footage: Crowd Control, clip # 00177_001_21.

that is a much smoother, nicer looking compound blur with more precise control than the **Compound Blur** that ships with After Effects. The Compound Blur in After Effects is very boxy and the default value of 20 for maximum blur is entirely too high.

## "Smallgantics," a.k.a. the Tilt-Shift Effect with Sapphire Rack Defocus or Other Blurs

Smallgantics is a term used in film production where the film-maker will use an extreme depth of field to miniaturize the video. Smallgantics is more commonly referred to as tilt-shift photography. Check out the video on YouTube for Thom Yorke of Radiohead's "Harrowdown Hill," which employs the use of Smallgantics.

**Figure 3.5** Original footage. Footage: Michele Yamazaki.

**Figure 3.6** After the Tilt-Shift effect. Footage: Michele Yamazaki.

To get the right effect, your photo or video should be a very wide shot with a lot of people, cars, boats, trees, buildings… anything that can be miniaturized into Mr. Rogers' Neighborhood cuteness.

*Project files are included on this book's DVD in a folder named Smallgantics.*

**Third-party plug-ins needed:**

- GenArts Sapphire

    1. Import the footage Vancouver.jpg, included on this book's DVD in the Smallgantics folder.
    2. Create a new Composition in After Effects using the "HDTV 1080 29.97 preset", 5:00 in duration, named Smallgantics.
    3. Drag Vancouver.jpg into the comp. Scale the image to 50.0% and position to fill the screen so that the edge of the window in the upper right corner doesn't show.
    4. Now we'll apply a hue/saturation effect and boost the saturation to give it a more playful, toy-like look. I used GenArts Sapphire S_HueSatBright and increased Saturation to 2.000. Any hue/saturation filter will work. (See Figure 3.7.)

**Figure 3.7** The saturation is increased to give the image a more toy-like look. Screenshot: Michele Yamazaki.

**Figure 3.8** A Rounded Rectangle is drawn around the midsection of the image on an Adjustment Layer. The Rounded Rectangle tool is shown in the flyout menu in the toolbar. Screenshot: Michele Yamazaki.

5. Layer > New > Adjustment Layer. Use the Rectangle tool and draw a rectangle around the area that you do not want to blur. In your timeline, set the mode of Mask 1 to Subtract or tick the Inverted box. Press the F key to bring up Mask Feather and set it really high, to 100 or 120. This number will vary whether you're using SD or HD footage but you just want a very soft feather. *Note*: You won't be able to see the effect of this mask until you add the blur. (See Figure 3.8.)

6. Apply a Sapphire S_RackDefocus to the Adjustment Layer (Effect > Sapphire Blur+Sharpen > S_RackDefocus). In the Effect Controls panel, increase the Defocus Width to 12.00. Increase Bokeh to 2.000 to bring a bit more detail back into the blurred areas. (See Figure 3.9.)

*Note*: Other blurs will also work here. Try them out until you find the right one. Adjust the blur settings, the mask positioning, and feather as needed. Also, if you add any animation to the shot (for example, blinking lights, moving boats), be sure to leave the Adjustment Layer on top of the stack in the timeline so that all layers below will be affected.

Figure 3.9 Sapphire S_RackDefocus is applied to the Adjustment Layer to blur the entire image. Screenshot: Michele Yamazaki.

## Motion Blur: RE:Vision Effects ReelSmart Motion Blur

Motion blur feels natural to the human eye, but there are certain times when you do not want motion blur. For example, high-action sports like soccer and hockey are often shot with a fast shutter to catch all of the action clearly. This is especially useful if the footage will be shown slow-mo, as the blur will hide the detail.

Figure 3.10 Original footage. Footage: Artbeats, clip # SW101.

Figure 3.11 After ReelSmart Motion Blur is applied. Footage: Artbeats, clip # SW101.

If you've ever tried to key greenscreen footage, you'll know that keying blur is very difficult and often impossible. In a composite, motion blur should look the same for the foreground and background elements for the most realistic look, but for better edges in your key, you might try reducing motion blur in your greenscreen shot by increasing shutter speed, and then replace the motion blur after keying with a tool such as **RE:Vision Effects ReelSmart Motion Blur** ($89.95 Standard, $149 Pro).

There are other times when adding motion blur can be used for dramatic effect, for example, a little motion blur on moving water can make it look like silk. When compositing 3D, adding motion blur will help it look more organic, but can be render intensive, especially if you have a large scene. Applying some motion blur in a compositing program like After Effects is a render-saving advantage.

RE:Vision Effects ReelSmart Motion Blur fills that need beautifully. RSMB focuses on movement in a shot without blurring static areas of the screen and can even remove blur if a negative value is used. How well the blur can be removed will differ from project to project, of course, but if you need to remove blur, this is a great option to try.

## Pro Tip

RSMB is made to work with progressive footage, so if your footage has fields, deinterlace it before applying the effect. It will work with interlaced material in After Effects, but check the RSMB manual for in-depth details on this topic.

**Figure 3.12** ReelSmart Motion Blur is applied to 3D text. Notice how the ends of the text are more blurred while the center, which doesn't move as much, is less blurred. Footage: Michele Yamazaki.

So, you may be wondering why you'd need ReelSmart Motion Blur if you can do the same thing with Timewarp? You'll get much nicer results with RSMB. For a smooth result you will need to increase the Shutter Samples with Timewarp, which slows screen redraw and render time, so RSMB is also a lot faster.

# Pro Tip: Create Motion Blur with After Effects Timewarp Effect

There is a great trick with the After Effects Timewarp plug-in to add motion blur to moving video footage without a third-party plug-in. The Timewarp plug-in is based on an older version of The Foundry's Kronos technology.

Apply the Timewarp effect to your footage (Effect > Time > Timewarp). Set the value of Speed to 100 so the speed does not change. Click the checkbox to Enable Motion Blur within the Timewarp Effect Controls. Set Shutter Control to Manual, and adjust the Shutter Angle and Shutter Samples until you get the desired results.

**Figure 3.13** Timewarp's Effect Controls panel. Screenshot: Michele Yamazaki.

*A Comparison of Timewarp and ReelSmart Motion Blur*

**Figure 3.14** Original footage.
Footage: Daniel Evans,
LifebloodSkateboards.com.

**Figure 3.15** The footage blurred with Timewarp. Footage: Daniel Evans, LifebloodSkateboards.com.

**Figure 3.16** The footage blurred with ReelSmart Motion Blur. Footage: Daniel Evans, Lifeblood-Skateboards.com.

## Bokeh

My favorite blur is Bokeh (pronounced bo-keh, Japanese for blur), which is a special kind of defocus where the lens creates circles in the out-of-focus area. This is commonly seen in shots with a shallow depth of field where the foreground is in focus and the background is filled with bokeh. Certain lenses can also create bokeh shapes such as hexagons. To recreate a bokeh effect in After Effects CS5 and earlier, try **Frischluft Lenscare Defocus**.

**Digieffects Delirium DE NightBloom**, while not a true bokeh since it works with luminance values, not lens focus, will blur and

**Figure 3.17** The circles formed from the blur are Bokeh. Footage: Michele Yamazaki.

**Figure 3.18** Digieffects Delirium DE NightBloom applied to a photo of the Las Vegas Strip at sunrise. Footage: Michele Yamazaki.

give the appearance of bokeh. There are options for different bloom shapes, including Flares, Hexagon, and Circular, and at low settings, DE NightBloom can look very natural.

With the release of After Effects CS5.5, Adobe introduced **Camera Lens Blur**, which replaced the Lens Blur effect. The new one is a lot faster and has new features such as Diffraction Fringe and Highlight. Also in the CS5.5 release, the Camera has several iris settings under Camera Options that work if Depth of Field is turned on, including Iris Shape, Iris Rotation, Iris Roundness, Iris Aspect Ratio, and Iris Diffraction Fringe. Highlight Gain, Highlight Threshold, and Highlight

| 1 | Camera 1 | |
|---|---|---|
| ▼ Camera Options | | |
| Zoom | 2666.7 pixels (39.6° H) | |
| Depth of Field | On | |
| Focus Distance | 2666.7 pixels | |
| Aperture | 25.3 pixels | |
| Blur Level | 249% | |
| Iris Shape | Pentagon | |
| Iris Rotation | 0x+80.0° | |
| Iris Roundness | 0.0% | |
| Iris Aspect Ratio | 1.0 | |
| Iris Diffraction Fringe | 0.0 | |
| Highlight Gain | 0.0 | |
| Highlight Threshold | 255 | |
| Highlight Saturation | 0.0 | |

**Figure 3.19** Camera Options in After Effects CS5.5 include several options to control the iris.

Saturation are other new options. These settings allow the user to create some interesting blur effects that weren't possible in earlier versions of After Effects without the use of third-party plug-ins.

## AN OVERVIEW OF FRISCHLUFT LENSCARE

**By David Torno**

**Figure 3.20** A 3D-rendered image of a destroyed bridge. Footage: David Torno.

**Figure 3.21** A Z-Depth render of the same bridge. Footage: David Torno.

Frischluft's Lenscare plug-in package for After Effects is by far the industry standard for a camera focus and depth-of-field post solution. Why make a post effect for this you ask? Well, if you have ever tried doing a 3D render with any amount of camera focus applied, you'll know what

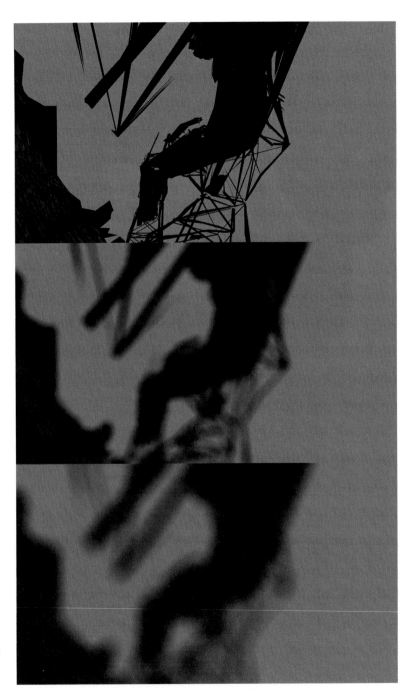

**Figure 3.22** Frishluft Lenscatre Out of Focus with the following Radius settings, Top image - Radius: 0; Middle image - Radius: 30; Bottom image - Radius: 60. Footage: David Torno.

I'm talking about. Most of today's 3D renders are pretty hefty to process, add any kind of blur to the mix and your render times can drastically increase, especially if you are going for photorealism. Other applications of this effect include adding focus changes and variations to practical footage after it has been shot. It is possible to do a rack focus on a shot

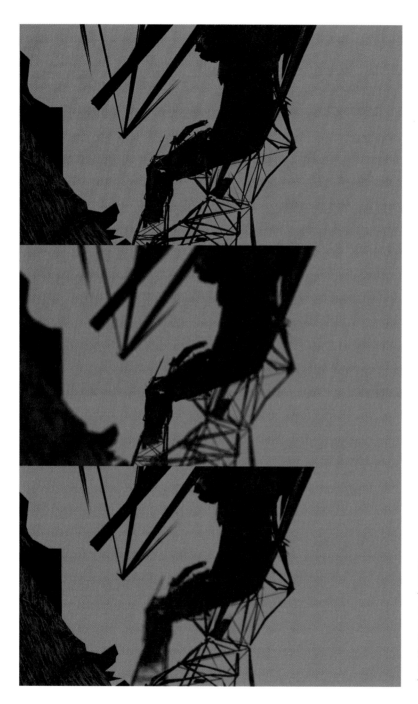

**Figure 3.23** Frischluft Lenscare Depth of Field with the following Radius settings and Focal Point settings. Top image - original image; Middle image - Radius: 30; Focal Point: 53; Bottom image - Radius: 30; Focal Point: 182. Footage: David Torno.

that never had one to begin with. Some detailed work can sometimes be required to accomplish it.

Lenscare comes as a two plug-in set: Depth of Field and Out of Focus. The main difference being that Out of Focus will simply just blur the whole image uniformly and Depth of Field will allow variations

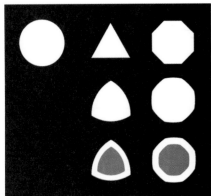

**Figure 3.24** *An example of how the iris shape. Left to right:*
Top Row: Facets: 3.0, 3.0, 8.0;
Rounded Facets: 1.0, 0.0, 0.0;
Middle Row: Facets: 3.0, 8.0;
Rounded Facets: 0.5, 0.5;
Bottom Row: Facets: 3.0, 8.0;
Rounded Facets: 0.5, 0.5;
Relative Border Brightness: 0.5,
0.5. Footage: David Torno.

of blurring on separate areas of your image based on Z-Depth information.

What is Z-Depth? Simply put, Z-Depth, also known as Z Buffer, Depth Map, and Depth Buffer, is a grayscale image representation of the distance within your 3D rendered scene from camera to any given object within the scene. The distance or depth is measured for each pixel. Traditionally black is represented as the closest to camera and white is the furthest away from camera, with all of the remaining shades of gray assigned to the in-between distances. A Z-Depth pass will end up looking like a foggy morning view of your 3D scene, but without textures. Most of today's 3D applications can render Z-Depth passes.

Frischluft included a fair amount of options for both plug-ins and they are setup almost identically. Out of Focus allows you to set the radius, iris, highlight selection, and a few other options. Depth of Field includes the same options in addition to depth layer selection and focal point.

Under the iris settings is facets, or the amount of iris facets that creates the aperture.

Here are a few tips when working with Frischluft Lenscare.

**Tip #1**: When adjusting focal point in Depth of Field, use the Sharp Zone option under the Show dropdown menu. This will allow you to home in on where you want your focus to be, in real-time, without AE trying to continually render the blur effect as you adjust it.

**Tip #2**: When using Depth of Field and Out of Focus on layers with alpha channels, keep an eye out for a white halo around the alpha edges. If you notice this, uncheck the Gamma Correction option and it will resolve this.

**Tip #3**: Use the Highlight Selection Only option under the Show dropdown menu and enable Highlight Selection to control how much specular points are used in the final blur. Very useful when creating defocused backgrounds that contain nighttime lights or cityscapes.

**Tip #4**: When using a Z-Depth pass that has too wide of a depth of field, you can narrow its coverage by adjusting the curve, black point, and white point in the Depth Buffer section of Depth of Field. This can give you some flexibility on the width of the focal depth area.

## Cycore FX CC Vector Blur

Cycore FX CC Vector Blur is an interesting effect, which actually falls more into the distortions category. Instead of just defocusing, it uses maps to define a vector field along which the blur will take place. The maps are taken from another layer, but it's also an interesting effect to use without a layer map.

Vector Blur ships with After Effects but is also included with **Cycore FX HD** ($299), which includes more plug-ins and other benefits.

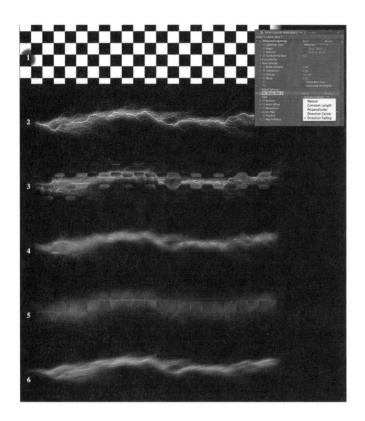

**Figure 3.25** Cycore FX Vector Blur is applied to Advanced Lightning. All vector blurred samples use the Checkerboard pattern as a map. The Checkerboard was generated with Noise Industries FxFactory Pro Checkerboard. (1) A checkerboard pattern; (2) Advanced Lightning only; (3) Vector Blur with Natural Type; (4) Vector Blur with Constant Length; (5) Vector Blur with Direction Center; (6) Vector Blur with Direction Fading. Screenshot: Michele Yamazaki.

**Figure 3.26** GenArts Monsters GT M_SpinBlur using the Fade Blur style. Footage: Crowd Control, clip # 00045_001_52.

## Radial Blurs and Spin Blurs

A radial blur will blur from a center point in all directions, while a spin blur will smear around a center point.

**GenArts Monsters GT M_SpinBlur** allows the user to isolate segments of a circle, giving a soft transition between the twirled and untwirled portions.

**Boris Continuum Complete BCC Radial Blur** gives more options than the Radial Blur that ships with After Effects. There are several presets and there's an Apply mode, Motion Tracker, and Pixel Chooser, which allows the user to isolate areas of the image based on a number of parameters.

**Figure 3.27** BCC Radial Blur has many presets and a built-in Motion Tracker. The center of the blur is placed at the center of the lantern. Footage: Michele Yamazaki.

## Light Effects: Light Rays, Glints, and Glows

Adding a bit of glow or a glint to an effect can really add something special or even become important to storytelling. Light rays can give life to a bland sky, signify the presence of an angel, give a logo more impact and add depth to underwater scenes. Glints can add a natural feel to shots of water and sparkle to ruby slippers or the angst-filled teenage vampire's skin. What would a light saber be without its colored glow?

Light effects are some of the most important and useful effects for a digital motion artist, and, like blurs, there are dozens of options from every manufacturer on the market.

### Dream Look with Boris Continuum Complete BCC Colorize Glow

The "dream look" is common for flashbacks and dreams in films. Red Giant Magic Bullet Looks has some lovely dream-look presets, but the following is a very easy recipe for giving your footage that dreamy otherworldly feel with **Boris Continuum Complete BCC Colorize Glow**.

**Figure 3.28** Boris Continuum Complete BCC Colorize Glow is used to create a Dream Look. Footage: Crowd Control, clip # 00087_004_25.

1. Bring your footage or composite into a comp in After Effects.
2. Add an Adjustment Layer (Layer > New > Adjustment Layer).
3. Apply BCC Colorize Glow to the Adjustment Layer (Effects > BCC Effects > BCC Colorize Glow). In the Effect Controls panel, apply the preset glowOverlay.bcp.
4. Twirl open Color Preset and choose violet-yellow.bcp from the preset menu.

## Pro Tip: Why Use an Adjustment Layer?

The advantage to using an Adjustment Layer as opposed to just applying the effect to the footage is that a Composite mode can be used with an Adjustment Layer for different looks. Also, if you have several elements in the composite, as long as the Adjustment Layer is placed on top of the stack in the timeline, effects on the Adjustment Layer will affect everything below it.

## Comparing Some After Effects Glows

There are so many different glow plug-ins that work differently and have multiple options that it's difficult to really compare them side-by-side. They just don't have the same output.

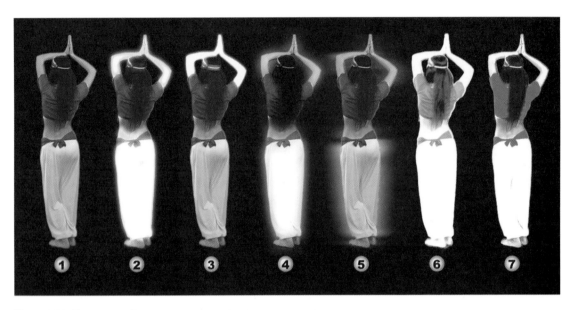

**Figure 3.29** Glow comparisons. Footage: Crowd Control, clip # 00368_002_30.

Figure 3.29 shows a sampling of a few of the options on the market, with descriptions listed below.

1. Original image.
2. **After Effects Glow** works either on the Color Channels, which can be used for creating a glow for full-frame footage, or Alpha Channels, for creating light-ray effects around layers with alphas such as text and logos. There are several good options but the look just isn't as nice as with the third-party glow options. It has no presets.
3. **Noise Industries FxFactory Glow (Box-Shaped)** is a nice looking glow, but there are no presets. Even at a Strength value of just 0.01, the effect is still viewable. This is a great plug-in for bright bloom transitions. There is a Use Image Colors option or you can choose a color with the eyedropper, a feature not included in a lot of glow plug-ins. There is a built-in Mask tool, which has custom mask shapes or the option to choose a path on the layer.
4. **Boris Continuum Complete BCC Glow** is a robust plug-in that comes with multiple presets and allows for the glow to be based on RGB Channels, Luminance, Lightness, Red, Green, Blue, or Alpha. There are the usual glow adjustments such as the radius, threshold, and compositing mode. BCC Glow has the added options of a built-in Motion Tracker, a Pixel Chooser to isolate areas of the shot, and Beat Reactor, to animate with audio input.

5. **GenArts Sapphire S_Glow** is interesting because it works with a background and matte layer, so it is made specifically for compositing. Width X and Width Y allow the glow to be stretched and this is not something seen in other glow plug-ins. Not only that, individual Red, Green, and Blue widths can be adjusted. It also has options to Glow From Alpha and Glow Under Source, so the glow can come from behind the text or keyed footage, not just on top of the image. There are no presets with S_Glow, but it's a solid choice.

6. **Digieffects Delirium DE Glower** does not have a lot of options but it does include the basics and the option to set Dark Color and Bright Color, or use Original Colors. There are a few presets as well.

7. **Tiffen Dfx Digital Filter Suite Glow** is a plug-in that doesn't seem too special on the surface but once Color Correct settings are pulled down, there are options not seen in other glow filters. There are Hue, Saturation, Brightness, Contrast, Gamma, and Red, Green, and Blue controls for the color of the glow and precise control of the color.

If I had to choose my personal favorite of the bunch, it's the GenArts Sapphire S_Glow.

## Light Rays, Glows, and Glints with idustrial revolution Volumetrix

**Figure 3.30** Three styles of Volumetrix. Footage: Michele Yamazaki.

Nothing jazzes up a bland logo like beautiful animated light rays and glows. **idustrial revolution Volumetrix** ($49) comes with a full library of presets. The plug-in is based on the FxFactory engine so it's lightning fast. Many of the presets are meant to animate so that text is revealed or the light rays move across or behind the text. Most importantly, Volumetrix looks beautiful

**Figure 3.31** Volumetrix's Effect Controls panel. Screenshot: Michele Yamazaki.

and it's a lot of fun to use. At the low price of $49, this is a plug-in every After Effects user should own.

*Note*: Volumetrix requires the free FxFactory installed to run, which can be downloaded at *www.noiseindustries.com*.

The plug-in is broken into sections, with the Presets at the top, then Source, Animation, Style, Light Rays, Glow, and Distortion.

- **Presets**: There are around 50 presets broken into Text and Video and some also will reveal as they wipe. They are named well so it's easy to find what you're looking for.
- **Source**: Allows the user to choose Opaque pixels (best for titles), Transparent pixels, Range of pixels (best for video), or Custom mask, which is pulled from another layer.
- **Animation**: The settings can be keyframed by selecting Progress (animate with keyframes) or auto-animate using Duration in Seconds or Duration of the Clip.
- **Style**: Choose which part of the text or video is affected and if and how a wipe will animate. Effect Width, Effect Softness, and Angle are set here.
- **Light Rays**: If the box is checked, Light Rays is enabled. Light Source can follow the effect or be in a fixed location and the position can be modified. Rays Color, Length, Strength, and Saturation are modified here.

- **Glow**: If the box for Glow is checked, it's enabled. Source colors or a specified glow color can be used. Glow Radius, Saturation, and Strength are keyframable.
- **Distortion**: Adds a bulgy effect to the transition or source of the light for interesting effects.

## Create a Creepy Atmosphere with Trapcode Shine and Digieffects Delirium DE Fog Factory

**Figure 3.32** Trapcode Shine is seen though fog. Footage: Michele Yamazaki.

I remember when **Trapcode Shine** ($99) was released and AE users were abuzz with excitement. It was the first light rays filter that wasn't a render hog. It has become the industry standard for light ray effects and is very easy to use.

This tutorial takes you through making a creepy scene with light coming through fog and around the silhouette of a tree, as if there's a single light moving behind the tree. The tree is a still image of a shot I took in Tokyo with my Canon Rebel XSi. *The project files are included on this book's DVD in a folder named Shine Spooky Tree.*

**Third-party plug-ins needed:**
- Trapcode Shine
- Digieffects Delirium
    1. Create a new composition using the "HDTV 1080 29.97" preset, 5:00 in duration. Name it "Spooky Tree" and make the Background Color black.
    2. Import spookytree.jpg (included on this book's DVD in the Shine Spooky Tree folder) into After Effects. Drag the image file into the Spooky Tree comp.

**Figure 3.33** Shine settings on the spookytree.jpg layer. Footage: Michele Yamazaki.

**3.** First we'll add the light rays. Apply Trapcode Shine to the spookytree.jpg layer (Effects > Trapcode > Shine).

Open the Effect Controls for Shine. First, let's set the Transfer Mode of Shine to Screen. This will Screen the light rays over the tree.

**Figure 3.34** The light rays from Shine appear to burst through the fog, generated with DE Fog Factory, and from behind the tree. Screenshot: Michele Yamazaki.

4. Twirl open Colorize. Set Colorize…to Aura with the pulldown menu. This gives the light rays a pinkish look.

Next, we'll make the light appear as if it's moving from left to right. Make sure you're at the first frame in the timeline. Place the Source Point of Shine to the left of the tree and enable keyframing. Go to the final frame and move the position of Source Point to the right of the tree.

Increase Ray Length to 10.0 and set Boost Light to 2.0 to give the light more oomph.

5. Twirl open Shimmer and set Amount to 20.0. Check the Source Point Affects Shimmer checkbox so that the light rays will slowly rotate as the Source Point moves.

Now you should see some beams of purplish light coming from behind the tree. Time to add some atmospheric fog with Digieffects DE Fog Factory. Fog can also be created with Fractal Noise, however I think DE Fog Factory is easier to set up and it looks nicer.

6. Create a new Solid layer (Layer > New > Solid). Make it comp size and name it Fog. Apply DE Fog Factory (Effects > Digieffects Delirium > DE Fog Factory). At the top of the Effect Controls panel, click the Effect Only checkbox so that the Solid layer is completely hidden and just the effect is seen. Leave the other settings at their defaults or change them as you wish. It's easiest to see the fog if the layer is soloed.

## Trapcode Shine Samples

Since the previous tutorial was not a typical use of Trapcode Shine, Figures 3.35 through 3.38 show a variety of Shine looks to showcase this versatile plug-in.

**Figure 3.35** Shine used on a Text layer that has been broken apart with Shatter. Footage: Michele Yamazaki.

**Figure 3.36** Shine used on a Trapcode Particular preset. Footage: Michele Yamazaki.

**Figure 3.37** Shine used on a sphere generated with CycoreFX CC Sphere. The sky was generated with BCC Stars. Footage: NASA.

**Figure 3.38** Shine applied to Digieffects DE Fairy Dust. Footage: Michele Yamazaki.

# Boris Continuum Complete BCC Light Zoom from within a Planet

**Figure 3.39** A planet made with all Boris Continuum Complete plug-ins. Footage: Michele Yamazaki.

For this quick tutorial we'll use **Boris Continuum Complete Light Zoom** with the tutorial "Make a Planet with Boris Continuum Complete BCC Granite & BCC Sphere." *Open the project named BCCPlanet.aep on this book's DVD in the BCC Planet folder and start from there, or jump ahead to the tutorial in Chapter 6 on page 214 "Make a Planet with Boris Continuum Complete BCC Granite & BCC Sphere." The finished comp is in the same folder and is named BCCPlanet-withLightZoom.aep.*

**Third-party plug-ins needed:**
- Boris Continuum Complete
    1. Once you've completed the tutorial mentioned in the paragraph above or opened the project files named BCC Planet, open the final Space Scene comp. Select the planet texture layer.
    2. Apply Boris Continuum Complete BCC Light Zoom to the planet texture layer (Effects > BCC Lights > BCC Light Zoom).

The default looks pretty decent, but we want the effect to appear stronger as if it's coming from within the planet. The effect is using the luminance values of the planet, so as it rotates and comes into the light, the effect has more intensity.

    3. In the Effect Controls panel for BCC Light Zoom, choose the preset Increase Intensity.bap. In the Animated Preset Options, choose Preserve Timing and First Frame. Click OK. Go to the second Intensity keyframe in the timeline for BCC Light Zoom, which is around 3:01. Set Intensity to 180.

In the Effect Controls panel, set Color to Colorize with the pulldown menu. Under Color Preset, choose red-yellow.bcp.

4. The planet stops moving before 3 seconds, so you may want to keep the spin going through the duration of the composition by dragging the Spin keyframe in BCC Sphere to the final frame of the comp and increasing the value.

5. To add some interest to BCC Light Zoom, we'll add some dust. Under Noise, choose Light in the pulldown menu. Twirl open Noise and check the Auto Animate box.

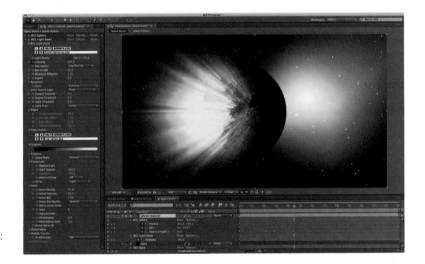

**Figure 3.40** The final settings for BCC Light Zoom. Screenshot: Michele Yamazaki.

## Glints

Need to add a sparkle in someone's eye or a glint off her lip-gloss? Use **Boris Continuum BCC Glint**, which is included in **Boris Continuum Complete** and **Boris Continuum Glitters**

**Figure 3.41** BCC Glint adds some lovely glints to the bright spots in the video. Footage: Crowd Control, clip # 00126_001_93.

**Figure 3.42** The frame of video rendered from Red Giant Psunami has Trapcode Starglow applied to the sunset on the right. Footage: Michele Yamazaki.

**Unit** ($99). Try the reallySmallRays.bcp preset. The trick is to have Glint Threshold set high enough so that it only appears in those brighter areas. If your actor is wearing a light color, the Pixel Chooser can help isolate the areas you want. There is also a built-in Motion Tracker.

**Trapcode Starglow** ($99) is a great plug-in to add some beautiful light reflections to water.

## Making Your Composition a Masterpiece

Do you remember the Robin Williams' film *What Dreams May Come?* (1998)? The effects in the afterworld looked like they were from a Van Gogh painting. This section deals with painterly effects and adding artistic effects. I'll also demonstrate some plug-ins and explain some techniques for making cartoon and comic-book looks.

### Creating and Applying Custom Brushes using RE:Vision Effects Video Gogh

**RE:Vision Effects Video Gogh** ($119.95) actually employs the same technology used in the film *What Dreams May Come?* In the latest version of the software, the user can now create custom brushes. The great thing about applying this sort of effect is that the composites don't have to be tidy. The effect will cover any flaws (but if you're transitioning to the effect, you're not so lucky).

Anything can be made into a brush: images, graphic elements, text. I'll design two types of brushes, one in Adobe Photoshop and one in After Effects using the shape tools, and I'll apply them to footage in After Effects. I'll be creating brushes with an alpha channel, but Video Gogh can also use the red channel, red and

**Web Link:**

See *http://bit.ly/ WhatDreams* for images and information about the visual effects from the film *What Dreams May Come?*

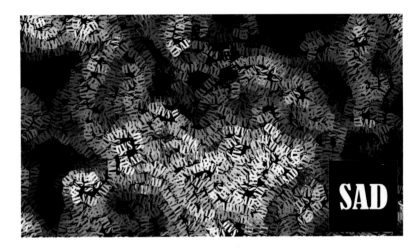

**Figure 3.43** A custom brush, created with simply a layer of text with an alpha channel, is used as a brush to create interesting effects with RE:Vision Effects Video Gogh. Footage: Crowd Control, clip # 00087_004_25.

green channel, the sprite direct, or the color of the sprite and luminance of the image. See the manual for more information on other brush mode options.

*The project files and a few custom brush images are included on this book's DVD in the Video Gogh folder in the subfolder named Custom Brushes within the Footage folder.* Try them out! This tutorial explains how to create your own custom brushes in Photoshop.

**Third-party plug-ins needed:**

- RE:Vision Effects Video Gogh
    1. In Photoshop, create a new square image that is 200 × 200 pixels, 72 ppi. You can create the brush at any size, but 200 × 200 is a good size to work with because you won't likely need a larger brush. (Figure 3.44.)
    2. Create a new empty layer for your brush on this layer. There are many ways to create the brush. Use a custom shape or text, paint on the layer, or a use photo. Just be careful of the

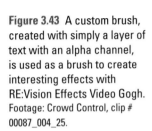

**Figure 3.44** Photoshop image settings. Screenshot: Michele Yamazaki.

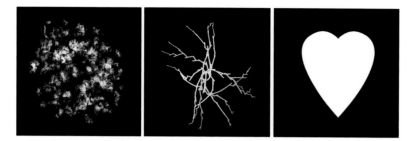

Figure 3.45 Examples of three brushes you could create, shown over black. The left and center were created with the Paint Brush tool in Photoshop. The one on the right is a Custom Shape in Photoshop. All are saved with Alpha channels. Footage: Michele Yamazaki.

edges of the image. If your image is cut off, the final artwork will show it. (Figure 3.45.)

3. After you're happy with your brush, delete the background. You'll have a regular floating layer with transparency built in. Save the file as a Photoshop document (.PSD).
4. Import the brush into After Effects as footage with Merged Layers enabled. You should not see any background behind your image. (Figure 3.46.)

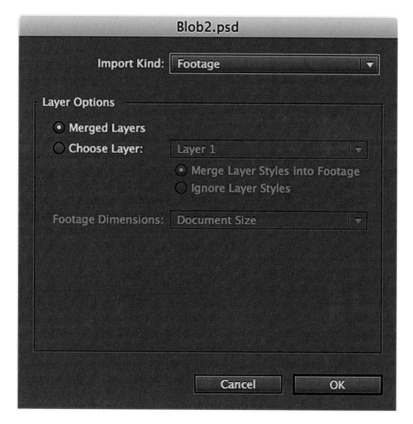

Figure 3.46 Import settings for the brush image. Screenshot: Michele Yamazaki.

5. When your composite is ready in After Effects, bring your brush into your comp by dragging the image into the composition. Turn off the visibility of the brush layer by clicking the eyeball in the Timeline panel. (Figure 3.47.)

6. Apply RE:Vision Effects Video Gogh or Video Gogh Pro to your footage (Effects > RE:Vision Plug-ins > Video Gogh). If you do have a multilayered composite, applying the effect to an Adjustment Layer will unify the look of your composition. Make sure the Adjustment Layer is placed on the top of the Timeline stack.

7. In the Effect Controls panel for Video Gogh, choose User-defined for Style. Under Custom Brushes, choose your custom brush for Brush 1 in the pulldown menu.

**Figure 3.47** The original composite. The background was generated with Fractal Noise and Tritone. Footage: Crowd Control, clip # 00087_004_25.

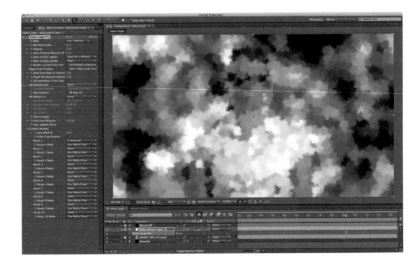

**Figure 3.48** Custom Brush is used in Video Gogh with the alpha channel selected. Max Brush Size is set to 0.25. Footage: Crowd Control, clip # 00087_004_25.

Multiple brushes can be selected for more unique looks by choosing them for Brush 2, Brush 3, and so on. Set the Brush mode to Use Alpha Chan or try one of the other settings in the pulldown menu. (Figure 3.48.)

## Pro Tip: Creating a Brush in After Effects

Brushes can also be made directly in AE too. Anything on a layer will work. Use the Custom Shape tool, the Type tool, or even the Paint Brush to create an element onscreen. Try using masked footage too. Anything with a soft edge will work. Again, if your image is cut off on the edges of the comp, the brush will show it. Name the layer appropriately.

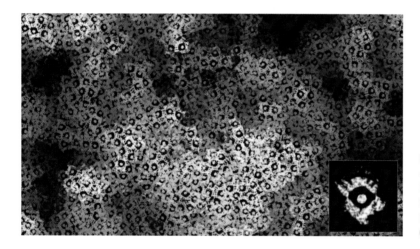

**Figure 3.49** Video Gogh with a custom blob brush, created in Photoshop. The Brush mode is set to Use Alpha Chan. Footage: Crowd Control, clip # 00087_004_25.

**Figure 3.50** A photo of a goose as a custom brush. The Brush mode is set to Use Sprite Direct. Footage: Michele Yamazaki.

8. Customize the look by adjusting the Max Brush Size, Extra Distance Between Brushes, and Paint over %Source settings. There is also an option under Custom Brushes to Vary Width %.

9. To animate the painting, adjust the values of Birth Grow Rate (in Frames) and Death Die Rate (in Frames). Alternate Motion Source can also be pulled from another layer of video or animation. Please see the manual for instructions.

## GenArts Monsters M_Brush

GenArts Monsters M_Brush has several presets for different styles of artwork, including Oil, Water, Chalk, Pastel, Pencil, Felt Tip, Splat, and others.

All aspects of the effect can be keyframed, including Brush Size, Number of Brushes, and Angle of the brush strokes.

**Figure 3.51** The original image is on top. The bottom sample has GenArts Monsters M_Brush with the Oil1 Type and Oil Style selected. Footage: Michele Yamazaki.

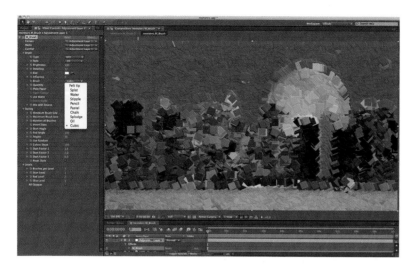

Figure 3.52 Monsters M_Brush with Cubic Style Brush. Screenshot: Michele Yamazaki.

## Storek Studio nVeil by FxFactory

**Storek Studio nVeil** ($99) falls somewhere between an artistic effect and a distortion filter. Simply apply it to your footage

Figure 3.53 The composite on the left is the original. On the right, Storek Studio nVeil has been applied with Built-in Veil set to the River preset. Footage: Crowd Control, clip # 00074_001_24.

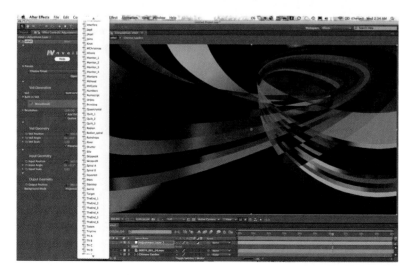

Figure 3.54 Storek Studio nVeil has dozens of built in Veil SVG files included. Footage: Crowd Control, clip # 00074_001_24.

and watch it work. It's a very simple plug-in to use with several presets and built-in Veils, or shapes to distort the footage. These built-in Veils are SVG files, and a custom SVG file, a vector format, can be used.

nVeil is great for creating interesting backgrounds for text builds and slates, and it also has some presets for picture frames. Text can be used in the form of an SVG file, to make some interesting titles.

It uses the Noise Industries FxEngine so it's fast, and the plug-in also works in Final Cut Studio.

*Note*: nVeil requires the free FxFactory to run, which can be downloaded at *www.noiseindustries.com*.

## Warhol-Style Art with Noise Industries FxFactory Pro Pop Art

The famous pop art style is a cinch to create with Noise Industries FxFactory Pro Pop Art. There are only a few presets, but all colors in each quadrant can be modified and Layer Threshold, Layer Distance, and Color Sharpness can be adjusted to taste.

*Note*: Pro Pop Art requires the free FxFactory to run, which can be downloaded at *www.noiseindustries.com*.

**Figure 3.55** FxFactory Pop Art. Footage: Michele Yamazaki.

## Cartoon Look

I'll be the first to admit that the cartoon look, as seen in the Charles Schwab commercials, is not exactly my favorite look. I have seen it used a few times, though, in an interesting manner. The title sequence for *The Pillars of the Earth* TV mini-series

Figure 3.56 Cartoon look comparison. 1. Original footage; 2. Red Giant ToonIt; 3. DVShade LiveToon; 4. Boris Continuum Complete BCC Cartoon Look; 5. GenArts Sapphire S_Cartoon; 6. After Effects Cartoon. Footage: Crowd Control, clip # 00033_001_98.

used a cartoon look and is a truly gorgeous animation. Also, the Temper Trap "Science of Fear" video (*http://tinyurl.com/2wkt9av*) shows an old car driving at night with yellow headlights and it is combined with hand-drawn trees and other elements.

Someone must really like cartoon look because there is no shortage of plug-ins on the market. There is one that ships with After Effects simply called **Cartoon**, however you can try many others including **Red Giant ToonIt**, **Boris Continuum BCC Cartoon Look** and **BCC Cartooner**, **DVShade LiveToon**, **Noise Industries FxFactory Pro Cartoon**, and **Sapphire S_Cartoon**. The filters vary greatly in speed and options.

Figure 3.56 shows a sampling of a few of the cartoon look plug-ins available, with descriptions listed below.

1. Original footage
2. **Red Giant ToonIt ($399)**. Of all of the cartoon look plug-ins on the market, Red Giant ToonIt has by far the most options, the most presets, and renders the quickest. It includes the main plug-in ToonIt Roto Toon, which gives the cartoon looks: Color Effects, Outlines, Comic Outlines, Shadow Outlines, Woodcut Outlines, Halftone Patterns, Stipple Pattern, and more. ToonIt Goth gives a posterization and three-color look. ToonIt Heat Vision creates the look of infrared video. ToonIt Blacklight Edges creates bright outlines of the video while making the video black. ToonIt Outlines is just what it says it is. ToonIt Roto Toon has several presets, broken into sections. When the options are not available for the preset, they are grayed out, which keeps the Effect Controls panel tidy.
3. **DVShade LiveToon** ($49) has presets for the common cartoon look as well as Charcoal Sketch, Comic Book, Graphic Novel, and more. There is an option to screen Dots, Lines, Hatches, and Circular patterns. Something I found a little odd about this plug-in is that higher values in some of the settings will decrease the effect. For example, increasing the value of Detail actually lessens the detail. This does not apply to all of the settings in the plug-in. That said, the plug-in is extremely easy to use, has useful presets, and is very fast.

# Pro Tip

Noise Industries FxFactory Pro Cartoon filter is a nice looking effect, but it has only a few presets and it ignores the alpha channel. There are actually quite a few filters that don't support alpha channels, so the effect will affect the area that should be hidden when applied to footage with an alpha channel. This is fine if you put the effect on an Adjustment Layer on top of the layer stack, effecting all layers of the composite. If you want to effect only a layer with an alpha channel, you have to work around this limitation. One method is to place another instance of the layer with the alpha channel (without the filter) above the filtered layer. Then, set the Track Matte to Alpha Channel to remove the area around the alpha channel. The layers must be perfectly lined up for this to work properly.

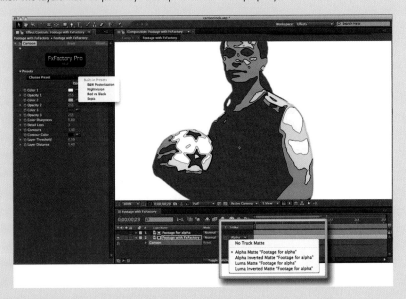

**Figure 3.57** The FxFactory Pro Cartoon filter ignores the alpha channel. As a workaround, place another instance of the layer with the alpha channel above the effected layer and set the Track Matte to Alpha. Footage: Crowd Control, clip # 00033_001_98.

4. **Boris Continuum Complete Cartoon Look** ($199) ships with four **Boris Continuum Complete** plug-ins: Cartoon Look, Pencil Sketch, Charcoal Sketch, and Watercolor. In Cartoon Look, there is a preset called "ChuckSchwab.bsp," which imitates the look from the commercials. Several of the presets animate, becoming a cartoon, or going back to reality. As with many of the Boris Continuum plug-ins, there is a Pixel Chooser to isolate areas of the footage.

Cartoon On and Lines On are separate so it's possible to have just the cartoon fill or outlines, and both parameters are customizable.

5. **GenArts Sapphire S_Cartoon**. Many of the cartoon look plug-ins have a default look with a thick and ugly black stroke

along the edges. Thinning or removing the outline entirely can definitely improve the look. Sapphire S_Cartoon gives you full control over the edges and even comes with a Suppress Small Edges option and an Edge Sharpen feature.

6. **After Effects Cartoon**. One of the catalysts behind After Effects' Cartoon filter was to exhibit the speed and power of OpenGL rendering, using the Adobe Pixel Bender toolkit. For more on Pixel Bender, see the section "Pixel Bender Plug-ins" on page 13 at the end of Chapter 1.

*Note*: LiveToon requires the free FxFactory to run, which can be downloaded at *www.noiseindustries.com.*

## Creating a Comic Book Look

As much as I dislike cartoon look, I love the comic book effect that is often seen in superhero movie title sequences. How is it done? Cartoon look can be mixed effectively with a half tone, super-saturated effect to create a comic book look. **Boris Continuum Complete** and **GenArts Sapphire** include both cartoon look filters and half-tone filters. To make it even easier, **Noise Industries FxFactory Pro Comic Book, DVShade LiveToon,** and **Red Giant ToonIt,** mentioned above, have the filter as an all-in-one, specifically made for a comic book look.

The thought bubble is made with **SUGARfx Bubble Buddy**, a plug-in that uses the FxFactory engine. Bubble Buddy generates talk bubbles, thought bubbles, balloons, and more. The colors, text, style and animations are completely adjustable and key-framable. It's laid out very logically so it's easy to start using it productively minutes after it is installed.

*Note*: SUGARfx plug-ins require the free FxFactory to run, which can be downloaded at *www.noiseindustries.com.*

**Figure 3.58** A comic book look created with Noise Industries FxFactory plug-ins. Footage: Crowd Control, clip #: 00074_003_47.

*The project files, including the footage, courtesy of Crowd Control, are included on this book's DVD in the ComicBook folder (Mac).*

**Third-party plug-ins needed:**

- Noise Industries FxFactory (Mac)
- SUGARfx Bubble Buddy (Mac)

1. Import the footage of the gunman, Crowd Control clip 00074_003_47.mov, into After Effects. Drag it to the Make a New Composition button at the bottom of the Project panel. A new composition opens. Rename the composition "Comic Book" by going to Composition > Composition Settings and editing the composition name.

2. We'll want to place a hold frame so that the gunman freezes in time. Go to 4:13 in the timeline, select the layer and go to Layer > Time > Freeze Frame. This applies Time Remap in the timeline and adds a Hold keyframe for 4:13.

   The Comic Book effect will be applied to both the footage and the background, so it will be applied as an Adjustment Layer. To get a better idea of the final look, we'll create the background first.

3. Create a New Solid, the same size as the comp (Layer > New > Solid). Make sure it is behind your footage. Apply 4-Color Gradient (Effects > Generate > 4-Color Gradient) and set the colors to shades of red, black, and yellow. Move around the points so that it looks like your actor is standing in a pool of light. (Figure 3.59.)

4. Add an Adjustment Layer and place it above the footage and background. Apply FxFactory Comic Book (Effects > FxFactory Pro Stylize > Comic Book). Start with the High Fidelity preset and modify the settings until you have a nice halftone look. I made the following adjustments (Figure 3.60):

   - **Shadows**: 0.14
   - **Brightness**: 0.10
   - **Saturation**: 2.00
   - **Sharpness**: 0.74

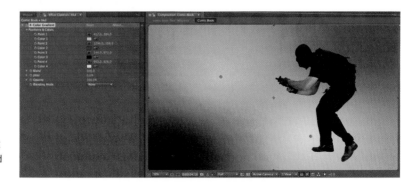

**Figure 3.59** The background is created with a 4-Color Gradient applied to a solid. Footage: Crowd Control, clip #: 00074_003_47.

**Figure 3.60** FxFactory Comic Book filter. Footage: Crowd Control, clip #: 00074_003_47.

5. Apply another Adjustment Layer and apply SUGARfx Bubble Buddy (Effects > SUGARfx > Bubble Buddy). It's important to use an Adjustment Layer as opposed to a Solid Layer because there is no alpha control and the solid color will show through.

- **Main Setup**: Set the position to a logical place onscreen (thought bubble coming from head, talk bubble coming from mouth, etc.).
- **Color Palette**: I am mainly using Colors 1–4. I set Color 1 to white, Color 2 to Yellow, Color 3 to Orange, and Color 4 to black.
- **Bubble:**
  **Graphic Style**: Square Round 2
  **Color**: Color 1
  **Additional Elements**: Around Stuff
- **Pointer**:
  **Style [Graphic]**: Bubbles

**Figure 3.61** FxFactory Pro Rounded Corners gives the comic a frame. Footage: Crowd Control, clip #: 00074_003_47.

> **Direction**: 84.0°
> **Pointer Flip**: Checked
> **Size Adjust**: −0.15
> - **Text**:
>   **Text Margin Width**: 1.50
> - **Text**: "DEVIL HAWK, WHERE ARE YOU?"
>   **Font Name**: Comic Sans Bold (yes, an appropriate use for Comic Sans!)
>   **Color**: Color 4
>   **Font Size**: 25

**Finishing Touches**: Drag this comp into the Make New Composition panel. Rename it as you wish. Apply FxFactory Rounded Corners (Effects > FxFactory Pro Distort > Rounded Corners). Adjust Uniform Margin, Radius, and Softness.

## Aged Film Effects

**Digieffects Cinelook** was the first plug-in on the market to simulate the look of old film and was a great tool for making your footage look like it had been stored in a garage or run over by a Mac truck. As cool as it was, Cinelook was very slow and ended up being sold to Red Giant in 2007, and is no longer being developed by either company.

Although Cinelook is no more, there are plenty of other options available for damaged film looks in After Effects. **Red Giant Magic Bullet Looks** comes with **MisFire** and has tools such as Deep Scratches, Displacement, Dust, Fading, Flicker, Funk, Gate Weave, Grain, and so on. With MisFire, each effect has to be applied separately. It's not a single plug-in. This allows the effects to be applied in any order that you like. It's easy to use but looks best when lightly applied and is not all that fast.

**Figure 3.62** The original shot used in the samples in this section. Footage: Michele Yamazaki.

**Digieffects Aged Film** ($49) also includes Grain, Dust, Scratches, Frame Jitter, and Color to give footage that timeworn look. There's a Random Seed setting for infinite assortment of looks. The 64-bit version includes loads of presets, found in the Effects & Presets panel. The presets include names such as 8 mm, Purple Rain, Old TV, Rose Colored Glasses, Shaky Projector, The '70, and Tipsy Camera Man. Aged Film renders pretty fast and is fun to use.

**Figure 3.63** Red Giant Magic Bullet Looks MisFire. Screenshot: Michele Yamazaki.

**Boris Continuum Complete BCC Film Damage** is very fast to render and comes with some nice presets. Options include Color, Flicker, Shake, Grain, Dirt, Hair, and Scratches; they can be turned on an off with a checkbox. If the parameter group is turned off, the options are grayed out, so it keeps the Effect Controls tidy and easy to navigate. As with many other BCC plug-ins, there is a built-in Motion Tracker and a Pixel Chooser, which allow the user to isolate the effect with masks or by channels.

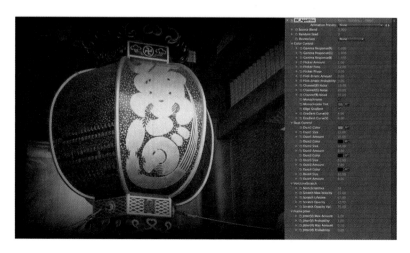

**Figure 3.64** Digieffects Aged Film. Screenshot: Michele Yamazaki.

**Figure 3.65** Boris Continuum Complete BCC Film Damage. Footage: Michele Yamazaki.

**Figure 3.66** GenArts Sapphire Film Damage. Screenshot: Michele Yamazaki.

Of all of the film damage plug-ins, **GenArts Sapphire S_FilmDamage** is my favorite, not because it has the most options, it just looks the nicest. Defocus and Hairs look completely organic, and it's fast.

## Creating an Edgy, Chaotic Look with Digieffects Aged Film and Digieffects Damage, by Joe Mason

In this section, Joe Mason, a Missouri-based motion graphic artist and owner of MyAfterEffects.com, shows you how to create a jittery, helter-skelter style using **Digieffects Damage** ($99) **Interference** and **Aged Film**. Digieffects Aged Film is available either à la carte or with Damage v2, along with Interference, Blockade, Artifact, Skew, Overexposure, and Destabilize. Instead of using Aged Film to create the old film look that you've seen a thousand times, Joe uses the effect to move elements of the composition. Interference is used to create even more chaos.

Figure 3.67 This project was a winning entry in the Digieffects/Motionworks Challenge and Joe Mason put together a tutorial to go along with it. Footage: Joe Mason.

*There is comp already built that you can apply the effects to on this book's DVD in a folder named Digieffects Damage + Aged Film.* Instead of copying exactly what is on the video tutorial, this section will dive into some great tips in working with Digieffects Damage and Aged Film. If you want to check out the full tutorial, it can be found on Vimeo: *http://vimeo .com/11721258.*

**Third-party plug-ins needed:**
- Digieffects Damage
- Digieffects Aged Film (included with Damage v2 or à la carte)

1. Open the project named Chaos.aep. Inside the folder are precomps, footage, and final comps already built. The final comp is named Main Comp – Final, but if you'd like to follow along using the tutorial below, use the comp named Main Comp – for Tutorial.

2. Select the Adjustment Layer named Digieffects Adjustment Layer and apply Digieffects Aged Film (Effect < Digieffects Aged Film < DE_Aged-Film) to give the comp a very cool, grungy look. (Figure 3.68.) Using the Frame Jitter parameter group settings, found in

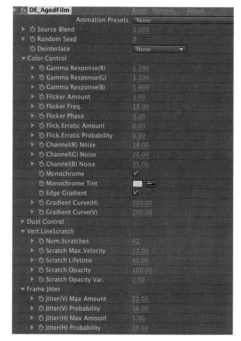

Figure 3.68 The settings for Digieffects Aged Film in this step. Footage: Joe Mason.

## Pro Tip: Digieffects Frame Jitter

Aged Film effects only the area of actual size of the element you're effecting. If you're applying the effect to full-screen footage, it's no problem, but if you're applying Aged Film to a logo that fills only 25% of the screen, the effect will only occur in that 25% area. A workaround is to precompose the logo in a larger composition and apply the effect to the precomp; the effect will fill the screen.

the Effect Controls panel for Aged Film, randomly offset the video. I love the fact that you can modify how much your overall frame jitters on individual axes. I used these settings:

**Figure 3.69** This is what the comp will look like after applying the Aged Film effect. Footage: Joe Mason.

# Pro Tip: Tinting and Vignetting with Digieffects Aged Film

No need to pull out another effect to tint or add a vignette to your footage. To tint, check the Monochrome Tint box in Aged Film and choose the Tint Color. Adjust Source Blend to pull some of the original color back into the footage. For a vignette effect, lower the Gradient Curve settings.

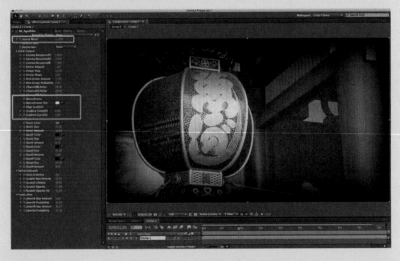

**Figure 3.70** Tints and Vignettes can be easily created within the Aged Film plug-in by adjusting the Monochrome Tint and Gradient Curve settings. Screenshot: Michele Yamazaki.

*Frame Jitter*

- **Jitter (V) Max Amount**: 22 (the maximum vertical jitter)
- **Jitter (V) Probability**: 16 (the probability of a vertical jitter)
- **Jitter (H) Max Amount**: 5 (the maximum horizontal jitter)
- **Jitter(H) Probability**: 33 (the probability of a horizontal jitter)

*Vertical Line Scratch*

- **Number of Scratches**: 42
- **Scratch Max Velocity**: 22
- **Scratch Lifetime**: 40
- **Scratch Opacity**: 100
- **Scratch Opacity Var.**: 0

Click the Monochrome Tint box, and set the Tint Color to light blue.

3. Apply **Digieffects Damage DE_Interference** (Effect > Digieffects > Damage > DE_Interference) to the same Digieffects Adjustment Layer. Damage will create a *signal loss* type of look. Here are the settings I used for Damage/Interference:
   - **Source Blend**: 70 (mixes the Damage Effect with the original source)
   - **Noise Level**: 29 (the amount of noise effect added)

You can use this look for any high-energy promo or project where keeping the attention of the viewer is critical.

**Figure 3.71 (a)–(d)** Still frames of the final animation with Digieffects Damage Interference applied. Footage: Joe Mason.

## Television Inspired Effects

Some of the things I'm asked about quite often by customers at Toolfarm are how to make channel change effects, switch a TV off, and make video look like it's on an old TV. We're talking old tube televisions with broadcast television, not a high-definition plasma screens with digital cable. Yes, you could create these types of effects with displacement maps and masks and other built-in filters, but it's so much easier with third-party plug-ins.

**Figure 3.72** Noise Industries FxFactory Pro Vintage TV filter. Footage: Michigan Film Reel.

**Figure 3.73** CoreMelt Channel Change applied to a clip as a transition. Footage: Crowd Control, clip # 00087_004_25.

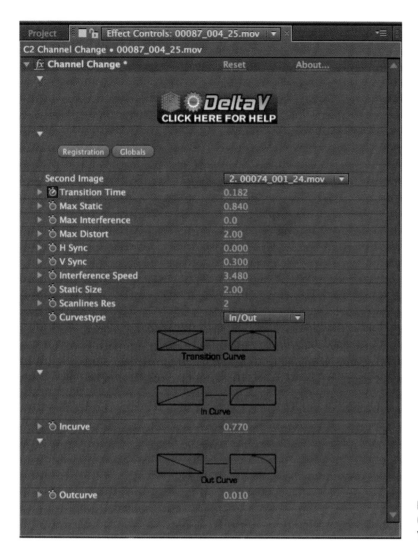

Figure 3.74 CoreMelt Channel Change. Screenshot: Michele Yamazaki.

## CoreMelt Channel Change

CoreMelt Channel Change is part of **CoreMelt Delta V – Motion Transitions** ($79). This tutorial explains how to do a cool Channel Change transition on prekeyed alpha footage. Project files are not included for this tutorial.

    **Third-party plug-ins needed:**
- CoreMelt Delta V – Motion Transitions
  1. Bring two keyed clips of people into a comp in After Effects. Turn off the visibility for one of the clips.
  2. Apply CoreMelt Channel Change to the clip that is visible. Apply Channel Change (Effects > C2 Delta V – Motion Transitions > Channel Change).

3. For the Second Image, choose the other clip that is not visible.
4. Go in about a second and place a keyframe for Transition Time with a value of 0. Jump ahead by 15 frames and increase the value to 100. Preview for timing.
5. Adjust the V Sync to 0.3 to add vertical roll to the effect.

## GenArts Sapphire S_TVChannelChange

Figure 3.75 GenArts Sapphire S_TVChannelChange applied to two clips. Footage: Michele Yamazaki.

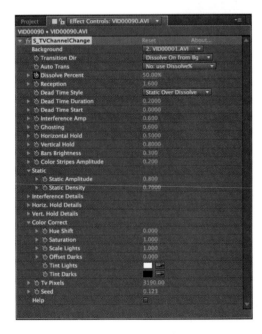

Figure 3.76 The GenArts Sapphire S_TVChannel-Change interface. Screenshot: Michele Yamazaki.

Create a completely different looking channel change effect with the GenArts Sapphire offering, S_TVChannelChange. This is a quick tutorial to show you how to go from one clip to another as if the clips are different channels on a television. Project files are not included for this tutorial so use two of your own clips or images.

**Third-party plug-ins needed:**
- GenArts Sapphire
  1. Bring two clips into a composition. Apply S_TVChannelChange to the top layer (Effects > SapphireTransitions>S_TVChannelChange).
  2. In the Effect Controls panel, set Background to the other clip in the pulldown menu.
  3. Set Transition Dir to Dissolve On from Bg. This will use the other clip instead of a solid color.
  4. Jump to the point in the timeline where you want the transition to begin. Set the Dissolve Percent to 0.00%. Go to the point where you want the transition to end and set it to 100.00%.

5. Dead Time Style is the look between channels. Set Dead Time Style to Static Over Dissolve so that the clips dissolve instead of dip to black.
6. The default noise is too large, in my opinion, so scale it by increasing TvPixels.

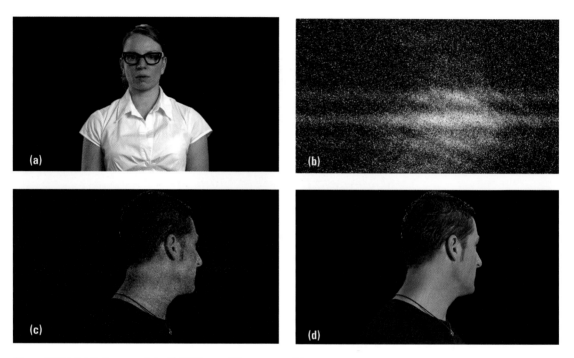

Figure 3.77 (a)–(d) Frames of the S_TVChannelChange transition. Footage: Crowd Control, clip # 00087_004_25 & 00074_001_24.

## Boris Continuum Complete BCC Damaged TV

As a child, my family had cable TV with one of those slider boxes. We didn't have all of the pay channels though, so when I wanted to see *Gremlins* or *The Goonies* on a channel we didn't have, it was scrambled (although, sometimes you could position the slider partway between channels and it would mostly unscramble!).

**Boris Continuum Complete BCC Damaged TV** can easily give that effect with a preset. In fact, there are about a dozen presets and full control of settings to give interference such as Noise, Scanlines, Ghosting, Distorted Edges, Degraded Color, Rolling, and more. The effects can be set to either auto-animate or they can be keyframed manually.

**Figure 3.78** Boris Continuum Complete BCC Damaged TV gives the look of scrambled cable channels. Footage: Michigan Film Reel.

## Closed Circuit Television with GenArts Monsters CCTV

Creating a fake surveillance tape can be done with built-in effects and scaling video but it's amazingly easy to just apply GenArts Monsters M_CCTV plug-in to a video layer and link three other videos. All aspects are easily adjustable including setting Hold Frames, Blur, Snow, and Brightness for each individual quadrant of video. It comes complete with text and time code for each quadrant.

Project files are not included on the DVD, so use four clips of your own to create your own closed circuit television.

**Third-party plug-ins needed:**
- GenArts Monsters GT
    1. Drag four video clips to a new composition. Make sure that the video you want to appear in the top left is the top layer. Apply M_CCTV to the top video layer (Effects > Monsters Stylize > M_CCTV).
    2. In the Effect Controls panel, set Clip 2, Clip 3, and Clip 4 to the other video layers. The CCTV section controls the entire look of the screen, as if you're looking at the monitor that has the four quadrants of video. Adjust the Border Width between quadrants, the Roll and Scan Lines, the Quality and Brightness, and whether Monitor is color or black and white.

# Hot Tip: Render Faster!

Click the eyeballs for clips that are hidden. For this tutorial, click the eyeball to hide the three movies below the top video layer. The effect is utilizing the three clips so they do not need to be visible. This should speed up render times since After Effects doesn't use its resources to composite all four layers.

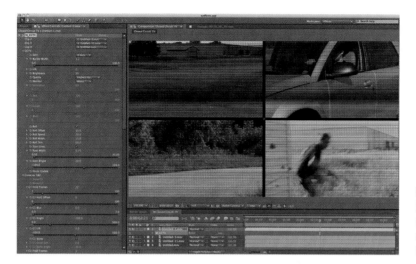

**Figure 3.79** GenArts Monsters M_CCTV effect is an extremely easy way to create the look of closed circuit television. Footage: Michigan Film Reel.

The Cameras 1&2 and Cameras 3&4 sections allow the user set Hold Frames, Blur, Brightness, and Snow for each individual quadrant.

The last section is Text, which will put TimeCode or an alternative in each quadrant. The Text Position, Text Scale, and Text Blend can be adjusted. To add text:

3. In the Effect Controls panel, twirl closed all parameter sections except Text near the bottom. Click the Add Text checkbox to activate text labels and TimeCode. (Figure 3.80.)

4. Set Text Position by clicking the crosshairs in the Effect Controls panel and click and drag the red crosshair around the screen. *Note*: The position will not be the same on the top and bottom. The Text Scale and Text Blend are global for all text windows.

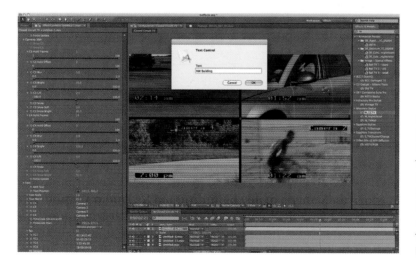

**Figure 3.80** The Text Control panel is for adding Text, such as location or TimeCode, to the video quadrants. Literally click the text to edit. In this case, click the text that says Camera 2 to type new text. The usual dotted underline to show that the parameter is clickable. Footage: Michigan Film Reel.

5. Click Text for Camera 1, Camera 2, Camera 3 and Camera 4 to set the text for each quadrant. This could be labeling each camera with a location or with the camera number.

6. Set the fps (frames per second) for the TimeCode in the video and then click each individual time code number to replace with your own time code. The TimeCode will increment as the video progresses. In this example, fps is set to 10. Do not worry if your video is 30 fps. It will not be out of sync. The video will just play slightly more stuttered at 10 fps, like a security camera might.

## Quick and Easy Reflections Using the Video Copilot Reflect Plug-in, by Joe Mercier

Adding a reflection to an element in After Effects can help tie the object to its environment by interacting with the ground plane. Reflections in After Effects give a lot of the look of a full 3D environment without the longer rendering time that comes of using a separate 3D program. While reflections are possible in After Effects by duplicating the layer to be reflected, flipping it vertically, and adding masks to control the falloff of the reflection, there are a few really nice plug-ins to create reflections. **Red Giant Warp** ($199) creates natural looking reflections for text or other elements. **Zaxwerks Reflector** ($99) will make any 3D plane reflective and reflect elements onto any floor, wall, or ceiling. It's fantastic for simulating mirrors too.

There's also a great free plug-in called **Video Copilot Reflect** which makes creating reflections almost a drag-and-drop affair. Making things easier and faster is pretty much the reason we look to plug-ins, and Reflect does what it promises. Joe Mercier, a Michigan-based independent visual artist, shows you Reflect in action!

**Figure 3.81** The final reflection created with Video Copilot Reflect. Footage: Joe Mercier.

## Pro Tip: Title/Action Safe

To turn on the Title/Action Safe overlay, use the pulldown menu for Grid and Guide Options at the bottom of the Composition panel. The Grids and Guides will not render on movies. It's only for reference. (See Figure 3.82.)

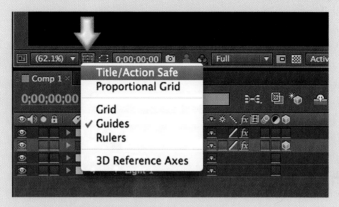

**Figure 3.82** The arrow points to the Grid and Guide Options. Screenshot: Michele Yamazaki.

*The finished After Effects file is on this book's DVD, along with the art used, in the VC Reflect folder.* The project is in After Effects CS3 but will work fine in newer versions of the software.

**Third-party plug-ins needed:**

- Video Copilot Reflect
  1. Create a new comp using the "HDTV 1080 29.97" preset.
  2. Import Reflection_Still.psd with the alpha channel. The file is found on this book's DVD in the VC Reflect folder. Drag it to the Composition panel and center it. Reflection_Still.psd is text created in Photoshop with layer styles. The file has an alpha channel. Change the scale to of the image to 80% to fit within the title safe zone.
  3. Apply the Video Copilot Reflect to the Reflection_Still.psd layer (Effect > Video Copilot > VC Reflect). (Figure 3.83.)

**Figure 3.83** The default settings of VC Reflect applied to the image. Footage: Joe Mercier.

p1675

**4.** In the VC Reflect Effect controls, adjust the Floor Position to bring the reflection to the distance below the image that you would like, depending on if you want your image to appear in contact with, or floating above the reflective floor. Let's have the reflection touch the image, so change the Floor Position from 410 to 386. (Figure 3.84.)

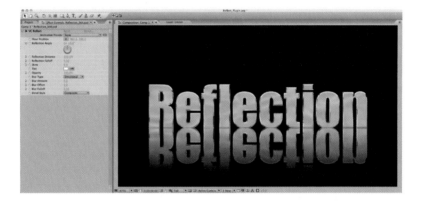

**Figure 3.84** Use Floor Position to adjust the position of the reflection. Footage: Joe Mercier.

p1680

**5.** We'll leave the Reflection Distance at 100% to reflect the full height of the art, and leave the Reflection Falloff at 0.50 to control where the reflection starts to fade. We'll lower Opacity to 60% to reduce the apparent strength of the reflection. The Opacity setting is the main way to control how strong or subtle the reflection is. A lower Opacity allows the reflection to be scaled back to not overpower the main art; left at 100% for Distance, Falloff, and Opacity, the reflection would be like a perfect mirror image. (Figure 3.85.)

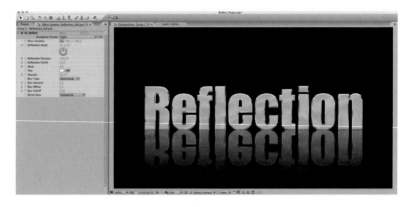

**Figure 3.85** Using Opacity to control the strength of the reflection. Footage: Joe Mercier.

**6.** You can also control whether the reflection is sharp or blurred with several options. In Blur Type, let's try Directional, and change the Blur Amount to 3.0. The Blur Falloff default of 0.50 blurs the reflection the farther it moves away from the image. (Figure 3.86.)

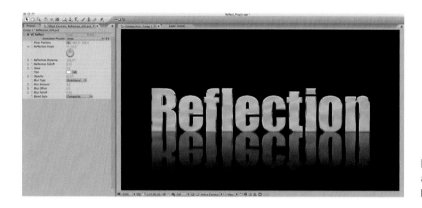

**Figure 3.86** Blur settings applied to the reflection. Footage: Joe Mercier.

7. The last detail in the VC Reflect plug-in is the Blend Style. It is subtle, but it affects how the reflection interacts with the image. The default is Composite, which puts the reflection in front of the original image if the reflection and image touch. Change the Blend Style to Behind Original, and the reflection will look more natural. A third option is Reflection Only, which will show just the reflection. If the reflection is chopped off using Reflection Only, adjust the Floor Position. (Figure 3.87.)

**Figure 3.87** Change Blend Style to Behind Original to place the reflection under the image. The image on the right shows the detail of the reflection moving behind the original image. Footage: Joe Mercier.

8. Let's put the object and its reflection in an environment. Go to the Layer > New Solid. Change to RGB Color Mode and set the color Red 22, Green 37, Blue 113. Move the new blue Solid Layer below the Reflection_Still layer to put the background behind the art.

**9.** To break up the solid color, apply Fractal Noise (Effect > Noise & Grain > Fractal Noise) to the background and change the settings to your liking. In this example we have used a Dynamic, Soft Linear settings with 26 Contrast to make a mottled background. (Figure 3.88.)

**Figure 3.88** Adding a mottled background puts the object in a setting. Footage: Joe Mercier.

**Figure 3.89** Add a vignette and pools of light to the background with Spot Lights. Footage: Joe Mercier.

**Finishing Touches**: To finish up, we'll add some lights to put highlights and add a vignette to the background. To have the lights affect the background, make the background a 3D layer by clicking on the 3D icon in the Timeline panel and set its Material Options to Accepts Lights. After adding a couple of Spot Lights, adjust the intensity, cone angle, and position of the lights to shape the pool of light in the background.

# DISTORTIONS, WARPS, TILING, AND TIME EFFECTS

This chapter is all about having fun with your video, being able to twist, turn, and deform your video footage, all in the name of art! Using distortion and warp filters, you can create lively abstract images or simulate disturbing sequences.

Still images, perhaps ones you have created in Illustrator, can be given life and a real-life look with the aid of distortion filters. For example, a simple image of a flag just doesn't look real moving back and forth on designated planes, but add a warp and a ripple, and that flag really comes to life! Your viewers will never know the scene wasn't shot under a giant flagpole.

Distortion to the level of destroying your footage can add elements of mystery or fright, well after the fact. The right music score and some video destabilizing, and your audience will be jumping right out of their seats. Even simple, low-budget scenes can turn into big-hit horrors with these plug-ins.

Even before Michael Jackson's music video *Black or White*, morphing was one of my favorite effects. This chapter relives the dream of turning one person into another right within After Effects.

And if you're wondering how time effects fit into this category, most time filters are a distortion or warping of time and help establish mood in a story as well. Plug-ins such as Twixtor, Kronos, and other time-remapping plug-ins, help accentuate and enhance the scene by focusing on specific parts of the footage in slow motion. This effect is widely used in sports or high-action shots.

## Create the Predator Effect, by Eran Stern

Eran Stern is an independent motion graphics and visual effects expert, host of SternFX.com, and author of After Effects video tutorials and training series for Creative COW, Artbeats, Digital Juice, Motionworks, and Adobe. I remember when I first saw the original *Predator* (1987) with Arnold Schwarzenegger. I was fascinated by the invisible shield look of the extraterrestrial. This was (and still is) an amazing effect, especially in the late '80s when CGI was only at its birth. The invisibility effect was achieved by having someone in a bright red suit that was the size of the Predator. Red was chosen because it was the farthest color in the spectrum from the green of the jungle and the blue of the sky. The red was removed by chroma keying, leaving an empty area. The take was then repeated without the actors, using a 30% wider lens on the camera. When the two takes were combined optically, the jungle from the second take filled in the empty area. Because the second take was filmed with a wider lens, a vague outline of the alien could be seen with the background scenery bending around its shape.[1]

Fast forward seven years or so to the birth of Adobe After Effects, and suddenly this unique effect, which took so long to film and prepare, has become something that everyone can achieve using a desktop computer.

We can create a similar looking effect but with a different technique by using displacement. The displacement effect is based on the idea of offsetting and distorting pixels based on another layer's pixel values. It has become very common, and almost every sci-fi production uses displacement mapping in some way or another.

If you want to reproduce the invisible look, here are the basic steps to follow. *A project file, which includes a prekeyed alpha clip from Crowd Control, is on the DVD in the Predator folder.*

**Third-party plug-ins needed:**
- **CycoreFX** (which ships with After Effects)
    1. Import the footage 00177_001_21.mov into After Effects. The clip is from Crowd Control and is prekeyed. (See Figure 4.1.)

**Figure 4.1** The footage you'll be using as your Predator. Frightening, I know. Footage: Crowd Control, clip # 00177_001_21.

2. Drag the footage to the Make a New Composition button at the bottom of the Project panel. Open Composition Settings (Composition > Composition Settings) to change the name of the comp to Predator. Click OK. (See Figure 4.2.)

*Note*: If you're using your own greenscreen footage, now is the time to use a keyer to remove the green pixels in your shot. See Chapter 12, "Keying and Compositing Greenscreen Footage" for instructions on keying.

[1]Source: *http://en.wikipedia.org/wiki/Predator_(film)*

**Figure 4.2** Predator
Composition Settings.
Screenshot by Michele Yamazaki.

3. To use a displacement map effect, its best to convert the footage to black and white at this stage. Apply the Tint effect to the footage to create a grayscale image (Effect > Color Correction > **Tint**). Leave the effect at its default settings. (See Figure 4.3.)

**Figure 4.3** Tint is applied.
Screenshot by Michele Yamazaki.

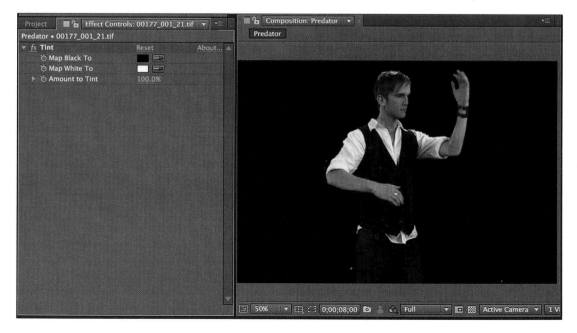

The final effect will use a height map to displace the actual geometric position of points over the textured surface. In other words, the pixels will be distorted where the grayscale values are different from mid-gray (R:128, G:128, B:128). The white pixels will lift the pixels up and the black pixels will lower them down.

In order to create a smooth map that will drive the distortion, we need to define where we want the effect to take place. In this case we want to see a distortion around the edges of the image.

4. Apply **Find Edges** to create edges around the footage (Effect > Stylize > Find Edges). To smooth it, you can use one of the many blur effects that ship with the software. We'll use **Cycore CC Vector Blur**, as it yields nice results (Effect > Blur > CC Vector Blur). Set Type to Perpendicular, with an amount of 10.0. Adjust Map Softness until you get a desirable result, which will vary depending on your footage. (Figure 4.4.)

5. In the Project panel, drag the Predator comp onto the Make a New Composition button to create a new composition with the same frame size and duration as the clip. Go to Composition Settings and rename it Main Comp.

6. For a background, import rainforest.jpg, and then drag it into the main comp behind the Predator layer. Position and scale the background so that it looks in proportion to the Predator. (Figure 4.5.)

7. Turn off the visibility of the Predator layer by clicking the eye for it in the timeline. It will serve only as a source for the distortion.

8. Choose the background rainforest layer and apply Effect > Distort > **Displacement Map**. Select the Predator comp layer

**Figure 4.4** Find Edges with CC Vector Blur. Screenshot by Michele Yamazaki.

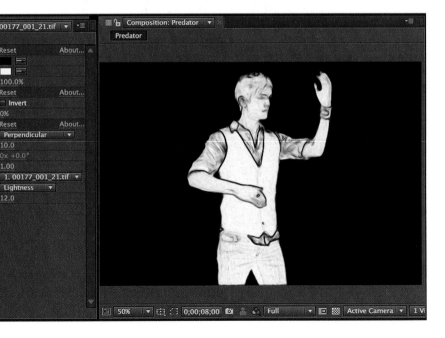

**Figure 4.5** Place the Predator image over the background. Background image courtesy of Michele Yamazaki.

that you prepared as the Displacement Map Layer. Choose Luminance for both Use for Horizontal Displacement and Use for Vertical Displacement. (Figure 4.6.)

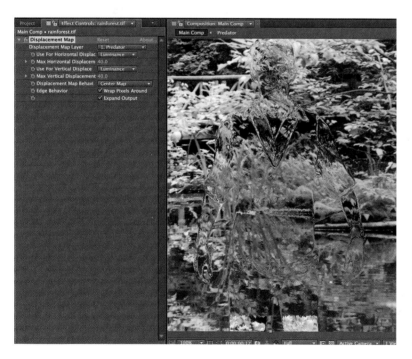

**Figure 4.6** The final look of the invisible Predator. Note that the values of Max Horizontal and Vertical Displacement are turned up so that they are more visible in print. Screenshot by Michele Yamazaki.

9. Set the Max value for each as desired for imitating the invisible predator look; a value of 10 to 20 works well. You will need to preview the effect in motion to see if these values are enough. Check the Wrap Pixels Around box for Edge Behavior to hide the bottom of the legs of the actor.

# The Push Effect with GenArts Sapphire Distortion Plug-ins

Eran Stern contributed quite a bit to this chapter on distortions, and he has a great technique for creating the famous look from the film *Push*, which looks like someone is pushing the air to generate a liquidy water effect around her. A similar effect also appears in many sci-fi films including *The Abyss, The Matrix, Terminator,* and more.

"When you want high-end cutting-edge distortions, look no further than **GenArts Sapphire** ($1699 node-locked, $2499 floating). The Sapphire Distort category is packed with more than 20 distortion effects that can warp, magnify, shake, and transform your footage in various artistic ways not available with plug-ins that ship with After Effects," says Eran.

Here is a short tutorial inspired by the technique Eran shared and using the plug-in **GenArts Sapphire S_DistortChroma**. *The project files are included on the DVD in the Punch – Sapphire Distort folder with a still image from Crowd Control.*

**Third-party plug-ins needed:**

- GenArts Sapphire
    1. Import the clip 00035_001_32.tif into After Effects. Drag it to the Make a New Composition button at the bottom of the Project panel. Open Composition Settings (Composition > Composition Settings) and rename the comp "Punch." Make the comp 5:00 in duration. (Figure 4.8.)
    2. Next we'll create a gradient background. Create a new Solid Layer (Layer > New > Solid, press Make Comp Size, then click OK. Place the layer below the boxer in the timeline. Apply **4-Color Gradient** (Effect > Generate > 4-Color Gradient)

**Figure 4.7** The final effect of the tutorial, which looks quite different in motion. Footage: Crowd Control, clip # 00035_001_32.

**Figure 4.8** Punch composition settings. Screenshot by Michele Yamazaki.

and choose whatever colors please you eyes. I'm going with shades of gray. (Figure 4.9.)

**Figure 4.9**  A 4-Color Gradient fills the background and gives it a polished look. Footage: Crowd Control, clip # 00035_001_32.

3. Next, we'll create the distortion map. Create a new Solid Layer in white named Distortion Map, press Make Comp Size, then OK. Apply **Wave World** to the layer (Effect > Generate > Wave World). (Figure 4.10.)

**Figure 4.10**  Wave World default settings. Footage: Crowd Control, clip # 00035_001_32.

4. Open the Effect Control panel. Under Wireframe Controls, set Vertical Rotation to 0x +90.0° so that the wave plane is facing forward. Increase the Vertical Scale as well. (Figure 4.11.)
5. Set View to Height Map so that you see black, gray, and white rings. To line the center of the punch up with the shot, we'll need to adjust the Producer 1 Position. To see the

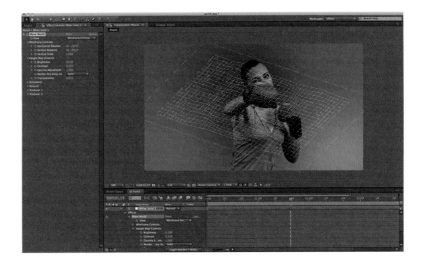

**Figure 4.11** Use the Wave World Wireframe controls to rotate the wave plane forward. Footage: Crowd Control, clip # 00035_001_32.

video below, lower the Opacity of the layer with Wave World applied, move the Producer 1 Position over the right boxing glove, the one giving the punch, then increase Opacity to 100 again. (Figure 4.12.) Also under Producer 1 are the controls to make the rings closer together and more contrasting. Set Amplitude to 1.000 and Frequency to 2.000. (Figure 4.13.)

6. Preview the comp to see how it moves. This will be the shockwave of air coming from a single punch, and because Wave World will keep cycling, we'll need to stop the movement by keyframing the Wave Speed. We will precompose the wave map and keyframe the Opacity to fade it out.

7. Select the Wave World layer and go to Layer > Precompose. A dialog box will pop up. Name the composition Wave Map. Select Move All Attributes into the New Composition, check Open New Composition, and click OK. (Figure 4.14.) We will

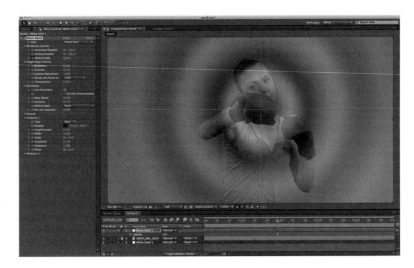

**Figure 4.12** Move the Producer Position 1 over the right glove. Footage: Crowd Control, clip # 00035_001_32.

Figure 4.13  Make the rings closer together and more contrasting by adjusting the Frequency and Amplitude. Screenshot by Michele Yamazaki.

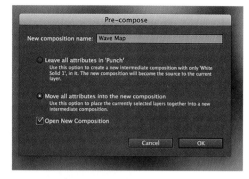

Figure 4.14  Precompose the Wave World layer. Screenshot by Michele Yamazaki.

need to fade out the effect. Eran explains, "For Sapphire distortions the black pixels will have zero distortion while the white pixels create maximum distortion." Basically, fade to black for zero distortion.

8. In the Wave Map comp that you've just created, add a new comp-sized Solid layer in gray with a brightness of 50% and have it start at 2:00. At 2:00 set a keyframe for Opacity with a value of 0%. At 3:00, set a keyframe for Opacity at 100%. (Figure 4.15.) *Note*: If you are using your own footage, time the fade of the effect to the animation. A still won't have nearly the impact of moving footage but it will demonstrate the technique. If you need to make the wave more or less contrasting, come back to this comp and make adjustments.

Figure 4.15  Keyframe the Opacity of a gray solid. Screenshot by Michele Yamazaki.

9. In the Punch comp, turn off the visibility for the Wave Map comp layer. This will be used as a distortion map so it doesn't need to be visible.

10. Create an Adjustment Layer (Layer > New > Adjustment Layer). In this case, we'll want to use an Adjustment Layer and place it above all other layers so all layers are affected. Apply **S_DistortChroma** to the Adjustment Layer (Effect > Sapphire Distort > S_DistortChroma). In the Effect Controls panel, set Lens to Wave Map in the pulldown menu. The effect is pretty strong, so adjust the Amount and other settings to your preference. I kept the effect strong, but lowered Amount to 0.500. (Figure 4.16.)

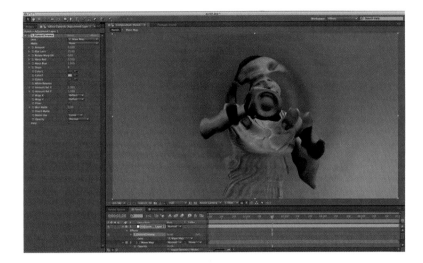

**Figure 4.16** The final effect. Footage: Crowd Control, clip # 00035_001_32.

# Pro Tip

You do not need to make a luminance distortion map for S_DistortChroma. You can use the source layer as a map too.

## AN INTERVIEW WITH ZBORNTOY CREATOR TIMUR "TARON" BAYSAL

**By Andrew Embury**

ZbornToy is a unique plug-in which uses grayscale depth maps to allow the user to adjust lighting and texture, refract backgrounds, and create caustic reflections onto other layers from within After Effects.

**Figure 4.17** A ZbornToy stereoscopic 3D render. Image: Timur Baysal.

Just define a depth map with the deeper areas (valleys) in black and the ridges in white. ZbornToy works in After Effects, Premiere Pro, and Combustion.

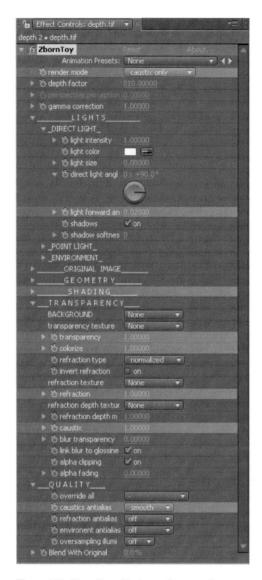

**Figure 4.18**  ZbornToy with the settings used to create the monster image. Screenshot: Timur Baysal.

**Andrew Embury: What prompted you to create ZbornToy?**

**Timur Baysal:** Frankly, it's the second plug-in I wrote for After Effects and started off as an experiment. I realized that, with all my 3D shader writing knowledge, I should be able to treat images the way I would treat textures and surfaces for a render engine. Additionally, I always had a different idea about shading parameters, for example, to simplify the ability to create consistency of surface properties by defining its glossiness and have everything that would relate to it act accordingly. Specular highlights as well as reflection images and refraction properties would all be as smooth or as diffuse as defined by the glossiness of the surface. This allows very easy access too much more realistic material appearances and, at the same time, is great fun to adjust and witness the changes.

In short, it became a playground for our ideas just as I had hoped it would. Together with Philipp Spöth of Frischluft, we created a very unique implementation of caustic light projections through the material onto a flat imaginary background plane or into ray length defined space. Even those respond properly to the glossiness settings of the surface, further helping to maintain consistency. But that's just a few aspects of it all.

**Andrew: What have you used ZbornToy for?**

**Timur:** I've used it in various ways on a few productions, while most importantly on a theme park venue that required a 10K resolution stereo 3D animation. The **ZbornToy** was used to create HUD elements and a female liquid face of a computer, making announcements. We only rendered depth image sequences of the face and did the entire rendering in nearly real-time with the ZbornToy, directly in After Effects. Using **Caustics** as a means to project the depth image from slightly different angles, I even created the stereo 3D sides at the same time. It was an invaluable asset.

I have also created force field effects with it directly in AE, using **Caustics** to create some nice sci-fi effects. Come to think of it, there were a number of places more where I used it in that show, mostly for refraction effects.

Another project were "half" digital mermaids for a permanent display loop. There I used it to create bubbles and some transitional refraction. Here, again, it was the speed, simplicity, and directness of it that made the **ZbornToy** a powerful helper and even design tool.

## Create an Instant Alien with Cycore FX Warps

Cycore FX distortion plug-ins, prefixed with a CC, ship with After Effects, so you already own them. They are powerful plug-ins that allow you to create some cool effects.

*The image of the actress from Crowd Control and project files are included on the DVD in the CC Smear – Alien folder.*

**Plug-ins needed:**

- **Cycore FX** (included with After Effects)
    1. Import 00045_001_52.tif into After Effects. Drag it to the Make a New Composition button at the bottom of the

**Figure 4.19** Use CC Smear to turn your actress into an alien. Footage: Crowd Control, clip # 00045_001_52.

Project panel. Open Composition Settings (Composition > Composition Settings) and rename the comp Alien. Make the comp 5:00 in duration.

2. Apply **CC Smear** (Effects > Distort > CC Smear) to the image. In the Effect Controls panel, click the crosshair and place it between the eyes of the actress. Click To and place it right in the center of her lips. (Figure 4.20.)

3. To set up the warp, go to 1:00 in the timeline and set a keyframe for Reach with a value of 0.0. Go to 2:00 and set Reach to 100. Set Radius to 70.0. (Figure 4.21.)

**Finishing touches:**

- Place a background behind your actress.
- For quick color correction, place an Adjustment Layer over the background and foreground and apply **Red Giant Magic Bullet Mojo**.

**Figure 4.20** Place the crosshairs for To over the lips of the actress. Footage: Crowd Control, clip # 00045_001_52.

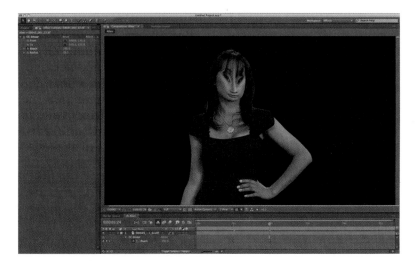

**Figure 4.21** The effect pulls down the actress' face, giving her alien features. Footage: Crowd Control, clip # 00045_001_52.

This tutorial uses a still image to animate the smear, but you may want do this effect with moving footage instead. If you use a movie, you'll need to use motion tracking software to track your actor then link the tracking data to the **CC Smear** effect points.

## Morphing in After Effects

Recently I've seen some excellent morphs in the *Twilight* series, with Jacob the human morphing into a werewolf in mid-pounce. Predating *Twilight*, this technique was made famous by Michael Jackson's *Black or White* video, still one of the coolest videos ever made.

In the mid to late 1990s, I remember spending endless hours with Elastic Reality, which was eventually acquired by Avid. One day I had a 26-frame morph and I remember leaving work for the day coming back the following morning to find that only 21 frames had finished rendering!

Today's morphing plug-ins are much faster and there are two to choose from: **Boris Continuum Morph Unit** ($199, also included with **Boris Continuum Complete**) and **RE:Vision Effects RE:Flex** ($595).

Boris Continuum Morph is OpenGL accelerated for real-time rendering and comes with three plug-ins:

- **BCC Warp** for animated or still image warps using After Effects masks
- **BCC Morph** for image morphs between still images
- **BCC Video Morph** for morphing between two video clips

RE:Vision Effects RE:Flex also uses After Effects masks, and includes a Smart Blend feature to help morphs look natural.

# Morphing with RE:Vision Effects RE:Flex

Image 1    Mid-Morph    Image 2

In this tutorial we'll do the Michael Jackson *Black or White* style morph, with one face morphing into another, using **RE:Vision Effects RE:Flex** ($595). We'll do a still–image-to-still–image morph, as opposed to a video morph. It's just a lot easier to explain in fewer pages. If you need to do a video-to-video morph, check out the RE:Vision Effects website or YouTube channel for tutorials.

*The still images of the faces and Morph project files are included on this book's DVD in the Morph folder.* The images are stills of video from Crowd Control. This tutorial is a quick morph, just to give you the idea of the process. Quality morphs can take a lot of time to be perfect. If you happen to take a morph effect job, budget the job accordingly. They can take an exorbitant amount of time.

**Third-party plug-ins needed:**
* RE:Vision Effects RE:Flex
  1. Import background.jpg and the stills of the men, Ralph.tif and Francis.tif, into After Effects. Select both men still tif images and drag them to the Make a New Composition button at the bottom of the Project panel. Both images are the same size at 1920 × 1080. Choose Single Composition. Use Dimensions From either image, since the images are the same size. Set the Composition Duration to 3:00. Click Okay. (Figure 4.23.)
  2. Match up the facial features as closely as you can by nudging the layers. Make sure the eyes line up and get the mouth and nose as closely lined up as possible. You may need to scale one layer slightly. To match them up even more closely, I flipped one of the layers horizontally

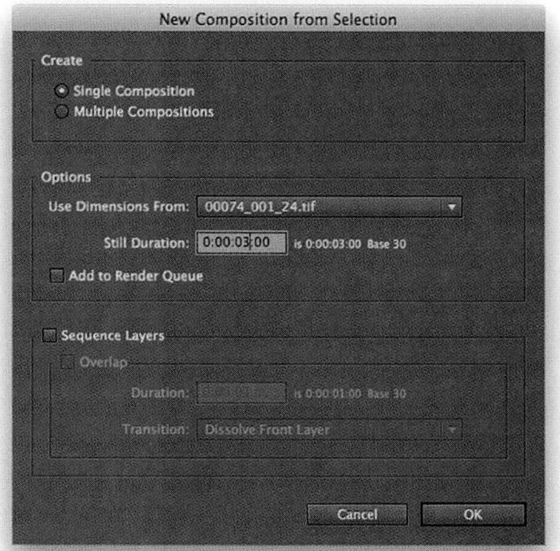

**Figure 4.22** The final morph effect, done with RE:Vision Effects RE:Flex. Footage: Crowd Control, clip # 00434_002_156 and 00074_001_24. Note that this is a quick morph and not meant to be a polished piece.

**Figure 4.23** The New Composition from Selection dialog box. Screenshot by Michele Yamazaki.

and rotated it slightly, nudging down the layer so that there would be no hard edge at the bottom of the clip. (Figure 4.24.)

3. We'll need to trim the duration of the images, put one image at the beginning and one at the end of the timeline, and then set up the morph to happen in the frames between. (Figure 4.25.) Go to 0:01 and select both layers and trim them so they are only two frames in duration. With both layers selected, use Opt (Alt)+ ] (right bracket) to trim both layers at once. Go to 2:28 (one frame from the end) and select the layer you want to morph to. Tap the [ key (left bracket) to move the in-point of the layer to 2:28.

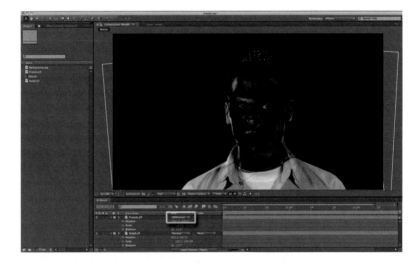

**Figure 4.24** The top layer is set to Difference Mode so that they can be more easily lined up. The object is to get the image as dark as possible. The darker the image, the fewer the differences. Footage: Crowd Control, clip # 00434_002_156 and 00074_001_24.

**Figure 4.25** The timeline has one clip in the beginning and one clip at the end, each one frame in duration. Screenshot by Michele Yamazaki.

4. Rename this composition "Morph Precomp" by going to Composition Settings (Composition > Composition Settings).

5. In the Project panel, drag the Morph Precomp to the Make New Composition button. Rename this new comp "Morph Final".

6. Apply RE:Flex Morph to the Morph Precomp layer. RE:Flex Morph will create the in-between morphing frames. In the Effect Controls panel, leave Display set to Warped and Blended.

7. Make sure you are at the first frame in the timeline. To create these interpolated morph frames, check Picture Key? box. This will enable keyframing for Picture Key? and add a Hold Keyframe at the first frame. Jump ahead to 0:01 and set another keyframe by clicking the Picture Key? checkbox again to turn it off. Go to the last frame and click the Picture Key? box again to add another Hold Keyframe. (Figure 4.26.) When you preview the comp, you should now see the image morphing back and forth a bit. If Picture Key? is set to On, it uses that frame as an image to morph. If Picture Key? is set to Off, it uses that space to create the morph. It will only morph if there are On keyframes on both sides of the Off keyframe.

8. To refine the morph, I like to mask areas and link them together. For example, I'll mask the left eye of one man at the first frame, set a keyframe for the mask, then go to the last frame and edit the Mask Shape to match up the existing points of the Mask to the left eye of the second man. Repeat this process with other features of the face, using open or closed splines. RE:Flex will automatically detect and use these masks. When a closed mask is added, the mode will automatically be set to Add. Change the mode to None so that you can see the contents of the image outside the mask.

**Figure 4.26** Picture Key? Hold Keyframes. Footage: Crowd Control, clip # 00434_002_156 and 00074_001_24.

# Hot Tip!

Set the top layer to Difference Mode so that you can see the layer behind it.

## Pro Tip

Colorize and name the masks so that it is easy to navigate between them. To rename a mask, select a mask, tap the return key, and type a new name. To change the colors, click the yellow box in the timeline and choose a new color. Choose a color that is easy to see over your imagery.

**Figure 4.27** Colorize masks to easily differentiate them. Footage: Crowd Control, clip # 00434_002_156 and 00074_001_24.

## Repeating Video with Cycore CFX Path Tools Rakka

**Cycore CFX Path Tools** ($199) contains two plug-ins, Rakka and Wiggle Stroke. Both use After Effects mask paths.

**Figure 4.28** Cycore CFX Path Tools Rakka uses a path to repeat an element from another layer. Footage: Crowd Control, clip # 00365_001_19.

Rakka is great for animations that repeat. With Rakka, a path is placed on the layer with the effect. The effect references both the path and another layer. For example, it's extremely easy to create the 1970s video feedback look that is still seen on public access channels, or to make a crowd of clones, like the single actor playing hundreds of Oompa Loompas in Tim Burton's *Charlie and the Chocolate Factory.*

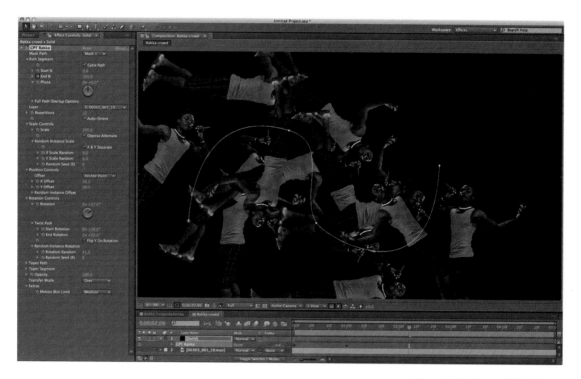

For more on Wiggle Stroke, see Chapter 8, "Text and Graphic Elements."

**Figure 4.29** Cycore CFX Path Tools Rakka has options to rotate, scale, and randomize the element on the path. Footage: Crowd Control, clip # 00365_001_19.

# Time Effects

The effects in this section use the fourth dimension: time. I love the look of extremely slowed footage, especially of natural elements like water splashing and bats flying in science shows, or of an athlete in motion. It really allows the viewer to see the detail of each and every movement that is normally too fast for the human eye to catch.

There are options built into After Effects to slow footage down, such as **Time Remapping** and the **Timewarp** effect, but third-party plug-ins can improve workflow, offer faster rendering, and just look better. **RE:Vision Effects Twixtor** is faster and gives beautiful results, if the footage is shot correctly. **The Foundry Kronos** uses the same Kronos engine as the After Effects Timewarp plug-in, but it's a newer version of the software and is faster.

## FURTHER READING: SLO-MO

Sometimes spelled slow-mo, slo-mo is an abbreviation for slow-motion, a term used in filmmaking where time is slowed down. The effect can be achieved while filming, by over-cranking the camera (running the film through the camera at a faster speed), or in postproduction by time-stretching.

A few tips about shooting for slo-mo:

- **Use faster shutter speeds to reduce motion blur**. Software, no matter how state of the art it may be, can have serious problems building in-between frames with footage that is motion blurred. And don't worry, you can add motion blur in post with RE:Vision Effects ReelSmart Motion Blur if you need to.
- **Lock down your tripod or use a Steadicam for smooth, slow moves**. If you have bumpy footage, smooth your footage first. See Chapter 13, "Tracking, Matchmoving, Motion Stabilization, and Rotoscoping" for instructions. If the shot is moving, you will probably experience warps in places when the slo-mo effect is applied.
- **Shoot at 60 fps for super slow motion effects.**
- **The better the quality of the footage, the better the result.** Don't shoot in low light, which causes noisy footage.

Time lapse, time displacement, freeze frames, jittery frames, and those trippy echo effects where frames of video blur together are all in the Time category.

## Creating Super Slo-Mo Effects with RE:Vision Effects Twixtor

*In this tutorial we'll be slowing down some skateboarding footage, courtesy of Daniel Evans of Lifeblood Skateboards. It's 720p/ 59.94 fps and included on this book's DVD in the Twixtor Skater folder.* We'll use frame blending in this project as well as **Twixtor**. Frame blending creates smoother motion on retimed footage. I use **Twixtor Pro** but the effect can also be created with the regular **Twixtor**.

   **Third-party plug-ins needed:**
- RE:Vision Effects Twixtor Pro
   1. Import the clip named Johnny Backside Air @ Hood River. mp4 into After Effects. Make a new Composition by dragging the clip to the Make New Composition button at the bottom of the Composition panel. Open Composition >

Figure 4.30 The final slo-mo shot with Red Giant Magic Bullet Looks applied, using Eric Escobar's Indie Looks presets. Footage: Daniel Evans, LifebloodSkateboards.com.

# Hot Tip: Twixtor Standard Versus Twixtor Pro

Twixtor Pro has advanced features that allow the user to utilize masks or animated objects as mattes. The masks need to be separated into foreground and background objects. Their purpose is to assist the tracking and help prevent ghosting. Twixtor Pro can track the foreground and background separately, and can animate position points to show where the objects are moving from frame to frame. Twixtor Standard does not have this feature. If users aren't sure which version they need, they can buy the standard and upgrade to the pro later, so they're not penalized.

Composition Settings and change the duration of the composition to 20:00.

2. The clip is much too long and needs to be trimmed. Double-click the clip in the timeline to open it in the Layer panel. Go to 6:26 and click Set IN point to current time layer. Go to 12:33 and click Set OUT point to current time layer. Bring the Composition panel forward when done. (Figure 4.31.)

3. Create a new solid (Layer > New > Solid) and click the Make Comp Size button. Name the Solid "Twixtor". The color of the solid is not important.

    Why apply it to a solid and not directly to the footage? If Twixtor is applied to a solid, the visibility of the solid layer can be toggled on and off to see the original footage below it, which is not slowed. The main reason I do it this way is because if the effect is applied directly to a clip, the clip is not physically stretched out to the end of the timeline. The footage will play slowed but once you reach the original out-point of the footage, the clip will end, whether the slo-mo effect is finished or not. By applying the effect to a solid layer

**Figure 4.31** Click the Set IN point and Set OUT point to the current time layer to trim the clip. Set IN point is shown. Footage: Daniel Evans, LifebloodSkateboards.com.

that reaches the end of the timeline, this is not an issue. Make sure the solid layer is placed above the footage layer.

4. Apply Twixtor to the footage (Effects > RE:Vision Plug-ins > Twixtor Pro). Set Source Control > Color Source to 2. Johnny Backside Air @ Hood River.mp4. You should now see the footage. (Figure 4.32.)

**Figure 4.32** Choose the source footage for Twixtor. Footage: Daniel Evans, LifebloodSkateboards.com.

5. Under Source Control > Input: Frame Rate, enter the exact frame rate of the clip. If you don't know the frame rate, go to the Project panel and select the footage. It will show up in the info area at the top of the Project panel. In this case, it's 59.94 fps. (Figure 4.33.) If your footage is 29.97 and interlaced, you can still create the effect but it won't be as smooth. Be aware that older versions of Twixtor would

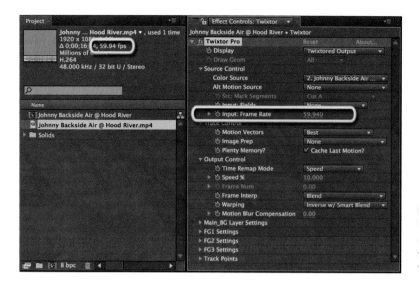

**Figure 4.33** Set the Input: Frame Rate to the exact value of the frame rate of the original footage. Screenshot by Michele Yamazaki.

separate fields itself and ignore the host application's field settings, so you would need to set Interpret Footage Separate Fields popup to Off. Twixtor 4 and newer use After Effects settings for Field Interpretation, so this is no longer a problem.

6. Next we adjust the speed settings for the clip. The idea is to have the skateboarder come in at full speed, then abruptly slow his speed to 10% while he is in the air. As his wheels touch the ramp, the speed is once again set back to 100%.

Select the solid layer and tap the E key to reveal Twixtor. Twirl Twixtor > Output Control open. Jump to 0:20 and set a keyframe for Speed % with a value of 100%. This should be at the point where the skateboarder is about halfway up the ramp. Go to 0:35 and set Speed % to 10%.

Find the point in the video just before he touches down on the ramp again, about 9:13 in the timeline. Set a keyframe again for Speed % with a value of 10%. Go ahead to 9:28 and set the value of Speed % to 100%.

Go to 10:49 in the timeline and set a keyframe for Speed % with a value of 100%. This should be at the point before he makes a jump. Move 15 frames ahead to 11:04 and set a keyframe with the value of 10%. At 18:44 set a keyframe with the value of 10%. Move another 15 frames ahead to 18:59 and set the value to 100% again.

Preview the effect a few times. You should be seeing the skateboarder go up the ramp at full speed, slow to 10% while he's in the air, then speeding back up to regular speed once his wheels touch back down on the ramp. (Figure 4.34.)

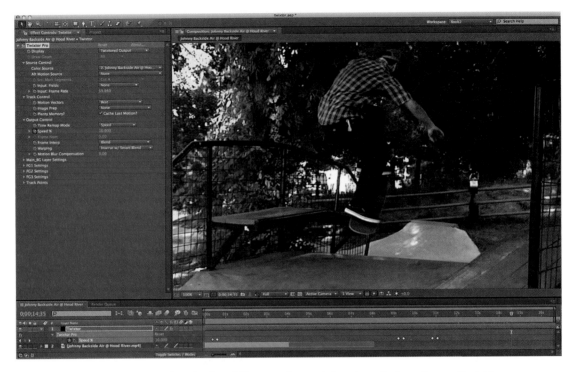

**Figure 4.34** Keyframes are placed on the Speed % to speed up and slow down footage. Footage: Daniel Evans, LifebloodSkateboards.com.

**Figure 4.35** Warping problems are occurring between the skateboarder's legs. Footage: Daniel Evans, LifebloodSkateboards.com.

This is a tough shot to get good results while slowing. The shot is not locked down and there is a lot of texture in the trees and pavement. In this shot, there is problem area between the legs of the skateboarder where warping is apparent. The trees between the legs are repeating and stuttering and this is most noticeable while the footage is playing. This happens when the shot is slowed down a lot and there is not enough information for frames to be rebuilt accurately. The easiest cure is to not slow the footage down so much.

If adjusting the speed isn't an option, Twixtor can address this problem in other ways. First, try setting Motion Vectors to Best and adjusting the value of Motion Sensitivity, which can be keyframed in the timeline through the area that is problematic. A better way to handle the issue, though, is by masking the problem area with a matte or vector. This process is explained in Twixtor's documentation.

**Finishing Touches**: There are areas of the sky that are washed out and too bright, so to give it a very stylized look, I applied **Red Giant Magic Bullet Looks**, using a preset from Eric Escobar's Indie Looks. This Look blows out the trees completely in some areas

**Figure 4.36** Before and after. The original is on the left. Magic Bullet Looks is applied on the frame on the right. Footage: Daniel Evans, LifebloodSkateboards .com.

and gives more focus to the skateboarder. This preset also camouflages some warping artifacts that were not fully fixed in Twixtor.

## User Story: Jeremy Hanke on RE:Vision Effects Twixtor

As with **Boris Continuum Complete Optical Stabilizer**, I worked with **RE:Vision Effects Twixtor** on the effects for *The Guardian* (2010), an independent film written and directed by Nick Denney. I was impressed with its overall quality and the options it made available. *The Guardian*'s effects sequences were shot at 30 fps at 1/120th shutter speed on the Panasonic DVX100, and early test renders turned out pretty well. As a fan of John Woo style action films, I wanted to get as close as I could get to the 120–200 fps he shot his films at. When I shot *Depleted: Day 419* (worldofdepleted. com), I shot it on the Panasonic HVX200A. As the max speed that camera can shoot at is 60 fps, I knew that it would take the power of something like Twixtor to get us close to where I wanted to be.

For *Depleted: Day 419*, we shot all of the action sequences in 60 fps at 1/120th shutter speed and utilized speed ramps to go from full speed into slo-mo and back again. The ability to add frame blur to slower than filmed or faster than filmed sequences meant that we didn't have to use **ReelSmart Motion Blur** (a RE:Vision Effects plug-in for blurring footage regardless of speed) very much. That was a huge thing for making the accelerated footage not look strobey (like the intro to *Gladiator*).

I learned a number of good tricks about Twixtor, both for production and postproduction:

1. **Try to record at as fast a shutter speed as you possibly can, in addition to as fast a frame rate as you can**. If you can record at a fast enough shutter rate, you will obliterate motion blur between frames, which makes it much easier for Twixtor to create pristine intermediate frames between them. It can blur

these frames as much as you want after the fact, so don't worry about them being *too* pristine. If you're shooting 60 fps, your goal is record it at 1/240th of a second or faster.

When we shot *Depleted: Day 419*, we were shooting indoors with a modest light kit and exposing an HVX200 camera (which only has 1/3" recording sensor) and a 35mm lens adapter (which further cuts down on light sensitivity). This meant that we couldn't shoot faster than 1/120th of a second, which resulted in more motion blur than we would've preferred. While these problems could've been corrected if we shot outdoors in full sunlight, a better option for the future is to try and get a camera with a larger recording sensor that can process more light. As of the time of this writing, the Canon 7D DSLR and the Panasonic AF100 both have much larger sensors and do not require a 35mm lens adapter to get film-like depth of field. As such, this is the way we will go for the *Depleted* feature.

2. **Be sure to consider the type of frame interpretation you want based on your needs**. I found for slow motion that Nearest was logical, because it forced Twixtor to create new frames based on the connect-the-dot principle of nearest pixels. For acceleration, I went with Blend as this helps blur the frames together.

3. **Motion sensitivity is a bit counter intuitive**. The initial preset of 70 is a bit choppy, in my experience. As far as I can tell, Motion Sensitivity describes the units of time that pass between when Twixtor checks for changes in the frame. I personally found setting it for 20 seemed to be the sweet spot for fluid transformations.

4. **Motion Blur Compensation**. While this can change based on how much you're slowing or accelerating your footage, I usually found somewhere between 2 and 3 was a good place to select.

## THE FOUNDRY KRONOS

In January 2011, I was lucky enough to get to see The Foundry's new office in London and chat with Jack Binks, plug-ins product manager at The Foundry. He gave me some in-depth information on the technology in The Foundry Kronos ($120 node-locked, $170 floating) and some overall good tips on how to get the best results with the plug-in.

**Michele Yamazaki: What makes Kronos a great product?**

**Jack Binks:** The BLINK framework allows Kronos to translate algorithms into CUDA, which can be run on the nVIDIA graphics card—the card that you can play Premiere Pro CS5's Mercury Playback Engine on nice and fast—which will speed up your retiming as well. I've seen it run on SD on a regular graphics card in real time. It's really amazingly powerful because one of the things I find about retiming is that generally it doesn't look perfect the first time around and you have to tweak a few parameters to make it look like you really want it to. Half of the time you're sitting there waiting for it to render. If you're doing it nearly in real time, it's going to really speed things up. That's the real key feature to Kronos.

Figure 4.37

Adobe licensed the original algorithm Kronos version 3 from Furnace version 3, which forms the basis for Timewarp inside of After Effects. The current Kronos uses the algorithm Kronos 4, which probably has three more years of research into motion estimation under the hood. It's a bit faster and shows less of the warping artifacts. The controls are very similar to Timewarp, so if you've spent a while getting familiar with Timewarp, you'll be able to translate your knowledge directly to Kronos, which is quite powerful.

**Michele: In the shot I used in the RE:Vision Effects Twixtor tutorial in the previous section, I experienced warping in the trees and in areas of the cement that can potentially be fixed using background and foreground mattes. How does Kronos deal with warping?**

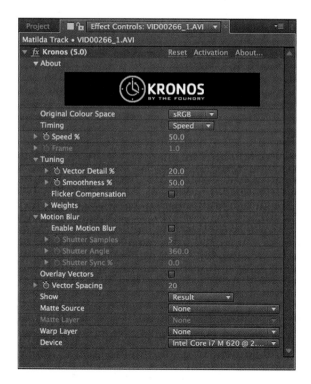

Figure 4.38  The Kronos Effect Controls panel. Screenshot by Michele Yamazaki.

**Jack:** The way to deal with warping artifacts is also with a matting component. Shall I get a bit geeky? Essentially when you have motion estimating, what you're trying to do is to build a field of vectors that shows how the pixels move from one frame to the next, so it's just like tracking, but rather than tracking one feature, you're trying to track every single pixel in the frame. You do it in blocks. The problem is that you can't actually show where pixels are occluded, where stuff disappears behind another thing, you can only show movement. So, often what you find is that the pixels that were appearing in one frame but disappear in the next get pushed along by this smoothing algorithm that gets run on top of the original vector field.

Instead of using a one dimensional vector field, what you have to do is a 2D field, so you use a matte to split the two areas, so you have the foreground movement and the background movement. It's the same in Timewarp and Twixtor. You can use whatever tricks you can pull to make the matte, whether it's Rotobrush or a bit of keying if you have some sort of luma key sky background—that I've seen work quite nicely on skateboarding footage in the past.

The other thing you might find handy is the Local Smoothness parameter, under Tuning. That governs that smoothing algorithm so essentially you're saying this scene has smaller objects moving more rapidly in different directions and a larger object with maybe just one of them moving. For people like me, who generally don't read manuals, I recommend trying both Vector Detail % and Smoothness % low and high to see if one of those looks better. Once you've done that on a few shots, you'll get a feeling how that percentage parameter relates to the size of the object in the scene. It's a bit of art and science.

**Michele: How is Kronos different from Twixtor?**

**Jack:** The key difference is the graphics card element of it, so being able to run the graphics card to make it run a whole load faster.

# CREATIVE TRANSITIONS: WHEN A SIMPLE CUT JUST ISN'T ENOUGH!

Transitions can be used in the traditional sense, such as a full-frame dissolve or wipe effect, and as effects in and of themselves, contributing to an overall design element.

A transition is easily one of the most used effects throughout video and broadcast. This chapter explains how third-party transitions move the viewer from one scene to the next. Transitions give you the style, and allow you to seamlessly bring all your pieces into one. That said, transitions can also be extremely hokey. Case in point: the infamous Kiki wipe, the idiosyncratic wipes in Wes Craven's *Swamp Thing*, and the cringe-worthy wipes in *Star Wars: Episode III—Revenge of the Sith*.

Although transitions are more often used in nonlinear editors, transitions can take on a whole new level in After Effects as a motion graphics and visual effects tool. Many plug-in developers have a vast array of options to choose from when it comes to transitions, and may include them as part of a larger bundle of effects.

Sure, everyone has seen a page turn used to transition from one piece of video footage to the next, but this chapter shows not only the power of plug-ins, but dives deeper into more creative uses of transition plug-ins.

## CoreMelt Complete Transitions: PolyChrome Transitions, TRX-Filmic and High-Color Transitions, and Delta V Motion Transitions

**CoreMelt Complete V2** ($399, Mac only) is an extensive package of 219 plug-ins aimed at saving editors time on the more tedious aspects of their workflow. **PolyChrome Transitions** ($129) represents the transitional plug-ins in the V2 package, made up of two transition package types that are also sold individually. Together they contain over 60 transitions (as of the publishing of this book). CoreMelt plug-ins use GPU accelerated architecture, allowing speedy previews and renders in Adobe After Effects, Final Cut Pro/Express, and Apple Motion.

**TRX-Filmic and High-Color Transitions**: Traditional film style transitions including blooms, luma and chroma dissolves, blur pans, and camera affects such as focus pull dissolves. These are great for more subtle effects where you don't want a loud or obvious transition. A few highlights are:

- **Chroma Drain Dissolve**: Pulls the saturation levels out of outgoing clip and transfers saturation levels to the next, resulting in a nice subtle transition effect. (Figure 5.1.)
- **Filmstrip**: Uses a filmstrip graphic as an in-between to pull one full frame to the next. (Figure 5.2.)

**Figure 5.1**  CoreMelt Chroma Drain Dissolve. Footage: Michele Yamazaki.

**Figure 5.2**  CoreMelt Film Strip. Footage: Michele Yamazaki.

- **Focus Pull Dissolve**: A blur dissolve that simulates a rack focus effect from one image to the next. (Figure 5.3.)
- **Camera Shutter**: Creates a snapping shutter effect from a still camera over the layer. (Figure 5.4.)
- **Sliders**: Uses the secondary clip to push the clip left or right out of the frame. (Figure 5.5.)

  **Delta V Motion Transitions**: Unique graphical transitions for a not-so-subtle effect. Recreates popular grunge, distortion, and

**Figure 5.3**  Focus Pull Dissolve. Footage: Michele Yamazaki.

**Figure 5.4**  Camera Shutter.
Footage: Michele Yamazaki.

**Figure 5.5**  Sliders. The arrow demonstrates the direction of the sliding movement. Footage: Michele Yamazaki.

**Figure 5.6** Acid Blotches. Footage: Michele Yamazaki.

**Figure 5.7** Pixelate Crossfade. Footage: Michele Yamazaki.

**Figure 5.8** Push Away and Spin. Footage: Michele Yamazaki.

3D motion graphics effects quickly and easily without leaving your editor. Some examples are:

- **Acid Blotches**: Similar to a film burn effect between clips. Edges glow using either the luminance from both clips or a selected color. (Figure 5.6.)
- **Pixelate Crossfade**: Clip distortion by degenerating the resolution between clips. (Figure 5.7.)
- **Push Away and Spin**: A three-dimensional effect that does as described—pushes and twirls in 3D the outgoing clip away from camera, while pulling the incoming clip into the frame. (Figure 5.8.)
- **Random Cloud Transition**: Breaks the clips into multiple stacked frames in 3D space, zooming from one full frame to the next. (Figure 5.9.)

**Figure 5.9**  Random Cloud Transition. Footage: Michele Yamazaki.

**Figure 5.10**  A sci-fi style wipe with CoreMelt C2 Film Blowout Wipe. Footage: Crowd Control, clip #00074_001_24 & 00087_004_25.

## Sci-Fi Wipe with CoreMelt C2 Film Blowout Wipe

**CoreMelt Film Blowout Wipe** is a plug-in in the **CoreMelt PolyChrome Transitions** bundle. This effect is great for sci-fi transitions between characters or showing a character become another character.

Still images of the Crowd Control clips and project files are included in the CoreMelt TRX Film Blowout Wipe folder on this book's DVD. This looks great with moving footage, so try your own chroma keyed footage. *The project files are included on this book's DVD in a folder named CoreMelt TRX Film Blowout Wipe (Mac).*

**Third-party plug-ins needed:**

• CoreMelt PolyChrome Transitions (Mac)

    1. Open the project folder on this book's DVD named CoreMelt TRX Film Blowout Wipe. Bring the footage into After Effects and drag both clips to the Make a New Composition button at the bottom of the Project panel. When two images are dragged to this panel, a New Composition from Selection dialog box will pop up. Under Create check Single Composition. Use Dimensions from either image because they're both the same size. Set Still Duration to 3:00, and then click OK. (Figure 5.11.) In the timeline, place 00177_001_21.tif on top.

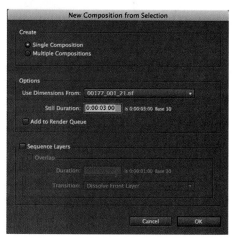

**Figure 5.11**  New Composition from Selection dialog box. Screenshot: Michele Yamazaki.

2. Apply CoreMelt C2 Film Blowout Wipe to the top clip, 00177_001_21.tif (Effect > C2 TRX-Filmic Transitions > Film Blowout Wipe). (Figure 5.12.) After the effect is applied, part of the screen will have a CoreMelt splash screen. This is indicating that you need to choose Second Image for the transition. (Figure 5.13.)

3. In the Effect Controls panel, choose 2. 00206_002_227.tif. for Second Image. You should now see the two clips mixed. (Figure 5.14.)

4. Turn off the visibility for 00206_002_227.tif in the timeline.

5. Go to 0:20 in the timeline. Set Transition Time to 0.000 and enable keyframing for this parameter. Go to 2:10 and set the value of Transition Time to 1.000. Under Wipe, set Angle to 0x –90.0° so that the effect moves from the top to the bottom. (Figure 5.15.)

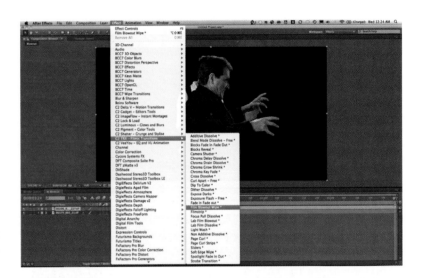

**Figure 5.12** Apply CoreMelt C2 Film Blowout Wipe. Footage: Crowd Control, clip #00074_001_24 & 00087_004_25.

**Figure 5.13** The Film Blowout effect is applied to one image. The other image has not yet been selected so the CoreMelt splash screen appears. Footage: Crowd Control, clip #00074_001_24 & 00087_004_25.

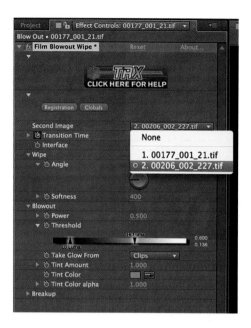

**Figure 5.14**  Second Image is chosen in the pulldown menu in the Effect Controls panel for Film Blowout. Screenshot: Michele Yamazaki.

**Figure 5.15**  The Wipe angle is set so that the wipe moves from top to bottom. Footage: Crowd Control, clip #00074_001_24 & 00087_004_25.

# Hot Tip

For the best results, use footage that matches up in position and frame size when using the CoreMelt Film Blowout effect. Alternately, reposition the footage in a precomp so the sizes and positions match.

## Allergy Ad Page Curl

You may have seen the Claritin commercials that show washed-out footage, then a page wipe occurs and takes the scene to full saturation, as if the allergy meds have kicked in. There are a couple of page curl plug-ins on the market, **Boris Continuum Complete BCC Page Turn** and **Cycore FX CC Page Turn** for example, but **CoreMelt TRX-Filmic Transitions Page Curl** works great for this type of effect.

**Figure 5.16** The Page Curl gives the look of a layer of fog peeling away. Footage: Michigan Film Reel.

*The project files and footage are included on the DVD in the CoreMelt Page Curl folder (Mac).*

**Third-party plug-ins needed:**

- CoreMelt TRX-Filmic Transitions

  1. Import Jason-CloseUp.mp4 and drag it onto the Make a New Composition button at the bottom of the Project panel. A new composition will open that is the exact size and duration of the footage.

  2. Duplicate Jason-CloseUp.mp4 in the timeline. On the top copy apply Levels (Effect > Color Correction > Levels). To wash out the video, increase the value of Output Black to about 45.0. (Figure 5.17.)

  3. Apply CoreMelt Page Curl to the top layer of footage (Effect > C2 TRX-Filmic Transitions > Page Curl).

     In the Effect Controls panel, set Second Image to Jason-CloseUp.mp4. This will be the layer that is below the peeled clip.

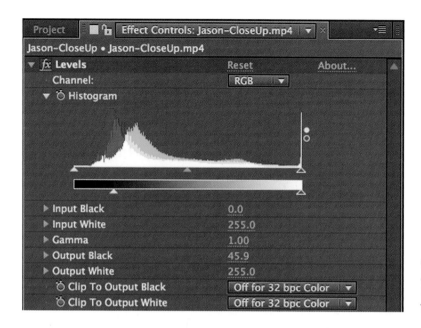

**Figure 5.17** The top instance of the video is brightened with Levels. Screenshot: Michele Yamazaki.

Go to 3:00 in the timeline and enable keyframing for Transition Time, with the value set to 0.000. At 5:00, set the value to 1.000. This will animate the page curl.

Set the Angle to 0x −128.0° and the Radius to 200. The Angle sets where the page curl comes from and the Radius is the width of the peel.

4. The Reflect and Backside settings are where this plug-in shines because there are so many options. Set Reflect Strength to 0.350, Backside Shading 1 and 2 Alpha to 0.140, and the color of Backside Shading 2 to white. (Figure 5.18.)

**Figure 5.18** The final Page Curl effect in mid-animation. Footage: Michigan Film Reel.

## Noise Industries FxFactory Transitions

**Noise Industries FxFactory** ($399, Mac only) is a great example of an all-inclusive package that has a plethora of transitions, containing over 160 filters, generators, and transitions, many with separate distinct components to allow customized effects and even more possibilities.

While you'll find the typical wipe, color, and gradient transitions here, FxFactory also contains a few unique transitional elements based on popular effects from movie titles, television, and commercial spots, even styles that mimic the OS X finder interface. Each transition option includes a sample thumbnail for easy browsing. Here are a few samples:

- **Agent**: Creates animated scaling transitions of clips, similar to the effect used in the television show *"24"*. (Figure 5.19.)

**Figure 5.19** Agent with a transition between three clips.
Footage: Michele Yamazaki.

- **Channel Switch**: A "bad video signal" effect, switching between channels on an old analog set, with scan lines and distortion. (Figure 5.20.)
- **Copy Machine**: A vertical wipe transition with an added glow effect; simulates a copy machine. (Figure 5.21.)
- **Glow Dissolve**: A luminance bloom effect, useful for camera "flash bulb" style transitions. (Figure 5.22.)
- **Mask Dissolve**: A simple way to add several types of gradient wipes and custom wipe effects. (Figure 5.23.)
- **Video Conference**: An OS X style browser effect with multiple gradient/mirroring options. (Figure 5.24.)
- **Whoosh**: A horizontal blur transition. Can be used to simulate a pan swish effect. (Figure 5.25.)

**Figure 5.20**  Channel Switch.
Footage: Michele Yamazaki.

**Figure 5.21**  Copy Machine.
Footage: Michele Yamazaki.

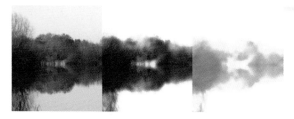

**Figure 5.22**  Six frames during a Glow Dissolve transition. Footage: Michele Yamazaki.

**Figure 5.23**  Three settings for Mask Dissolve. *From left*: Bar Mask, Gradient Mask, and Oval Mask. Footage: Michele Yamazaki.

**Figure 5.24** Video Conference.
Footage: Michele Yamazaki.

**Figure 5.25** Whoosh, before, during, and after the transition. Footage: Michele Yamazaki.

## idustrial revolution ParticleMetrix Sci-Fi Teleportation Effect

**idustrial revolution ParticleMetrix by FxFactory** ($99) is one of the coolest, most fun plug-ins on the market. Just apply it to video, keyed footage, text, or logos and ParticleMetrix will turn your source into particles. It's great for wiping on and off text and creating fancy transitions. The presets are fantastic and can be easily fine-tuned.

I had to blow away a 3D rendering of an Angus Young statue like dust for AC/DC's world tour a few years back, and used the **Shatter** plug-in that ships with After Effects. It worked but cranking the effect up to so many pieces made my computer drag. This same sort of effect is seen in *Scott Pilgrim vs. The World* where the minions of the evil exes explode into sand. This same effect can be created with ParticleMetrix, which is better than Shatter and unbelievably fast, since it's built on **Noise Industries FxFactory** engine and is OpenGL accelerated.

This Sci-Fi Teleportation effect is very easy to create in After Effects with ParticleMetrix. *The project, including the greenscreen footage, is on this book's DVD in the ParticleMetrix Teleport folder (Mac).*

**Figure 5.26** idustrial revolution ParticleMetrix is used to wipe on keyed footage for a futuristic effect. Footage: Michigan Film Reel.

**Third-party plug-ins needed:**
- **The Foundry Keylight** (or a keyer of your choice)
- **idustrial revolution ParticleMetrix (Mac)**
    1. Import the greenscreen footage included in the Particle-Metrix folder on this book's DVD, JasonGoggles.mp4, and key it in your program of choice. Don't add a background. *Note*: the project on the DVD was keyed with The Foundry Keylight; for more information on Keying, see Chapter 12, "Keying and Compositing Greenscreen Footage."
    2. Apply ParticleMetrix to the JasonGoggles.mov footage (Effect > idustrial revolution > ParticleMetrix).
    3. In the Effect Controls panel, set Video to the Heart Sinks preset. This preset will be customized for a completely unique look. I like to start with a preset that has the movement, or some other aspect, that I want, and then modify it to my liking. It can really speed up workflow and be a great way to try out designs. (Figure 5.27.) First we'll change the look of the particles from a heart to a pixel. Under Particles, change the Built-in Particles to One Pixel. Change the Start Color to a forest green and the End Color to aqua. Lower Particle Size to 0.06. (Figure 5.28.)
    4. ParticleMetrix has the option to auto-animate or be set up manually to animate with keyframes. To auto-animate the effect, go to Animation in the Effect Controls panel. Set Animation Time to Duration in Seconds (secs). Set Duration (secs) to 2.00. To adjust timing, try a few of the Animation Curve settings. (Figure 5.29.)

**Finishing Touches**: Add a background layer and apply a black to dark-gray gradient. I used a simple Ramp applied to a solid layer.

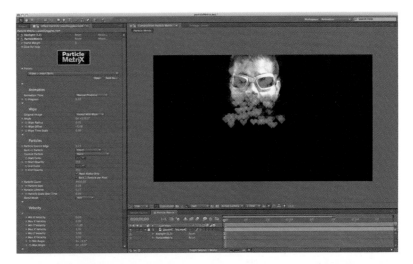

**Figure 5.27** ParticleMetrix Heart Sinks preset. Footage: Michigan Film Reel.

**Figure 5.28** *Left*: the look of the effect before changing Particle Size; *center*: the One Pixel preset; *right*: choosing the pixel color. Footage: Michigan Film Reel.

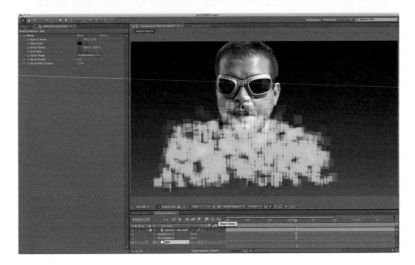

**Figure 5.29** Animation settings and the final look of the wipe animation. Footage: Michigan Film Reel.

**Figure 5.30** Examples of Pixelan CreativEase. Courtesy of Michael Feerer, Pixelan Software, pixelan.com.

## Pixelan CreativEase Transitions

**Pixelan CreativEase** is a set of transition plug-ins for After Effects (Microsoft Windows only), which is broken into 12 categories such as:

- **ChromaWarp**: color distortions and warp effects
- **OrganiBlur**: spin blurs, fluid liquid effects, swirls
- **SpatterFlex**: artsy, grain looks to create debris, swarms
- **StepTime**: stop action, strobe effects, echoes

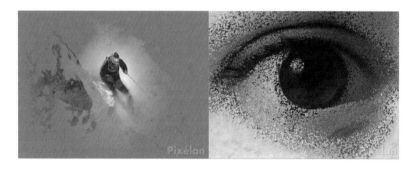

**Figure 5.31** More samples of Pixelan CreativEase. Courtesy of Michael Feerer, Pixelan Software, pixelan.com.

Pixelan is custom-built for artists, so it is designed to be very easy to use. Users will be able to jump right in and start using it with a very short learning curve.

## Boris Continuum Complete Wipes and Transitions

**Boris Continuum Complete** is one of my favorite plug-in bundles. It includes several plug-ins for transitioning from one shot to another. This section contains tutorials for a couple of the transitions that I find the most useful or interesting.

**Figure 5.32** Footage shattered to particles with Boris Continuum Complete BCC 2D Particles. Footage: Crowd Control, clip # P1020749.

## Footage Shatter with Boris Continuum Complete BCC 2D Particles

It's great fun to shatter footage into a million little pieces with plug-ins. My daughter adores the Gene Wilder film *Willy Wonka and the Chocolate Factory* and this effect could be used to recreate the "broadcast" of Mike TeeVee, where Mike is broken into particles and floats above everyone's heads before being reassembled and miniaturized.

*The project files, including the footage (clip # P1020749 courtesy of Crowd Control), are included on this book's DVD in the BCC 2D Particles Shatter folder.*

**Third-party plug-ins needed:**
- Boris Continuum Complete
1. Import P1020749.mov, which is in the BCC 2D Particles Shatter folder on this book's DVD. Drag P1020749.mov, onto the Create a New Composition button at the bottom of the Project panel.
2. Apply BCC 2D Particles (Effects > BCC Distortion Perspective > BCC 2D Particles) to the P1020749.mov layer. (Figure 5.34.)
3. Apply the AutomateActions.bap preset. It's an animated preset so there will be a popup dialog for Animated Preset Options. For Stretching, check Preserve Timing and for Offset click First Frame. (Figure 5.35.)

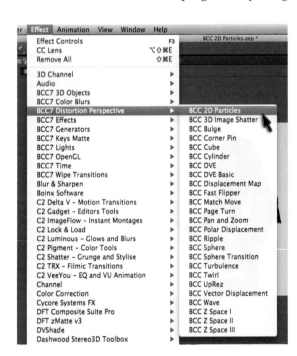

**Figure 5.33** BCC 2D Particles in the Effects menu. Screenshot: Michele Yamazaki.

4. If you play the Comp through, it looks very cool except the footage doesn't start out intact. To make it start at full video and break into particles, go to 2:00 and enable keyframing for Speed. Go to the first frame and set the value of Speed to a value of 0.00. (Figure 5.36.)

**Finishing touches**: Add a drop shadow and a gradient background. For the example, I used BCC Drop Shadow and BCC Mixed Color for the background.

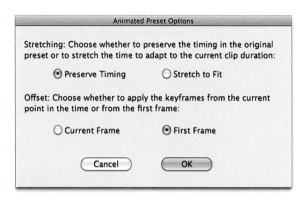

Figure 5.34 Animated Preset Options. Screenshot: Michele Yamazaki.

Figure 5.35 Keyframe the Speed so that the video starts whole and breaks apart. Although Speed was the only option that we keyframed, the AutomateActions.bcp preset added other keyframes. Footage: Crowd Control, clip # P1020749.

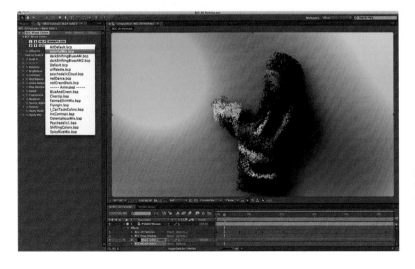

Figure 5.36 The final project with BCC Drop Shadow applied to the footage and BCC Mixed Color applied to the background, a Solid layer. Footage: Crowd Control, clip # P1020749.

## "Orbing" with Boris Continuum Complete Particle Array 3D

The television show *Charmed* has lots of great particle effects, with witches "orbing," or teleporting, in and out of scenes as magical balls of light whoosh around them. This tutorial is a take on that type of effect, using **Boris Continuum Complete Particle Array 3D**, which is a new plug-in introduced in BCC7.

**Figure 5.37** Boris Continuum Complete Particle Array 3D is used to create an effect similar to the "orbing" effect on *Charmed*. Footage: Crowd Control, clip # 00154_002_36.

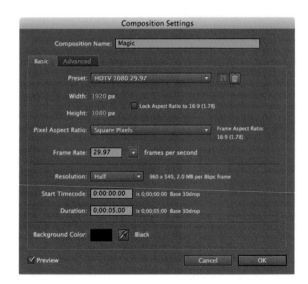

**Figure 5.38** Composition Settings. Screenshot: Michele Yamazaki.

*The project file is included on this book's DVD in the BCC Orbing Particles folder. It includes a still image of the Victorian lady, which is from a Crowd Control clip.*

**Third-party plug-ins needed:**

• Boris Continuum Complete

1. Import the still image of the Victorian lady, 00154_002_36.tif, into After Effects. Drag the image to the Create a New Composition button at the bottom of the Project panel. A new Composition panel will open with the footage. Open Composition Settings (Composition > Composition Settings), rename the comp "Magic," and set the duration to 5:00. Depending on the last settings used, the comp may be shorter or longer than five seconds. Click okay. If the comp was too short, extend the footage to the duration of the clip. (Figure 5.39.)

2. Create a new solid (Layer > New > Solid), click the Make Comp Size button and name it "Magic." Select this Magic layer and

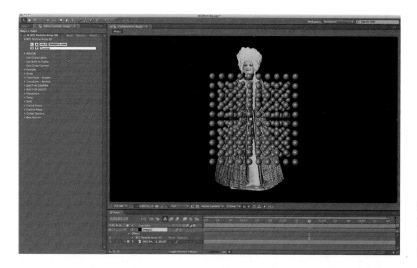

**Figure 5.39** The gray spheres is the default setting for BCC Particle Array 3D. Footage: Crowd Control, clip # 00154_002_36.

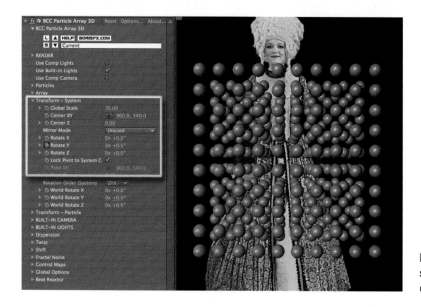

**Figure 5.40** Transform – System settings. Footage: Crowd Control, clip # 00154_002_36.

apply BCC Particle Array 3D (Effect > BCC OpenGL > BCC Particle Array 3D). In the Comp panel, you'll see a cube grid of blue spheres with several rows appear. Make sure Use Built-in Lights is checked in the Effect Controls panel for BCC Particle Array 3D. (Figure 5.40.)

3. Go to the first frame of the composition. In the Effect Controls panel, twirl down Transform – System and enable keyframing for Rotate Y with a value of $0x + 0.0°$. Jump to the last frame and set the value of Rotate Y to $3x + 0.0°$. This will cause the cube grid to spin. Set Global Scale to 70 to make the orb/particles smaller. (Figure 5.41.)

**Figure 5.41** Keyframe Shift to move the orbs from the bottom of the screen to the top of the screen. The point in time is marked in the lower left corner of each frame. Footage: Crowd Control, clip # 00154_002_36.

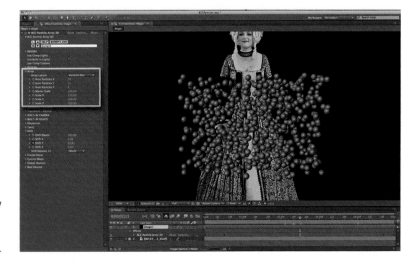

**Figure 5.42** Adjusting the Array settings will give the particles variety in position. Footage: Crowd Control, clip # 00154_002_36.

4. Since this effect has so many parameters, twirl Transform – System to keep things tidy and easy to find. Go to 0:15. Twirl open the Shift section in the Effect Controls panel. Drag the value of Shift Y so that the cube grid is moved off the bottom of the screen (about 500.00) and enable keyframing for Shift Y. Go to 4:21 and drag Shift Y so that the grid moves off the top of the screen (–500.00). Hold down shift while dragging Shift Y for a live preview in the Comp panel. (Figure 5.42.)

5. Twirl open the Array section in the Effect Controls panel. Set the Array Layout to Random Box. This will vary the position of the spheres so they're no longer in a tidy grid. Also under Array, set the following (see Figure 5.43):
   - **Num Particles X**: 13 (adds more particles on the *x*-axis)
   - **Num Particles Y**: 13 (adds more particles on the *y*-axis)
   - **Num Particles Z**: 4 (adds more particles on the *z*-axis)
   - **Master Scale**: 120 (increases the size of the array of particles)
   - **Scale X**: 150 (spreads the array wider)

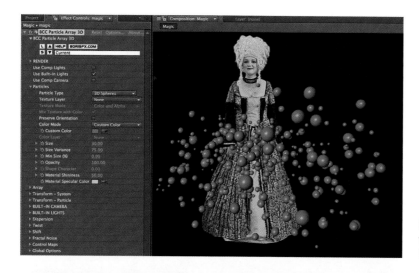

**Figure 5.43** Size and colorize the particles. Footage: Crowd Control, clip # 00154_002_36.

**Figure 5.44** Apply a Linear Wipe to make the actress appear. Footage: Crowd Control, clip # 00154_002_36.

- **Scale Y**: 90
- **Scale Z**: 225

6. Twirl open the Dispersion section in the Effect Controls panel. Set Disperse Master to 325.00. This will spread the particles out more from the center. Twirl Dispersion closed, as well as Shift and Array closed if they're still open.

7. Time to make the particles look magical. Under Particles, set Size Variance to 75 to vary the size of the particles. Set Custom Color to a royal blue and Material Specular Color to turquoise. (Figure 5.44.)

8. The actress will need to disappear as the particles move up the screen; this can be easily accomplished with a wipe. Select the Victorian lady layer and apply **Linear Wipe** to the footage (Effect > Transition > Linear Wipe). Go to 1:12 on the timeline. Set Wipe Angle to $0x + 0.0°$ and Feather to 120.0,

then enable keyframing for Transition Completion with a value of 0.0%. At 3:25, set Transition Completion to 100%. The idea is to match the wipe with the moving particles, so preview the wipe a few times and adjust the Transition Completion keyframes as necessary. (Figure 5.45.)

9. Select the Magic layer. At the very top of the Effect Controls panel, twirl open Render. Set Motion Blur to Smoothest in the pulldown menu. This will give the animation a natural blur as it moves, but it will also kill the RAM Preview and screen redraw speed, hence it's saved for last. (Figure 5.46.)

**Finishing Touches**: To give the particles a bit more magic, apply BCC Colorize Glow to the magic layer (Effects > BCC Effects > BCC Colorize Glow). Select the blueGlow.bcp preset. Increase the intensity to 250.

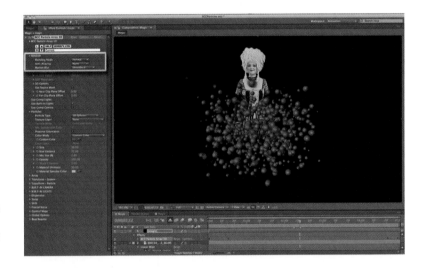

**Figure 5.45** Set Motion Blur to Smoothest for the nicest look to the particles. Footage: Crowd Control, clip # 00154_002_36.

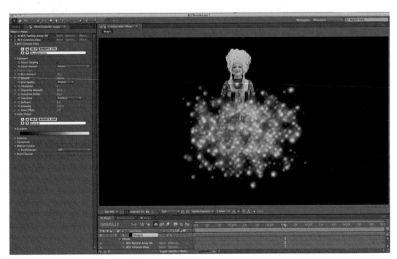

**Figure 5.46** BCC Colorize Glow adds magic. Footage: Crowd Control, clip # 00154_002_36.

Figure 5.47  A scene transition using GenArts Sapphire S_SwishPan. Footage: Michigan Film Reel.

# GenArts Sapphire S_SwishPan Transition

Have you ever needed to make a quick pan between two clips and make it look like they were shot in the same scene? Another use for this effect is to transition from scene to scene as they do on Disney Channel's *The Wizards of Waverly Place*.

There are a few plug-ins to create a swish pan effect, including **Boris Continuum Complete BCC Swish Pan**, **Noise Industries FxFactory Whoosh**, and **GenArts Sapphire S_SwishPan**. Sapphire S_SwishPan is extremely easy to use when keyframed, but it also has an automatic animation function (which I find difficult to control the speed of the wipe with). We will be keyframing the wipe in this tutorial.

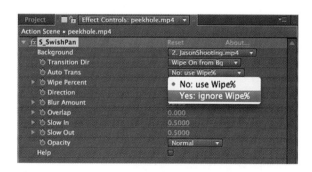

Figure 5.48  Sapphire S_SwishPan can be auto animated by setting Auto Trans to Yes Ignore Wipe%, which tells the effect to auto-animate and ignore any Wipe Percent values. Screenshot: Michele Yamazaki.

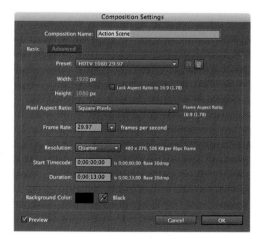

Figure 5.49  Action Scene composition settings. Screenshot: Michele Yamazaki.

*The footage for this tutorial is provided by Michigan Film Reel and is included on this book's DVD with the project in the GenArts SwishPan Folder.*

**Third-party plug-ins needed:**

- GenArts Sapphire

  1. Import two clips from the GenArts S_SwishPan project folder, titled JasonShooting.mp4 and peekhole.mp4, into After Effects.

  2. Make a new Composition (Composition > New Composition). Name the composition Action Scene. Use the HDTV 1080 29.97 preset and set the duration to 13:00. Click OK. (Figure 5.50.)

  3. Drag JasonShooting.mp4 and peekhole.mp4 into the Action Scene composition, starting at the first frame. The clip JasonShooting.mp4 is 8:00. We want peekhole.mp4 to transition in beginning at 5:22 where Jason's shirt is fully on screen. Go to 5:22 and select the peekhole.mp4 layer, and then tap the [ key (left bracket). (Figure 5.51.)

  4. Apply GenArts Sapphire S_SwishPan to peekhole.mp4 (Effect > Sapphire Transitions > S_SwishPan). In the Effect Controls panel, set the Background to JasonShooting.mp4. Set Transition Dir to Wipe On from Bkd, which will make this layer, peekhole.mp4, wipe on from the background layer, JasonShooting.mp4. (Figure 5.52.)

**Figure 5.50** JasonShooting.mov and peekhole.mov clips overlap in the timeline. Screenshot: Michele Yamazaki.

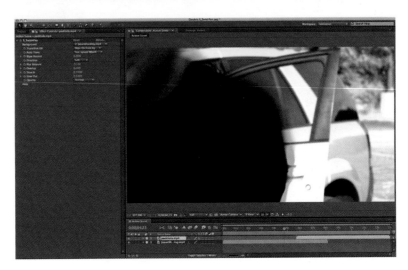

**Figure 5.51** Applying the GenArts S_SwishPan effect. Footage: Michigan Film Reel.

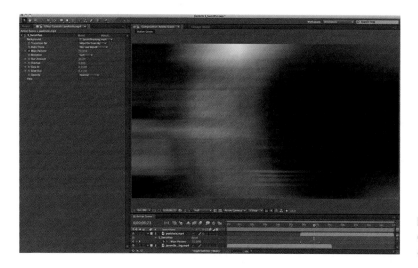

**Figure 5.52** The swish pan effect lasts about a second and a half. Footage: Michigan Film Reel.

**5.** At 5:22, at the first frame of peekhole.mp4, enable keyframing for Wipe Percent with a value of 0.00%. Go to 7:07 and set the value of Wipe Percent to 100.00%. Preview the comp for timing. If you'd like the swish pan effect to happen faster, move the second keyframe to a few frames earlier in the timeline. If you'd like it to happen slower, move the second keyframe to a later point in the timeline.

You can also adjust the values for Slow In and Slow Out to give more of a speed curve to the effect, as Easy Ease does. A positive value gives a more gentle transition. A lower value will cause the effect to start faster. Because these are action shots with someone with a gun, I set Slow In and Slow Out to 0.1500 so that the effect kicks in quickly.

Lastly, I set Blur Amount to 25.00 so that more detail can be seen in each shot as it transitions.

# GENERATORS

This chapter deals with plug-ins that generate something from nothing—elements like lens flares, particles, strokes, and more.

## Lens Flares

Where would we be without the lens flare? Probably one of the hardest things to focus on and study, a lens flare will quickly come and go, generated by fractions of light. A properly placed lens flare can generate a feeling of depth and realism. Sci-fi movies and shows such as *Star Wars* and *Battlestar Galactica* rely heavily on lens flares, often used as a surrounding for planets and when a spaceship flies by, for a look and feel of being in space where light is precious.

J.J. Abram's *Star Trek* (2009) features some beautiful, and often excessive, use of lens flares. Many of the flares in *Star Trek* were created with powerful spotlights, mirrors, and specific lenses; they gave the film a definite mood and atmosphere. I read an interview with Abrams where he equated the lens flares in the film to "another actor in the scene."[1]

*Scott Pilgrim vs. The World* (2010) also uses anamorphic film style lens flares predominantly throughout the film, most notably during the fight scenes.

In the following tutorials, we'll look at Video Copilot Optical Flares, Boris Continuum Adv. Lens Flare, Red Giant Knoll Light Factory, FxFactory SUGARfx Lens Flare, and GenArts Sapphire Lens Flare. We'll mimic a glare from the sun, create a faux concert stage light set up, and bring a monster's eye to life. After Effects does have its own subpar flare, but there are robust third-party options that allow you to make your own flares, many of which produce superb results.

### Comparisons of Lens Flare Plug-ins on the Market
*After Effects Lens Flare ($0)*

> **Pros**: Simplicity at its best.
> **Cons**: Bare bones. Not many looks that can be created with it.
> **Notes**: Ships with After Effects.

[1]See: *http://on.io9.com/trekflares*.

**Figure 6.1** Sunflower with After Effects Lens Flare. Footage: Michele Yamazaki.

### Video Copilot Optical Flares ($124.95)

**Pros**: Layer your flares as deep as you like to control the look of each and every parameter. A vast variety of looks can be created, from very natural to anamorphic lens looks, and other special effects. Contains a 3D flare and a flare that can be attached to a camera.

**Cons**: Separate elements of the flares can't be keyframed individually.

**Notes**: The favored overall for a well-designed user interface; endless variety of options and speed.

**Figure 6.2** Sunflower with Video Copilot Optical Flares. Footage: Michele Yamazaki.

### Boris Continuum Complete Advanced Lens Flare ($99, or $995 for Boris Continuum Complete)

**Pros**: Several nice presets, some animated. Elements of the flare can be easily turned on and off. Built-in Motion Tracker and Beat Reactor for working with audio.

**Cons**: Believe it or not, no real downsides to this lens flare.

**Notes**: Boris Continuum Lens Flare Advanced is a close second to Video Copilot Optical Flares.

### Red Giant Knoll Light Factory ($399)

**Pros**: Loads of presets and a custom lens editor make KLF a great tool. It's very fast and the flares are beautiful and clear.

**Figure 6.3** Sunflower with Boris Continuum Complete Lens Flare Adv. Footage: Michele Yamazaki.

**Figure 6.4** Sunflower with Knoll light Factory EZ. Footage: Michele Yamazaki.

**Cons**: A bit expensive compared to the competition for a product that does a single thing (not a bundle).

**Notes**: The auto-obscuration feature turns a flare "off" when something passes between the source and the viewer. It's very useful.

### SUGARfx Lens Flare (FxFactory) (included in SUGARfx Lens Pack, $79)

**Pros**: Very fast and no learning curve. The beams are really nice looking and make a great sun replacement.

**Cons**: This one is a bit more difficult to control individual elements of the flare. Reflections can be turned on and off but not really controlled.

**Notes**: Requires the free FxFactory to run, which can be downloaded at *www.noiseindustries.com*.

**Figure 6.5** Sunflower with SUGARfx Lens Flare. Footage: Michele Yamazaki.

*GenArts Sapphire Lens Flare*

> **Pros**: Several nice looking presets ship with Sapphire. Everything is keyframable. Two versions of the Lens Flare, one contains a motion tracker.
>
> **Cons**: All settings are in one big list. Not easy to layer elements of the flare. Expensive, but it does come with a full bundle.

**Figure 6.6** Sunflower with GenArts Sapphire S_LensFlare. Footage: Michele Yamazaki.

## Faking a Sun with Video Copilot Optical Flares

If you're filming in a place that doesn't always have bright sunshine and you need to add some warmth to your footage, **Video Copilot Optical Flares** gives you an easy way to add some sun shine to your shot. We'll track a shot of a sunflower (shown in the comparisons in the previous section) and apply the flare in 2D mode to fake a sun. We'll keep the sun mostly offscreen so we just see the flares, something that was done in J.J. Abrams *Star Trek* (2009) to give the idea that big things were happening offscreen. *This project is included on the DVD in a folder named VC Optical Flares – Sunflower folder.*

**Figure 6.7** The final render of a fake sun with a lens flare, created with Video Copilot Optical Flares. Footage: Michele Yamazaki.

**Plug-ins needed**:

- Video Copilot Optical Flares

    1. Bring the sunflower footage, sunflower.mp4, into After Effects and then drag it to the Make a New Composition button at the bottom of the Project panel.

    2. Create a new Solid (Layer > New > Solid), call it Solar Flare, and make it the same size as your composition.

    3. Apply **Video Copilot Optical Flares** to the solid. The default flare appears. Set the Render Mode at the very bottom of the Effect Controls panel to On Transparent so that you can see the Sunflower footage below. Alternatively, instead of using On Transparent, the flare can be applied to a black Solid layer with the Blending Mode set to Screen, Lighten, or another for compositing.

    4. Set the Preview BG layer to sunflower.mp4. This will be useful for examining the colors and other elements of the flare once we're in the actual Optical Flares interface. If you do not select a Preview BG layer here, you will not be able to see the flare over a selected background in the Optical Flares interface. You can choose any layer as a BG layer, but you can only choose one. Save your project.

    5. We will track the shot of the sunflower with **Imagineer mocha for After Effects**. Please read the section "*Depleted*: Tracking with Imagineer mocha for After Effects" in Chapter 13 for details on the process. Our tracking target is the area of the sky near where the sun would be. For most of the shot, the sun will actually be offscreen so we'll choose an area bordering the edge. These trees are extremely difficult to track with After Effects' built-in tracker (I had no success with it). mocha for After Effects, however, works amazingly well. Instructions on using mocha for After Effects are in Chapter 13, "Tracking, Matchmoving, Motion Stabilization, and Rotoscoping."

    6. Bring the mocha tracking data into After Effects by selecting File > Export Tracking Data. Simply copy the text data from mocha for After Effects to your clipboard, switch to After Effects, and paste them to the Position parameter of a small solid (with visibility turned off). Later, you will pick whip the XY Position of the flare to the position of this solid. Select all of the position keyframes of the track in After Effects and nudge them to the appropriate position. While this could be done with an expression, it's easy enough to select them all and move them.

    7. Once positioned, the flare needs to be edited. Click Options at the top of the Optical Flares Effect Controls panel. The full interface will open. Some users don't care for different interfaces, preferring to work in After Effects native effect control interface, however, this one is particularly well-designed and easy to use. I might even call it "cool." (Figure 6.8.)

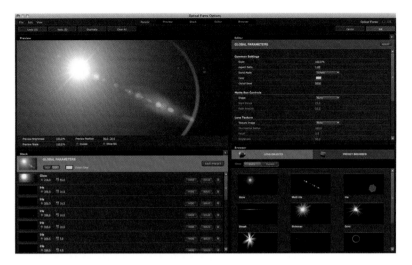

Figure 6.8 Video Copilot's Optical Flares Options interface.

8. The top section of Optical Flares is the flare Preview panel. If you check the Show BG box below it, you should see the background layer behind the flare, previously selected in the Effect Controls panel. You can drag the flare around the window interactively, but you can't keyframe anything in this interface. Below the Preview panel is the Stack list, which shows all of the pieces as a building block. Along the top of the window you can choose Panels, which are clickable tabs for Preview, Stack, Editor, and Browser. The Editor allows you to edit and customize the flare. The Browser shows you available presets. With Optical Flares, browse for a preset that is close to what you want, then click on the Editor and make adjustments or add and remove elements of the flare. If you design a keeper, simply click the Save Preset button and name it. It will show up in the preset gallery under "_Custom Presets".

9. Once you are happy with your flare, which is supposed to simulate the sun, click OK and the interface window will close. You should see your new flare superimposed on the sunflower image. (Figure 6.9.)

10. To make the flare's position, follow the motion tracker data, Option (Alt) + click to add an expression to the XY Position parameter name, then drag, releasing the pick whip icon over the Solid Layer's Position parameter (holding the pasted tracker keyframes from earlier). (Figure 6.10.)

11. Adjust the scale and brightness of the flare. I added some flicker to the flare and customized the rotation to my liking. Play it through and if you need to make changes to the flare, simply click Options in Optical Flares Effect Controls panel.

Figure 6.9  The Optical Flares interface. Footage: Michele Yamazaki.

Figure 6.10  Pick whipping the Position parameter.

## Quick and Dirty Concert Lights with Video Copilot Optical Flares

*Scott Pilgrim vs. The World* had several scenes of Scott's band playing onstage with serious flares from the stage lights. Video Copilot Optical Flares allows you to attach flares to comp lights very easily with a feature called Track Lights, allowing you to

Figure 6.11  The final shot with a composited performer, some Digieffects Delirium Fog Factory for ambience, and some Red Giant Magic Bullet Looks for color effects. Footage: Crowd Control, clip# 00365_001_19.

recreate the background scenes in *Scott Pilgrim*. The film used mainly blue anamorphic film flares and chroma hoops. *This little project, which is included on the DVD in a folder named VC Optical Flares – Concert Lights, will literally take you ten minutes to put together and looks really cool.*

**Third-party plug-ins needed:**

- Video Copilot Optical Flares
    1. Create a new Composition using the HDTV 1080 29.97 preset named Flare. Add a New Solid Layer (Layer > New > Solid), click Make Comp Size and name it Optical Flares. Apply Video Copilot Optical Flares to the Solid layer (Effects > Video Copilot > Optical Flares). Although you will be adding 3D Lights to the comp, the Solid layer will remain 2D.
    2. Under Positioning Mode in the Effect Controls panel, choose Track Lights for the Source Type. (Figure 6.12.)
    3. Add a Light to the comp (Layer > New > Light). Name this light "A-Light 1" and set the Light Type to Spot. Set Intensity to 75%, Cone Angle to 90°, and Cone Feather to 50%. Set the light Color to white. Click OK to close the Light Settings dialog popup. (Figure 6.13.)
    4. Place the Position for the light in the upper left corner of the Comp panel. The light should look like the default flare and

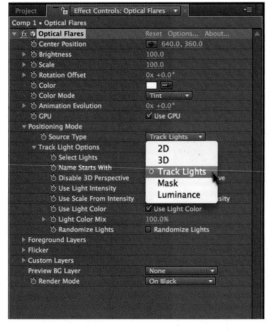

Figure 6.12 Video Copilot interface.

Figure 6.13 Light settings.

that's fine for now. The letter A will be used to tie it to the lens flare design in a future step. (Figure 6.14.)

5. *Note*: Depending on other steps taken previously, when you add a 3D Light with no 3D layers in your comp, you may receive a warning message. Just ignore it.

6. Duplicate A-Light seven times so that you have eight lights total. Spread the lights evenly across the top of the Comp panel by adjusting the position parameter. (Figure 6.15.)

7. To give it some interest, add some gentle camera movement. Create a new camera (Layer > New > Camera). Use the 35mm preset and click OK to close Camera Settings. (Figure 6.16.)

8. Use the Unified Camera tool (C) to position the camera. Set keyframes to animate the position of the camera.

9. To adjust the look of the flare, click Options at the top of Effect Controls for Optical Flares, opening the custom GUI. Under Browser, in the Light presets, choose the preset called Main Lights. Double-click to select the preset, modifying the flare as you wish, and click OK when you are happy with the flare. (Figure 6.17.)

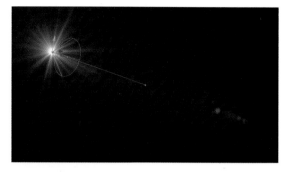

Figure 6.14 The default flare.

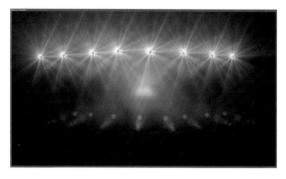

Figure 6.15 The lights spread across the screen.

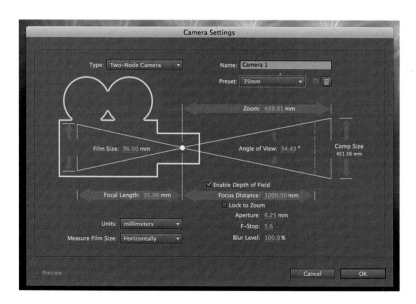

Figure 6.16 Camera settings.

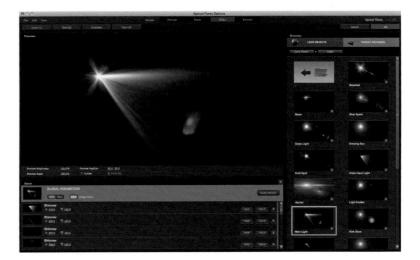

**Figure 6.17** Main Lights.

10. Using more than one flare style in a composition is quite simple and it has to do with how the lights are named. Under Positioning Mode > Track Light Options there is a pulldown menu called Name Starts With. The list includes Anything, the letters A–I, and Light. Simply rename every other light "B-Light" and use the corresponding setting on the Optical Flares Effect. To set this up with two or more different styles of lights, Lights 1, 3, 5, and 7 should be called "A-Light" and Lights 2, 4, 6, and 8 should be named "B-Light".

11. On the Optical Flares effect, change Name Starts With to A. You should see half of the flares shut off—the B-Lights. (Figure 6.18.)

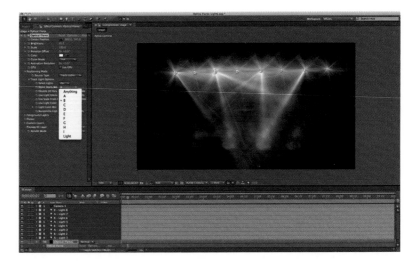

**Figure 6.18** Using multiple flares linked to lights in Optical Flares.

12. Duplicate the Solid Layer with Optical Flares applied to it. Change the duplicate solid's Name Starts With effect control to B. The lens flares will turn back on for B-Lights. You will not see any difference yet because the flares on the two layers are exactly the same. Click Options and change to another flare preset, then modify the lens flare as you like. I used one called Red Light. Click OK and you will see two different styles of flares linked to the lights. (Figure 6.19.)

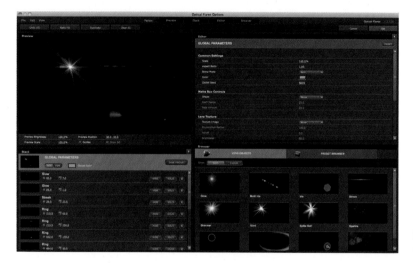

**Figure 6.19** Video Copilot Optical Flares Interface.

13. To add more interest to the shot, I added a camera and keyframed the position.

## Creating a Glowing Eye with Boris BCC Lens Flare Advanced

A nice feature of **Boris Continuum Complete BCC Lens Flare Advanced** is the built-in Motion Tracker. It's a 2D point tracker and is very fast and impressively accurate. The tracker is built into several BCC plug-ins and there is a nice help PDF included—just click Help under the Tracker Settings.

For this project, which is included on the DVD, I'll quickly go through how to track a simple eye onto an enormous art deco sculpture of the Loch Ness monster (affectionately known as Nessie). Nessie was one of the top pieces in the 2009 ArtPrize competition in Grand Rapids, Michigan. At night her eye glowed green and this tutorial will take you through an exaggerated version of her glowing eye, looking like Nessie on a foggy Scottish loch in the early morning.

*The project is included on this book's DVD in the BCCLensFlareAdv Nessie folder.*

# Pro Tip

This plug-in may give the illusion of volumetric light, but remember that it is just creating flares at points. With Optical Flares applied to a light, the rotation of the light will not rotate any flare elements, even when pick-whipped to a null object. The entire light can be parented to a Null and rotated but it will move the entire light, not just pan the light angle.

**Figure 6.20** Video Copilot Optical Flares used on Track Lights. Footage: Crowd Control, clip# 00365_001_19.

**Third-party plug-ins needed:**

- Boris Continuum Complete
    1. Import the Nessie.mp4 footage into After Effects and drag the Nessie.mp4 clip onto the Make a New Composition button at the bottom of the Project panel. As always, preview the clip through a few times to see what you'll be creating.
    2. Apply BCC Lens Flare Adv (Effects > BCC Open GL > BCC Lens Flare Adv). First we'll take care of the tracker, then we'll choose the look of the eye. Near the bottom of the BCC Lens Flare Advanced plug-in settings in the Effect Controls panel, twirl down Motion Tracker. Under Preprocess, check the View Preprocessed box so you can see the tracker

**Figure 6.21** The final look of Nessie sculpture with the glowing eyes, created with Boris Continuum BCC Lens Flare Adv. Footage: Michele Yamazaki. Sculpture by Nessie Project: *http://nessieproject.wordpress.com.* Used by permission.

parameters. At the first frame of the composition, place the Tracker Center KF at the center of Nessie's eye. Drag out the target width to surround her whole eye and a bit of her head. Drag the outer Search Width box, to span the area where the eye moves throughout the clip's duration. The eye is out of the shot at about 6 seconds, so set the End Tracking Frame to 180. Click the Track On-The-Fly checkbox and the Show Motion Path box so you can see it as it tracks. Make sure you're still on the first frame in the timeline then click the Play button in the Preview palette. Watch it track and make sure it stays on track. (Figure 6.22.)

3.  Once your track is finished, uncheck the View Preprocessed box, which will turn off the tracking boxes and motion path view. To make things simple, choose the BCC Lens Flare Advanced preset greenGlow.bcp, which will create a surreal, stripy flare. There are many settings to play with in BCC Lens

**Figure 6.22** The Boris Continuum Tracker in action. Footage: Michele Yamazaki. Sculpture by Nessie Project: *http://nessieproject.wordpress.com.* Used by permission.

Flare Advanced and I encourage you to get in there and see what it does. The plug-in is a lot of fun to use and you can create a huge variety of different flare looks. (Figure 6.23.)

**Figure 6.23** Boris Continuum Advanced Lens Flare presets and Effects control. Footage: Michele Yamazaki. Sculpture by Nessie Project: *http://nessieproject.wordpress.com*. Used by permission.

**Finishing touches**: To enhance the shot even more, I applied **BCC Color Correction** with the addPopSuble.bcp preset with Brightness lowered to −30.0 and Saturation lowered to −20.0. BCC Color Correction is placed in effect order before BCC Lens Flare Advanced, to give it a desaturated, presunrise look. On top of that I added a bit of fog using **BCC Clouds** with the foggy.bcp preset with the Speed and Billow Speed turned down and the Sky Type set to Composite on Original, to hopefully give it the look of a foggy Scottish loch. I also toned down the Global Intensity and Stripe length of the flare so it's not quite so over the top.

**Figure 6.24** Nessie, with the final touches of Magic Bullet Looks and BCC Clouds to create fog. Footage: Michele Yamazaki. Sculpture by Nessie Project: *http://nessieproject.wordpress.com*. Used by permission.

## A Simple Light Array Backdrop with Knoll Light Factory by Harry J. Frank

In this tutorial you'll learn how to set up a custom flare design in Knoll Light Factory that not only adds punch, but also has a dual nature almost like two flares in one. In addition, we'll construct a simple light array as a backdrop, and then load a preset flare file into Knoll Light Spectacular. *Project files are in the KLF from Scratch folder on this book's DVD.*

**Figure 6.25** The final render with flares (left) and the original 3D render. Footage: Harry J. Frank.

**Third party plug-ins needed:**
- Red Giant Knoll Light Factory
    1. Create a new Composition using the HDTV 1080 29.97 preset. Add a New Solid Layer (Layer > New > Solid), click Make Comp Size and name it "Main Flare". Apply Knoll Light Factory> Light Factory. Click Options... in the Effect Controls for Light Factory to open the Knoll Light Factory Lens Designer. Click the Delete button several times to remove the default elements. (Figure 6.26.)
    2. First, click Add Element and add a Stripe. Scrub over the values to set the Length to 1.0, increase the Brightness a little, and set the Outer and Center colors to a light blue. Repeat this process to create a second stripe, and then set the position of this stripe to −1, which will have it "mirror" the motion. (Figure 6.27.)

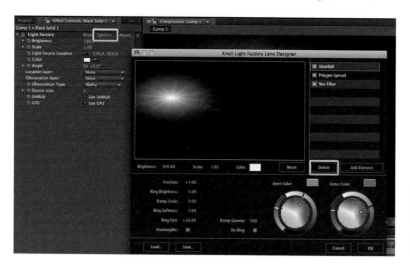

**Figure 6.26** To open Knoll Light Factory Lens Designer, click Options.... Click Delete to remove the default elements. Footage: Harry J. Frank.

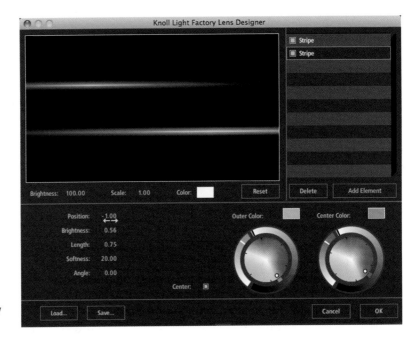

Figure 6.27 Click and drag on the Position parameter to change the value. Footage: Harry J. Frank.

3. Next, we will repeat the steps with Disc elements. Discs are a great way to add a soft glow, but have more parameters to adjust than the standard Glow element found in the Lens Designer. Add the two Disc elements, one with position set to –1. Check the Anamorphic checkbox to stretch the disc out a little, and set the colors to a similar shade of blue. (Figure 6.28.)

Figure 6.28 The flare with added Disc elements. Footage: Harry J. Frank.

4. To add a bit of a more "digital" feel, I am going to add a heavily adjusted Chroma Fan that will render two small light streaks that follow the lens position, as well as add a circle and polygon spread.

5. Add the Chroma Fan element, and you'll immediately see that there's a lot of tweaking to do. Initially it looks a bit like a soft vertical rainbow. However, the Chroma Fan element can be tweaked to achieve a lot of different looks. (Figure 6.29.)

6. First, rotate the angle to +90. Then lower the Chroma Spread to 1.00, which will squeeze the spectrum into a white light. Set the Brightness to 0.20 and the Scale to 0.50. Increasing the Cycles can yield many light elements if you turn it up, but this case, I've lowered it to 1 cycle, which yields one light streak on either side of the Light Source Location.

7. It might seem a bit light at this point, but that is because the Chroma Fan is still fanned out quite a bit. Condense the Spread and Radial Offset settings both to 125. Then, pick your color to taste. I've simply used the same blue I've been using for the other elements. The default position of 1 will have it follow the Light Source Location exactly. I find it more interesting to have it lag the position a little bit by using a position around 0.8 or so. (Figure 6.30.)

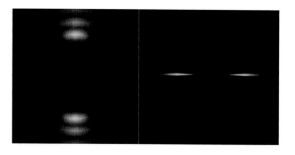

**Figure 6.29** *Left*: The default Chroma Fan settings. *Right*: The modified settings. Footage: Harry J. Frank.

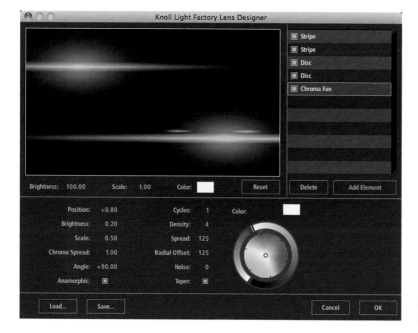

**Figure 6.30** The Chroma Fan modified. Footage: Harry J. Frank.

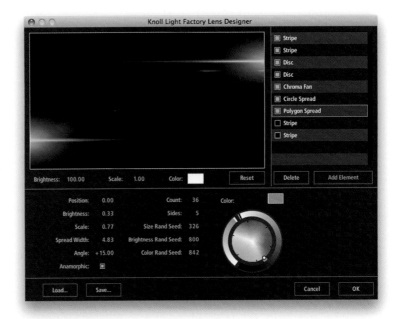

**Figure 6.31** The Polygon Spread and Circle Spread applied to the flare. Footage: Harry J. Frank.

**Figure 6.32** Two more Stripes, rotated 90° add more depth to the flare. Footage: Harry J. Frank.

8. Adding a Circle Spread will add some small specks of light bridging the two sides of the two flares. We can fill it in more by increasing the Count to 40.

9. Adding a Polygon Spread will add a similar spread, but using softer light orbs (polygon spread uses shapes with a finite number of sides, allowing shapes like triangles, squares, or hexs.) For the Polygon Spread, increase the Count to about 30. For both the Circle Spread and Polygon, tweak the color to taste, and also adjust the Color Rand Seed so that you end up with a color variation that you are happy with. (Figure 6.31.)

10. As a finishing touch on this lens flare design, we'll add two small vertical Stripes. They will be almost identical to the first two stripes added with the following differences: The angle will be +90 and the length will be 0.10 on one and 0.20 on the other. Then adjust the Position to place them somewhere between 0 and 1. (Figure 6.32.)

11. That wraps up this element! Click OK to close the Knoll Light Factory Lens Designer.

12. In the Effect Controls panel, check Use Unmult for this flare and the upcoming layers so that the elements blend with the background. Also, I would suggest setting this layer to a

Screen blending mode to blend the elements placed below it in the timeline more subtly. (Figure 6.33.)

13. Next, we'll add an array of lights as a backdrop, which is actually very simple. On a new Solid Layer (click Make Comp Size and name it "Array"). Just as before apply Light Factory and go into the Options. Delete the default elements and add a Glowball. Set the Inner and Center colors to blue, check the Anamorphic checkbox, and lower the Ramp Scale to 0.50. From here, with this element at the Position of +1.00, we just need an array of them at 0.80, 0.60, 0.40, 0.20, .0, −0.20, etc. (Figure 6.34.)

14. Also, I think it helps to add a couple other elements to help sell the realism of a lens flare. Try adding other elements like a Stripe and a subtle Circle Spread. Click OK to close the Lens Editor.

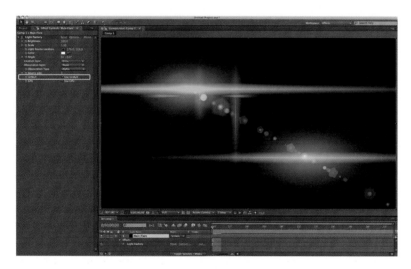

**Figure 6.33** Check Use Unmult to remove the background color. The black background isn't removed because there is no layer placed behind the Knoll Light Factory layer. Footage: Harry J. Frank.

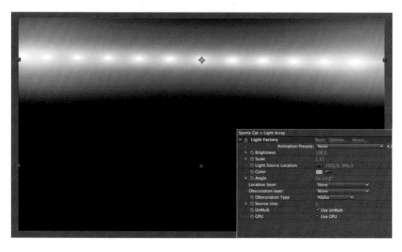

**Figure 6.34** An Array of Glowballs is spaced out evenly. Footage: Harry J. Frank.

# Hot Tip

In the Preview panel, the cursor becomes a hand. Grab onto one of the Stripe Flares and drag it to view the flare from another angle. It will not render at this angle. This is just for reference.

**Figure 6.35** The Knoll Light Factory Lens Designer. Footage: Michele Yamazaki.

**Figure 6.36** The final flares, placed over a 3D rendered car. Footage: Harry J. Frank.

15. In the Effect Controls for the Array layer, position the Light Source Location in the middle of the solid, and move the solid up to the top third of the screen.

16. Although we've been using the same colors all along, we can easily adjust the color to add some slight variation. In the Light Factory Effect Controls panel, adjust the color a little bit more toward a greenish blue. Don't forget to check the Unmult option and set the Mode to Screen.

17. Place a background element, stacked below the flare layers in the Timeline panel to finish the project. (Figure 6.36.)

# Pro Tip

Unfortunately, in Knoll Light Factory for CS5 there isn't an easy way to duplicate edited elements. In the CS4 version, one can simply drag an edited element to the New Element icon, and it will be duplicated. This feature has been omitted from the CS5 version (hopefully it will be back soon). One workaround is to save your settings using the Save… button and then to reload it with the Append checkbox checked.

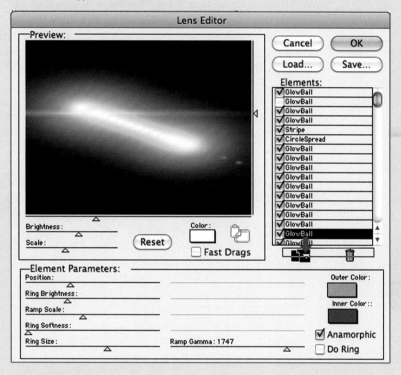

**Figure 6.37** CS4 Lens Editor. Footage: Harry J. Frank.

# Particle Systems: Fire and Bubbles and Snow Flakes, Oh My!

It's surprisingly easy to make particle elements with third-party plug-ins and there are a lot of options on the market.

What can you do with particles? What can't you do! Here is a short list of the possibilities:

- **Weather**: torrential downpours, blizzards, hail, fog, clouds, tornadoes
- **Space elements**: Stars, meteor showers and comets, warp speed, an asteroid field
- **Fire elements**: flaming swords, smoking eyes, sparking electrical wires, explosions, fireworks

- **Water elements**: Bubbles, water droplets, gushing fountains
- **Groups of things**: swarms of bees, crowds of people, herds of cats, blowing hearts
- **Background elements**: Sparkles, ethereal background miscellany, graphical backgrounds
- **Text effects**: Letters flying around the screen, raining reverse Katakana (as seen in *The Matrix* title) or the B notes from the bass as seen in *Scott Pilgrim vs. The World*
- **Cool random transitions**

When Particle Playground was introduced to After Effects, people were excited. There were tutorials on the web about creating different effects with it and how to use some of the very complex settings, but this plug-in has not really been updated since it was introduced. If you've used it for more than five minutes you'll know that it's difficult to use and extremely complex; I've personally had poor results with it. I've made decent looking smoke with it but not much else.

If you need to make particles in After Effects, third-party plug-ins are the only way to go, and you're in luck because the plug-ins available are awesome. That said, the problem with some of the particle generators is that many of the particles do not look all that natural on their own, especially in the plug-ins that have been on the market for years. You can spend a lot of time tweaking the settings, but the addition of effects, such as a blur, can make all the difference.

Toolfarm did a plug-ins survey in early 2010 and Trapcode Particular won the poll by more than double the votes of the second most popular plug-in, as it should because it's a powerful plug-in. Another more recent entry into the After Effects particle arena is **wondertouch particleIllusion AE**, now sold by GenArts. There are also very nice particle systems that come with some of the bigger bundles, like **Noise Industries FxFactory, Boris Continuum Complete, GenArts Sapphire**, and **Cycore FX HD** (the 8-bit version of Cycore FX ships with After Effects).

## VIRUS23: Distorted Text with Trapcode Form (Part 1 of Tutorial)

My friend Dru Nget generously shared a gorgeous movie title project file with about 20 precomps and containing 24 effects. He used mainly **Trapcode Form** and **Trapcode Particular, Red Giant Holomatrix, Video Copilot Twitch**, and several built-in plug-ins. It's an amazing example of what can be achieved with multiple plug-ins, but instead of going through the entire project, which would be a book in itself, I will go into detail on certain aspects of the project. *There are two versions of the project included on this book's DVD: VIRUS23-Dru, which is the original,* *and VIRUS23-simplified, which requires only Trapcode Form and Trapcode Particular.*

We'll look at VIRUS23-simplified in two parts. The first portion of the tutorial explains how to use Trapcode Form as a displacement map to distort text.

**Third-party plug-ins needed:**

• Trapcode Form

1. Create a new comp with the HDTV 1080 29.97 preset called VIRUS23 Logo, 5:00 in duration. Use the Type tool to create the words VIRUS23 in the center of the Composition panel in large font in white. (Figure 6.38.)

**Figure 6.38** The VIRUS23 Text. Footage: Michele Yamazaki. Design by Dru Nget.

2. In the Project panel, drag VIRUS23 Logo to the Make New Comp button. Go to Composition Settings and rename this new composition "VIRUS23 Title Precomp".(Figure 6.39.)

3. Add a Layer > New > Solid, the same size as the comp. Call it "Form Particles" and apply Trapcode Form (Effect > Trapcode > Form).

4. First we need to set up the base form and make the particles fill the width and height of the Composition, which is 1920×1080. Under Base Form, set Size X to 1920, and Size Y to 1080. We do not want to fill the depth with particles, so set Size Z to 0. (Figure 6.40.)

5. Now you'll set the number of particles in each dimension.
   – **Particles in X:** 500
   – **Particles in Y:** 500
   – **Particles in Z:** 1

6. Turn off the visibility of the VIRUS23 Logo layer by clicking the eyeball in the Timeline panel.

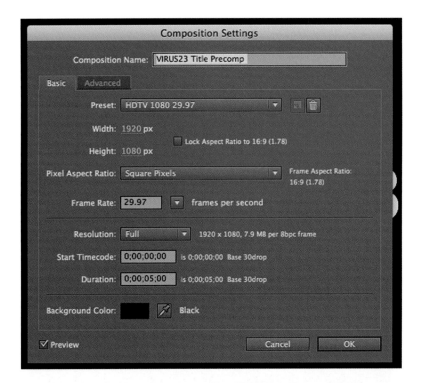

**Figure 6.39** Composition Settings. Footage: Michele Yamazaki. Design by Dru Nget.

**Figure 6.40** The Base Form settings with a close-up of how the particles will look at this point. Footage: Michele Yamazaki. Design by Dru Nget.

7. Under Layer Maps > Color and Alpha, choose 2. VIRUS23 Logo in the Layer pulldown menu. Under Functionality, choose A to A. A to A is short for Alpha to Alpha and will give you the ability to use the colors from Quick Maps, which will be explained in a future step. Set Map Over to XY since we set up the particles to fill the X and Y dimensions. You should now see the text filled with what looks like a window screen. (Figure 6.41.)

8. Under Layer Maps > Displacement, choose Individual XYZ in the Functionality pulldown menu. This will give you control of each axis, instead of just the group as a whole. Choose 2. VIRUS23 Logo for all three: Layer for X, Layer for Y, and Layer for Z. Set Strength to 0. There will not be any visual changes at this time as you change Displacement settings. (Figure 6.42.)

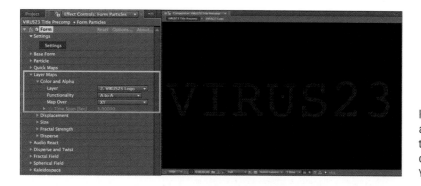

**Figure 6.41** Layer Maps Color and Alpha brings the texture through the alpha channel of the text. Footage: Michele Yamazaki. Design by Dru Nget.

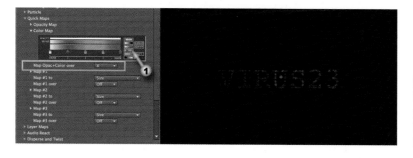

**Figure 6.42** Base Form settings. Footage: Michele Yamazaki. Design by Dru Nget.

9. Under Quick Maps > Color Map, choose a preset or design your own color map. I chose the yellow to purple preset, which is fourth from the top. Set Map Opac+Color over to X. (Figure 6.43.)

**Figure 6.43** Quick Maps Color Map settings. 1. Check the yellow to purple preset. Footage: Michele Yamazaki. Design by Dru Nget.

10. Twirl all sections closed. Open Disperse and Twist and Fractal Field. This is where we start keyframing. Under Fractal Field, set Displacement Mode to XYZ Individual.
11. Go to 2:02 in the timeline. Set keyframes for the following (Figure 6.44):
    - **Affect Size:** 38
    - **X Displace:** 0

**Figure 6.44** Keyframe values at 2:02. Footage: Michele Yamazaki. Design by Dru Nget.

**12.** Go to 2:04 and set the following values (Figure 6.45):
- **Affect Size:** 62
- **X Displace:**−616

**Figure 6.45** Values at 2:04. It will look very distorted at this point. Footage: Michele Yamazaki. Design by Dru Nget.

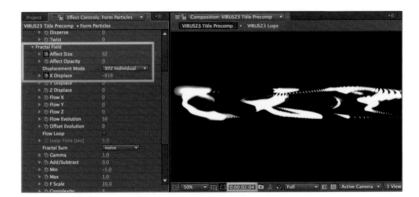

**13.** Go to 2:06. Change the following values:
- **Affect Size:** 42
- **X Displace:** 0
**14.** We're going to select all of these keyframes for X displace between 2:02 and 2:06 and paste them further down the timeline. Select them all and copy them to your clipboard. Go to 2:12 and paste. (Figure 6.46.)

**Figure 6.46** Copied keyframes. Footage: Michele Yamazaki. Design by Dru Nget.

15. To vary how Affect Size finishes, change the value to 18 at 2:16.
16. Under Disperse and Twist, set the following keyframes for Twist:
    – 0 at 2:02
    – 1 at 2:04
    – 0 at 2:06
17. Copy these keyframes. Go to 2:12 and paste, so you have keyframes for Twist at 2:12, 2:14, and 2:16.
18. Select all of the keyframes and apply Easy Ease (Animation > Keyframe Assistant > Easy Ease). (Figure 6.47.)

**Figure 6.47** 1. Select all keyframes. 2. Apply Easy Ease. Footage: Michele Yamazaki. Design by Dru Nget.

19. Scrub through the timeline. You should see the logo forming and displacing.
20. Turn on the visibility for VIRUS23 Text. We're going to make it rapidly blink on and off. Set the following keyframes for Opacity:
    – 100% at 2:02
    – 0% at 2:03
    – 100% at 2:04
    – 0% at 2:05
    – 100% at 2:06

Copy these Opacity keyframes to your clipboard. Go to 2:11 and paste. There is no need to Easy Ease these keyframes since they are so close together. (Figure 6.48.)

**Figure 6.48** Opacity keyframes. Footage: Michele Yamazaki. Design by Dru Nget.

Figure 6.49 Keyframes for Twist, Affect Size, and X Displace. Footage: Michele Yamazaki. Design by Dru Nget.

## VIRUS23: Explode Text into Particles with Trapcode Particular (Part 2 of Tutorial)

This section explains how Dru Nget created the text exploding into cells with **Trapcode Particular**, shown in the storyboard frames. *The project files are included on this book's DVD and using the comp titled 04. VIRUS23 Particular for this tutorial and continued from the previous tutorial.* Below is the basic technique, simplified.

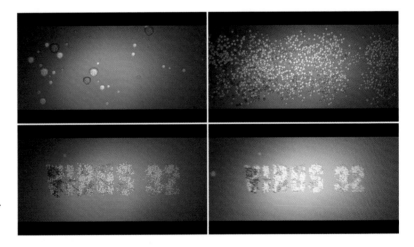

Figure 6.50 Storyboard frames of titles for VIRUS23. (Design by Dru Nget, designreactunite.com). Footage: Michele Yamazaki. Design by Dru Nget.

**Third-party plug-ins needed:**
- Trapcode Particular
  1. Drag the VIRUS23 Title Precomp, made in the previous tutorial, into the Make a New Composition button at the bottom of the project window. Rename this composition "Main Title". Make this layer 3D by checking the 3D Layer box in the Timeline panel under Switches.
  2. Add Layer > New > Solid (Make Comp Size). Name the solid Particles.
  3. Apply Trapcode Particular to the layer.

4. Select the Particles layer; go to Particular in the Effect Controls panel. Twirl down Emitter > Emitter Type and choose Layer from the pulldown menu. (Figure 6.51.)

**Figure 6.51** The Form Emitter with the VIRUS23 Title Precomp layer selected. Footage: Michele Yamazaki. Design by Dru Nget.

5. Under Layer Emitter, choose VIRUS Title Precomp. An emitter light will automatically appear in the timeline. (Figure 6.52.)
6. Still under Emitter, set the Particles/sec to 18,000 and zero out the values for Velocity, Velocity Random [%], Velocity Distribution, and Velocity from Motion. (Figure 6.53.)
7. Go to 2:00 in the timeline. Under Physics > Air set a keyframe for Wind Z to a value of 0. Jump ahead 10 frames and set Wind Z to –3000, so that the particles come toward you. Turn off the visibility for the VIRUS23 Precomp layer to see the effect. (Figure 6.54.)

**Figure 6.52** When an emitter layer is chosen (1), an Emitter Light will automatically appear in the Timeline panel (2). Footage: Michele Yamazaki. Design by Dru Nget.

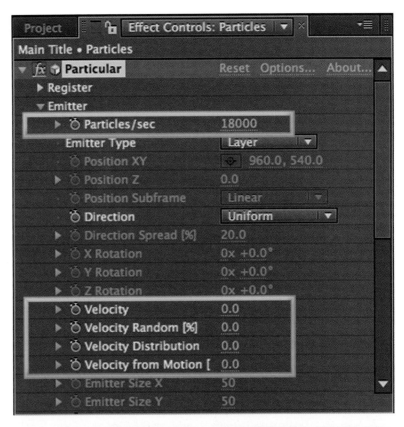

**Figure 6.53** Trapcode Particular Effect Controls. Footage: Michele Yamazaki. Design by Dru Nget.

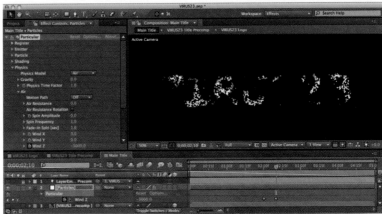

**Figure 6.54** Particular Physics settings. Footage: Michele Yamazaki. Design by Dru Nget.

8. Go back to 2:00 and set a keyframe for Spin Amplitude with a value of 0. Go to 3:00 and set the value of Spin Amplitude to 400. (Figure 6.55.)

9. Again, go back to 2:00. Back under the Emitter, set a keyframe for Velocity with a value of 0. Go to 3:00 and increase the value to 10,000. This is what gives you the speed as it explodes. Use what works best for your animation. (Figure 6.56.)

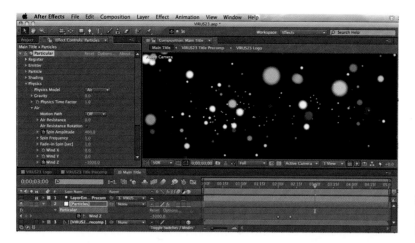

**Figure 6.55** Spin Amplitude.
Footage: Michele Yamazaki. Design by Dru Nget.

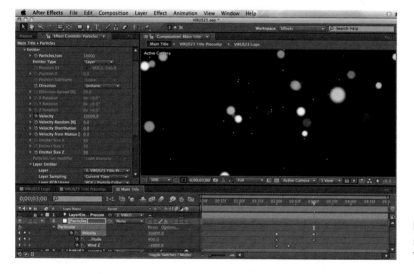

**Figure 6.56** Particular Emitter settings. Footage: Michele Yamazaki. Design by Dru Nget.

10. Go to 2:00. Tap the letter T to bring up Opacity. Set a keyframe for Opacity at 100%. Go to 1:00 and set the value of Opacity to 0.

11. Under Particle > Life Random [%], set the value to 20 to vary the life of the particles.

12. Select the Particles layer and tap the letter U to bring up all keyframes on the layer. Select the second keyframe on each parameter and add an Easy Ease In (Animation > Keyframe Assistant > Easy Ease In). (Figure 6.57.)

**Figure 6.57** Easy Ease In the keyframes to smooth them.
Footage: Michele Yamazaki. Design by Dru Nget.

Time to make a custom particle. We could spend a lot of time making a custom cell in Photoshop or Illustrator but instead, apply a circle mask with a few standard After Effects plug-ins.

13. Create a new Composition named "Cell", 200×200 pixels and 5 seconds in duration. Add a new solid. Layer > New Solid (Make Comp Size). A nice shortcut is to select the Solid layer, and then double-click the Ellipse tool in the toolbar to apply a mask that completely fills the solid layer.

14. To make it more cell-like, apply Fractal Noise and Tritone with custom colors. To give the cell some movement, apply Wave Warp. Experiment until you create something you like. (Figure 6.58.)

15. Drag the Cell comp into your Main Title comp. Turn off the visibility for the Cell layer.

16. In the timeline, jump to around 3:00 so that you can see the cells. On the Particles layer, under Particular, go to Particle. Set Particle Type to Sprite in the pulldown menu. Under Particle > Texture, set the Layer to your Cell layer. The cell you created should now replace the plain particles. To offset the time of the cells so that they are not exact copies, set Particle > Texture > Time Sampling to Random – Loop.

**Figure 6.58** Easily create a cell in After Effects with a few built-in plug-ins: Fractal Noise, Tritone, and Wave Warp. Footage: Michele Yamazaki. Design by Dru Nget.

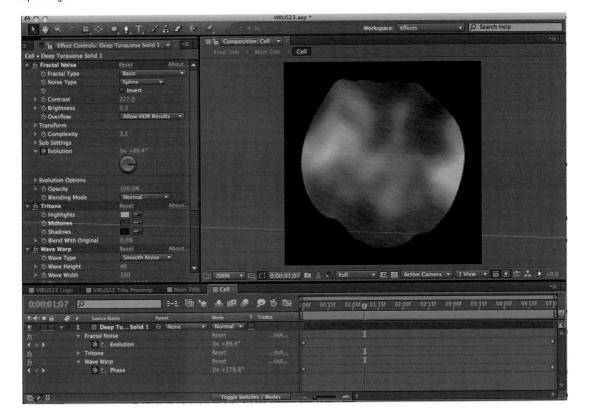

Change the value of Random Seed. For even more random-ness, set Particle > Random Rotation to 100.0. (Figure 6.59.)

17. Next, you'll keyframe the visibility of the Logo so that it fades out as the Particles layer begins to explode. Turn on the visibility of the VIRUS23 Title Precomp layer and drag it below the Particles layer. At 2:00, set a keyframe for Opacity with a value of 100.0% on the VIRUS23 Title Precomp layer. At 2:02, set the value of Opacity to 0.0%. (Figure 6.60.)

18. *Note*: If your computer is having a difficult time with so many particles, lower the Particles/sec. Turning down the resolution of the comp will also help with slow RAMPre-views. If the particles are too small, go to Particle > Size and increase the value just a bit.

19. In the Project panel, drag the Main Title comp to the Make New Composition icon to create a new comp. Rename the

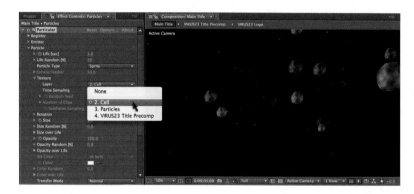

**Figure 6.59** Particular's settings in the Effect Controls panel for this project. Footage: Michele Yamazaki. Design by Dru Nget.

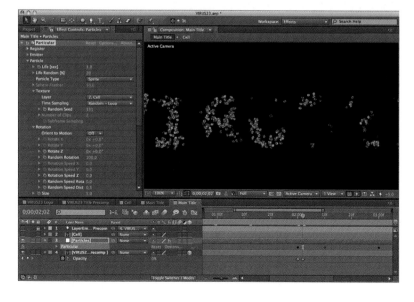

**Figure 6.60** This is how the cells and text should appear at this point. Footage: Michele Yamazaki. Design by Dru Nget.

comp "Final Title" by going to Composition > Composition Settings. Click OK.

20. To make the logo form out of particles, you need to play the layer backward. Select the Main Title Layer and go to Layer > Time > Time Reverse Layer.

**Finishing touches:** To finish the project, I applied the same Fractal Noise and Tritone effects and settings that I applied to the

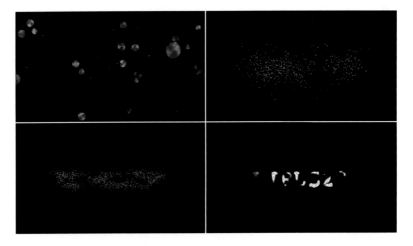

**Figure 6.61** Frames of the final simplified version. Footage: Michele Yamazaki. Design by Dru Nget.

Wondertouch particleIllusion AE by GenArts
vs. Trapcode Particular

| Features | Wondertouch particleIllusion AE by GenArts | Trapcode Particular |
|---|---|---|
| 2D/3D | particleIllusion AE is a 2D particle system. | Particular is a 3D particle system that is able to follow the camera and lights in After Effects. |
| Preview | Nice motion previews in the video window. There is a free particleView application if you want to see the particles before buying the plug-in. | No previews of presets or the effect, not even with Adobe Bridge. A ram preview or render is needed to see what's being created. |
| Presets & Emitters | Ships with thousands of emitters and more than can be downloaded for free or purchased. Presets can be searched by title but not by keyword with particleView. | Comes with around 40 SD and HD presets, but more can be purchased or found online. |
| Ease of Use | Very easy to use. | Physics and Aux Systems can be confusing at first but starting with a preset makes it fairly easy to jump right in. |
| Physics variations | About infinite. So many variables that can be adjusted but they are similar for each element of the emitter. | You will never run out of ways to vary Particular. |
| Price | $299 | $399 |

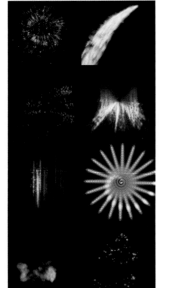

**Figure 6.62** particleIllusion emitters. Footage: Michele Yamazaki.

**Figure 6.63** Wondertouch particleIllusion for After Effects by GenArts vs. Trapcode Particular. Footage: Michele Yamazaki.

cell to the original text layer in the VIRUS23 Precomp Logo comp. This helped them to match.

## Wondertouch particleIllusion for After Effects by GenArts versus Trapcode Particular

Wondertouch particleIllusion for After Effects (pIAE) is another quality particle generator for After Effects. It is a 2D particle generator that comes chockfull of presets—over 3000 emitters, and every month users can download new packs of preset particles from wondertouch.com. particleView is a free application to view emitter libraries.

## Making a Title Animation with Noise Industries FxFactory Particle System

**FxFactory Particle System** includes just a few presets but with a nice variety to get the user started quickly. The downside of this plug-in is that only still frames can be used for particles, so no animated QuickTime movies or gif animations. You also can't randomly vary the angle or shape of the particle over time. But, if

**Figure 6.64** A lower third title animation using Noise Industries FxFactory Particle System for particles and a matte for the letters. Red Giant Magic Bullet Mojo was used as a final touch to colorize the scene. Man Footage: Crowd Control, clip#00074_001_24.mov. Background: Michele Yamazaki.

you're looking for something fast and simple that looks good, this is an excellent choice and it's part of a strong bundle.

For this title animation, we'll create a lower third title, as in the opening title sequence of a cop show. We'll take a preset and modify it, using it as a track matte for a title. Second, we'll duplicate the effect, modify it, colorize it over time to look like flashing lights on a police car, and place it behind the text. This effect is very versatile, with modification, and can be used for lower thirds or full-page titles. *This project is included on this book's DVD in the FxFactory Particles Title folder (Mac), and includes a still of the headshot, provided by Crowd Control.*

**Third-party plug-ins needed:**

- Noise Industries FxFactory Pro (Mac)

1. File > New > Composition with the HDTV 1080 29.97 preset, 4:00 in duration, with a black background color. Drag the image FxFactory Particle System headshot.tif and IMG_1128.JPG into the Timeline panel and arrange them so that the headshot is over the street scene. Scale the street scene as needed. Turn off the visibility of these layers for now so that you can have a clear look at the particles as you're working through the next few steps. (Figure 6.65.)

**Figure 6.65** The headshot of the actor over the background plate. Man Footage: Crowd Control, clip#00074_001_24.mov. Background: Michele Yamazaki.

2. Create a single line of text with the Type tool that says "Raul C. Peligroso" (or any other fictitious name) in 124pt. Arial in white with a 1px gray outline.

3. Create Layer > New > Solid titled "Particle Matte". Make the width 1920 px and the height 200 px. In the end this will be a bar of particles. Position this bar in the lower third of the Composition panel. Apply Noise Industries FxFactory Particle System (Effect > NI Generators > Particle System). Apply the preset Glowing Wire by selecting it in the Presets pulldown menu in the Effect Controls panel. (Figure 6.66.)

4. Make sure the Particle Matte is above the text layer. In the Modes area of the Timeline panel, set the TrkMt for the text layer to Luma Matte Particle Matte. The visibility of the Particle Matte layer should now be turned off. When you RAM Preview you should see your text showing through the matte. (Figure 6.67.)

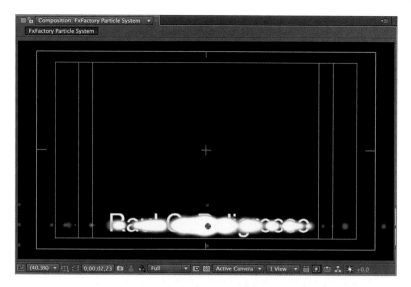

Figure 6.66 The Glowing Wire preset. Footage: Michele Yamazaki.

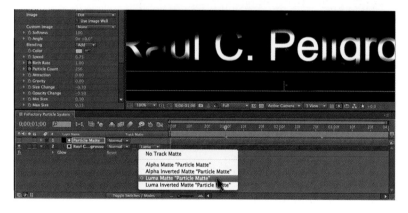

Figure 6.67 By setting TrkMt to Luma Matte for the text layer, you will be able to see the text come through the particles, giving it an ethereal look. The comp is zoomed to 100% so that you can see the detail. Footage: Michele Yamazaki.

5. Play the animation through a few times. You'll need to keyframe the Particle Count and the Birth Rate so that the particles come on strong and then fade.

6. At 1:00, set a keyframes for Birth Rate with a value of 1.00 and Particle Count, with a value of 256. At 2:10, set the value of Birth Rate to 0:00. This is where the particles will start to die out. Keep previewing and moving the keyframes around until the text is on screen long enough to be fully readable. Adjust the Speed, Size Change, and Opacity Change to give it a random and interesting effect.

7. Once you are satisfied, duplicate the Particle Matte layer. Rename it "Particle Large" and drag it below your text. Make sure it is visible by clicking the layer's eyeball in the timeline. Increase the Size Change parameter for the layer a bit.

8. We want to cycle the particle colors to make them look a bit like flashing police car lights. Set the Color

to red and add a keyframe for Color at the first frame. Jump to frame 16 and change Color to a bright blue. Select both keyframes and make them hold keyframes by going under Animation > Toggle Hold Keyframes. This will stop the red and blue from fading into each other and giving shades of purple. Copy and paste the Color keyframes through the end of the timeline. (Figure 6.68.)

**Figure 6.68** Color Hold keyframes. Footage: Michele Yamazaki.

9. Adjust the position of the keyframes for Particle Count and Birth Rate on the Particle Colors layer so that it differs slightly from the original matte layer. If the background and matte particles are the same, there won't be that offset that creates the depth and interest we're looking for. Adjust the Speed and Opacity to your liking.

10. Duplicate the Particles Large layer, renaming the layer Particles Medium. Slide the keyframes around so that the Speed, Opacity, and Color differ from Particles Large. Lower the value of Size Change so that you can see two very different sizes of particles stacked on each other. (Figure 6.70.)

11. Duplicate Particles Medium and name the new layer "Particles Small". Make sure it is above Particles Medium in the layer stack. Again, adjust Speed, Opacity, and Size Change, making the particles even smaller. You should now have a beautifully layered stack of particles behind your text.

12. Turn on the visibility of the headshot and street scene. Preview it a few times and make adjustments to the particles as you see fit. Try different Layer modes for the Particle layers so that they pop from the screen.

# Pro Tip

There is an easy Expression for looping keyframes. After you have the first two keyframes set, instead of cutting and pasting more keyframes through to the end, you can loop these two infinitely. Option + click Color, then type the following in the Expression area to loop the keyframes:

```
loopOut(type = "cycle")
```

**Figure 6.69** Loop cycle. Footage: Michele Yamazaki.

**Figure 6.70** The Particle layers and the effect settings. Footage: Michele Yamazaki.

If your particles and text aren't fading out as you want them to, keyframe the Opacity of the layers at the end of the timeline.

**Finishing touches**: If you need your text to pop a bit more, apply NI Glow to the text layer (Effects > NI Glow > Glow). I used a blue glow and made it soft and barely there, just to give it a bit more oomph.

I added **Red Giant Magic Bullet Mojo** on an Adjustment Layer over the top of all particle, image, and text layers to give it a gritty urban look. I then tweaked the colors of the particles.

**Figure 6.71** The FxFactory Particles particle system plug-in is used as a matte for text and layered in varied sizes underneath the text. Man Footage: Crowd Control, clip#00074_001_24.mov. Background: Michele Yamazaki.

## Willowglow: Sparkling Text Wipe-on with Digieffects Delirium Fairy Dust

Wiping on text with a sparkle is an effect seen in commercials, especially around the holidays. It goes together quickly with a bit of modification of a preset in Digieffects Delirium. The new version of Fairy Dust in Delirium v2 is remarkably faster and looks much better in HD.

**Figure 6.72** Digieffects Fairy Dust is an easy way to make a fancy sparkly wipe-on for text. Footage: Michele Yamazaki.

This project was inspired by my daughter's love of Disney's *Tinker Bell*, which is quite appropriate for a plug-in called Fairy Dust. Imagine that this is a new straight-to-DVD *Tinker Bell* title called *Willowglow* (these are extremely popular among elementary school aged girls). Colorful fairy dust will wipe on text and bounce all over the screen. *The project is included on this book's DVD in the Delirium – Fairydust folder.*

**Third-party plug-ins needed:**
- Digieffects Delirium V2
   1. Create a new Composition with the HDTV 1080 29.97, 6 seconds in duration, and name it Willowglow.
   2. Use the Type tool and type the word "Willowglow" on screen in a whimsical but easy-to-read font. I chose Charlemagne Std, 230 px in white, placed directly in the center of the screen. To stylize the text, apply all Layer Styles (Layer > Layer Styles > Show All). It is easier to add them all and then remove the styles that are not used instead of applying them one by one. I've added Drop Shadow, Inner Shadow, Outer Glow, Inner Glow, and Gradient Overlay. Adjust to taste. (Figure 6.73.)

**Figure 6.73** The Layer Styles applied to the text really give it some class. Footage: Michele Yamazaki.

3. Create a new solid, the same size as the composition, called Fairy Dust. Make sure that it is on top of the text layer. Apply DE Fairy Dust (Effects > Delirium > DE Fairy Dust). Change the Dust color to pink and increase the Dust Amount to 12.

4. At the first frame, drag the Dust Point so that it is off the left side of the screen, vertically centered. My point is –534, 544. Enable keyframing for Dust Point. Go to 1:00 and drag the Dust Point off the right side of the screen. My point is 2700.0, 544.0. The fairy dust will fly through the screen very quickly. If you'd like it slower, drag the second keyframe to a later point in the timeline. (Figure 6.74.)

5. Apply a Linear Wipe to the text layer (Effect > Transition > Linear Wipe). Set the Wipe Angle to 0x290.0°, then keyframe the Transition Completion to match with the moving particles. Feather as needed. (Figure 6.75.)

6. Play it through a few times and then modify the timing as needed.

Although it looks good, it needs more magic! The idea is that the fairy wiped on the text with magic, flies offscreen, and flies back onscreen behind the text. We'll use Motion Sketch on a null object and another instance of Fairy Dust to add a "Fairy" behind the text.

7. Although we didn't change many of the settings, duplicate the Fairy Dust layer and drag the duplicate below the text. Rename the layer "Fairy" by tapping the return key with the layer selected, then typing. Go to a point after the text is fully on screen, in my case this is about 1:03. Select the Fairy layer and then press the [ (left bracket) to move the layer's in-point to this point. Tap the U key to bring up the keyframes and delete them by clicking the stopwatch.

8. Go to the point in time where your Fairy layer begins. Add a Null Object to the timeline (Layer > New > Null Object).

**Figure 6.74** The DE Fairy Dust Dust Point. Footage: Michele Yamazaki.

**Figure 6.75** Feather the wipe so there are no hard edges along the text. Footage: Michele Yamazaki.

Make sure that it begins at the same point in the timeline as your Fairy layer. If it does not, press the [ (left bracket) again to slide the in-point to that point in time. Tap the letter B to set the beginning of the work area, so that Motion Sketch will only add keyframes to the work area. This is important because we don't want the Fairy to just pop onscreen but to come from offscreen, so it needs to start the capture at the appropriate time.

9. Open Motion Sketch (Window > Motion Sketch). Increase the value of smoothing to 10. This will create less keyframes in the timeline. If you'd like to see the background while you are capturing, click the Background checkbox in the Motion Sketch panel.

10. With the Null Object selected, press the Start Capture button in the Motion Sketch panel. The capture will begin as soon as you click in the Composition panel. Motion Sketch is capturing data to the Position parameter of the Null. Drag the cursor around in a looping manner and not too quickly.

11. If you are having a hard time because you're using a mouse, undo, then adjust the Capture Speed and try again. A lower value will capture more slowly and produce more keyframes; a higher value will capture less keyframes. (Figure 6.76.)

**Figure 6.76** Capturing position data with Motion Sketch onto a null object. Footage: Michele Yamazaki.

12. Select all of the Position keyframes on the Null Object layer and copy them to your clipboard. On the Fairy Layer, add a keyframe to Dust Point and tap the U key. This will bring up only keyframed parameters and is an easy way to isolate parameters. Paste the data from your clipboard. The Dust Point is compatible to Position so data can be copied between them. It's important that Dust Point is selected to target the point, otherwise, the data will be pasted to the Position of the layer instead of the Dust Point.

    The Fairy Dust needs a bit more excitement and style, and DE Glow is a great tool to give it that final touch. Not only will it add a bit of glow, but also will allow us to have multicolored sparkles, something that is not possible with the Fairy Dust plug-in alone. If you change the color of the dust particles, it will change all of the particles at once, not individual particles.

13. Select the Fairy Dust layer and move to a point in the timeline where you can see the sparkles, probably around 0:15. Apply DE Glow (Effects > Digieffects Delirium > DE Glow).

14. Under Glow Layer choose Use Channel Matte in the pulldown menu. This will allow multiple colors to show up.

15. Under Colorize, click the Enable checkbox, then choose Rainbow from the Color Presets.

# Pro Tip

It's a lot easier to create smooth Motion Sketch paths with a tablet. It can be done with a mouse, of course, but a tablet is a must-have item! It will make painting and rotoscoping that much easier too. (Figure 6.77.)

**Figure 6.77** The position keyframes captured with Motion Sketch onto a null object. Footage: Michele Yamazaki.

16. Under Size, set the value of Size to 40. (Figure 6.78.)
17. Select DE Glow in the Effect Controls panel or in the timeline. Copy it to your clipboard. Select the Fairy layer and paste. All settings should be copied so your colors will match.

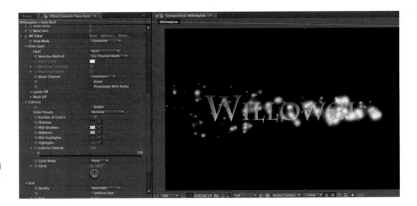

**Figure 6.78** DE Glow allows you to create multicolored sparkles. Footage: Michele Yamazaki.

18. To finish it up, add a new Solid named "Background" and place below the other layers. Apply DE GradientDesigner (Effects > Digieffects Delirium > DE GradientDesigner). Under Basic Shape, set Shape to Vertical. Under Color Presets, set it to Blue. Under the Gradient Interface, select the blue box on the right side. Using the sliders, make the blue less saturated.

19. To give it the cloudy appearance, Apply DE Fog Factory on the Background layer. Check Effect Only at the top. Set the following (Figure 6.79):
    - **Fog Wispiness:** 4
    - **Blend Top:** 15
    - **Blend Bottom:** 50
    - **Blend Original:** 90

**Figure 6.79** The background is created with DE Gradient Designer and DE Fog Factory. Footage: Michele Yamazaki.

## A Tornado with Cycore FX CC Particle World

Tornadoes are more difficult to create than you might think, but with **Cycore FX HD CC Particle World**, it goes together very easily.

Cycore FX ship with After Effects and have for many versions, but there is also a very popular HD version available. *The project on this book's DVD, which is in the CCParticleWorld – Tornado folder, uses the standard version of Cycore FX, which is included with After Effects.* If you have the HD version of Cycore FX, the project will automatically load in the HD version and render it with greater bit depth.

**Third-party plug-ins needed:**
- Cycore FX
  1. Make a new Composition called Tornado Comp, 2800 × 2000, 10 seconds long, with a white background, so that you can easily view the tornado. Yes, this is a vertical composition, wider than it is tall.

**Figure 6.80** A tornado is one of the infinite particle effects that can be created with Cycore FX CC Particle World. Footage: Michele Yamazaki.

2. Add a new layer, the same size as the composition, and call it tornado.

3. Apply CC Particle World to the tornado layer (Effect > Simulation > CC Particle World). Set the Birth Rate to 2.8 and the Longevity (sec) to 1.54.

4. To get the conical shape, twirl down Physics. Set Animation to Vortex in the pulldown menu.

5. Drag the Position crosshairs down or increase the value of Producer > Position Y until the tornado fills the composition.

6. Go to the first frame of the composition. Under Extras, set the distance to 4 and Rotation X to −4.0. Set a keyframe for Rotation Y, keeping the value at $0x$ +0.0°. Set FOV (Field of View) to 50.

7. Twirl down Floor and move the Floor Position so that the grid is at the base of the tornado.

8. Under Particle, set the Birth Color and Death Color to dark brown and black.

9. Scale the layer to 100.0, 200.0 to stretch the tornado and make it taller.

To create some debris at the bottom of the funnel and along the sides of the tornado, we'll apply CC Particle World to another layer with different settings.

10. Create a new solid the same size as the composition and name it Debris. Apply CC Particle World. Under Physics, set Velocity to 0.89, Gravity to 0.180, and Extra to 0.41. Set the Birth Color and Death Color to brown and black. Under Producer, set Position Y to 0.66 so that it lines up with the bottom of the tornado. Set the Render Animation to Reflected on Floor, Floor Action to Bounce, and increase Bounciness, Random Bounciness, and Bounce Spread to the highest values possible.

11. Duplicate the Debris layer and adjust the settings so that the Emitter is as tall as the tornado, shooting debris from the center, by adjusting the Producer settings.
12. To give the tornado some wriggly movement, apply Wave Warp (Effect > Distort > Wave Warp). Since we want the effect to be a huge wave and not zigzagged waves, change the following settings:
    – **Wave Height:** 107
    – **Wave Width:** 623
    – **Wave Speed:** 0.5
    – **Pinning:** Bottom Edge

Now that the tornado is created, it needs to be composited into the shot. The image of the field out of the airplane window is included in the project.

13. Make a new Composition called Final Tornado and use the HDTV 1080 29.97 preset, 6 seconds in duration.
14. Drag field.JPG into the comp and scale so it fills the comp.
15. Drag the Tornado Comp into the Final Tornado Comp.
16. Because CC Particle World starts from nothing, we'll need to apply Time Remap to reset the start time. Drag the Start Point of the layer to −2:00 so it has some preroll time.
17. Make the layer 3D by checking the Make 3D box, which will help you position in Z space. Use the Pan Behind tool to drag the Anchor Point to the bottom of the funnel. To give the tornado a bit of jump, press the letter A to bring up Anchor Point. Option + click the stopwatch to apply the expression: `wiggle(0.5,2)`. (Figure 6.81.)

**Figure 6.81** Wiggle. Footage: Michele Yamazaki.

18. Go to the first frame and position the tornado toward the left side of the frame. Set a keyframe. Go to the last frame and position the tornado toward the right side of the screen.
19. To darken the tornado, apply CC Toner (Effect > Color Correction > CC Toner). Set the Highlights, Midtones, and Shadows to shades of brown and black and adjust the Blend. Original to about 65.0%.
20. Apply Fast Blur to the tornado with a value of 40, but make it higher if you think it needs more blur. (Figure 6.82.)

**Finishing touches**: I've added some basic clouds, created with Fractal Noise, applying a feathered mask to the layer so that clouds fill only the sky.

To make everything blend and give the sky a bad-weather look, I added an Adjustment Layer with Curves. This scene

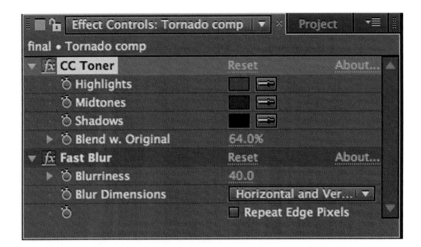

**Figure 6.82** CCToner and Fast Blur. Footage: Michele Yamazaki.

**Figure 6.83** Fractal Noise is applied to create dark clouds in the sky. Footage: Michele Yamazaki.

could be made even more realistic by adding rain, objects blowing by (cows, houses, wicked women on bicycles), and adding camera shake. This tutorial is just meant to get you started and spur some ideas.

## Backgrounds and Textures

Generating backgrounds is one of the most important functions of After Effects for those working in the realm of corporate video. At my first post-college job, I created a lot of text bullet builds over a gradient or simple texture background.

Textures are often needed for special effects and for use with 3D elements, text builds, sports graphics, news bumpers, and so on. Textures can be used in displacement maps or gradient wipes, and to fill text.

This section deals with plug-ins and methods of generating backgrounds and textures for multiple uses.

## Gradients and Ramps

Gradients are a simple way to class up a flat background or lower third. Every large bundle of plug-ins seems to have a ramp plug-in too, so there is no shortage of options.

One I particularly like is **Noise Industries FxFactory Banding-Free Gradient** because it includes some subtle noise to eliminate banding. The plug-in allows for two or three color linear gradients or a radial 2-color gradient.

There are gradient plug-ins that ship with After Effects. Good old **Ramp** has been around since early versions of After Effects. Under Generate, **4-Color Gradient** is not as well-known but a very useful plug-in.

**GenArts Sapphire** has a couple of nice gradient plug-ins. **Sapphire S_Gradient** is a 2-color ramp tool with a built-in Add Noise function, but just has a linear ramp option. Secondly, **Sapphire S_GradientRadial** is a robust 2-color radial ramp, which allows the user to click and drag on an oval for the inner and outer radius and position the ramp right in the Comp panel. **Sapphire S_GradientMulti** allows up to six colors in a gradient.

**Figure 6.84** Noise Industries Banding-Free Gradient. Footage: Michele Yamazaki.

# Pro Tip

Banding occurs in the colors in a gradient when there's only a small color-change over a large area. Sometimes adding effects, a lot of saturation, or contrast can make banding worse. There are a few things you can do to reduce problems with banding. The first is to add a little noise to break up the banding. Second, if you're working in 8-bit mode, set the project to 16-bit or higher. Most plug-ins now work in 16-bit so this shouldn't give you any problems. Lastly, modify the colors in the gradient so that there is a larger color change.

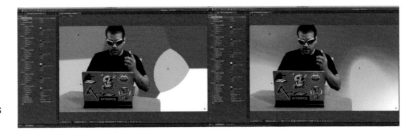

**Figure 6.85** GenArts Sapphire S_GradientMulti gradient. The image on the left has no blur while the image on the right has blur. Footage: Michigan Film Reel.

The plug-in allows for a lot of control, including softness between colors that can be animated.

**Luca Visual Effects Light Kit (FxFactory)** ($49) has an interesting gradient tool called Multicolor Gradient that uses multiple colors and custom shapes. The gradient can be animated in several ways. The downside of this one is that it is difficult to select specific colors and it needs to be applied to video or an image with multiple shades. It will not work on a solid color. These are not straight-up ramp generators, but instead give the background a bit of texture.

**Red Giant Image Lounge** ($299) and **Red Giant Key Correct** ($399) each contain a plug-in called **Alpha Ramp**, which allow you to directly affect the transparency of a layer. This gives the alpha channel a smooth radial black and white matte,which is great for vignettes and soft edges.

**Zaxwerks The Werks Vol. 1** ($199) also has a quality gradient tool in the package named GradientWerks, which has its own Gradient Editor GUI. It allows for multiple colors and styles of gradients. The user can set up the gradient to repeat and shift phases for complete control of the look of the gradient. The Werks Vol. 1 also contains Glintwerks and Easy Glow.

## Recipes for Ethereal Moving Backgrounds

There are so many plug-ins out there that will generate background textures. Noise plug-ins are a great place to start when used in combination with blurs and colorizers. Here are a few quick ways to make random ethereal backgrounds that are great for text builds and corporate video.

**After Effects Fractal Noise** and **Turbulent Noise** are both included with After Effects and are powerful ways to generate cloudy or noisy elements in the background. Others included with AE are **Cell Pattern** and **Brush Strokes**. These effects

# Pro Tip

Some of these effects can be render intensive so if you're making several title slides, prerender the background before applying the text.

coupled with Tritone or Tint can make some really interesting background elements.

**Noise Industries FxFactory Perlin Noise** background:

1. Apply Perlin Noise (Effect > FxFactory Pro Generators > Perlin Noise) to a solid and use the Waves preset. Adjust the Scale and Speed.
2. Apply the Tritone filter (Effect > Color Correction > Tritone) that ships with After Effects to add some color.
3. Make the layer 3D and apply a light. Adjust the position of the light to give interesting edge shadowing.

**Digieffects Delirium DE VanGoughist + DE Colorize:**

**Digieffects DE VanGoughist** gives the appearance of strokes using different patters such as dapples, swishes, water, mesh, swirls, cylinder, and more. It does need to be applied over something that is moving, so any sort of texture below it will work.

1. Apply Fractal Noise to a solid (Effect > Noise & Grain > Fractal Noise). Increase Contrast, turn down the complexity, and keyframe the Evolution.
2. Apply DE VanGoughist (Effect > Digieffects Delirium > DE VanGoughist) and select a Brush Type. The example uses Boxes. Increase the Horizontal and Vertical Size to taste.
3. Apply **Tritone** or **Digieffects DE Colorize** and set colors.
4. Again, to give it some depth, make the layer 3D and apply a light. Adjust the position of the light to give interesting edge shadowing.

**GenArts Sapphire S_TextureCells:**

1. Apply S_TextureCells to a solid (Effect > Sapphire Render > S_TextureCells). Scale up the cells by lowering the Frequency and slow down the movement by lowering the value of the Rotate Speed.
2. Give it a little blur with Sapphire S_BlurMotion (Effect > Sapphire Blur+Sharpen > S_BlurMotion). If you like, adjust and keyframe the values of several of the parameters to give a unique look.
3. To color the layer, try Sapphire DuoTone (Effect > Sapphire Adjust > S_DuoTone).
4. For added depth, make the layer 3D and apply a light. Adjust the position of the light for edge shadowing.

**Figure 6.86** FxFactory Perlin Noise
Footage: Michigan Film Reel.

**Figure 6.87** A background created with Digieffects DE VanGoughist.
Footage: Michele Yamazaki.

**Figure 6.88** A background created with Sapphire S_TextureCells.
Footage: Michele Yamazaki.

**Boris Continuum Complete BCC Noise Map:**

1. Apply BCC Noise Map to a layer (Effects > BCC Generators > BCC Noise Map). Slow down the Flow Speed and the Morph Rate and make other adjustments.

2. Apply BCC Colorize Glow (Effects > BCC Effects > BCC Colorize Glow). Try some gradient presets or make your own. Crank up the Blur Amount, Softness, and Intensity.

3. Apply Pyramid Blur (Effects > BCC Color Blurs > BCC Pyramid Blur). Use a fairly high value for Blur so that there is not a lot of detail and the text will pop.

4. Make the layer 3D and apply a light. Adjust the position of the light to give interesting edge shadowing.

**Figure 6.89** A background created with Boris Continuum Complete BCC Noise Map. Footage: Michele Yamazaki.

## Make a Planet with Boris Continuum Complete BCC Granite and BCC Sphere

I was watching *The Universe*, the series on The History Channel that explores all aspects of the cosmos, and noticing the gorgeous renderings of planets and stars. It's very fast and easy to create similar effects in After Effects with Boris Continuum Complete. First we'll create a planetary texture with BCC Granite, which is also part of the **Boris Continuum Materials Unit** ($199), and map the texture to a sphere with BCC Sphere. *The project file is in a folder named BCC Planet and is included on the DVD.*

**Third-party plug-ins needed:**

- Boris Continuum Complete
  1. Create a new comp that is 2000 × 1000, 10 seconds in duration. Name it Planet Texture. By making the comp a 2:1 aspect ratio, the texture will wrap properly when BCC Sphere is applied later in the tutorial.
  2. Layer > New > Solid. Name it "Texture". Make the layer 2000 × 1000.
  3. Apply BCC Granite (Effect > BCC Generators > BCC Granite) and select pittedTexture.bcp from the presets pulldown menu. Modify the colors for Color 1, Color 2, and Background Color to shades of brown. Adjust the Border Blend, Mutation, Cellularity, Coarseness, and Detail to taste.
  4. Twirl down 3D Bump Mapping and click the checkbox for Use Bump Map. Change the Light Type to Distant and adjust the Position and Intensity of the light until it looks like natural rock. (Figure 6.90.)
  5. In the Project panel, select the Planet Texture comp and drag it to the Make New Comp button at the bottom of the Project panel. A new comp will open the same size and duration

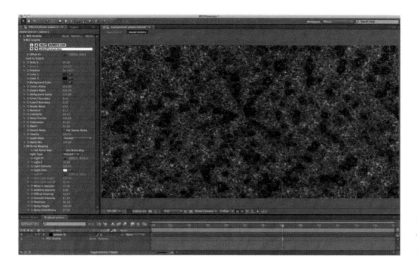

**Figure 6.90** BCC Granite, made to look like natural rock. Footage: Michele Yamazaki.

as the first comp with the Planet Comp nested. Name this new comp "Space Scene".

6. Apply **BCC Sphere** (Effect > BCC Distortion Perspective > BCC Sphere). Apply the preset named Orbit1.bap. Choose Stretch to Fit and First Frame so that the animation will last the entire duration of the comp and begin at the first frame.

7. Under Faces set the Source to 1. Planet Texture and the Wrap to Back & Forth Repeat. (Figure 6.91.)

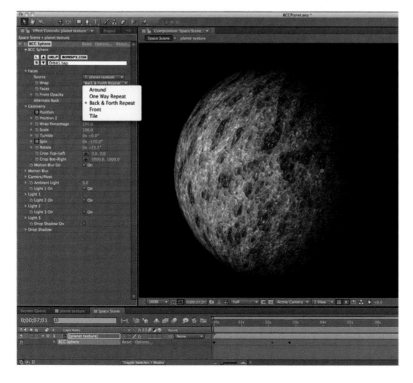

**Figure 6.91** BCC Sphere. Footage: Michele Yamazaki.

**Figure 6.92** BCC Stars. Footage:
Michele Yamazaki.

8. Add a new solid named Stars and make it the same size as the comp. Drag it below the planet layer. Apply BCC Stars and choose the preset shiningStarsCloseGalax.bcp. (Figure 6.92.)

# INVISIBLE AND NATURAL EFFECTS

Natural effects like rain, snow, fog, and so on, are also generators, and are needed for several reasons. Their use allows the filmmaker to choose the ideal filming location, and to stay warm and dry! With the magic of After Effects, you can realistically generate rain, and quickly change a scene from a sunny day, to a cold, dark, rainy day. You are in control: Should you want to increase the amount of rain coming down just a little, you can add those elements after the fact in postproduction with the use of generators.

Much of this chapter deals with adding movement to a still photo by adding natural effects. There are many reasons you may want to add movement to a still photo. Maybe you need a quick background of Bali for some greenscreen footage and you can't afford to take a trip to shoot there. Maybe you just love a certain photograph. The benefit of using a photo is that the resolution is often better than video.

Whatever the reason, it's easy to add some natural looking movement to a still image, especially nature photos with large skies or water. This chapter walks you through a few tricks to add some realistic movement to still images using a variety of third-party plug-ins. In many of the examples, I use the same photo of the harbor in Vancouver, British Columbia, bringing it to life in a couple of different ways. I use GenArts Monsters GT and Boris Continuum, and also give alternate options.

## Generating Water

Creating a flood or a tsunami on set can be very dangerous to your expensive cameras and electrical gear near. It is a lot more cost-effective to create this sort of cataclysm with visual effects. Water is a very commonly generated effect, but creating photo-realistic water in postproduction used to be a feat. A few well-known films that use water generated with visual effects are *2012*, *A Perfect Storm*, *Waterworld,* and *Titanic*. After Effects ships with **Wave World** and **Caustics**, both of which can be used to create some nice looking water. In keeping with this book's focus, we'll look at third-party plug-ins here. For more on Wave World and

Caustics, there are several great resources, including After Effects' help documents, Chris and Trish Meyers' books on After Effects, or just plain Google.

## Creating Photorealistic Water with Red Giant Psunami

**Figure 7.1** The SteamPig Experiment uses Red Giant Psunami beautifully. Image: Alicia VanHeulen, *http:// vimeo.com/14433603.*

A most realistic solution for generating truly realistic water and waves in After Effects is **Red Giant Psunami** ($199), an outstandingly powerful plug-in. It has been used in many films, including the Academy award-winning *The Aviator*. Psunami uses Arete Image Software's RenderWorld ray-tracing engine. With this plug-in, the user can generate ultra-realistic water, waves, and skies, with control over all aspects of the water including wind atmospheric effects such as haze, sun, and rainbows, air and ocean optics, swells, lights, reflection mapping, displacement mapping and swell controls. It comes with several presets such as Stormy Seas, Arctic Dunes, Moonlight, Polluted Lake, and Swimming

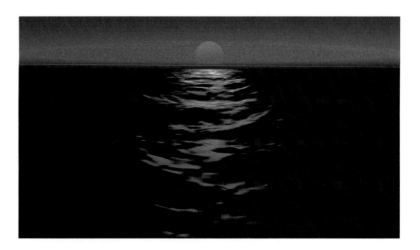

**Figure 7.2** Psunami. Footage: Michele Yamazaki.

Pool, which are very handy in getting started quickly. The built-in camera is fully animatable, allowing the camera to fly over, under, and through the surface of the water. One of the coolest features of the camera is the Bobbing Platform Size, which mimics the camera floating on the water and bobbing on the waves. A downside of Psunami is that it doesn't use the After Effects camera.

Psunami works in After Effects CS3 and higher, Apple Final Cut Pro, and Motion.

Psunami, originally developed by Digital Anarchy and acquired by Red Giant Software in 2008, first generates an accurate wireframe of the water surface, and renders realistic ray-traced water, complete with depth of field. Because it is render intensive, here are a couple of tips to speed up workflow, screen redraw, and rendering time.

- Work in the Grayscale or Texture (No Geometry) mode. The water won't be drawn as accurately and the waves look quite a bit different than Realistic mode, but it's a heck of a lot faster. Set the mode to Realistic or Too Realistic when you need to see a precise render.
- To work with and preview wave animations, use Wireframe mode, and again, use Realistic or Too Realistic when you need to see accuracy.
- Work at Half Resolution and only set it to Full Resolution when you need to see the scene accurately.
- Create seamless loops of water, which will save a lot of time if you need to show a calm lake or rolling waves for an extended period of time. Psunami will automatically loop the water. Under Render Options for Psunami, set the Loop Time (S), which is set in seconds.

**Figure 7.3** The Psunami interface. Screenshot: Michele Yamazaki.

## Simulating Water Movement with Boris Continuum Caustics and Fractal Noise

Caustics allows you to generate water movement. There is a built-in Caustics plug-in in After Effects, but **Boris Continuum ($999) BCC Caustics** is more robust and has a lot more options. It can create fractals of water movement that are very realistic when composited properly. When creating naturalistic realism, remember that subtlety is key.

We want to match the angle of the plane of water, as well as texture and movement of the existing water in the image. There are several noise generators available, but here we will use the Fractal Noise filter that ships with After Effects. This will be pre-composed and used as a Luma Matte. *This project is on this book's DVD in the BCC Caustics folder.*

**Figure 7.4** Plug-in–generated weather. Footage: Michele Yamazaki.

**Third-party plug-ins needed:**
- Boris Continuum Complete
    1. Create a new Comp in After Effects with the HDTV 1080 29.97 preset (1920 × 1080), 5:00 in duration. Name it Vancouver, BC.
    2. Bring the Vancouver.tif photo into the comp. Scale the photo to 50%.
    3. Layer > New Comp (Make Comp Size). Name it Fractal Noise.
    4. Apply **Fractal Noise** (Effect > Noise & Grain > Fractal Noise). Crank up the Contrast. Under Transform, uncheck the Uniform scaling box and scale the Height down to about 30. Keyframe the Evolution so that when you preview it is not moving too quickly. Leave all of the other settings for Fractal Noise at their defaults.
    5. Make the Fractal Noise layer a 3D layer by clicking the Make Layer 3D box under Switches. Adjust the X Rotation so that the plane of the water and the plane of the solid match. You may need to make the width of the solid layer larger to span the width of the comp. (Figure 7.5.)
    6. We'll be adding a Ramp effect so that the Fractal Noise filter fades as it moves further toward the horizon. Duplicate the Fractal Noise Layer and rename this layer Ramp. Delete the Fractal Noise effect from the Ramp layer, which should be above the Fractal Noise layer. Apply a Ramp (Effect > Generate > Ramp). The default settings should be fine. Set the mode of the Ramp layer to Multiply in your timeline.
    7. Select the Fractal Noise Layer and Ramp Layer together by shift + clicking them in the timeline, then go to Layer > Pre-Compose. In the popup window, name your precomp "Water", check the Move All Attributes radio button, and uncheck Open New Composition. (Figure 7.6.)

**Figure 7.5** Fractal Noise and Caustics. Footage: Michele Yamazaki.

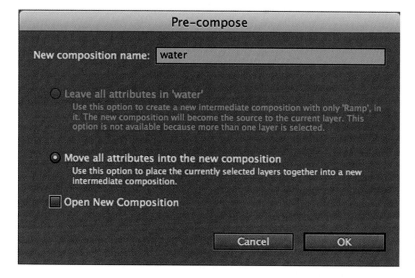

**Figure 7.6** Pre-compose dialog box. Screenshot: Michele Yamazaki.

8. Turn off the visibility of the Water precomp in your main Composition. (Figure 7.7.)

9. Add an Adjustment Layer named "Ripples" (Layer > New > Adjustment Layer). Use the Pen tool to draw a mask on the Ripples layer to isolate the water in the Vancouver.tif layer. Feather the mask by tapping the F key to bring up Mask Feather in the timeline. Set it to 23.

10. Apply **BCC Caustics** to the layer. Select the AltDefault.bcp preset. Set the Wave Source to Aux Layer, the Color Source to Filtered Image, and the Aux Layer to the Water layer. Set the Wave Height to 1.00 so that there is subtle movement. Preview and make adjustments as needed. (Figure 7.8.)

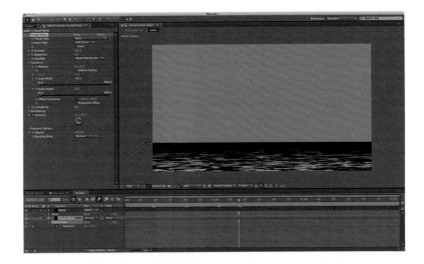

**Figure 7.7** Fractal Noise and a simple ramp create the map for the water movement. Screenshot: Michele Yamazaki.

**Figure 7.8** BCC Caustics links to the Water map to add natural looking water movement to the still image. Footage: Michele Yamazaki.

**Finishing touches**: Add rain, lightning, and clouds with BCC Rain, BCC Lightning, and BCC Clouds.

## Generating Moving Water with GenArts Monsters Pool3D

Another filter that can make nice Caustic-style effects is the **GenArts Monsters ($999 node-locked or floating) M_Pool3D** plug-in. Follow the instructions for **Boris Continuum BCC Caustics** up to Step 6. Instead of applying **BCC Caustics**, apply **GenArts Monsters M_Pool3D** filter. Use the following settings to get a similar effect as the one we created with BCC Caustics. *Project files are in the DVD in the back of this book in a folder named Monsters Pool_3D.*

**Third-party plug-ins needed:**
- GenArts Monsters
  1. Set the Region Map to the Water layer.
  2. Under Pool3D, adjust the center to the bottom left of the screen. Set the following:
     – **Radius:** 1.17
     – **Frequency:** 12.1
     – **Speed:** 0.12
     – **Mix with Source:** 44
     – **Use Matte:** On.
  3. Under Lighting:
     – **Lighting:** On
     – **Light Bright:** 13.0
  4. Under Perspective: Check Use Perspective and set the corner points to match the horizon of the water and bottom of the screen.
  5. Tweak the settings as needed but remember that the effect is supposed to be subtle.

**Finishing touches**: Add clouds with GenArts Monsters M_Cumulo.

**Figure 7.9** GenArts Monsters M_Pool3D uses to the Water map as a reference to create moving water in the still image. Footage: Michele Yamazaki.

# Generating Rain

There are a multitude of rain plug-ins and particle generators that can create rain, and some look more realistic than others. I'll talk a bit about five of them: **GenArts Monsters GT M_Rain**, **Boris Continuum BCC Rain**, **Cycore CC Rain**, **Digieffects Delirium Rainfall ($49 à la carte or included in Delirium)**, and **Trapcode Particular ($399)**.

With any of the rain effects, I find it most natural to add rain generators to two or three layers and scale the size of the drops so it looks like there are bigger drops closer and smaller drops in the distance. Also, most rain looks computer-generated so adding a bit of motion blur makes a lot of difference. *Note*: The samples in this section have the rain effects turned up so that they will be visible in print.

The most robust plug-in specifically for rain, **GenArts Monsters GT M_Rain** allows you to place the directional source where you want by placing crosshairs for the left and right sides of the plane. There are presets for Rain type, including Squall, Light, Drizzle, Sheet, and Bouncing Rain. You can adjust the Gravity and Friction, Light and Color of the rain as well. As with the others, **Monsters M_Rain** looks best when carefully composited into the video. Turn down the opacity and blend it with the original to make it look believable and not too obvious.

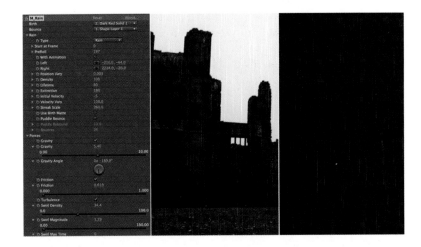

**Figure 7.10** GenArts Monster GT M_Rain. Footage: Michele Yamazaki.

**Cycore CC Rain** ships with After Effects and there is also an HD version of the plug-in. CC Rain is very easy to use and fast,

**Figure 7.11** CycoreFX CC Rain. Footage: Michele Yamazaki.

but the parameters are much more limited than with **Boris Continuum BCC Rain** or **GenArts Monsters GT M_Rain**. Adjust the speed and amount as necessary to give a realistic rain, and, of course, turn down the Rain Opacity to make it believable.

**Boris Continuum BCC Rain** comes with several rain presets and rain's lifespan is adjustable as with **GenArts Monsters GT M_Rain**. There's a feature to add a Splash Layer or to Splash on Ground. BCC Rain also includes the Pixel Chooser, which is included in most of the BCC plug-ins; it allows for more control in selecting and masking exactly where you want an effect to appear.

**Figure 7.12** Boris Continuum Complete BCC Rain. Footage: Michele Yamazaki.

**Digieffects Delirium Rainfall** is a robust plug-in with a splash mode, so that rain can bounce off of a surface (via another layer). Gravity, Wind, and Gusts are also options. There are several presets that come with Delirium, including Anime Rain, Light Rain, Waterfall, Hard Rain, and Splashing Rain.

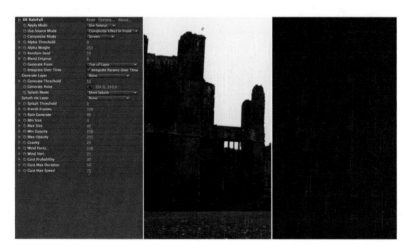

**Figure 7.13** Digieffects Delirium DE Rainfall. Footage: Michele Yamazaki.

Lastly, **Trapcode Particular**, while not a plug-in specifically for rain, makes some darn nice rain. Again, turning down the opacity and layering the rain will enhance the effect.

**Figure 7.14** Rain created with Trapcode Particular. Footage: Michele Yamazaki.

## Replacing Skies and Cosmos

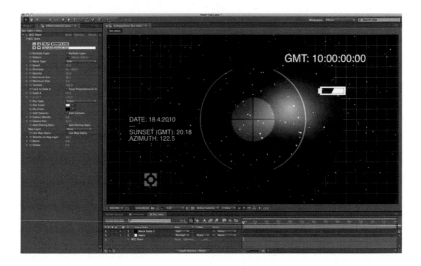

**Figure 7.15** Boris Continuum Complete BCC Stars with a galaxy and SUGARfx HUD OSD (On Screen Display) to give the look of a digital telescope. Screenshot: Michele Yamazaki.

Sky replacement is a very common task in visual effects for many reasons. Shooting on a bright, sunny day gives harsh shadows, so shooting on an overcast day will offer much more diffuse light on your actors. That bland overcast sky can be replaced with gorgeous blue skies with white fluffy clouds, or storm clouds, if the scene requires it. Also, night skies are very difficult to shoot. Those tiny stars just don't put out enough light to be captured on video. It's also simple to create a larger, more dramatic moon in post.

There are a few plug-ins to generate star fields. **Boris Continuum Complete BCC Stars** has some presets and basic stars. There are settings for the Movement Type, Speed, Direction, Density, Size, and Twinkle, as well as color settings and Galaxy settings. This plug-in is great for night sky replacement or stars moving by the spaceship window.

If you are looking for something more robust, **GenArts Monsters M_NightSky** makes beautiful stars and has some really interesting features, such as the ability to set the city and date so that you can match the actual sky from a certain date, time, and place. This allows you to animate timelapse nightscapes

**Figure 7.16** GenArts Monsters M_NightSky with the New York Location selected on August 1, 2020 at 3:12 am (during a blackout, obviously!). The oversized moon was created with GenArts Monsters M_Luna. Footage: Michele Yamazaki.

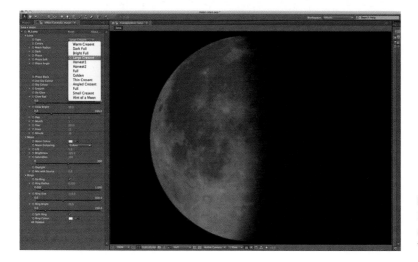

**Figure 7.17** GenArts Monsters M_Luna with the preset menu open. Screenshot: Michele Yamazaki.

accurately. There are even Longitude and Latitude settings if your city is not in the list.

**GenArts Monsters M_Luna** renders a photo-accurate moon, with several presets for full moons, harvest moons, and crescents. The Moon and Sky Colour, Glow, and Rings are keyframable, but the coolest feature is the phases that can be animated, and like the **M_NightSky** plug-in, the date can be programmed in for accurate historical moon phase. If you need to match the moon phase the night that Paul Revere made his historic ride, you do not need to consult an almanac, just type in the date.

## Recreating Long Exposure Star Trails

**Figure 7.18** Fake long exposure nighttime photography with GenArts Monsters. Footage: Michele Yamazaki.

It's fast and simple to fake a long exposure style photo in After Effects with a few plug-ins. This type of effect is often seen in on reality shows to represent a passage of time overnight. **GenArts Monsters GT M_NightSky** creates beautiful skies, with plenty of options for customization. *The project files are included on the DVD in the back of this book in the Monsters StarsTimelapse folder.*

**Third-party plug-ins needed:**
- GenArts Monsters GT
- GenArts Sapphire (for finishing touches only)
    1. Create a new comp called Stars, 10 seconds in duration and use the HDTV 1080 29.97 preset. Create a black solid the same size as your comp. Apply GenArts Monsters M_Night-Sky (Effects > Monsters Render > M_NightSky).
    2. Set the Type to Plough Bold and zero out the values of Longitude D, Longitude M, Latitude D, and Latitude M. This will place the center of star movement in the center of the screen, so think of it as the camera pointing directly at the North Star.

3. Go to 0:11 and set a keyframe for Move Over Time with a value of 0. Go to the last frame and set Move Over Time to 50. Select the first keyframe at 0:11 and apply Easy Ease Out (Animation > Keyframe Assistant > Easy Ease Out).
4. Under Style, set DrawStyle to Bright Point. Set Add Twinkle to On, On Black to Off, and All Opaque to On. (Figure 7.19.)

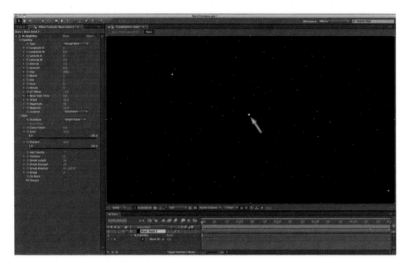

**Figure 7.19** M_NightSky applied to a solid with the Longitude and Latitude set to 0, spinning around Polaris, the North Star, which the arrow points out. Screenshot: Michele Yamazaki.

5. In the Project panel, drag Stars to the Make New Comp button at the bottom of the window. Go to Composition Settings and name this new comp "Stars Timelapse Final".
6. Apply M_SpinBlur (Effect > Monsters Blur + Sharpen > M_SpinBlur). Place the center point on a star at the middle.
7. Go to 0:11 and set a keyframe for Speed with a value of $0x$ 90.0°. Go to the last frame and set a keyframe with a value of $0x$ –90.0°. Select the first keyframe at 0:11 and apply Easy Ease Out.
8. Set Mix with source to 1.0 to show a bit of unblurred star.
9. Apply M_Lighten to boost the brightness of the stars (Effect > Monsters Adjust > M_Lighten). Set Size to 2 and Boost Highlights to 2.00. (Figure 7.20.)

**Finishing touches**: To add some nice sky color, apply a gradient that allows for multiple colors. Create a new solid that's the same size as the comp and drag it below the stars. I used **GenArts Sapphire ($1699 node-locked, $2499 floating) S_GradientMulti** with blacks, browns, and oranges placed around the Solid.

If you have a tree silhouette photo, set the mode to Multiply and place it over the top of your layer. The image I chose works well because the sky is light and the trees are dark. By using multiply, it ignores the lighter areas and compounds the darker areas, giving the appearance of a silhouette.

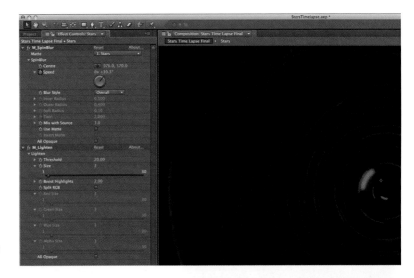

**Figure 7.20** GenArts Monsters M_SpinBlur. Screenshot: Michele Yamazaki.

**Figure 7.21** The original photo, on the left, has Levels applied to create more contrast between the sky and trees. On the right, the tree image is set to Multiply mode, so that the sky is removed. Footage: Michele Yamazaki.

**Figure 7.22** The final project with Sapphire S_GradientMulti applied to a solid and a silhouette of trees. Footage: Michele Yamazaki.

## Replacing a Sky with CoreMelt Pigment Sky Replace

**Figure 7.23** The original sky is on the left, and the new sky, on the right, was replaced with CoreMelt Pigment Sky Replace. Footage: Michele Yamazaki.

Replacing overcast sky is extremely fast and easy with **CoreMelt Pigment Sky Replace**.

    **Third-party plug-ins needed:**
- CoreMelt Pigment
    1. Apply CoreMelt Pigment Sky Replace to footage. The effect will immediately replace your sky if it's close to the Old Color. If it's not, turn off the effect by clicking the FX box for the layer, and choose the Old Color with the eyedropper.
    2. If the shot has similar colors as the sky in other areas of the shot (like the building reflecting the sky in the example), use the Key to refine the selection. Under Key, check Show Key to view the black and white matte. Adjust the

**Figure 7.24** The Key for Sky Replace. Footage: Michele Yamazaki.

Tolerance, Softness, and Blur Key. It is not necessary to have a completely black and white matte as you would when you're keying greenscreen footage, you'll just want to make sure that areas that should not be part of the sky are black. (Figure 7.24.)

3. Adjust the New Color, New Color Alpha, Amount of color, Diffuse Gradient, and the position of the Sky Top and Sky Bottom.

## Clouds Generators

There are many ways to generate clouds in After Effects with **Fractal Noise** and **Turbulent Noise**, but if you want something specifically made to make clouds with more options than the freebies, there are a few third-party options available.

**Figure 7.25** GenArts Sapphire S_Clouds. Footage: Michele Yamazaki.

**Figure 7.26** Monsters GT Clouds. Footage: Michele Yamazaki.

**Boris Continuum Complete BCC Clouds**, **GenArts Sapphire S_Clouds**, and **GenArts Monsters GT M_Cumulo** are all useful cloud generators with different looks. Just like rain, the trick to faking movement in a scene that already has clouds is to make the movement and opacity barely noticeable: just a layer of wispy stratus clouds in the foreground.

These tools are cloud generators, not sky replacement tools, so you will need to rotoscope or key the sky, feather the matte, and place the sky behind. Color correct to match the foreground and sky.

**Figure 7.27**  BCC Clouds. Footage: Michele Yamazaki.

# Need to remove a sky?

Many plug-ins do not include automatic compositing tools to remove or isolate the sky. The Rotobrush, a mask, or a luma key must be used to isolate the bland sky so that a new sky can show through.

## Sun

Just because you live in the dreary dark north doesn't mean you can't add some sun to your video projects!

**Noise Industries FxFactory Sun**, a plug-in included with the full bundle of **FxFactory** ($399), is a simple and fast plug-in to add a sun to footage. Track the center point to a moving shot. For other methods of creating the sun, check out the Lens Flares section of this book, beginning on page 163.

**Figure 7.28** A sun created with Noise Industries FxFactory Sun plug-in with the Hottest Day preset. The sky was first replaced with CoreMelt Sky Replace. Red Giant Magic Bullet Mojo gives it a dramatic color effect. Footage: Michele Yamazaki.

# Other Atmospheric Effects

You can't have *The Wizard of Oz* without a rainbow, and the chances of Mother Nature creating one on cue are slim to none. What if you decide you need fog in postproduction? Reshoot with a fog machine? No way! There is a multitude of plug-ins to add natural atmosphere footage and we'll explore them in this section.

## Spooky Title Animation with Digieffects Delirium Fog Factory and Trapcode Shine

This title animation mimics the look of a generic horror film title, with lights coming through thick fog and the title panning. **Digieffects Delirium ($299) Fog Factory** is perfect for creating this type of effect with multilayered fog. *Project files are on this book's DVD in the Deathfog folder.*

**Third-party plug-ins needed:**
- Digieffects DE Fog Factory
- Trapcode Shine
    1. Create a new composition with the HDTV 1080 29.97 preset, 5 seconds in duration with a black background. Name it "Death Fog".
    2. Use the Text tool and type the words DEATH FOG in all caps in a large white font, and positioned in the center of the Composition panel. The text will be filled with black with a

**Figure 7.29** A generic horror film title animation made with Digieffects DE Fog Factory and Trapcode Shine. Footage: Michele Yamazaki.

layer style, but making it white will make it easy to see while positioning and animating the camera.

3. Click the Enable the 3D Layer switch and then keyframe the Y Rotation so that the text rotates slowly for the duration of the composition.

4. Add a new camera to the composition. Keyframe the Z Position so that there's a slight push in with the camera.

5. Create a new black solid, the same size as your composition. Name the solid Fog and drag it to the bottom of the stack.

6. Apply DE Fog Factory (Effects > Digieffects Delirium > DE Fog Factory). Change the following settings (Figure 7.30):
   - **Speed Close:** 20 (adjusts the speed of the fog layer in front)
   - **Wispy Strength:** 0.3 (controls the wispiness; a lower value has less detail)
   - **Blend Top:** 0 (set to 0 to make the top of the screen fogless)
   - **Blend Bottom:** 61 (lowering the value gives less dense fog near the bottom)
   - **Blend Bias:** 15 (adjusts where the blend happens)
   - **Detail Close:** 34 (a lower number gives less detail to fog in the foreground)
   - **Random Seed:** Set it to anything you like

7. Duplicate the Fog layer and drag the copy above the text. Check the Adjustment Layer switch in the Timeline panel. It looks like a circle that is half black and half white. You should now be able to see the text behind the Fog layer. Press UU to bring up the values that have been changed from default. Change the following values:
   - **Speed Close:** 6
   - **Blend Bottom:** 25
   - **Blend Bias:** 47
   - **Detail Close:** 47
   - **Random Seed:** Change the value to whatever you like.

# Turning an Adjustment Layer into a Solid Layer

So what happened in step 7 after the Adjustment Layer switch was clicked? It turned the Solid into an Adjustment Layer. Now DE Fog Factory is being applied to a composite of all layers below it, but only where the fog is not transparent.

**Figure 7.30** Fog Factory gives multiple layers of depth of fog. Footage: Michele Yamazaki.

1. The front layer of fog isn't visible over the white text, so we'll apply Layer Styles. Select the DEATH FOG text layer, then go to Layer > Layer Styles and add Bevel and Emboss and Color Overlay. Set the Color Overlay color to black. Adjust the Bevel and Emboss settings until you find something you like.

2. Add an Adjustment Layer (Layer > New > Adjustment Layer). Place it on top of the other layers and Apply Trapcode Shine (Effects > Trapcode > Shine). At the bottom of the Effect

**Figure 7.31** Trapcode Shine is added to send light rays through the fog from behind the text. Footage: Michele Yamazaki.

Controls panel, set Transfer Mode to Add. At the top of the panel, set Ray Length to 11.8. Under Colorize, set the Colorize to the Chemistry preset to give it a green shade. Under Shimmer, keyframe the values for Amount and Phase. Set Boost Light to 7.5. Preview and adjust settings as you see fit. (Figure 7.31.)

## Lightning and Electrical Arcs

**Figure 7.32** After Effects Advanced Lightning. Footage: Michele Yamazaki.

If you have played with **Advanced Lightning** in After Effects, you'll have noticed that the defaults can be a little cheesy. Realistic lightning is actually quite difficult to recreate. I recommend going out and shooting the real thing or finding some footage of lightning and analyzing it. Notice where the lightning starts and ends, how long the flicker lasts, how it lights up the surrounding area, how it branches, the color of the lightning, the size of the lightning, the position of the lightning in the sky, and so on. Then copy that look and feel.

No matter which plug-in you use, apply the lightning filter to a black solid layer and use a layer mode set to Add or Screen.

**Boris Continuum BCC Lightning** is OpenGL accelerated and has a ton of options and a lot of presets. The easiest way to get started is to find a preset that is close to what you are looking for, then position it, adjust the wiggliness, forks, and glow. Trim the duration of your Adjustment Layer to control the duration of the lightning. You will not want it on screen more than a second or two. BCC Lightning has an Obstacle Control filter that will allow you to have lightning attracted around an object like text.

Chris Meyer, technical editor of this book, made a comment to me about BCC Lightning versus After Effects' built-in lightning, to the effect that BCC Lightning doesn't look as good as AE's

Advanced Lightning because the branching isn't right. After doing a few tests and trying to match the look of photos of lightning from Google, I have to agree with that assessment. The branching often looks strange when BCC Lightning's direction is moved.

**Figure 7.33** Boris Continuum BCC Lightning. Footage: Michele Yamazaki.

## Pro Tip

### Chris Meyer's Technique for Creating Realistic Looking Lightning

Lightning comes from within a cloud and usually strikes something, like the ground or (less often) another cloud. A feathered mask overlapping the origin point can help give that emerging-from-within feeling.

*Dueling Magicians with BCC Lightning, CC Particle World, and CC Vector Blur*

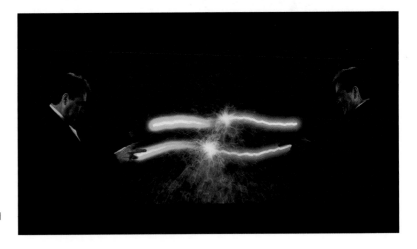

**Figure 7.34** A recreation of the type of lightning effect in the duel between Harry Potter and Voldemort in *Harry Potter and the Goblet of Fire*. Footage: Crowd Control, clip # 00206_002_227.

In *Harry Potter and the Goblet of Fire*, the very dark wizard duel scene where Harry Potter and Voldemort are zapping each other with magic is pretty intense. They are at a standoff and sparks are flying. This tutorial recreates that effect with dueling evil twin magicians. *The project file is included on this book's DVD in the Magician Duel folder*, but uses a still frame of the Crowd Control clip # 00206_002_227, with one magician flipped and the frames offset. To do this project with moving footage you will need to track the position of the magician's hands. This tutorial focuses on creating the lightning effect, but check out Chapter 13, "Tracking, Matchmoving, Motion Stabilization, and Rotoscoping" for more information on how to track the footage.

**Third-party plug-ins needed:**

- Boris Continuum Complete
- Cycore FX CC Particle World (included with After Effects)

1. Import the magician footage, 00206_002_227.tif.
2. Create a new composition using the HDTV 1080 29.97, 10 seconds in duration. Name it "Magicians" and drag the magician footage into the comp.
3. First we'll set up the magician on the left. Create a new solid the same size as the comp and make it black, named "Lightning". Drag this layer below the magician layer. Apply BCC Lightning (Effects > BCC OpenGL > BCC Lightning). Pin the Source point at the magician's front hand by clicking crosshairs and placing it on his hand. Set the Dest (Destination) point midway between the magicians. Change the following settings for BCC Lightning. There is no need to keyframe anything (Figure 7.35).
   - **Seed:** 150.00
   - **Core Wiggly Amount:** 15.00

**Figure 7.35** BCC Lightning settings. Footage: Crowd Control, clip # 00206_002_227.

- **Taper Amount:** 0
- **Under Fork Control:**
  **Max Level:** 1
  **Max Length:** 35.00
  **Max Width:** 5.00
  **Max Angle:** 8.00
  **Wiggliness:** 4.80
- **Glow Control** > **Outer Color:** Set it to bright blue
- **Obstacle Control** > **Obstacle Type:** Alpha
- **Apply** > **Apply Mode:** Lighter

4. Rename the layer "blue back" in the timeline. Duplicate the layer and rename it "blue front" and drag the copy above the magician. Reset the Source Point and Dest point. Adjust the value of the Seed to vary the movement.

5. Select both blue back and blue front by option + clicking them. Duplicate both layers and rename them "purple front" and "purple back". Adjust the Source point points accordingly but leave the Dest points where they are. They will perfectly line up with the blue lightning. Change Glow Control > Outer Color to a bright purple and, again, change the value of Seed. (Figure 7.36.)

6. Create a new solid, the same size as the comp. Name it "Sparks" and make sure it's above the lightning bolts in the timeline. Apply CC Particle World (Effect > Simulation > BCC Particle World). Nothing will need to be keyframed, so just change the following settings:
   - **Birth Rate:** 1.5
   - **Longevity (sec):** 0.52

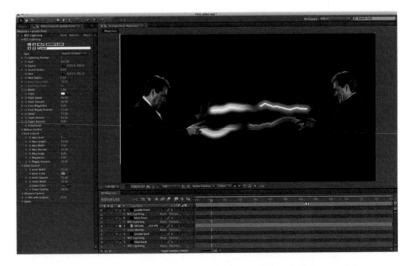

**Figure 7.36** Four layers of BCC Lightning, one for each hand of the magicians. Footage: Crowd Control, clip # 00206_002_227.

- **Under Producer:**
  **Position X and Position Y:** Position so that the sparks are produced where the front lightning bolts meet.
  **Radius X, Radius Y,** and **Radius Z:** 0.000
- Under Physics:
  **Animation:** Viscous
  **Velocity:** 1.32
  **Inherit Velocity** %: 37.0
  **Gravity:** 0.280
  **Resistance:** 1.7
- Under Particle:
  **Birth Color:** White
  **Death Color:** Bright blue
- **Extras** > **Depth Cue** > **Type:** Fog

7. The spark effect where the lightning bolts meet is supposed to have a lava type flow. Apply CC Vector Blur to the Sparks layer (Effects > Blur & Sharpen > CC Vector Blur). Set the Amount to 23.0.

8. Apply Glow (Effect > Stylize > Glow) and leave it at the defaults.

9. Duplicate the Sparks layer. Under CC Particle World, move Position X and Position Y under Producer point so that it lines up with the back hands. Change Physics settings values just slightly to vary them from the front sparks.

10. Under CC Vector Blur adjust the Amount slightly. Change the Angle Offset, Ridge Smoothness, and Map Softness to vary the effect.

This duel takes place in a cave, so the next step is to create a rock texture for the background. I'm creating the texture in a new comp so that the **Red Giant Key Correct ($399) Color Matcher** will bring the colors of one layer to the colors of another layer. If it's applied to a solid in the same comp, it will match to the color of the solid, not the colors in the rock texture. If you don't want to use the Color Matcher plug-in to match colors, you can manually color-correct using the plug-ins of your choice.

11. Create a new composition named "Cave". Use the HDTV 1080 29.97 preset and make it 10:00 in duration.

12. Create a new solid, the same size as the composition and name it "Rock".

13. Apply BCC Granite (Effects > BCC Generate > BCC Granite). Choose the paintedRock.bcp preset. Change the scale to 69.00. Change Color 1, Color 2, and Background Colors to shades of dark gray and black. Under 3D Bump Mapping, turn Use Bump Map to On. Set the Light Intensity to 167.00. (Figure 7.37.)

14. To finish the look of the composition, go back to the Magician comp. Nest the Cave comp into the Magician comp and drag the layer to the bottom of the stack.

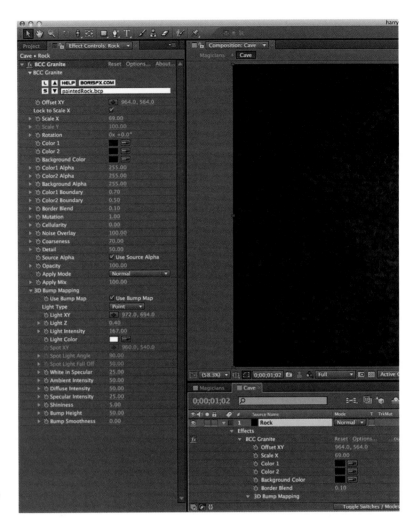

**Figure 7.37** BCC Granite is used to make the cavern background. Screenshot: Michele Yamazaki.

**Finishing touches**: Apply Red Giant Key Correct Color Matcher to the magician footage. If you don't have this plug-in, darken the footage so it looks more natural in a dark cave.

Additionally, I added an Adjustment Layer and placed it on top of the stack and applied **Red Giant Magic Bullet Looks'** **($399)** Blockbuster preset. If you don't have Looks, color correct using your own method.

Lastly, I added a letterbox effect by creating a new black solid, the size of the comp and dragging it to the top of the stack. Use the Rectangle tool to draw a Rectangular Mask Shape through the middle of the screen to make a reverse letterbox. Then tap the M key to bring up the Mask settings for the layer. Set the Mask Path Mode to Subtract or use the Invert switch to make the letterbox correct.

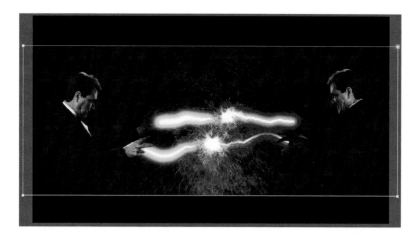

**Figure 7.38** Color correct the scene and add a letterbox to finish the look of the scene. Footage: Crowd Control, clip # 00206_002_227.

## Rainbows

**Figure 7.39** The rainbow is created with Monsters GT M_Rainbow. Footage: Michele Yamazaki.

Animate an overlaying rainbow with **Monsters GT M_Rainbow** filter. Add fog, a flock of birds, or even a boat floating by. When you're adding these elements, keep the final color correction in mind. A nice "cheat" is to add an Adjustment Layer over the top and apply **Magic Bullet Looks** or **Quick Looks ($99)** to bring all of the colors into the same realm and give it all a "mood."

**Tiffen Dfx Digital Filter Suite Rainbow** is another filter that can generate very natural looking rainbows. It has settings for adjusting all aspects of the rainbow's thickness, softness, radius, and position, as well as crop settings to adjust the bottom of the rainbow … you know, where the pot of gold is waiting.

**Figure 7.40** A double rainbow created with Tiffen Dfx Digital Filter Suite Rainbow plug-in. (*Note*: In the real world, in a double rainbow effect the colors would be reversed in the outer rainbow, see *http://en.wikipedia.org/wiki/Rainbow* for details. The filter does not have the option to reverse the colors.) Footage: Michele Yamazaki.

## Aurora Borealis

**GenArts Monsters GT** has so many great filters for recreating natural phenomena. The **M_Aurora** plug-in gives hundreds of settings for creating natural looking auroras. The auroras are completely customizable in every aspect imaginable.

**Figure 7.41** An aurora created with GenArts Monsters M_Aurora plug-in. The stars were created with Monsters M_NightSky. Footage: Michele Yamazaki.

This plug-in is great for creating groovy, fractalesque background elements like you might see in the scene changes for *That '70s Show* or *Wizards of Waverly Place*, lower thirds texture fills, and magic inside a crystal ball.

**Figure 7.42**  GenArts Monsters GT Aurora used with Noise Industries FxFactory Pro Glass Lozenge filter to make a lady in a crystal ball. Footage: Crowd Control, clip # 00154_002_35.

## Fire and Fireballs

Fire is a very dangerous to deal with on set and it can be expensive to burn props, so it's no surprise that there are several fire plug-ins. Fire plug-ins can be used to create simple flames or raging forest fires, it's great for special effects like flaming eyeballs, and the bonus is, no one gets burned!

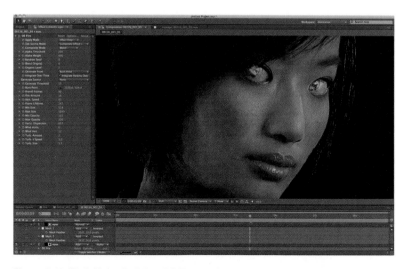

**Figure 7.43**  Digieffects Delirium DE Fire applied to a solid and appearing through masks. Footage: Crowd Control, clip # 00126_001_93.

Fire can be built with After Effects' **Turbulent Noise** or **Fractal Noise**, but there are some third-party plug-ins made specifically for fire, so there is less tweaking and masking.

**Digieffects Delirium DE Fire** ($49 à la carte or included in Delirium) is very easy to use and position but it doesn't have nearly the parameters of **GenArts Monsters GT M_Fire** or **Boris Continuum Complete BCC Fire**. With DE Fire there are no settings for the amount of smoke or the color of fire, but there are controls for Wind, Turbulence, Fire Amount, and Flame Lifetime.

**Figure 7.44** GenArts Monsters GT M_Fire. Footage: Michele Yamazaki.

GenArts Monsters GT M_Fire has more robust options for Fire, Winds, Vortices, Barriers, and Colour, and presets for a Base Fire, Wilder, Bold Smoke, and more. Instead of just rendering over a

**Figure 7.45** GenArts Monsters GT **M_FireBall** used to create a flaming soccer ball. Footage: Crowd Control, clip # 00033_001_98.

scene, M_Fire attaches itself to highlights in the scene. It's excellent for creating flaming text effects.

For ease of use and intuitiveness, Boris Continuum Complete BCC Fire wins hands down. It is extremely easy to position, adjust the Shape, Color, Smoke and Wind, and it comes with the Pixel Chooser so the fire can be isolated to masks and mattes.

**Figure 7.46**  Boris Continuum Complete Fire. Footage: Crowd Control, clip # 00087_004_25.

## Muzzle Flash

A muzzle flash is the expanding gas that looks like fire when a gun is shot. There are a couple of plug-ins available specifically for creating muzzle flashes: **Digieffects Delirium DE Muzzle Flash** and **FXhome MuzzlePlug** are two. It's easy enough to create with any fire and smoke plug-in as well, just a bit more work.

**Figure 7.47**  Digieffects Delirium Muzzle Flash with the 357 Handgun Muzzle Type preset. Footage: Michigan Film Reel.

Digieffects Delirium DE Muzzle Flash is as easy as a muzzle flash can possibly get. I like to apply it to an Adjustment Layer as opposed to the original footage so that it's easy to trim the in- and out-points. DE Muzzle Flash has three presets for Muzzle Type: 357 Handgun, M-16 Rifle and 12-Gauge Shotgun. These presets are extremely helpful for people like me who know absolutely nothing about guns. The trick to a good muzzle flash is to make it very fast, just a frame or two; this can be set with Flash Lifetime and Flash Spacing. There are crosshairs to pinpoint the Flash Point and Gun Butt so that the muzzle flash comes out at the correct angle. This plug-in auto-animates using settings such as Auto Fire and Burst Count.

# TEXT AND GRAPHIC ELEMENTS

Whether you are delivering a high-budget movie, producing a documentary or corporate video, or just delivering a home movie, in most cases you will need to add text that gives information, provides explanation, or simply gives background texture. After Effects text plug-ins give you added creative control and drive the message home.

Artists have gotten creative with opening movie credits since the invention of film. Instead of just names printed on the screen, the words often pop out at you, seemingly part of the movie, or appear as sideways text, 3D text, or even as names written on side of buildings in graffiti! This ability to animate text can change how the audience views the show, and the presentations have become mini artistic set pieces in themselves.

Documentaries and corporate video have an in-built need to deliver textual information such as names, statistics, and so on. Without lower thirds and animated text, they may as well get into the newspaper business. After Effects plug-ins not only allow you to animate and characterize your text, they can also deliver 3D Extruded Text and Shapes, for even more dynamic content.

A few plug-ins we'll look at in this section are **Boris Continuum Complete Type On Text, idustrial revolution Decimal Counter, Yanobox Motype**, and **Noise Industries Futurismo Titles**.

## Text Elements

Working with the built-in Text Engine in After Effects definitely has its upsides. It's fast, there are a lot of presets, and it comes with After Effects. It can be tough to understand how to manipulate for new users to After Effects. Most importantly, though, After Effects Text Engine works in 2D. Although words and individual letters can move in 3D space, there is no thickness to the characters. This is the main reason to choose a third-party plug-in for text, for real beveled edges and depth.

### Create a Custom Side and Bevel in Boris Continuum 3D Objects Type On Text

**Boris Continuum Complete** 6.0 introduced **3D Objects**, a set of 3D plug-ins for After Effects and other hosts. Each of the five plug-ins come with custom bevels, extrusions, bump maps, and

**Figure 8.1** Boris Continuum Complete 3D Objects Type On Text generates gorgeous "real" 3D text right within the After Effects native interface. Footage: Michele Yamazaki.

textures; built-in 3D warps, including bend, ripple, and shatter effects; multiple presets. They use the native After Effects Camera and Lights, and are OpenGL accelerated. The plug-ins include:

- BCC Extruded Text
- BCC Extruded EPS
- BCC Type On Text
- BCC Extruded Spline
- BCC Layer Deformer

They come with the full Boris Continuum Complete bundle or can be purchased as a set as the **Boris Continuum 3D Objects Unit** ($399).

BCC Type On Text is a full-featured 3D text extrusion tool that can be automated or keyframed to animate text or type text onscreen. Because it's also OpenGL accelerated, previews are fast, even live previews of moving the path in a custom bevel, as we'll be doing in this tutorial. *Project files for this tutorial are located in the BCC Type on Text folder.*

**Third-party plug-ins needed:**

- Boris Continuum Complete
  1. Create a New Composition named "BCC 3D Text". Use the HDTV 1080 29.97 preset, set the Duration to 5:00 and make the Background Color black.
  2. Add a new comp-sized solid. The color is unimportant. Name it Text.

     *Note*: Although we will be creating 3D text that will work with the comp camera, do not enable 3D for the layer. If you do, the effect will look wrong because both the effect and the layer will be giving the change in perspective. The effect needs to be applied to a 2D layer. We will check the Use Comp Camera option so that the effect will follow the After Effects Camera.

3. Apply the BCC Type On Text plug-in to the Text solid (Effects > BCC 3D Objects > BCC Type On Text). A text dialog will come up. Type "HAPPY HOLIDAYS" in an easy to read, bold serif font. I chose Book Antiqua Bold, 96 pt. (See Figure 8.2.)

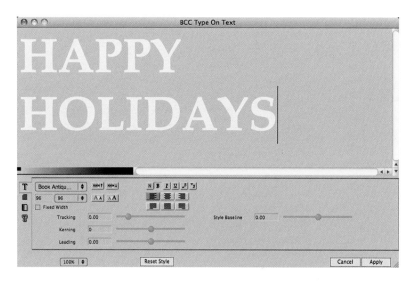

**Figure 8.2** This text dialog box is the only time you have to leave the native After Effects interface. To re-edit these elements, click Edit TEXT at the top of the Effect Controls panel.

4. At the very top of the Effect Controls panel there's a pulldown menu containing the presets. Select the preset on-off-drop down and jump.bcp. (Figure 8.3.)

**Figure 8.3** The Type On Text preset menu. Notice that some say "on", "off" or "on-off". This refers to whether the preset text is transitioning onscreen, offscreen, or onscreen then offscreen.

5. Go to 2:00 in the timeline so that the text is fully viewable onscreen. In the Effect Controls panel check the box for Use Comp Camera. Add a New Camera, using the 35mm

preset. Feel free to move the camera around so that you can see that this is indeed "real" 3D text, not a flat postcard on an angle. Undo any camera moves you have made or twirl open Camera 1 in the timeline and click Reset. Leave the camera at the default settings for now. (Figure 8.4.)

**Figure 8.4** Click Reset to put the Camera at the default settings.

6. By far the easiest way to get started in any of the BCC 3D Objects plug-ins is to start with a preset. There are hundreds included with BCC and they will save loads of time. Under Extrusion Style, choose the preset color-plastic 2 tone.bcp which will make the text red with a gold bevel. (Figure 8.5.)

**Figure 8.5** The Extrusion Style preset color-plastic 2 tone.bcp is very classic holiday look.

7. The sides of the text are difficult to see, but this is easy to remedy. Under EXTRUSION, set Extrusion Depth to 5.50. To give the text a beautiful, shiny look we'll add a smooth texture and some reflection. Under BEVEL/SIDE MATE-RIAL, set the following (Figure 8.6):
   - **Side Texture File:** metallic-Bronze Armor.jpg
   - **Ambient Intensity:** White
   - **Highlight Amount:** 100.00

- **Reflection:** Horizon Fire (creates a nice reflection on the text)
- **Reflectivity:** 22.00 (the amount that the reflection reflects)
- **Reflection Scale:** 100.00
- **Two-Sided Lighting:** Checked (lights both the front and back of the text so that if the item rotates, the back is also lit and not dark)

8. The custom side and bevel will be taken from a path that you create. The best way to illustrate how this works is to make three or four mask paths next to each other. Press the G key to bring up the Pen tool. Make a small-zigzagged path, a curvy path, and a crazy path, right on the same layer as your text. Between paths, switch back to the Selection tool so that you can create a completely new, unconnected path. (Figure 8.7.)

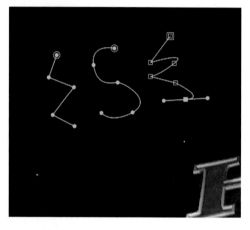

**Figure 8.7** Three paths that will be used as beveled edges.

   Don't worry if the paths won't look right after they are applied because they can easily be modified.

9. First, let's set up the custom side since it's currently just a big flat surface. Under EXTRUSION, set Side Style to Host Path. Set Side Host Path to Mask 1, Mask 2, or Mask 3. Try them all out to see what you like the best. If one is close, select it, and drag the points around so you can see the live update. It's really useful to watch how the bevel and side react as points are pulled on a path that is applied to a side or bevel. Delete points if needed. (Figure 8.8.)

10. Repeat the process for the Bevel. Under EXTRUSION, set Bevel Style to Host Path, and choose the mask you wish

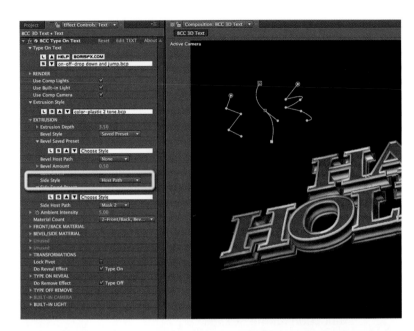

**Figure 8.8** Mask 2 is used as the Side Host Path.

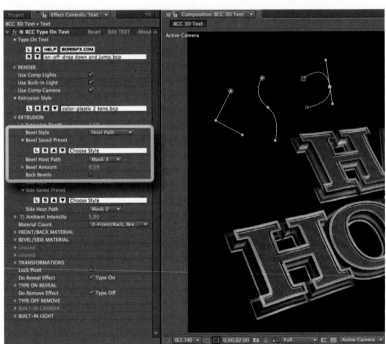

**Figure 8.9** Mask 3 is used as the Bevel Host Path.

to use for Bevel Host Path. Drag the points or delete to achieve the look you want. It is helpful to move the camera to see the front bevel better. (Figure 8.9.)

**Finishing touches:** We'll add some stars and some glints to give it a finished look. You'll need the full Boris Continuum Complete bundle for the following steps.

# Hot Tip

If you create your own animation and you'd like to save it for later use, click the S button at the top of the Type On Text's controls to save it and L to load your preset. (Figure 8.10.)

**Figure 8.10** Click the S button to save a custom preset.

1. Layer > New > Solid (Make Comp Size). Name it "Background" and click OK. Place it behind the Text layer. Apply BCC Stars and use the default settings (Effects > BCC Generators > BCC Stars).
2. To add some shine to the text, apply BCC Glints (Effects > BCC OpenGL > BCC Glint). Use the reallySmallRays.bcp preset.

   This effect will remove the transparency from the text layer, making the Background layer not visible. To fix this problem, twirl open Pixel Chooser in the Effect Controls panel, under BCC Glints. Twirl open Matte and set Channel to Alpha. (Figure 8.11.)
3. Adding some camera movement by keyframing the Position parameter of the Camera 1 will also give the project more interest.

**Figure 8.11** BCC Glint adds some nice light reflections to the text.

## FxFactory Type Plug-ins

**Noise Industries FxFactory** is a free plug-in management system that "fourth party" developers use to create very fast plug-ins which use your graphics card for hardware-accelerated previews and rendering. FxFactory-based plug-ins need to have the free FxFactory installed to run, which can be downloaded at *www. noiseindustries.com.*

FxFactory plug-ins support Apple Final Cut Pro, Final Cut Express, Motion, and, of course, After Effects. This section contains a few of my favorite text plug-ins that utilize FxFactory's FxEngine.

## idustrial revolution Decimal Counter

**Figure 8.12** idustrial revolution Decimal Counter makes counting a series of numbers very easy. Footage: Michele Yamazaki.

One of the big problems with the Numbers plug-in that ships with After Effects, which is now pretty much obsolete, is that the numbers will bounce around if a monospaced font is not used and Proportional Spacing is chosen. This can be somewhat remedied by checking the Proportional Spacing box, but then the Tracking is wide around the decimal point. Tracking can't be adjusted per character. It's a clunky, obsolete plug-in.

Far better is **idustrial revolution Decimal Counter** ($29), an inexpensive and easy-to-use counting plug-in. It looks nicer than Numbers, with a built-in drop shadow and tricolor gradient background tool. A currency symbol can be added in a pulldown menu, but it seems to only apply a U.S. dollar symbol (no Yen! no Euro! no Pounds Sterling!). The kerning, spacing, and position can be modified and easily keyframed, and because there is a Prop/Mono setting for proportional spacing or monospacing, any font with numbers can be used without the problem of the numbers shifting.

*Note*: To run Decimal Counter, you will need to install the free FxFactory engine, available at *www.noiseindustries.com*.

## Yanobox Motype (FxFactory)

**Figure 8.13** The Yanobox Motype interface. Footage: Michele Yamazaki.

If you're on a tight budget or on a tight schedule and need to make some marvelous title animations, **Yanobox Motype** ($99) will be your new best friend. It comes with several cool presets, all of which can be modified and keyframed to your specifications. The look can be anything from high-tech/modern to classic and corporate, all in one tool.

Motype is extremely fast and auto-animates text, graphic elements, and built-in particles. It's broken down into sections:

- **Presets:** 40 presets with a variety of looks in SD and HD
- **Help:** Click to go to the manual on the Motype website
- **Drop Shadow:** Enable to add a drop shadow with the usual settings
- **Random Characters:** Animate random characters like *The Matrix* title sequence, or scramble letters that form into the title
- **Motion Mixer:** Adjust the Position, Rotation, and Origin of the text movements; set the Attraction, Duration, Opacity, and Origin Type
- **Trailing Blur:** Creates interesting blur effects, which trail before or after the text; auto-animating or keyframable
- **Particles:** Several built-in particle presets with textures like Multi-Circles, Gradient Target, Mecanic Circle, Multi-Squares, Grids, and more; the image input can also take the text from the main title or a custom image; the emitters are completely

customized, using sliders for Count, Size, Lifetime, Opacity, Velocity, and Color

- **Camera:** A 3D camera to zoom and pan around graphics; can auto-animate or be keyframed
- **Cyclorama:** Allows a floor to be placed in the animation, with adjustable spotlights, colors and textures
- **Options:** Canvas Start Frame is the only option here; allows you to choose which frame the animation starts

*Note*: To run Motype, you will need to install the free FxFactory engine, available at *www.noiseindustries.com*.

**Figure 8.14** Yanobox Motype preset options. Footage: Michele Yamazaki.

## Futurismo Titles

If you're looking for something fast, fun, and unbelievably easy, try **Futurismo Titles** ($49), which are more "template" than "plug-in." Futurismo Titles, which is another that uses the FxFactory FxEngine, includes eight plug-ins: Bound, Fireworks, Flip, Flying, Magnet, Reverse, Slice, and Spring.

Each plug-in has a couple of presets and can animate automatically. The duration, delay between character, wobbliness, font, colors, spacing, angles, and background gradient can be modified.

*Note*: To run Futurismo Titles, you will need to install the free FxFactory engine, available at *www.noiseindustries.com*.

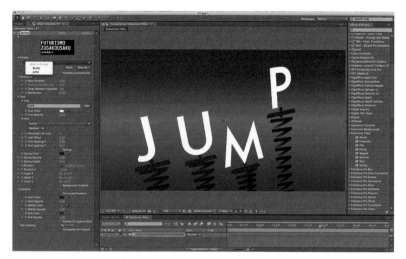

**Figure 8.15** Futurismo Titles
with the Spring plug-in applied.
Screenshot: Michele Yamazaki.

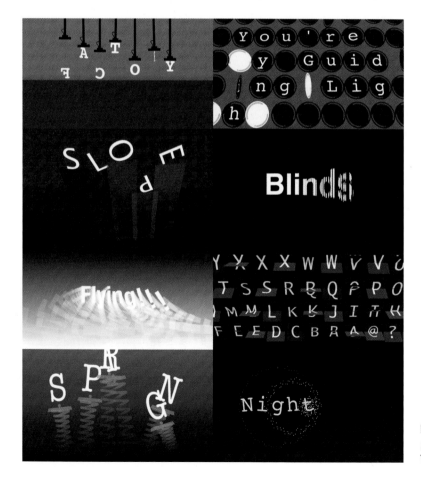

**Figure 8.16** Futurismo Titles
presets. Screenshot: Michele
Yamazaki.

# Creating a Mock User Interface or Heads Up Display

In 2009, I attended the Motion Conference in Albuquerque, New Mexico (*www.motion.tv*). My favorite presentation was by Mark Coleran, titled Screen Design: Imaginary Visual Interfaces. Mark has designed computer interfaces and graphical systems for film, and he has a prolific résumé including *The Bourne Ultimatum, Mission Impossible 3, Mr. & Mrs. Smith, The Island, Blade II*, and *Lara Croft: Tomb Raider*.

It is very rare that a computer screen seen on the big screen is a real, unmodified operating system. That is where interface designers like Mark Coleran come in to create screen graphics that serve as computer interfaces, HUD (Heads Up Display), or just set dressing, used as storytelling elements within a film.

In his presentation, Mark described the different styles of interfaces: realistic, which function and appear like current software; semi-realistic, which use visual references from current systems, but push the limits of reality; and "fluff" systems that are cutting-edge, slick, state-of-the-art conceptualizations.

## Red Giant Text Anarchy

**Figure 8.17** A faux HUD can be created using Red Giant Text Anarchy. Footage: Crowd Control Clip# 00074_001_24.

**Red Giant Text Anarchy** ($199) is a particle system for text that includes a variety of plug-ins for creating interesting and dynamic text animations, often like you see in the movies. For example, the Text Matrix plug-in can fairly easily recreate the look of *The Matrix* title sequence, with the falling letters.

Not only does Text Anarchy allow for creation of interesting text animations, but it animates graphic elements as well. Text

Anarchy was acquired from Digital Anarchy, along with Geomancy and Anarchy Toolbox, and the three products were combined into what is currently Red Giant Text Anarchy. Geomancy includes the GridSquares, GridLines, and HairLines plug-ins.

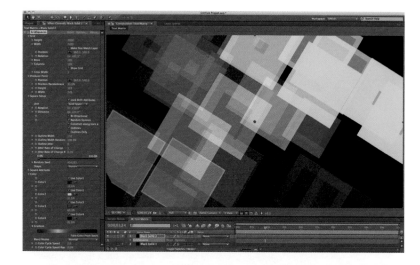

**Figure 8.18** Grid Squares. Footage: Michele Yamazaki.

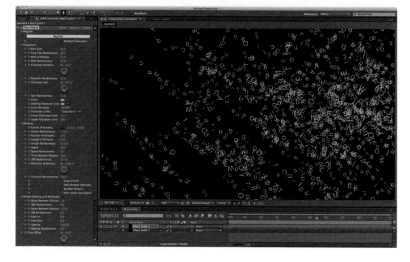

**Figure 8.19** Text Matrix. Footage: Michele Yamazaki.

# Hot Tip: ASCII Tables for Text Anarchy

Some plug-ins in Text Anarchy include the option to set the Lower Character Limit and Upper Character Limits. This allows users to isolate numbers, capital letters, and so on. Use an ASCII table to reference these limits. For example, if you wanted to use only capital letters, capital "A" has a value of 65 and the capital "Z" has a value of 90. The Lower Character Limit would be set to 65 and the Upper Character Limit to 90.

There is a reference ASCII table available at *www.asciitable.com*.

## SUGARfx HUD by FxFactory

If you're looking for an incredibly easy, automated way to create a HUD, check out **SUGARfx HUD** ($79), which contains three plug-ins: Binoculars, OSD (On Screen Display), and Target. Each plug-in has tons of options including presets, editable colors lines and shapes, video effects, text options, and more. It's a lot of fun and useful if you're working on an espionage or science-fiction project.

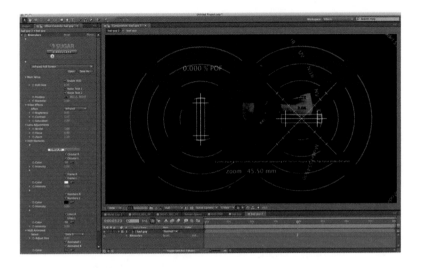

**Figure 8.20** SUGARfx HUD Binoculars. Footage: Crowd Control, clip # 00074_003_47.

## London Underground Station Graphic Animation with Yanobox Nodes (FxFactory)

Have you ever tried to recreate those tag clouds you see on WordPress blogs with After Effects? How about the Visual Thesaurus from Thesaurus.com? Both can easily be recreated with **Yanobox Nodes** ($99). With Nodes it is easy to create cool, complex data visualizations or info graphics. *Note*: To run Nodes,

**Figure 8.21** Yanobox Nodes is used to make a complex network of logos attached by a line. Footage: Michele Yamazaki.

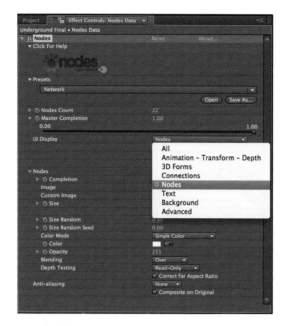

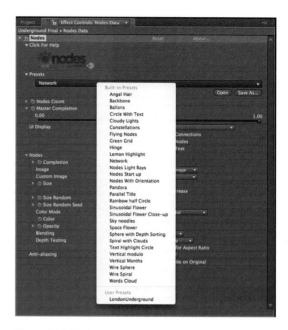

**Figure 8.22** The Nodes section is isolated for easy navigation of the plug-in. Screenshot: Michele Yamazaki.

**Figure 8.23** Nodes presets. Screenshot: Michele Yamazaki.

you will need to install the free FxFactory engine, available at *www.noiseindustries.com*.

Yes, there are a lot of options in the plug-in, but the UI of the plug-in is broken down logically into sections: Animation, 3D Forms, Connections, Nodes, Text, Background, and Advanced. Data can be typed, pasted, or brought in from an external list into the Text area. The text can be attached to nodes like circles, Xs, airplanes, flowers, or other symbols that are included as presets in the Nodes area. Alternately, the user can import or create custom nodes, shown in this tutorial. Under Connections, the nodes can be linked to each other or to a spot on the screen by lines or tubes. Nodes can be auto-animated or keyframed to move in 3D space in the Animation area of the UI. There are several presets to the user get started and I highly recommend doing so. The plug-in auto-animates but the presets are very well designed and a great jumping-off point.

In this tutorial we recreate the logo for the London Underground and list the stations in Zone 1. These stations are linked together in a network of lines, making a graphical representation of London linked together by the Tube. *The project is on this book's DVD in a folder named Nodes Underground folder (Mac).*

**Third-party plug-ins needed:**
- Yanobox Nodes (Mac)
    1. First we'll create the Node—the London Underground logo. Create a New Composition that is 1024 × 1024 for SD, or 2048 × 2048 for HD, square pixels. We'll use the SD setting here. Name the comp Logo and set the duration to 1 second. Click OK.

2. Turn on Title/Action Safe by using the grids and guides options at the bottom of the Comp panel. We'll use the crosshairs at the center to line up the logo perfectly in the center. (Figure 8.24.)

**Figure 8.24** Use the Ellipse and Rectangle tools to recreate the London Underground logo, sans text. Screenshot: Michele Yamazaki.

3. Use the Ellipse tool to create a circle Shape Layer in the Comp. It should fill about half of the comp (use the screenshot as a guide). Shape Layer 1 will be created. In the timeline, twirl down Contents > Ellipse 1. Delete Fill 1. Twirl down Stroke 1 and set the Color to a medium red. Set the Stroke Width to 95.

4. Deselect the layer so that the rectangle shape you'll be creating is not on the same layer. Use the Rectangle tool and drag a bar across the center of the circle. Twirl down the Contents > Rectangle 1 then delete Stroke 1 and set Fill 1 > Color to royal blue. Make sure the blue rectangle is on top of the red circle.

5. Create a New Composition named Underground Final, using the HDV/HDTV 720 29.97 preset. Set the duration to 10:00. Click OK.

6. Add a new comp-sized solid named Nodes Data. Apply Yanobox Nodes to the solid layer (Effects > Yanobox > Nodes).

7. Select the Nodes Data Layer and click the E key to bring up the Nodes effect in the timeline. Double-click it to open the Effect Controls panel. Choose the Network preset. (Figure 8.25.)

8. First let's add the text data. To keep things nice and tidy, under the UI Display choose Text. Click the Import Text

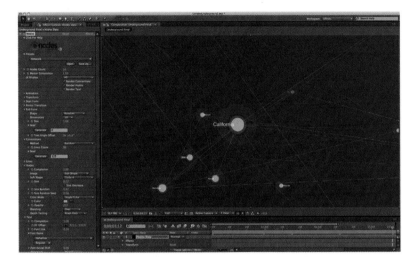

**Figure 8.25** The Network preset in Nodes. Screenshot: Michele Yamazaki.

File button and navigate to LondonUnderground.txt, included on the DVD with the project in the Nodes Underground folder. Click Import. This list uses carriage returns as a delimiter but there are other options such as commas, spaces, or custom characters. (Figure 8.26.)

In the Text settings, set the Font Name to Arial or Helvetica. Set the Alignment to Centered and the Color to White. (Figure 8.27.)

9. Now let's add the logo. Drag the Logo comp into the Underground Final Comp. Make sure it is placed below the Nodes Data layer. Disable the logos visibility by clicking the eyeball.

10. Under the UI Display choose Nodes. Twirl down the Nodes options. Under Image, choose Custom Image. In the Custom Image pulldown choose 2. Logo. Adjust the size as needed in conjunction with the size of the text. Set the Color to White so the graphic won't be tinted.

11. Back under the Text UI Display, set the XY Offset to 640, 360, which centers the text over the graphic. (Figure 8.28.)

**Figure 8.26** A text list can be imported into Nodes to save time. Screenshot: Michele Yamazaki.

Figure 8.27 Nodes Text.
Screenshot: Michele Yamazaki.

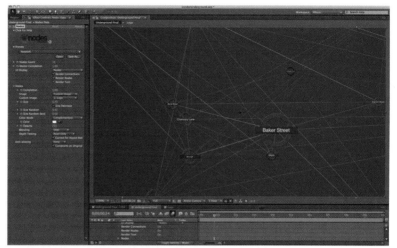

Figure 8.28 Adjusting the offset. Screenshot: Michele Yamazaki.

12. Under UI Display, choose Connections. Twirl down Connections and choose the Method named Serial. This will cut down on the number of connections but still leave them connected. Twirl down Lines and adjust the Thickness to 3 or 4. Change Primitive to Curved Tube. Adjust the Start and End Opacity as you see fit. If you want the lines to have a bit of curve, adjust the Control Start Point and the Control End Point for X, Y, and Z. Be warned: a small change has a huge impact on the curvature of the lines. Set the Blending to Over to see brighter lines.

13. Next let's adjust the background. Under UI Display, choose Background. Twirl down Background and choose Gradient in the Background pulldown menu. Choose something in the blue or gray family or something else you like. (Figure 8.29.)

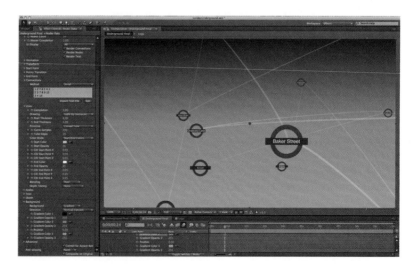

Figure 8.29 Settings for the Connections, Lines, and Background. Footage: Michele Yamazaki.

**14.** Under UI Display choose Animation – Transform – Depth. Twirl down Animation. Before changing any values, play the comp through a few times. Set Oscillator to XYZ, and leave Oscillator Speed at 0.80, and Oscillator Amplitude at 0.10. Set Auto Animate to Rotation Y and adjust Auto Animate Speed to taste.

Under Transform, keyframe the rotation. This is where you can get those *Matrix*-style effects where something freezes in midrotation, and then either continues to rotate or rotates the opposite direction. To achieve this kind of effect, use a hold keyframe at the point where you want it to freeze. Select the keyframe and go to Animation > Toggle Hold Keyframe. Give it a try. (Figure 8.30.)

**Figure 8.30** Animation settings for the project. Footage: Michele Yamazaki.

# Lines and Paths

Lines and paths are used in a multitude of creative ways in motion graphics, from growing lines with arrowheads, lines on maps and globes, to animated glowing lines, which have become very popular as background elements for text or keyed elements, especially after the release of Trapcode 3D Stroke.

After Effects contains a Stroke plug-in that can be applied to a path and animated; as an added bonus, it's very easy to use. Also, Shape Layers have Strokes that have many options such as dashed lines and dots, wiggle, or animated paths. There are third-party plug-ins that can make workflow easier and give you many more options. In this section we'll be looking at **Cycore CFX Path Tools** and **Cycore Sphere Utilities, Yanobox Nodes**, and, of course, **Trapcode 3D Stroke**. Other options are **Red Giant Text Anarchy GridSquares, GridLines**, and **HairLines**.

## Create an Animated Spirograph-Style Animation with Cycore CFX Path Tools Wiggle Stroke

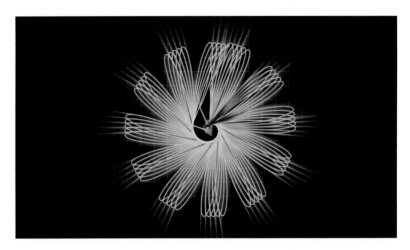

**Figure 8.31** Cycore Path Tools Wiggle Stroke with Trapcode Shine. Footage: Michele Yamazaki.

When I was a kid, the Spirograph was my favorite toy. I used to spend hours with those interlocking plastic wheels, using different colors of pens to create flowers, stars, and weaving lines. This type of effect is easy to create with **Cycore CFX Path Tools** ($199), which contains two plug-ins, Rakka and Wiggle Stroke. Both use After Effects Mask paths. Wiggle Stroke creates, obviously, a wiggling path, so animations can go way beyond a basic flower drawing on. (For more on Rakka, see Chapter 4, "Distortions, Warps, Tiling, and Time Effects.")

This is really more of a recipe than a tutorial. With recipes you're encouraged to improvise. *The project file can be found on this book's DVD in a folder called WiggleStroke – Spirograph.*

**Third-party plug-ins needed:**

- Cycore CFX Path Tools
    1. Create a new Composition using the HDTV 1080 29.97 preset, 10:00 in duration, named Spiro.
    2. Add a dark background of your choice, such as a dark-colored Solid layer or a dark image with a pattern. I've added a Solid layer with a green grid, created with the Grid plug-in, then added a vignette around the edges. The stroke will be white, so a dark background will help it pop.
    3. Add a new comp-sized Solid Layer named Stroke. Using the Ellipse tool, draw a circle path in the center of the layer.
    4. Apply Cycore Path Tools Wiggle Stroke to the Stroke solid layer (Effects > Cycore Systems FX > CPT Wiggle Stroke). In the Effect Controls panel, set Mask Path to Mask 1. (Figure 8.32.)
    5. Under Wiggle Position, set Wiggle Type (P) to Sine Wave.

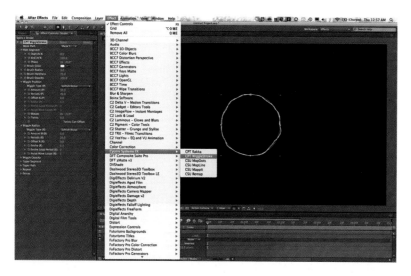

**Figure 8.32** The default settings of Wiggle Stroke applied to a circle path. Screenshot: Michele Yamazaki.

Instead of including a complete tutorial here, I recommend that you experiment by placing keyframes along your timeline and adjusting the values. Check the manual, which is included in the download, for in-depth descriptions of each parameter.

Under Wiggle Position, keyframe the following values to get a Spirograph-style animation.

- **Amount (P):** Will increase or decrease the scale of the design
- **Periods (P):** Adjusts the amount of detail
- **Offset (P):** Rotates the design
- **Twists (P):** Loops and twists the stroke
  Under Repeat:
- Set keyframes for the number of Repetitions. Many of the values for Repeat will be grayed out until the number of Repetitions is 2 or higher.

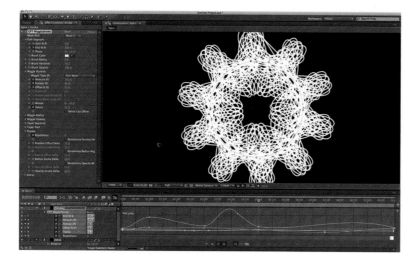

**Figure 8.33** The keyframes are adjusted in the Graph Editor. Footage: Michele Yamazaki.

Under Path Segment:

- Set keyframes for Start At % or End At % to animate the stroke drawing on or off. To soften the stroke, adjust Brush Hardness.

After setting keyframes, smooth them with Easy Ease and adjust in the Graph Editor. (For in-depth instructions on using the Graph Editor, see the book *Creating Motion Graphics with After Effects* by Chris and Trish Meyer, 2010.)

## A Newsreel Style Globe with a Travel Path with Cycore Systems Sphere Utilities Map Lines, Cycore FX CC Sphere, and Boris Continuum Complete Film Damage

**Figure 8.34** The final newsreel globe. Footage: NASA.

I always loved the animated lines on the globe showing where Indiana Jones was going. That look can be mimicked with a stroked path but it's made even easier with **Cycore Sphere Utilities** ($99). CSU MapLine, one of the plug-ins included with the package, follows the natural curvature of the earth. For example, if a plane flies from Chicago to Tokyo, it will not travel in a straight line following the latitude lines of the earth, but will instead take the shorter route over Alaska and Canada. Another nice feature is that the plug-in will automatically wrap off the left and right side of the screen when applied to a Mercator projection of the earth.

The Mercator projection is from the NASA Blue Marble Series and is free to use (American tax dollars at work!). *The project files are included on this book's DVD in a folder named Newsreel MapLines.*

**Third-party plug-ins needed:**

- Cycore FX Cycore Sphere Utilities
- Cycore FX CC Sphere (included with After Effects)
- Boris Continuum Complete (or other plug-ins for star generation and old film effects)

1. Import 136054main_bm_072004.jpg into After Effects. Drag it to the Make New Composition button at the bottom of the Project panel. Go to Composition Settings (Composition > Composition Settings) and rename it "Map Projection" and set the comp to 5:00 in duration.
2. Apply CSU MapLines (Effects > Cycore Systems > CSU MapLines). Set the Start Point crosshair to the U.S.A. (I used Chicago) and the End Point crosshair to somewhere in Asia (I used Tokyo). Notice that it wraps around the image automatically. Bonus! (Figure 8.35.)

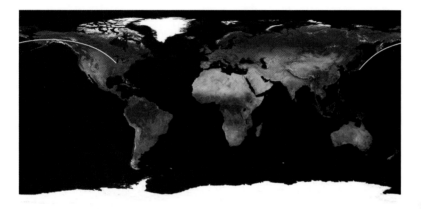

Figure 8.35  CSU Maplines. Footage: NASA.

3. Set the Hardness to 50% to soften the line a bit.
4. Now we'll animate the line from the U.S. to Asia. At the first frame, keyframe the value of End At % to 0. Go to 4:00 and set the value to 100%.
5. If you'd like to make the line dashed, twirl open Dash. Set the Gap % higher. 50% gives a nice dash. For shorter dashes, lower the value of Length (Degrees). If you'd like the dashes to move along the line, keyframe the value of Phase.
6. To make a spherical globe, create a New Composition using the HDTV 1080 29.97 preset, 10 seconds in duration, black background. Name it "Final Globe".
7. Drag the Mercator-projection comp into Final Globe. Apply CC Sphere to the Mercator-projection layer (Effects > Perspective > CC Sphere). There is a version that ships with After Effects and there's also an HD version named Cycore FX HD. The effect will make a perfectly matched sphere if the map lines up properly. The map is 2000 × 1000—an aspect ratio of 2:1, which is ideal for wrapping around a sphere. (Figure 8.36.)

**Figure 8.36** CC Sphere applied to the Mercator projection, which is a nested comp layer. Footage: NASA.

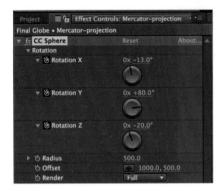

**Figure 8.37** CC Sphere Rotation and Radius settings. Screenshot: Michele Yamazaki.

Jump to 9:00. Set a keyframe for End At % with a value of 100.0. Go to 0:00 and set End At % to 0.0. Select both keyframes and apply Easy Ease (Animation > Keyframe Assistant > Easy Ease) to smooth out the movement.

8. Go to the first frame. Set a keyframe for Radius with a value of 500.0.

   Under Rotation, set Rotation X to $0x +13.0°$, Rotation Y to $0x +80.0°$, and Rotation Z to $0x -51.0°$, and set a keyframe for Rotation Y and Z parameters. At 9:29, the final frame, set Rotation Y to $0x +223.0°$ and Rotation Z to $0x +0.0°$. (Figure 8.37.)

Select all Rotation parameters and the Radius parameter for CC Sphere and Easy Ease the keyframes.

The final map is done at this point. The next steps involve enhancing the final composite.

9. The lighting is a bit dark. Think of the light as the sun. If you've ever flown west, the sun will be up almost the whole time, so increase the Light Height, under Light, to 100.0. Under Shading, increase Ambient to 200.0, its maximum value. This may seem like too much but the old film effect will darken the scene considerably.

10. For the background, add a star field. Try **Boris Continuum Complete BCC Stars** or **GenArts Monsters GT M_Night-Sky**. Over-exaggerate the stars and galaxies, as they did in the old film reels. Another option is to download a public domain image of a star field from NASA.gov.

11. Using the Type tool, add some large type that says "NEWS-REEL" in an old-style font, such as Bernard MT Condensed at 350 px. Add a thick black Drop Shadow (Effects > Perspective > Drop Shadow). Do not soften it. (Figure 8.39.)

**Figure 8.38** Boris Continuum Complete BCC Stars is used to make very bright stars and galaxies. No, it does not look very good now, but bright settings will be needed for the old film effect. Footage: NASA.

**Figure 8.39** Text with a Drop Shadow is added. Footage: NASA.

This is a bit crisp for an old film reel. Add an Adjustment Layer (Layer > New > Adjustment Layer) and apply Box Blur (Effects > Blur & Sharpen > Box Blur) with a Blurriness of 2.0.

12. For the old film look, apply an old film filter to the Adjustment Layer. There are several options out there including **Boris Continuum Complete BCC Film Damage, Digieffects Aged Film, Red Giant Magic Bullet Looks** with **Misfire, GenArts Sapphire S_FilmDamage,** and **Tiffen Dfx Filter Suite Faux Film**. I used BCC Film Damage with the mackTruckDamage.bcp preset. (Figure 8.40.)

# Pro Tip

An even cooler effect is to put the line and map in separate comps then layer the two comps. Apply CC Sphere to each with the line sphere slightly larger. This will give you an interesting 3D look with the line floating above the earth.

**Figure 8.40** Boris Continuum Complete BCC Film Damage and Box Blur finish the look of the old newsreel. Compare mode is turned on for BCC Film Damage, so the left side of the comp is unaffected by Film Damage, while the right side shows the effect. Footage: NASA.

## Swooshing Lines with Trapcode 3D Stroke

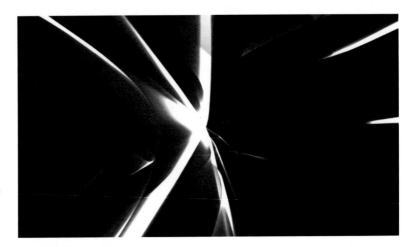

**Figure 8.41** Trapcode 3D Stroke with Trapcode Shine can mimic the look of the Mac screensaver. Footage: Michele Yamazaki.

The moving lines and cycling colors of the Mac screensaver can be hypnotic. This is a recipe for creating that sort of look. *The project is on the book's DVD in the 3D Stroke Screensaver folder.*

**Third-party plug-ins needed:**
- Trapcode 3D Stroke
- Trapcode Shine

1. Create a New Composition named "Lines". Use the HDV/HDTV 720 29.97 preset. Set the duration to 30:00. Click OK.

2. Apply Trapcode 3D Stroke to the Solid layer (Effects > Trapcode > 3D Stroke).

3. Draw a simple path using the Pen tool or use one of the Presets in 3D Stroke. The stroke will automatically draw on the path. There is no need to select it. You can draw multiple paths if you wish and the stroke will apply to all paths if the Use All Paths box is checked. (Figure 8.42.)

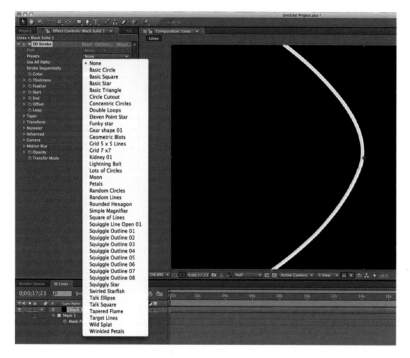

Figure 8.42  A mask path with 3D Stroke applied. Screenshot: Michele Yamazaki.

4. Lower the value of Thickness to 4 and set Feather to 100. With Trapcode Shine applied you will not want the stroke to be too thick. Feathering the stroke here, although you won't notice a lot of difference, will give a smoother appearance.

5. Let's jump down to Repeater so you'll have a more accurate gauge of the lines. Click the Enable checkbox and set the number of Instances. I set mine to 7. Adjust the X Displace, Y Displace, and Z Displace, as well as X Rotation, Y Rotation, and Z Rotation. You may want to keyframe these values in the timeline to give them some movement.

6. Under Transform, keyframe any of the values you like throughout the timeline. I keyframed Bend, X Rotation, Y Rotation, and Z Rotation. Preview the comp a few times and adjust as necessary. (Figure 8.43.)

7. Apply Trapcode Shine (Effects > Trapcode > Shine). Increase the values of Ray Length and Boost Light by quite a bit.

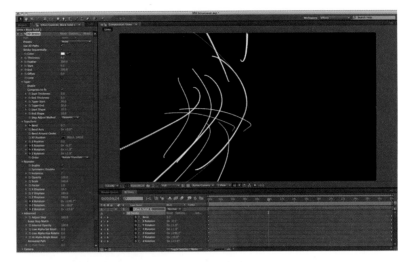

**Figure 8.43** Enabling and keyframing the values under repeater creates many more lines. Screenshot: Michele Yamazaki.

8. Under Colorize, use the 3-Color Gradient setup. Keep the Highlights color set to White, but keyframe the values of Midtones and Shadows throughout the timeline. Watch the comp through to tweak color selection. Easy Ease the keyframes and offset the keyframes in the timeline to vary the timing. (Figure 8.44.)

9. Duplicate the Solid Layer. Modify the values of the keyframes for both 3D Stroke and Shine on the duplicated layer.

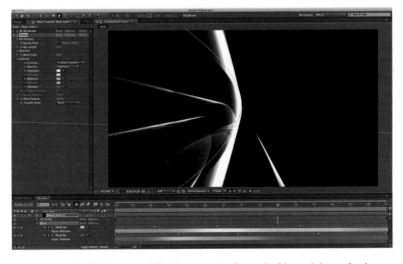

**Figure 8.44** The Midtones and Shadows are keyframed with a rainbow of colors. Screenshot: Michele Yamazaki.

**Figure 8.45** The example on top is in 8 bpc. Notice the banding in the purple area. The example on the bottom is 16 bpc and there is no banding. Screenshot: Michele Yamazaki.

10. If banding is a problem, set the project to 16 bpc. To do this, at the bottom of the Project panel, click on the 8 bpc button to open Project Settings. Under Color Settings > Depth, select the 16 bits per channel setting. The shortcut is to Option+click (Alt+click) on the 8 bpc button at the bottom of the Project panel; this will toggle through the available color depth options. (Figure 8.45.)

# GENERATING 3D ELEMENTS IN AFTER EFFECTS

When one thinks of 3D, several things come to mind, including funny glasses. However, in the world of After Effects and 2D video footage, 3D means something completely different. 3D elements within After Effects deal with objects and shapes in 3D space within a 2D world. In other words, while the object can be rotated and positioned in 3D space, the layer itself remains a 2D layer with no thickness or depth (often referred to as a "postcard in space"). Camera positions with extruded and beveled edges will help to simulate 3D in a 2D space.

The use of 3D objects is frequently found in text and logos. EPS or EPS vector logos, usually from Illustrator, can start life as a flat image and become extruded 3D with depth and beveled edges with the help of a plug-in.

## Creating Unique Structures in Zaxwerks 3D Invigorator by Joe Mason

Figure 9.1 The final structure. Screenshot: Joe Mason.

In this tutorial, I'll show you how to create unique structures or shapes in Zaxwerks 3D Invigorator. I had always wanted to create shapes or structures similar to those that I had seen on

**Figure 9.2** A unique custom structure from 3D Invigorator. Screenshot: Joe Mason.

different network opens. With a little imagination, you can create just about any shape using Zaxwerks plug-ins. This software is fast and easy to use, and can add a great deal to your motion graphics toolkit. We'll be alternating between different wireframes and shiny solid materials to create a look that will separate your work from others'.

**Third-party plug-ins needed:**

• Zaxwerks 3D Invigorator

1. Make a new Composition that is 960 × 540 pixels, 20 seconds in duration.
2. Create a new solid (Layer > New > Solid), and name it "Zax Layer". Make the new solid the same size as the comp.
3. Apply Zaxwerks 3D Invigorator to the solid (Effect > Zaxwerks > 3D Invigorator). In the popup window for 3D Invigorator, choose Create a New Scene. (Figure 9.3.)

One of the great features of Zaxwerks 3D Invigorator or Zaxwerks ProAnimator is that you can create your own shapes either within the plug-in or in Adobe Illustrator, and then modify and tweak it until it creates a unique, attention-grabbing object or structure. In this case, I simply created a segmented circle (dashes) in Adobe Illustrator. If you create shapes in Illustrator, be sure to save as an .ai file, with compression turned off.

4. In After Effects, go to the Effect Controls panel of the Zax Layer, and click on the red ball. This will open up the Invigorator Set-Up window.
5. Go to Object Mode, and select Open Illustrator File. (Figure 9.4.)
6. Select the .ai file that you have created, and it will appear in your Invigorator Set-Up window. (Figure 9.5.)

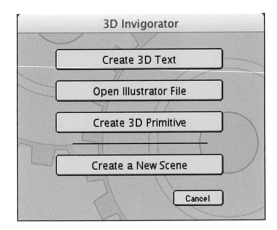

**Figure 9.3** The 3D Invigorator popup window. We'll choose Create a New Scene. Screenshot: Joe Mason.

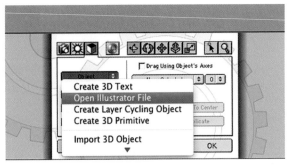

**Figure 9.4** Object Mode with Open Illustrator File selected. Screenshot: Joe Mason.

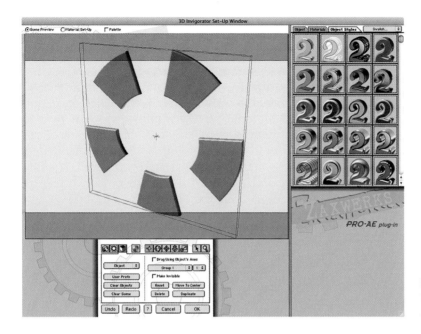

**Figure 9.5** Offsetting the shape in 3D Invigorator. Screenshot: Joe Mason.

7. Our object is fairly flat and lifeless right now. So we need to modify it in order to give it the depth and dimension that it needs to look great in 3D. In the upper right corner of the Invigorator Set-Up window, select the Object tab. This will open up the settings so that we can modify our object. Change the Depth Value to 500 to create an elongated structure. Set the Edge Scale to –13, and the Edge Offset to –2, so they taper inward slightly in the middle. (Figure 9.6.)

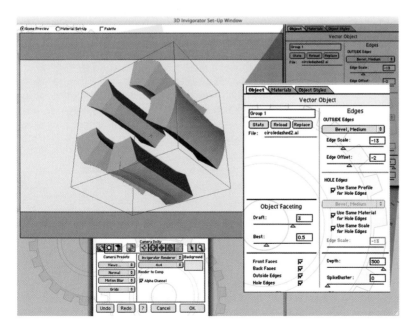

**Figure 9.6** Extruding Depth in 3D Invigorator, with the Vector Object box zoomed in. Screenshot: Joe Mason.

8. Next, we need to modify the edges of our object. In the same object tab, you can click on the Outside Edges pulldown menu and see many choices. I chose Special Purpose > Deco 2. Now you'll see some interesting pleats or edges that will start to give our structure a unique look. (Figure 9.7.)

9. Next to the Object tab is the Materials tab. Click on it, and then open the Material Set-Up window, which is next to the Scene Preview window. This shows us a top view of our object. We can now start assigning materials to each edge. I've chosen three materials that seem to work well. The first is a shiny blue material with a custom reflective texture map. I've made it a Wireframe Material by clicking on Wireframe in the Materials tab. (Figure 9.8.).

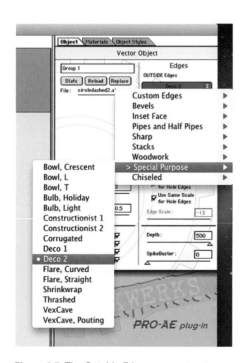

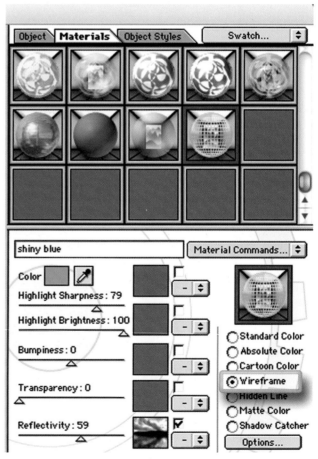

Figure 9.7 The Outside Edges menu structure in 3D Invigorator. Screenshot: Joe Mason.

Figure 9.8 The Materials tab with Wireframe selected. Screenshot: Joe Mason.

10. The second material is a shiny gold wireframe, with a Transparency value of 38 and using the Punchy Reflections material swatch that is included with the plug-in. The Reflectivity value for this material is 80. The third material is similar, only it is solid instead of wireframe, and blue in color. I gave it a Transparency value of 41 and used the Punchy Reflections material swatch again. The Reflectivity value is 63. (Figure 9.9.)

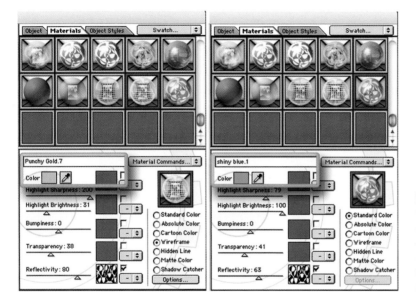

**Figure 9.9** The Materials tab. On the left, the Punchy Gold.7 color is selected. On the right, Shiny Blue.1 is chosen. Both use the Punch Reflections material swatch. Screenshot: Joe Mason.

11. Next we need to assign our materials to the edges (each surface) of our object. While in the Material Set-Up window, drag each material swatch down into the object's Material Assignments. Then click on the red arrowhead. Start clicking on each intersection or corner of the object. This assigns a green number to each surface. Alternate the green numbers in numeric order all along the edge of the object. By alternating materials along the surfaces of the object, we get an interesting look. It's important to remember to put a wireframe material on the front and back surfaces, so that the viewer can see through the object to the other surfaces. (Figure 9.10.)

12. The more detailed your object is, the better it will look in a close-up camera shot. Press OK in the Invigorator Set-Up window and After Effects will render a frame of our object, and we can see how it looks. (Figure 9.11.)

**Finishing touches:** This gives you an idea of how to create unique structures, which can be used for opens, logo animations, or anything else to grab the viewer's attention. From this point,

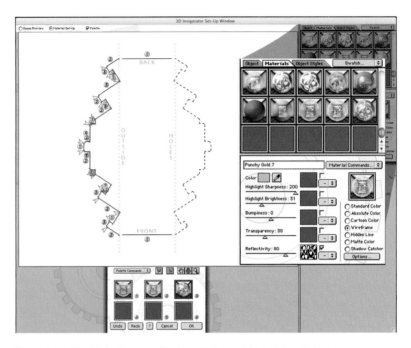

**Figure 9.10** The 3D Invigorator Set-Up window, with the Materials palette zoomed in. Screenshot: Joe Mason.

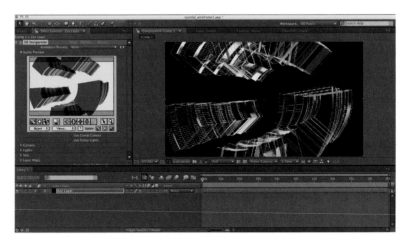

**Figure 9.11** The unique structures from 3D Invigorator, rendered in After Effects. Screenshot: Joe Mason.

you can do several things. I typically render out three or four camera moves in a scene, then edit them together to form an open or sequence. Obviously you can add elements to the scene such as a company logo or whatever else would be appropriate. You can add **Trapcode Shine ($99)** to enhance the look, and maybe drop in some background elements.

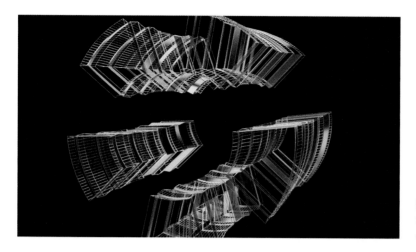

Figure 9.12 The final look of the unique structures. Screenshot: Joe Mason.

## Gnarly Man-Eating Devil Flowers with Zaxwerks 3D Serpentine

3D Serpentine isn't the most intuitive plug-in, but what it produces is pretty amazing and there's nothing else on the market like it. I'll go through a pretty basic procedure to get you started with the plug-in and go over a few of the features. We'll use a Cross Section shape to give the line a flower shape as it grows. We'll add a gradient as a color map for the stem of the flower and a bump map to give it some creepy texture. These are not pretty flowers but gnarly, man-eating devil flowers.

Figure 9.13 Evil looking flowers created with Zaxwerks 3D Serpentine. Footage: Michele Yamazaki.

3D Serpentine gets its thickness and positioning of path information from a 3D Solid layer, so that's where we'll start. This tutorial will also explore working with Custom Shapes in Photoshop, where we'll acquire the flower shape.

*The project file is included on this book's DVD in the 3D Serpentine Flower folder.* You'll need texture.tif, included in the folder, for this project if you're starting from scratch.

**Third-party plug-ins needed:**

- Zaxwerks 3D Serpentine

  1. Make a new Composition using the HDTV 1080 29.97 preset, 5 seconds in duration, called Flower comp. Make the background color light blue.

  2. Create a new solid, 50 × 50 and white. Name it "Path 1".

  3. Make the layer 3D by enabling the 3D Layer Switch in the Timeline panel. At the first frame, drag the position of the square straight down to the center bottom of the screen. Go to 4:00 and position the square somewhere in the top half of the screen.

  4. Go to the first frame and set a keyframe for Z Rotation with a value of 0x 0.0°. Go to 4:00 and set a value of 3x 0.0° for Z Rotation. This will make the path twist as it grows.

  5. We're going to separate dimensions for positions so that they're easier to control. This is a new feature added in After Effects CS4 and is something that a lot of people still don't realize they can do with the program. This will be easier to see with multiple views set up. (Figure 9.14.)

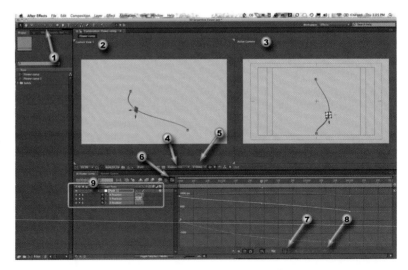

**Figure 9.14** Separating dimensions and viewing in multiple views will help you control the path. 1. Camera Tools; 2. Custom View panel; 3. Active Camera view; 4. 3D View popup; 5. Selection of 2 Views – Horizontal; 6. Graph Editor button; 7. Separate Dimensions button; 8. Easy Ease button (grayed out); 9. A solid layer with the X Position, Y Position, and Z Position parameters separated. Footage: Michele Yamazaki.

  6. At the bottom of the Composition panel, make sure the 3D View Setup is set to Active Camera. To the right of that Camera choose, select 2 Views – Horizontal for Select View Layout. Click on the new view and set it to Custom View 1. This will allow you to position the view as you like with the Camera Tools. This is just a view, not an active camera, so it's for monitoring only. Set the Magnification popup in the lower left corner of the Comp panel to Fit up to 100%.

7. Use the Camera Tools to position the camera onscreen so that you can see another angle on the path. If you cannot see the path, choose your layer in the timeline. Tap the M key to bring up the Mask path.

8. Tap the P key to bring up Position keyframes, and then click the Graph Editor button at the top of the timeline. The timeline should now have one diagonal line through it if you have Position selected.

9. Click on the word Position to select all keyframes (they will turn yellow when selected). At the bottom of the Graph Editor click the Easy Ease button. This will be grayed out if the keyframes are not selected. Your Position line should now be curved.

10. Click the Separate Dimensions button at the bottom of the timeline. You should now see X Position, Y Position, and Z Position. If you do not, tap the P key to bring them up. Select each individually to see the graphs for each dimension.

11. Go to 2:00 and adjust the positions for X, Y, and Z. Drag any or all of the Position parameters to give them some curve. Keep an eye on both Composition panels so that nothing gets too far out of whack. The idea is to make a smooth curved path that moves in 3D space. Select Position X, Y, and Z individual and adjust the Bezier curves. Make sure the path curves are smooth by dragging the Bezier handles. (Figure 9.15.)

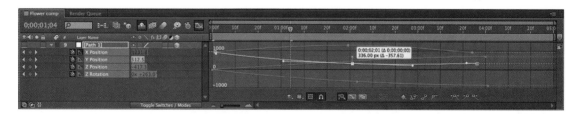

12. Once you are happy with your path, duplicate the layer. Open the Graph Editor and repeat. Keep the first keyframes close together and as the motion paths get toward the top, spread them out, like flowers in a bouquet. Repeat until you have 5 solids with different motion paths that fall open as they rise. Clearly name the layers Path 1, Path 2, Path 3, Path 4, and Path 5. Rotate the camera on the Custom View anytime you need to see a different perspective.

13. Drag the keyframes back or forth by a few frames so that all of the movement doesn't happen at exactly the same frame for each path. You may find this easier to do in the regular timeline, so click the Graph Editor button again to go back to the timeline. (Figure 9.16.)

**Figure 9.15** The Graph Editor with parameters selected. A point on the Y Position graph line (green) is being dragged and the Bezier handles are visible. Footage: Michele Yamazaki.

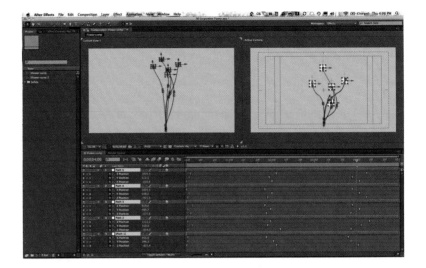

**Figure 9.16** The paths of the five solid layers with the position keyframes offset slightly. Footage: Michele Yamazaki.

Before creating the 3D Serpentine effect, let's go to Photoshop and prepare the flower shape, which will be used as the Cross Section Shape in 3D Serpentine. Figure 9.17 shows a reference image in Photoshop, if you're not familiar with the tools I am describing.

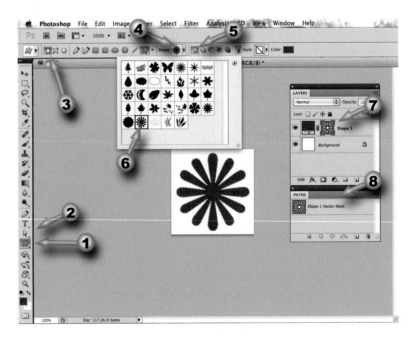

**Figure 9.17** Working with the Flower 7 shape in Photoshop. 1. Custom Shape tool in the toolbar; 2. Direct Selection tool; 3. Shape Layers; 4. Shape (with Flower 7 selected); 5. Create New Shape layer; 6. Shape presets menu (with Flower 7 selected); 7. Layers palette (with Flower 7 on the layer); 8. Paths (with Flower 7 Vector Mask). Footage: Michele Yamazaki.

14. Open Photoshop and create a new document that is 50×50 pixels. Press and hold down the Rectangle tool in the toolbar to pop out a menu of shape options, and select the Custom Shape tool. On the Application bar at the top

of the screen, open the Shape presets first then click on the small arrow to select Nature from the pulldown menu. Click the Append button to add the shapes to the existing set. Choose Flower 7, then click and drag the mouse across the canvas to draw the shape. Hold down the shift key as you drag to keep the square aspect ratio. Center the flower and then use the Direct Selection tool to select the middle dot. Just select a single point and then click the delete key twice—once to delete the point you selected and again to delete the entire center path. (Figure 9.18.)

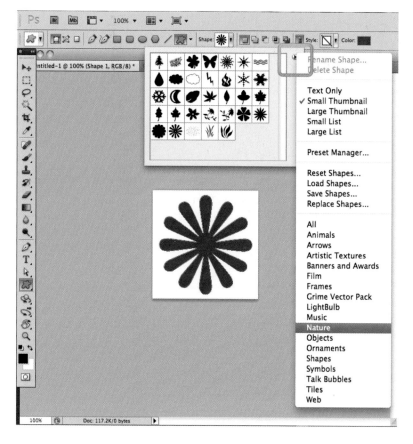

Figure 9.18 The Shapes preset menu in Photoshop. Footage: Michele Yamazaki.

15. Option (Alt) + click any point to select all the points in the flower vector path. Alternately, switch to the Path Selection tool and select the path. Copy the vector points to your clipboard.

16. Back in After Effects, create a new red Solid called Flower, $50 \times 50$. The only reason to make it red is so that it's easy to find quickly in the timeline. Paste the flower vector path on the layer. It will show up as a mask. (Figure 9.19.)

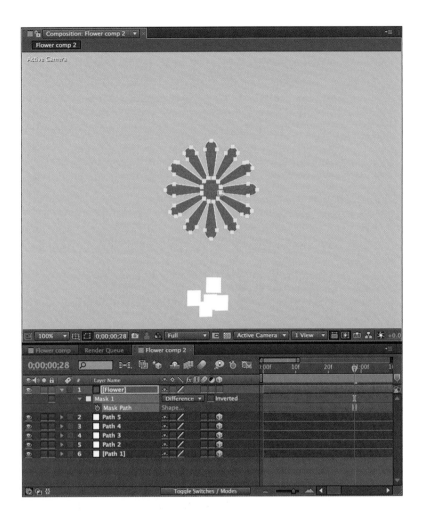

**Figure 9.19** The Flower mask pasted on a red Solid. Footage: Michele Yamazaki.

17. Turn off the visibility for the Flower layer, as well as Path 1, 2, 3, 4, and 5. Your Composition panel should appear empty.
18. Add a New Solid (comp sized) and make it green so that it is easy to find in the timeline with just a quick glance. Name the Solid layer "3D Serpentine".
19. Apply 3D Serpentine to this solid (Effects > Zaxwerks > 3D Serpentine). At the top of the Effect Controls panel, under Serpent 1(Globals) set Extrude Path to Path 1. You should now see a blue extruded path. (Figure 9.20.)
20. Add a new camera, frame the path as you see fit, and then set keyframes at the beginning and end so that the camera pans, tilts, and zooms slightly.

Before we form the flower, let's make a color map to give the stems varied color. Nothing says evil like splotchy, uneven color! We will also bring in a bump map to give the body and flower head a rough, creepy texture. (Figure 9.21.)

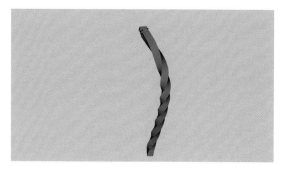

**Figure 9.20**  The 3D Serpentine default extrusion, applied to Path 1. Footage: Michele Yamazaki.

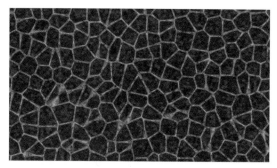

**Figure 9.21**  This texture, generated with Boris Continuum Complete BCC Reptilian, is called texture.tif and is included on the DVD in the 3D Serpentine Flower folder. Footage: Michele Yamazaki.

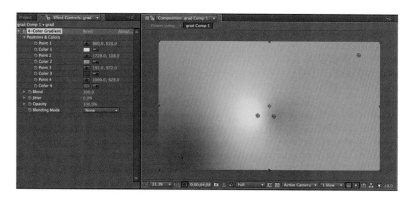

**Figure 9.22**  A comp with 4-Color Gradient applied to it will be used as the Body Color Map. Footage: Michele Yamazaki.

21. Create a new comp using the HDTV 1080 29.97 preset, 5 seconds in duration and name it "Grad Comp". Apply 4-Color Gradient (Effects > Generate > 4-Color Gradient). Set the points with shades of yellowish-green. Close this comp when you're finished setting up the gradient. (Figure 9.22.)

22. Drag texture.tif and Grad Comp into the Flower comp. Turn off the visibility for texture.tif, but leave Grad Comp visible. Make sure they are both at the bottom of the layer stack. We'll be using both of these layers in the 3D Serpentine effect.

23. In the Effect Controls panel for 3D Serpentine, set the following (Figure 9.23):
    - **Cross Section Shape:** Use Cross Section Layer
    - **Cross Section Layer:** Flower
    - **Auto Orientation:** None
    - **Head End Cap:** Domed
    - **Head End Cap Size:** 436
    - **Head End Cap Offset:** 0
    - **Color > Body Color > Body Color Map:** Grad Comp
    - **Color > Head Color:** Red

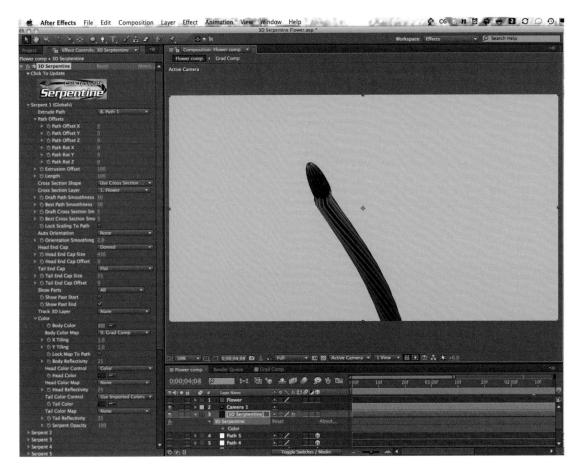

**Figure 9.23** The end of the path is shaped with the Flower Cross Section Shape and colored red. The body is colored with a Color Map from a gradient.
Footage: Michele Yamazaki.

24. For Serpent 2, 3, 4, and 5, choose the corresponding path for Extrude Path. If you would like all of your flowers to be red, then you are all set. If you'd like to make them other colors, uncheck Use Globals and repeat the process of setting the colors. If Globals is checked you will not be able to change flower color.

25. At the bottom of the Effect Controls panel for 3D Serpentine, set the following:
    - **Specular Brightness:** 100
    - **Bump Map:** Texture
    - **Bump Height:** 100

Play the animations through. If any of your paths are looking a little funky, you can try smoothing them out. Click the Update button to get Serpentine to see the new path. I asked Zax Dow of Zaxwerks about this and he explained that plug-ins cannot talk to After Effects in a two-way loop so it requires the user to click an Update Button. To get your flowers to grow a bit more, keyframe Extrusion Offset under Serpent 1.

Figure 9.24  The final render of the creepy flowers. Footage: Michele Yamazaki.

There's a button at the bottom of the Effect Controls panel to go directly to Online Docs at Zaxwerks' website, so if you want to learn about other features of 3D Serpentine, click and go!

## AN INTERVIEW WITH ZAX DOW ABOUT 3D

I asked Zax Dow, president of Zaxwerks, a few questions about working with a 3D application versus his plug-ins, a few of which you've already been introduced to earlier in this chapter. He also gave me a quick tutorial to get new users started with **Zaxwerks ProAnimator** ($649).

**Michele Yamazaki: Why would someone choose the ProAnimator plug-in for After Effects over a full-blown 3D application?**

**Zax Dow:** The world is 3D. You can't avoid it. If you are doing video or graphics for a living you have to have some kind of a 3D tool in your toolbox or else you'll start losing jobs to someone who does. After Effects has 3D layers but they're limited to postcards in space. So the question becomes how much time do you have to devote to learning a 3D program? A typical 3D program has thousands of controls and can take months to learn how to use. And yet, to get work you have to have some kind of 3D capability.

The modeling part is usually the slowest thing in 3D work but with ProAnimator it's automatic. Also, the 3D is right inside the After Effects Composition panel so you never have to leave AE.

**Michele: What do most people use ProAnimator for?**

**Zax:** ProAnimator is specialized for text and logo work, the kind of 3D graphics you'll get paid for the quickest, and can help upgrade your image.

**Michele: Can you explain the timeline in ProAnimator?**

**Zax:** ProAnimator doesn't use the After Effects timeline. Instead it has its own timeline that is much easer to use and can control all of these objects from a single track. Click the Animation Workspace button to switch to the animation controls.

**Michele: Thanks for putting together the tutorial, Zax!**

**Figure 9.25** Solid settings for the project. Screenshot: Zax Dow.

# Jumping into 3D the Painless Way by Zax Dow of Zaxwerks

**Third-party plug-ins needed:**

- Zaxwerks ProAnimator
    1. Inside After Effects create a Composition (Composition > New Composition.) Add a Camera (Layer > New > Camera) and then a Solid (Layer > New > Solid). Make sure the Solid is the same size as your Comp and click OK. (Figure 9.25.)
    2. Next, add the ProAnimator to the Solid (Effects > Zaxwerks > ProAnimator). (Figure 9.26.)
    3. You'll see an options window asking you decide whether to create 3D text, turn an Adobe Illustrator file into instant 3D objects, or do other things. Click on the Create 3D Text button. (Figure 9.27.)
    4. A text window will open, so let's type something. Type "Plug-in with After Effects". The width is a little large so select it and set the Size to 50. Once that's done, select the text and choose a font. (Figure 9.28.)

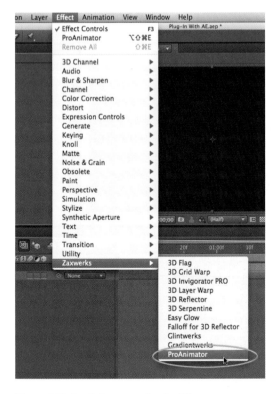

**Figure 9.26** ProAnimator under the Effects menu. Screenshot: Zax Dow.

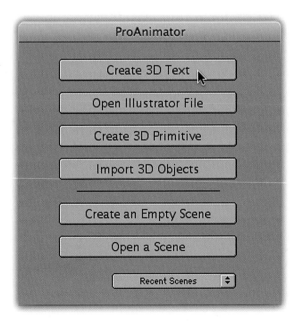

**Figure 9.27** The ProAnimator popup window. Screenshot: Zax Dow.

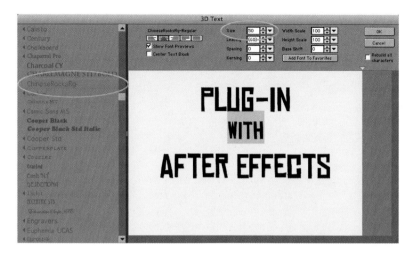

**Figure 9.28** Type "Plug-in with After Effects" in the 3D text window. Screenshot: Zax Dow.

5. Since you're working in 3D, a lot of the coolness of a 3D object comes from the edge bevels you apply to the lettering. Bevels tend to fatten things up, so if you have a choice, pick a thinner font at this stage.

6. The font used for this book title is already bold, so applying thick bevels will make the edges overlap. I'll show you how to handle this in a little bit.

7. Click the OK button to close the Text window and you can see that the 3D model is already extruded and beveled. (Figure 9.29.)

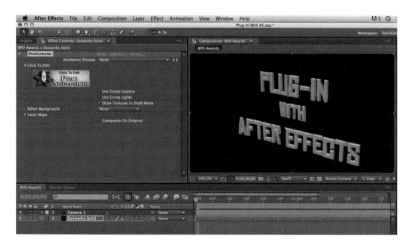

**Figure 9.29** The default rendered text. Screenshot: Zax Dow.

8. Next is setting the look of the 3D objects. Click ProAnimator's Click To Edit button to open up the main interface. (Figure 9.30.)

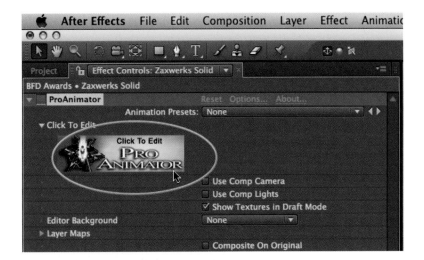

Figure 9.30 The Click to Edit
button in the Effect Controls
Panel. Screenshot: Zax Dow.

Figure 9.31 The Materials
workspace button. Screenshot:
Zax Dow.

9. Once inside, click the Materials workspace button so you'll see the same screen layout as you see in the picture here. (Figure 9.31.)

10. You can set the depth, bevels, and colors separately if you want, but the real power is in using Object Styles. An Object Style is like a text style but in 3D, so it gives you the bevel type, thickness, splits the object into surface areas, and applies materials all with one click. Choose one from the Object Styles Swatches panel. I'll use the one called Layered Metal. It uses three different materials to give the letters a

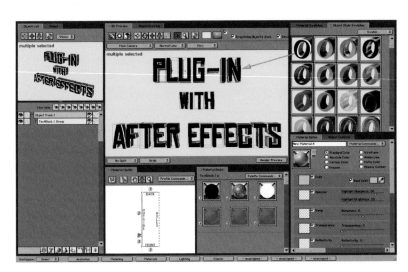

Figure 9.32 Click on an Object
Styles Swatch to apply it to the
text. Screenshot: Zax Dow.

cool look and it doesn't fatten up the letters, so the logo police will be happy. Drag it from the bin and drop it onto the selected objects. (Figure 9.32.)

11. Click the Animation button to animate. (Figure 9.33.).

**Figure 9.33** The Animation button in the ProAnimator interface. Screenshot: Zax Dow.

12. You can see in the Object List that this text block was placed into Object Track 1 by default. That's fine. We'll just leave it there. What we'll do next is select an Object Animation preset. An animation preset is like an Object Style for animations. It sets the positions, keyframes, motion paths, and timings for an entire track in one little preset. ProAnimator comes with lots of these. They're a great place to get started and they're easy to change. Select the one called Crazy Swing (Animation Timeline Panel > Object Animations > Crazy Swing). (Figure 9.34.)

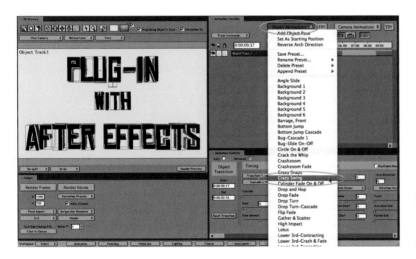

**Figure 9.34.** Crazy Swing is selected in the Object Animation presets. Screenshot: Zax Dow.

13. As soon as we select an Object Animation preset, the program sets up poses and transitions, and the animation starts playing in real time. Watching it play, you can see everything sitting a little low on the screen. That's because this animation wasn't made to fit a three-line title. To fix it, tap the spacebar on your keyboard to stop the playback, then drag the yellow time thumb so it's above the dark blue bar at about 4.5 seconds. This is your money shot where the full title is presented. (Figure 9.35.)

14. Now, go to the 3D Preview panel and select the Camera button and the Track tool. (Figure 9.36.)

**Figure 9.35** The Animation Timeline in ProAnimator. Screenshot: Zax Dow.

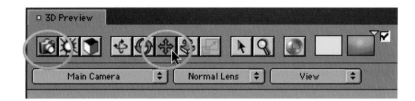

**Figure 9.36** The 3D Preview panel. The yellow circle on the left is highlighting the camera button and the circle on the right shows the track tool. Screenshot: Zax Dow.

**15.** In the 3D window, click and drag upward to center the title. When you have it where you like it, release the mouse and tap the spacebar to restart the playback. Now everything fits a little better. (Figure 9.37.)

**Figure 9.37** Position the title in the center by clicking and dragging it into position. Screenshot: Zax Dow

**16.** With that done we're ready to make the rest of your comp. Click the OK button to exit back to After Effects. Now as you scrub through your After Effects timeline you'll see the animation you created inside ProAnimator. This animation plays as an element on a single After Effects layer so you can do anything you want with the rest of your comp. (Figure 9.38.)

Figure 9.38 The ProAnimator animation in an after effects comp. Screenshot: Zax Dow.

So there you go—a very fast and very easy way to make that jump into profitable 3D work.

### FURTHER READING: REAL OR FAKE 3D?

Boris Continuum Complete 3D Objects and Zaxwerks plug-ins are plug-ins that generate 3D and can use the 3D Camera and Lights. They're not really 3D but 2D, and can't interact with "the real 3D" layers in AE (those with the 3D Layer switch enabled). They use their own 3D renderer to render objects, and then send the render back to After Effects as a 2D layer for compositing. This topic is covered in depth in Chris and Trish Meyer's book *Creating Motion Graphics with After Effects* (5th Edition) in the chapter titled "Parallel Worlds."

## Create a Spooky 3D B-Movie Title with Boris Continuum Complete 3D Extruded Text

**Boris Continuum Complete 3D Objects** is an easy way to create real 3D elements in After Effects—not just flat postcards moving through 3D space. It works right in After Effects' native interface and is OpenGL hardware accelerated so it's fast. It also works with the camera and lights within After Effects so the Boris 3D objects can appear integrated with your regular 3D layers. However, there are a few caveats with compositing (see the sidebar "Real or Fake 3D?" in the previous section for more details).

In this tutorial we'll create a fully extruded B-movie title that auto-animates and has a bumpy texture. We'll create a custom bevel on the edge and add BCC Film Damage to give it an old

**Figure 9.39** A frame from the final render of Siege of the Bedbugs, created with Boris Continuum Complete 3D Extruded Text, BCC Film Damage, and BCC Wood Planks. Footage: Michele Yamazaki.

drive-in movie look. We'll be depending on a lot of the presets, while still making the title completely unique. *The project files are included in the BCC 3D Objects—Bedbugs folder.*

**Third-party plug-ins needed:**

- Boris Continuum Complete
  1. Make a new Composition using the HDTV 1080 29.97 preset, 5 seconds in duration with a beige background. Name it "Siege of the Bedbugs".
  2. Go to Layer > New Solid (Comp Sized) and name the Solid layer "Siege".
  3. Apply BCC Extruded Text to the Siege layer (Effects > BCC 3D Objects > BCC Extruded Text). When the Type window comes up, type "Siege of the Bedbugs" in 96 pt. Buffied font, centered. Click Apply. (Figure 9.40.)
  4. To get started quickly, use the ArcJitter.bap preset. This preset gives a bit more style to the text, gives it a slight rotation, and a bit of jitter. When the Animated Preset Options dialog box comes up, choose Preserve Timing and First Frame.
  5. Play the animation through a few times to get a feel for the preset. The text movement is good but the type needs to be larger at the end of the animation. Go to the first frame. Twirl down TRANSFORMATIONS in the Effect Controls and set keyframes for Scale X and Scale Y with a value of 100. Jump to 3:20 and set the values of both Scale X and Scale Y to 130.
  6. To set the look of the Extrusion, use the metal-side ridges. bcp preset for Extrusion Style. Twirl down EXTRUSION and choose the raised trim 1.bcp preset for Bevel Saved Preset.
  7. We'll create our own custom bevel with a Host Path. Select the Pen tool and draw a backward S. Under EXTRUSION, set

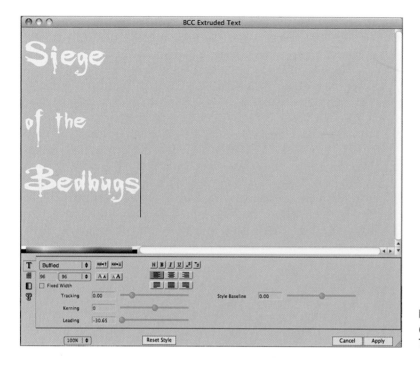

**Figure 9.40**  The window for entering text in BCC Extruded Text. Footage: Michele Yamazaki.

Side Style to Host Path. In the pulldown menu for Side Host Path choose Mask 1. Use the Selection tool to pull points around, and watch as the bevel automatically updates. Adjust the path until you like the look. Note: If your path crosses over itself, it will have unpredictable effects on the extrusion. Twirl EXTRUSION closed. (Figure 9.41.)

8. Set Ambient Intensity to 72.00 to get some reflection along the sides.

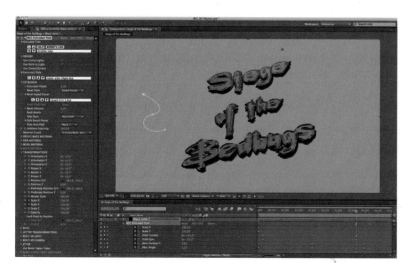

**Figure 9.41**  Draw a backward S-shaped mask and use it as the Side Style. Footage: Michele Yamazaki.

9. Twirl open FRONT/BACK MATERIAL and choose color-blue plastic.bcp under Material Preset. For Front Texture File, choose stone-BlackStar.jpg. Set the Front Bump file to stone-Marbled Crystal.jpg and the Bump Strength to 100. We are not going for subtle! Twirl FRONT/BACK MATERIAL closed. (Figure 9.42.)

10. Twirl SIDE MATERIAL open. Choose stone-marble-bcp for the Material Preset. Twirl SIDE MATERIAL closed.

11. Twirl BEVEL MATERIAL and choose Alt Default.bcp for the Material Preset. Set the Ambient Light color to black. Twirl BEVEL MATERIAL closed. (Figure 9.43.)

We'll add a wood plank background, made very large to give the feeling of tiny bugs on the floor. We'll also add light to give it a vignette, and add a drop shadow. The After Effects Lights

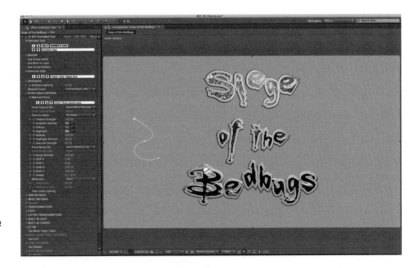

**Figure 9.42** FRONT/BACK MATERIAL settings give texture and color to the front. Footage: Michele Yamazaki.

**Figure 9.43** SIDE MATERIAL and BEVEL MATERIAL settings. Footage: Michele Yamazaki.

**Figure 9.44** A close-up of the side view of the bevel. Footage: Michele Yamazaki.

and Camera work fine with BCC 3D Objects if the check box is checked at the top of the Effect Controls panel, but the Boris title will not cast a 3D shadow on regular layers (see the sidebar "Real or Fake 3D?" on page 297 for the explanation). We'll apply the Drop Shadow effect as a workaround. Lastly, we'll finish the look off with BCC Film Damage to give it the old film look.

Make sure that Use Comp Lights and Use Built-in Light are both checked the top of BCC Extruded Text in the Effect Controls panel.

12. Create a new solid, the same size as the comp and drag it below the text. Check the 3D Layer box in the Timeline panel so that it will accept Lights. Apply Boris Continuum Complete BCC Wooden Planks (Effects > BCC Generators > BCC Wooden Planks). Set the Plank Length to 1.50 and the Plank Width to 0.50. (Figure 9.45.)

**Figure 9.45** BCC Wooden Planks, made really large, from a bug's perspective. Footage: Michele Yamazaki.

13. Add an Adjustment Layer on top of both layers. Apply BCC Film Damage (Effects > BCC Effects > BCC Film Damage). Use the preset oldBWIncBright.bcp.
14. Add a Spot Light with the Intensity at 100%, the Cone Angle at 90°, and the Cone Feather at 50%. Set the Color to White. Position the light so that there is shadowing around the edges of the background but the light is not directly center. (Figure 9.46.)
15. Select the Text layer and apply BCC Drop Shadow (Effects > BCC Effects > BCC Drop Shadow). Change the Shadow Distance to 100.

**Figure 9.46** BCC Film Damage, a spot light, and BCC Drop Shadow finish the title. Footage: Michele Yamazaki.

## Animated Cables with Trapcode 3D Stroke

Several years ago while working at Postworks, a client asked me to create eye candy for Dow Cable and Wire for a tradeshow video monitor. There would be no audio to support the video. Now,

**Figure 9.47** The final animated cable. Footage: Michele Yamazaki.

wires are not exactly the most interesting thing in the world, but with the help of Trapcode 3D Stroke, I was able to create a fun two-minute loop of eye-catching content. This tutorial covers the basic technique I used to give the stroke depth.

*The project is included on this book's DVD and is in the 3D Stroke Wire folder.*

**Third-party plug-ins needed:**

• Trapcode 3D Stroke

1. Make a new Composition with the HDTV 1080 29.97 preset with a 95% white background and 10 seconds in duration, and name it "Wire Comp".

2. Create a new solid, the same size as your composition, and name it "Wire". Color is not important.

3. With the Wire solid selected, select the Pen tool and create a smooth mask path on your Wire solid. Enable the Rotobezier checkbox to auto-smooth your path. You want the path to not be too complex but have a bit of curve and have both ends of the path hanging offscreen so you will not see the ends once the stroke is applied. (Figure 9.48.)

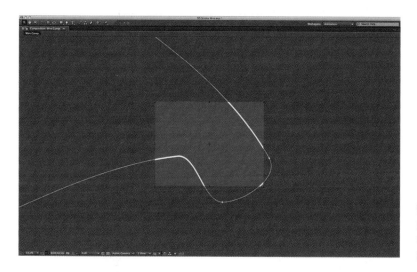

**Figure 9.48** The stroked mask path with the ends of the path outside of the Composition panel. Footage: Michele Yamazaki.

4. Apply 3D Stroke to the Wire solid (Effect > Trapcode > 3D Stroke). A white stroke will appear on your path. If your background is slightly off-white you should be able to see it. In the 3D Stroke Effect Controls panel, change the Color to Royal Blue. Increase Thickness to about 30 to fatten up the cable. (Figure 9.49.)

5. Add a Camera (Layer > New > Camera) and choose the 35mm preset. Use the Camera Tools to position your camera. Keyframe the camera with a short pan. In 3D Stroke's Effect Controls panel, under Camera, enable the Comp Camera

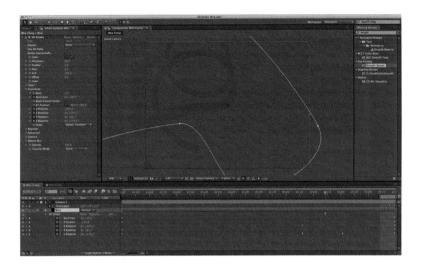

**Figure 9.49** The stroked path in blue and thickened. Footage: Michele Yamazaki.

box. You may not even use the camera but it is nice to be able to move both the wire layers together in the next few steps.

6. Under Transform in the 3D Stroke settings, keyframe Bend and Bend Axis until you get some interesting movement. If you want to hide the ends of your cable just drag the path further out. Also, keyframe the X, Y, and Z Rotation and Positions as you feel necessary. Apply Easy Ease or use the speed graph to get smooth movement on your wire. Don't worry if the cable looks too big and flat onscreen. We will be giving it some depth in the next step. (Figure 9.50.)

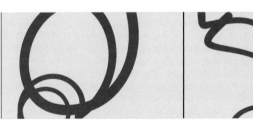

**Figure 9.50** Bend and Position are keyframed to give the cable interesting shape and movement. Footage: Michele Yamazaki.

7. Once you are happy with the movement of your wire, duplicate the Wire layer. The only settings you need to change on the top layer's 3D Stroke Effect are the color—make it a lighter blue; the Thickness—take it to about 20; and the Feather—crank it to 100.

8. If you need to go back and change the position and movement of the wire, you must change both layers. First try moving the camera.

**Finishing touch**: Put something nice in the background—perhaps a gradient or some ethereal looking background that will really show off your cable.

**Figure 9.51** The Stroke has been duplicated and the top layer feathered and lightened to give the impression of a three-dimensional cable. Footage: Michele Yamazaki.

# Extruding Mountains from a 2D Picture of the Earth with an Elevation Map and Digieffects FreeForm or FreeForm 3D Displacer by Dustin Klein

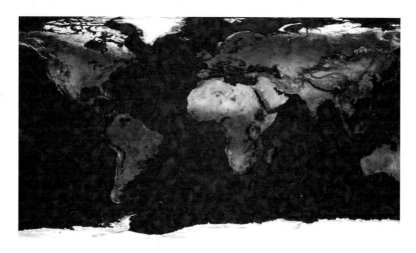

**Figure 9.52** The final earth elevation. Footage: NASA, Dustin Klein.

This tutorial will show you how to take a two dimensional picture of the earth and give it real three-dimensional topographical shape with Digieffects FreeForm 3D Displacer or Digieffects FreeForm. FreeForm ships with After Effects CS5, but if you haven't yet upgraded, FreeForm can be purchased for $299 or 3D Displacer for $99. Digieffects sold FreeForm from 2009 to May 2011, but it is now developed and sold only by Mettle.com. FreeForm 3D Displacer is one of three portions of FreeForm and is available à la carte. This tutorial uses FreeForm but the effect will work equally as well with FreeForm 3D Displacer.

We will use a grayscale topographical elevation map as a displacement map to tell 3D Displacer how to change the flat earth projection to one with extruded mountains and valleys, keyframed so that the mountains grow from the earth. Afterwards, we will use some solid layers with Fractal Noise, Blending Modes, and lowered transparency to generate the clouds above the earth.

*Project files are included on this book's DVD in the FreeForm Earth folder.*

## FURTHER READING

Lutz Albrecht has a very deep discussion of grayscale maps, which is included as bonus material on this book's DVD.

**Figure 9.53** *Top:* Colored version of the map. *Bottom:* The displacement layer. The images used for this tutorial were taken from the Blue Marble Collection on NASA's Visible Earth website (*http://bit.ly/nasablue*). Footage: NASA.

**Third-party plug-ins needed:**
- Digieffects FreeForm AE (ships with After Effects CS5 and CS5.5)
  1. Import both the colored earth image and the black and white earth elevation map into the project.

**2.** Create a new composition using the HDTV 1080 29.97 preset, 5 seconds in duration and name it "FreeForm Earth". Drag both earth images into this comp, placing the color version on top and turning off the visibility of the black and white image by clicking the eyeball switch in the Timeline panel. We don't need it except for the way that it's referenced in the FreeForm effect. (Figure 9.54.)

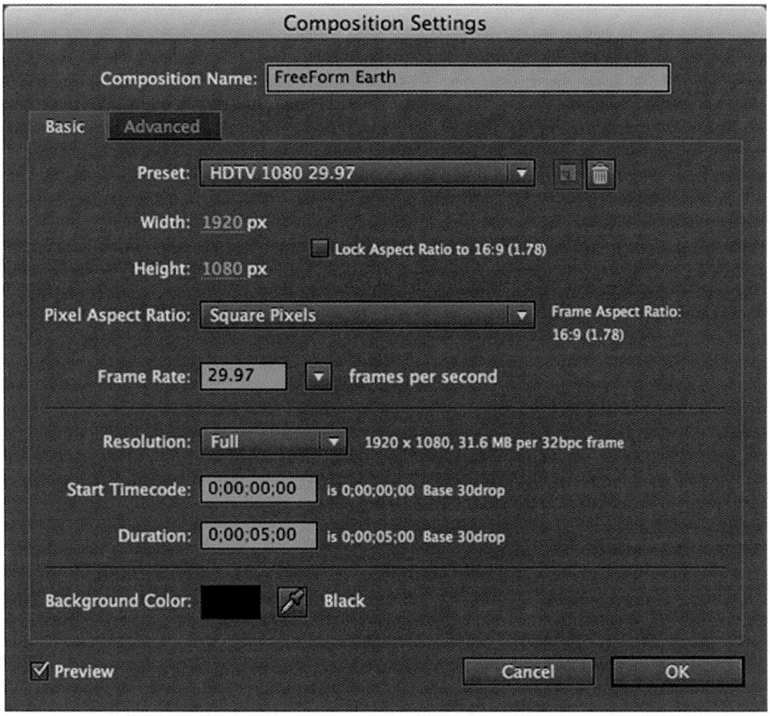

Figure 9.54 Composition settings for the project. Screenshot: Dustin Klein.

**3.** Apply **Digieffects FreeForm AE** to the colored map. Go to the Effect Controls and twirl down the Displacement Controls. In Displace Layer, select the Grayscale Displacement Map.

**4.** Create a Point Light (Layer > New > Light) with the intensity of 100% and white in Color. Make sure the Casts Shadows checkbox is checked. Shadow Darkness is set to 100% and Shadow Diffusion to 0 px. This will make a bright light with harsh shadows.

**5.** Next in Effect Controls, at the first frame, set a keyframe for Displace Height with a value of 0. At 1:00, set Displace Height to 80. This will start extruding the layer in 3D. (Figure 9.55.)

**6.** The Surface Controls allow you to change the way that light reacts with the surface of your layer. To make the land appear more realistic, drop the Specular value to 15% and raise the Roughness value to 75%. (Figure 9.56.)

**Figure 9.55** The mountains start to rise from the flat earth when Displace Height is increased. Footage: NASA, Dustin Klein.

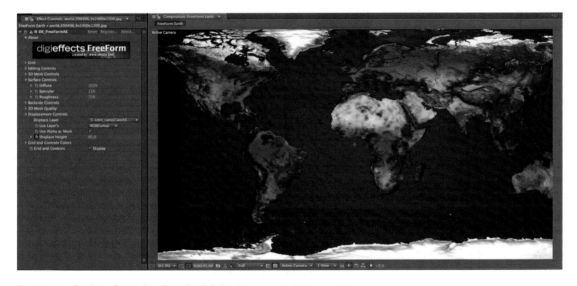

**Figure 9.56** Surface Controls adjust the lighting. Footage: NASA, Dustin Klein.

# Hot Tip

It's always a good idea to make the displacement map the same size as the layer, which it is displacing. Also, if a layer has effects applied to it must be precomposed to work as a displacement layer. Using 16 bpc compositions will work noticeable better. Lastly, any time you add FreeForm to a scene you will also want to add a light. The shadows created by the light dramatically enhance the 3D appearance of FreeForm.

# Pro Tip

If you notice that the quality is not very high, increase Mesh Subdivisions, under 3D Mesh Quality. The higher your Mesh Subdivisions, the longer your render will be and the slower your computer will work.

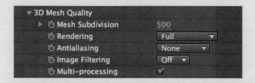

**Figure 9.57** 3D Mesh Quality settings. Screenshot: Dustin Klein.

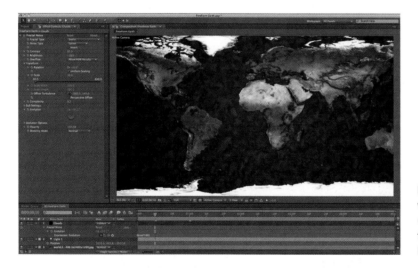

**Figure 9.58** Clouds are created with Fractal Noise. Add the expression time*180 to Evolution to make the clouds move. Footage: NASA, Dustin Klein.

There you have it, making mountains and valleys with Digieffects FreeForm AE!

**Finishing touches**: If you would like to add some clouds to the comp for added realism, it's a simple process with **Fractal Noise**.

Create a new comp-sized Solid layer named "Clouds". Apply the effect Fractal Noise (Effects > Noise & Grain > Fractal Noise). Change the Fractal Type to Swirly and the noise type to Spline to make the noise look like clouds.

Next, drop the contrast to 95 and the Brightness to –18 to let it blend better. Under Transform Options in Effect Controls, change Scale to 30. Adjust Complexity to get the look you desire. I used 8.2. Lastly, lower the Opacity to 20% and change the Blending Mode to Lighten.

To get the clouds moving, Option (Alt) + click on the stopwatch next to Evolution and type the Expression: (time*180)

# WORKING WITH THE 3D CAMERA

3D layers and camera were introduced way back in 2001 in After Effects version 5.0, since which time plug-ins have popped up to help users get more from the camera and 3D. The now defunct **Buena Software** started it off with **Depth Cue**, a collection of plug-ins that added depth effects to 3D layers based on the location of the lights, camera, and the layer itself. The set included **Falloff Lighting, Depth, Fog, 3D Composite, Rack Focus, Camera Mapper**, and **Flipside**. Buena was acquired by Toolfarm in 2006, and acquired by Digieffects in 2007. Digieffects split Depth Cue into single plug-ins sold à la carte: Camera Mapper, Depth, Falloff Lighting, and Fog (now called **Atmosphere**). We really thought Depth Cue could be at the end of its life, then Digieffects released **Buena Depth Cue v2** at the end of 2010, with some of the most useful camera tools out there.

**Digital Anarchy 3D Assistants** was a package of 16 keyframe assistants managing multiple 3D layers in After Effects. Red Giant acquired the video plug-ins from Digital Anarchy in 2009 and 3D Assistants is now known as **Red Giant PlaneSpace**. PlaneSpace lets the user animate an unlimited number of layers with ease. It's a great tool for creating video walls, cubes, and other complex shapes.

**Zaxwerks Layer Tools** is a 3D workflow tool and a huge time-saver for working with 3D layers. It simplifies distributing and moving layers in Z-Space without changing their screen size. It allows the user to scale, rotate, and move several layers at once. It even lets users match frames between 2D and 3D layers, which can be a challenge.

**Trapcode Horizon** is a mapping tool that ties the camera to a 3D world, creating "Equirectilinear Image Mapping," meaning that the camera can pan a full 360°, creating QuickTime VR-like effects.

**Evans & Sutherland Digistar 3 Virtual Projector** is an After Effects plug-in for creating domed presentations for planetariums with tools for synchronizing imagery and audio. **Sky-Swan DomeXF** is another tool for making domed projections for planetariums, allowing users to create a virtual dome in After

**Figure 10.1** The final render of a Van Gogh painting, animated in After Effects with the help of Digieffects Camera Mapper and Depth. Footage: Mark Eaton.

Effects, including tools for working with panoramic footage, which is distorted to look correct when projected in a dome. Both of these tools are for Windows only.

Addressing the recent resurgence of 3D in theaters, **Dashwood Stereo3D Toolbox** is a tool to help users set up the cameras for stereoscopic 3D.

This section explores some of these plug-ins and others that work in one way or another with the After Effects Camera.

## Digieffects Camera Mapper

**Digieffects Camera Mapper** ($79) allows the user to create camera projections from 2D still images by mapping parts of the image onto 3D solids. For example, a user can take a photo of a square building, shot on an angle, and map the front to one solid, the side to another solid, the ground to yet another solid. These solids are then positioned in 3D space with projected images and the camera can be rotated or zoomed, creating a parallax effect. Parallax is how we distinguish objects in the distance. As we move by them, objects closer to us seem to move faster than more distant objects. The user can bring still images to life, rotating the camera's view a bit and giving it some perspective without having to recreate the scene in a 3D program.

Camera Mapper is a complex plug-in, considering how simple the interface is. Projects with Camera Mapper can be multifaceted, depending on the complexity of the image or footage and how many elements are combined.

Before you dive into Camera Mapper, there are a few things you should know. There are four elements to each Camera Mapper Project:

1. **An image file or footage** that is securely locked down or stabilized.
2. **The Projection Camera**, which will need to point straight forward, so just leave it at the default settings for whichever camera you use. Choose the One-Node Camera type in the Camera Settings dialog box because it's easier to animate.
3. **One or More Solid Layers** onto which to map the image, positioned and rotated in perspective to a plane in the image.

With Camera Mapper, you can have well over 30 solid layers for complex projects. It's imperative that everything is named purposefully.

4. **A Render Camera** to animate. This camera will need to have the same settings as the Projection Camera, so it's best to duplicate the Projection camera, rename it Render Camera, then move it to the top of the stack in the timeline. After that, animate the settings of the camera, such as Position and Orientation.

The basic process of Camera Mapper takes place in just a few steps. There are no project files, as this is just an overview of the basic process, not a full tutorial. Images in this overview are from Mark Eaton's Van Gogh video tutorial, which can be found at *http://digieffects.com/support/tutorial/ vangough_depth_camera_mapper*.

1. Bring your image into a composition. This will be the Projection Layer. (Figure 10.2.)

**Web Link**

Mark Christiansen has a fantastic introductory video tutorial on Camera Mapper featuring the Golden Gate Bridge. Check it out on Vimeo: *http://vimeo .com/8905949*.

**Figure 10.2** This project uses a Van Gogh painting as the Projection Layer. Footage: Mark Eaton.

2. Add a new Camera named Projection (Layer > New > Camera).
3. Duplicate the Projection Camera and rename it "Render Camera". Drag it to the top of the stack. Leave the settings the same for now. (Figure 10.3.)

**Figure 10.3** Two cameras with identical settings are added. Footage: Mark Eaton.

4. Create a new Solid Layer (Layer > New > Solid). Name it appropriately to the plane you will be mapping it to, for example, "Ground" or "Left Wall".
5. Enable the 3D layer switch for the Solid Layer.

6. Apply Camera Mapper to the Solid Layer (Effects > Digieffects Camera Mapper). You should now see the content mapped on your Solid. (Figure 10.4.)
7. Turn off the original image or footage layer so that you only see the mapped Solid Layer.
8. Rotate and position the Solid Layer in perspective to a plane your mapping to. (Figure 10.5.)
9. Repeat steps 4 through 7 until all of the planes are set up.
10. Animate the Render camera. (Figure 10.6.)

**Figure 10.4** Camera Mapper applied to a layer. Footage: Mark Eaton.

**Figure 10.5** Solid Layers with Layer Masks, isolating the planes. Footage: Mark Eaton.

**Figure 10.6** Animate the render camera. Footage: Mark Eaton.

# Pro Tip: Alpha Handling

Camera Mapper can handle alpha channels quite nicely. I find it easiest to create the alpha channels on each layer in Photoshop with Layer Masks.

Mark Eaton's tutorial also uses **Digieffects Depth** ($49), another plug-in pulled from Buena Depth Cue, which allows the user to easily create depth maps in After Effects. A depth map is basically a grayscale elevation rendering which shows the distance from the camera of the video. This is great for adding depth of field to video that is completely in focus.

## Trapcode Horizon

I remember going to Walt Disney World in Florida as a kid and seeing a travel film in the 360° panoramic theater. I was right in the center of a gondola in Venice. The gondola driver was behind me and the scenes of Venice and the canals and bridges were around me at every angle (as well as 100 other people in the theater!)

Trapcode Horizon can do the same type of effect by putting the view right in the scene. Horizon allows you to take spherical maps or panoramic views and move through them in 3D space using the Comp Camera. Other elements such as text and particles can be mixed into the scene, and they will move with the panoramic scene.

In this tutorial we'll use Red Giant Psunami to create a world to pan around with. I have provided a prerendered still scene so you won't need the Psunami plug-in. Because Psunami is limited to a 175° view (and things start getting warped and streaked after about 150°), we'll be duplicating and masking a comp and making our own panoramic video.

This is a very simple use of Horizon, and the plug-in can get very interesting results with a lot of camera movement and added elements in the scene, such as fireballs, snow, fog, and so on. I really wanted to create a 360° view but had quite a few problems with getting it to work to my liking. I talked to David Torno, visual effects artist and supervisor at Ghost Town Media in Los Angeles, who gave me some great advice.

*Horizon works strictly as a background generator that reacts to AE camera movement. It has very limited movement as Horizon only translates X and Y camera movement. So a POV look around type shot or a simple pan move works best. You have to cheat forward or backward movement through the footage itself, like in your case of Psunami, having the water rush toward camera as if doing a flyover, then use that rendered plate as the Horizon source. So, if you turn the camera left and right it feels as if you are looking around as you fly over the water.*

This is in fact, what we'll be doing in this tutorial. *The Psunami image, which uses the Psunami preset "In a Blue Fog," and the project files are located on this book's DVD in a folder named Horizon Project.*

**Third-party plug-ins needed**:

• Trapcode Horizon

1. Create the final comp using the HDTV 1080 29.97 preset, name it "Horizon Final", and give it a duration of 10 seconds. Make the Background Color white. Drag the Psunami. tif file into this new composition.

2. Apply **Trapcode Horizon** to the Psunami layer. Once applied you'll notice the layer has turned into a gray gradient. We will not be using the Gradient feature of this plug-in, but for more information on using the Gradient parameter, see the Horizon Getting Started Tutorial video at redgiant-software.com.

3. Twirl open Image Map in the Effect Controls panel for Horizon. Set Layer to 1.Psunami. Set H Coverage to 180 and V Coverage to 90. (Figure 10.7.)

There are parameters for Orientation and Distort, which will rotate the scene right within Horizon; using a comp Camera will allow other elements to be viewed in 3D space with the panorama.

**Figure 10.7** The Horizon comp.
Footage: Michele Yamazaki.

There are a couple of things want to achieve with the camera. We would like to pan around the empty stretches of rolling sea, focusing on the text floating in the water that we'll be adding shortly. We also want to add some bob to the camera to give the feeling that we're on a raft lost at sea. There are options to set up a bobbing platform in Psunami but we want to be able to control the position with the camera in this comp so other elements will match.

4. Apply a New Camera (Layer > New > Camera). Below are the settings I used (Figure 10.8).

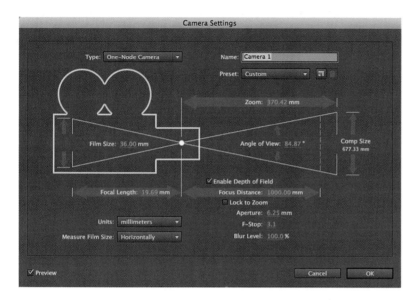

**Figure 10.8** Camera settings.
Footage: Michele Yamazaki.

- **Type**: One-Node Camera (it's easier to control)
- **Film Size**: 36.00 mm
- **Focal Length**: 19.69 mm
- **Zoom**: 370.42 mm
- **Angle of View**: 84.87
- **Enable Depth of Field**: Checked
- **Focus Distance**: 1000.00 mm
- **Aperture**: 6.25
- **F-Stop**: 3.1
- **Blur Level**: 100.0%

5. In the timeline, twirl open Camera 1 settings, or hit AA, the shortcut for Camera settings. Under Camera Option, set Zoom to 1000.0. (Figure 10.9.)

6. Under Transform, Option (Alt) + click the stopwatch for Z Rotation to apply an expression. Type the following in the timeline:

```
wiggle(0.2,10)
```

Next, we want to add text that moves with the camera. We'll be adding pauses during the camera spin where titles will be bobbing in the water. The text we'll be adding is "MISSING",

**Figure 10.9** Wiggle. Footage: Michele Yamazaki.

"SUMMER 2012". We will be modifying an After Effects Text Preset and adding a mask to the text to give it the appearance that it's sitting on the surface of the water.

7. Make sure you're at the first frame of the composition. Open the Effects & Presets panel. Twirl open * Animation Presets > Text > Organic. Double-click the Ocean Tide preset to apply the preset. Using the Text tool, select the default text and type "MISSING" over it in all caps. Set the font to something large and bold. I used Bernhard MT Condensed at 212 point in white with a 1 pixel gray outline.

8. Click the Enable 3D box in the timeline for the text layer. (Figure 10.10.)

**Figure 10.10** The Ocean Tide text preset was modified and masked so that it looks like it's bobbing up and down on the surface of the water. Footage: Michele Yamazaki.

9. This preset is much too busy, so select the text layer and tap the E key to bring up the Effect sliders that were part of the preset. Change the Slider for Frequency to 1.0 and Magnitude to around 50.00. This will lessen the movement of the text so that it bobs gently, not frenetically. Yes, it's a storm but you want the text to be readable, right?

10. Apply a Mask to the layer, selecting all but the bottom 10% of the text. Make sure that the mask is wider than the text so no horizontal movement is cut off. (Figure 10.11.)

11. Duplicate the MISSING text layer, which will be named "MISSING 2". Move the text so that you can see both layers separately. Double-click the text layer to select it and then type "SUMMER 2012" over "MISSING".

12. Now let's position the camera and text elements. Go to 3:10 in the timeline. Using the Unified Camera Tool, pan the position of the camera so that you're seeing the background as far to the left as possible, without showing any of the background. I set the Camera's position to 1581.7, 511.4, −586.1 and the orientation to 355.7°, 314.1°, 356.9°. This may be different on your project, depending on other settings.

13. Position MISSING so that it is about center screen. Set a keyframe for Position.

14. Go to 4:20 in the timeline. Pan the camera so that it is as far right as it will go without showing any of the background color. If MISSING is showing, move it offscreen to the left, so that it floats away during the camera move.

15. At 4:20, position SUMMER 2012 so that it is about center screen. Jump back to 3:10 and if SUMMER 2010 is showing, move it to the right so that it will appear to be floating onscreen during the camera move.

16. Select the Position keyframes for the camera and text layers and apply Easy Ease (Animation > Keyframe Assistant > Easy Ease). These keyframes can be finessed later. (Figure 10.12.)

**Figure 10.11** What exactly is Horizon doing? Basically it is creating a huge curved background with the Psunami layer. *Note*: The camera is zoomed out for demonstration and your comp should not look like this. Footage: Michele Yamazaki.

**Figure 10.12** Still frames of the camera move. Footage: Michele Yamazaki.

17. To make the scene more realistic, we'll add some fog layers, generated with **Fractal Noise**, applied to solids. Add a new Solid layer (Layer > New > Solid) that is $5000 \times 2000$ and name it "Fog". Apply a Layer Mask that is not full frame. Feather it

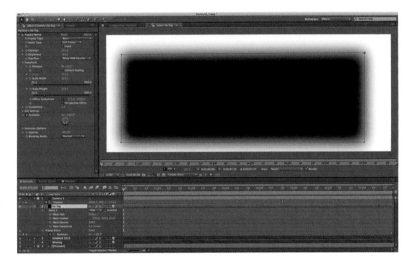

**Figure 10.13** The mask on the Fog layer is very soft and feathered. The image shows the feathering in the Layer panel so it's easy to see the Layer Mask feathering. Footage: Michele Yamazaki.

so that the edges are very soft but not cut off, about 300. If the edges are cutting off and you see hard lines, scale the mask. (Figure 10.13.)

18. Enable 3D for the layer, and then apply Fractal Noise to the layer and set it so that it looks like fog. I changed the following settings:

    • **Contrast**: 212
    • **Brightness**: –42
    • **Transform > Scale**: Uncheck Uniform Scaling
    • **Transform** > Scale Width: 277.5
    • **Transform** > Scale Height: 133.7
    • **Complexity**: 4
    • **Evolution**: Keyframe to taste
    • **Sub Settings > Sub Offset**: Keyframe the X parameter only

19. Set the Opacity of the Fog layer to 10%, then position the Fog layer so that it fills the screen at the first frame.

20. If you were to preview the comp, the fog would become warped as it rotates sideways. To remedy this problem, we just need to set the layer so that it will auto-orient toward the camera. Select the layer and go to Layer > Transform > Auto-Orient. Choose Orient Towards Camera and click OK. (Figure 10.14.)

**Figure 10.14** Auto-orient the Far Fog layer toward Camera. Footage: Michele Yamazaki.

21. Rename this layer "Far Fog". Duplicate the layer and rename the copy "Medium Fog". Select the layer, grab the Z position handle, and drag it toward you.

22. Duplicate the layer and rename it "Close Fog". Select the layer, grab the Z position handle, and drag it toward you again. Adjust the opacity.

# Hot Tip

If you're having problems positioning when using Horizon, zoom out the camera in a Custom View. You will not see the curvature of Horizon, but you can see the edges of the sea and fog images. (Figure 10.15.)

**Figure 10.15** Zoom out the camera in Custom View to get some perspective while positioning. Footage: Michele Yamazaki.

**23.** Preview the comp to make sure that you do not have any strange edges showing on the fog layers. It is likely you wilzl need to keyframe the position for the camera move.

**24.** Feel free to modify settings on the fog layers so they are not identical. Adjust the opacity as needed.

**25.** To give it some mood, apply a couple of Spot Lights (Layer > New > Light). Position them on different sides of the text but with their Point of Interest on the text. Adjust the Color, Intensity, and Cone Feather for each light.

**26.** The Psunami layer will not pick up lights. Remember that it is not a 3D Layer. The Text layers and Fog layers will use the lights, however. (Figure 10.16.)

**Finishing touch**: To add more excitement and realism to the shot, use Psunami as it's animating or render a movie of Psunami with the waves tumbling. It is processor intensive for a project like this but it looks fantastic. A less intensive option is to add rain, clouds, and other natural elements to the shot.

**Figure 10.16** Camera: The light positions. Footage: Michele Yamazaki.

# User Story: One-Click 3D Workflow with Zaxwerks Layer Tools by Matt Silverman

Oftentimes it's the little things that make you happy. Here at Bonfire Labs (bonfirelabs.com), the majority of our After Effects comps utilize 3D layers. As we build up a complex project it doesn't take long before the camera is at an odd position and no longer facing straight along one axis. Inevitably we run into a situation where we need a 3D layer, such as a UI screen, to face precisely at the camera. Trying to line this up manually is nearly impossible, since the layer needs to be positioned and rotated on all three axes. At these times I always wished for a 3D version of After Effects' built-in Fit to Comp function, which is Command (Ctrl) + Option (Alt) + F. Luckily my dream came true a few years back when we discovered **Zaxwerks Layer Tools** ($149), which does precisely what I needed and a whole lot more.

The relevant plug-in in the Layer Tools set is called Fit and Face, and it acts more like an AE Script than a traditional plug-in. With a few clicks in its custom palette, Fit and Face gives me all the tools to make this near-impossible task possible. It even has options for doing it, which I'll talk about as we go through the steps. Here's how it works.

Say you have a comp such as the one shown in Figure 10.17.

Notice that the camera has been offset and rotated and my job is to rotate the 3D layer to exactly face the camera.

I apply ZW Layer Fit and Face (Animation > Keyframe Assistant > ZW Layer Fit and Face). A Custom UI Panel opens, which can be docked into your workspace (Figure 10.18).

After selecting the layer and the camera, I can choose one of the four options for repositioning my layer to face the camera.

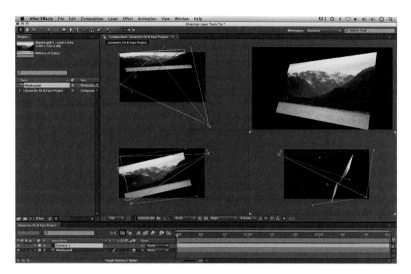

**Figure 10.17** 4 views of the camera. Screenshot: Zax Dow.

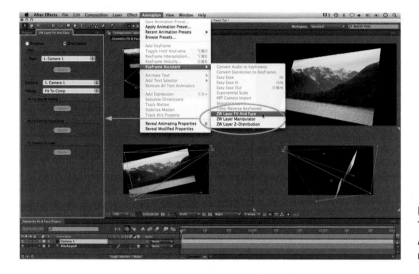

**Figure 10.18** To apply Layer Tools, go under Keyframe Assistants, not the Effects menu. Screenshot: Zax Dow.

The first option is simply called Face. As the word says, clicking this button will make the layer face the camera. You'd use this option when you are building your composite and need to rotate the layer so it faces the camera, but not change the overall size of the layer (Figure 10.19).

The second option is called Fit To View By Scaling. It rotates the layer just like the previous option, but also scales the layer to fit the camera's viewport (Figure 10.20).

The third option fits the layer to the camera's viewport like the previous option, but it does so by bringing the layer closer to the camera while leaving the scale intact (Figure 10.21).

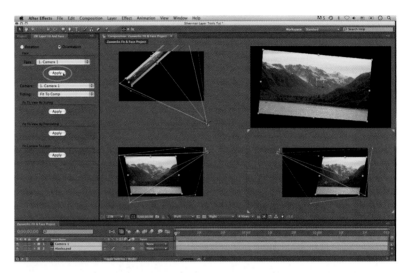

**Figure 10.19** The Face Option.
Screenshot: Zax Dow.

**Figure 10.20** Fit to View by
Scaling Option. Screenshot:
Zax Dow.

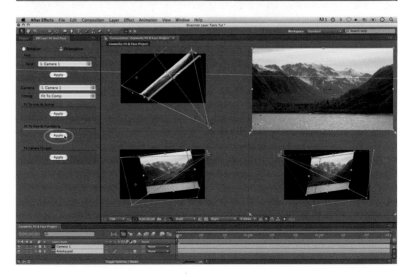

**Figure 10.21** Fit to View by
Translating Option. Screenshot:
Zax Dow.

The final option doesn't move the layer at all. Instead, it rotates and repositions the camera to fit the layer. This option is great when the layer is part of a bigger composition so it can't be moved or scaled. It lets you set keyframe to animate the camera right over to the picture (Figure 10.22).

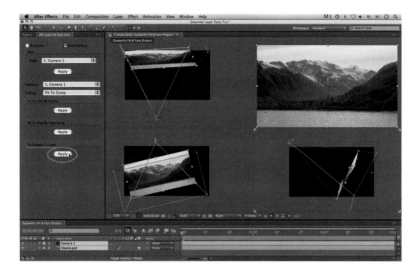

**Figure 10.22** Fit Camera to Layer Option. Screenshot: Zax Dow.

It also help in your workflow, like when you have a big, spread-out comp and you need to move a working camera so you can see a part of the comp with a specific picture in it. In this case, you would just select the picture from the AE timeline, then click the Fit Camera To Layer button. Zap, you're there. We use this one all the time.

That's it. One-click happiness. It seems really simple but I can't tell you how much time this one little plug-in ends up saving us.

## Stereoscopic 3D in AE

Stereoscopic 3D is everywhere if you haven't noticed. The NAB Shows in Las Vegas in 2009 and 2010 were overrun with 3D cameras, televisions, and software. I took my daughter, Lily, to see Toy Story 3D and most previews of upcoming films were in 3D. To me, 3D is a bit annoying. 3D glasses give me a headache and the films where the 3D is done after the film is shot do not look so great. Lily, of course, insists on seeing every film in 3D, but spends most of the film with the glasses pushed down on her nose! Do you think this 3D film trend will last? The kids seem to like it.

A 3D Glasses plug-in was introduced to After Effects that allows you to create a stereoscopic video effect quite easily.

**Figure 10.23** The final 3D Glasses effect. Footage: Michele Yamazaki.

Although this is not a third-party plug-in it seems beneficial to highlight it alongside other stereoscopic 3D plug-ins on the market. While at Toy Story 3D, two of the trailers for other films showed 3D snow, so it seemed like a nice idea to show how to create this effect. You'll need the red and blue 3D glasses to view it properly.

**Dashwood Stereo3D Toolbox** is a third-party option that comes in an LE version ($99) and a full super-powered version that retails for $1499 and has every bell and whistle you might need for creating amazing stereoscopic 3D. I'll walk you through the basics of using the LE version.

## 3D Snow in After Effects with Digieffects Snowstorm and 3D Glasses Plug-in

Get out those red/cyan 3D glasses! We'll be using **Digieffects Snowstorm** ($49), a plug-in included in the **Digieffects Delirium** ($399) bundle or à la carte, to create snow, then use After Effects 3D Glasses to offset the 3D.

*The project files are included on this book's DVD in the 3D Snow folder.*

**Third-party plug-ins needed**:

- Digieffects Delirium (or Digieffects Snowstorm, now available à la carte)

1. First, create a new comp in After Effects and use the HDV 1080 29.97 preset, 10 seconds in duration. Name it "Snow Comp". Our final output will only be HDV/HDTV 720 29.97, but by making it larger we will have room to scale the comp and not see the edges when it's precomposed.

2. First we'll create the background layer, which will have a cloudy blue effect (Layer > New > Solid). Make it 3000 × 1700 and name it "Background Clouds" with the Color set to Black. The reason that it needs to be so large is that there will be a camera move and we don't want to see the edges of the Solid. Enable 3D for the layer by clicking the 3D Layer Switch in the Timeline panel.

3. Add some clouds in the background by applying **Fractal Noise** (Effect > Noise & Grain > Fractal Noise). In the Effect Controls panel for Fractal Noise, lower the Contrast, Brightness, Complexity and Opacity and keyframe Evolution to add some movement.

4. Apply **Tritone** to add some color (Effect > Color Correction > Tritone). Set the Midtones to Royal Blue. Enable 3D for the layer by checking the 3D Layer Switch. (Figure 10.24.)

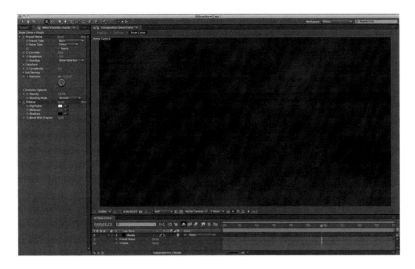

**Figure 10.24** Fractal Noise and Tritone make some simple clouds. Footage: Michele Yamazaki.

5. Next we'll create the first snow layer. There will be three snow layers altogether: Snow Near, Snow Mid, and Snow Far. Make this layer also 3000 × 1700 and name it "Snow Near" with the Color set to Black. This will be the snow nearest to the Camera. Enable 3D for the layer by checking the 3D Layer Switch.

6. In the Effects & Presets panel, twirl open *Animation Presets > DE_Delirium_V2. Drag the preset named DE_Snowstorm-blizzard onto the Snow layer (Figure 10.25). In the Effect Controls panel, change the following settings:
   - **Alpha Threshold**: 150 (a lower level will incorporate the background, a higher level will make the alpha tighter)
   - **Alpha Weight**: 300 (a higher level makes the snow more opaque)

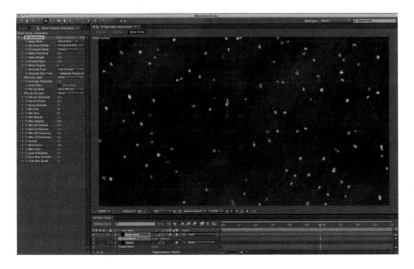

**Figure 10.25** DE Snowstorm applied to a solid to make the first layer of snow, which will be nearest to the camera. Footage: Michele Yamazaki.

**Figure 10.26** Three layers of snow. Footage: Michele Yamazaki.

- **Blend Original**: 0 (the amount that the snow blends with the Solid color)
- **Snow Generate**: 40 (will lessen the amount of snow)
- **Min Size**: 50 (the minimum size of the flakes)
- **Max Size**: 65 (the maximum size of the flakes)

7. Duplicate Snow Near and rename it "Snow Mid". Change Min Size to 20 and Max Size to 40. Change the value of Random Seed to any value that looks good to you.

8. Duplicate Snow Mid and rename it "Snow Far". Change Min Size to 10 and Max Size to 40. Change the value of Random Seed on this layer as well. (Figure 10.26.)

9. The basic snow animation is complete and the cameras are set up. Make adjustments to the snowflakes by bringing the flakes closer to you and randomizing them. Now is the time to add any embellishments to the composition such as text and lights. Have fun with it and make it interesting. Don't forget to save!

10. The next step is to separate the layers of snow and the background in 3D Space. At the bottom of the Comp panel, set the View Layout to 2 Views – Horizontal. Click on the Comp panel on the right and set the 3D View popup to Custom View 1. Use the Unified Camera Tool to rotate the view and zoom out. *Note*: This view can't be rendered. It is just for your reference. (Figure 10.27.)

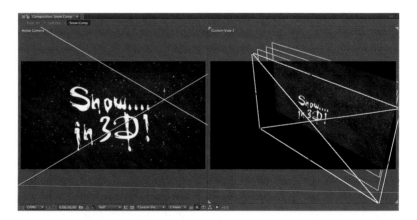

**Figure 10.27** 2 Views is selected in the 3D View popup. Footage: Michele Yamazaki.

11. Drag the Z position arrow in the Comp panel for each of the layers, placing Snow Near closest to the camera, then Snow Mid, followed by Snow Far. Behind that is the background. Keep an eye on the Active Camera view so that you don't position the elements so far back that you see the edges of any of the layers. Adjust the view position in the Custom View with the Camera Tool if you need to see a different angle. (Figure 10.28.)

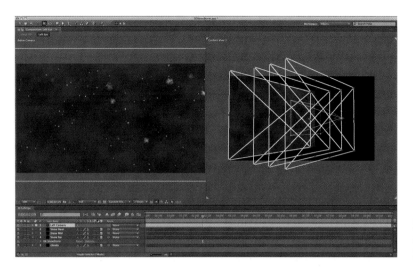

**Figure 10.28** The layers are separated in Z space. Footage: Michele Yamazaki.

12. In the project panel, drag Snow Comp to the Create a New Composition at the bottom of the Project panel. Rename this new composition "Left Eye".

13. Open the Left Eye Composition. Enable 3D for the Snow Comp layer by checking the Enable 3D switch. Also, click the Collapse Transformations checkbox so that the depth set up in the nested comp will be seen in this comp.

14. Add a New Camera (Layer > New > Camera). (Figure 10.29.) I used the following settings:
    - **Type**: One-Node Camera
    - **Film Size**: 36.00 mm
    - **Name**: Left Camera

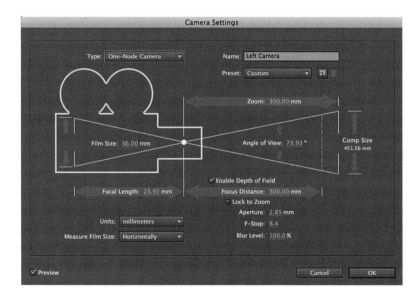

**Figure 10.29** My camera settings. Footage: Michele Yamazaki.

- **Zoom**: 300.00
- **Angle of View**: 73.93
- **Enable Depth of Field**: Checked
- **Focus Distance**: 300 mm
- **Aperture**: 2.85 mm
- **F-stop**: 8.4
- **Blur Level**: 100.0%

15. Modify the position of the Camera and keyframe the Orientation to add a pan or movement to the shot. This will make the final animation look more interesting. Make sure you do not show any edges of the background or snow layers as you move the camera. (Figure 10.30.)

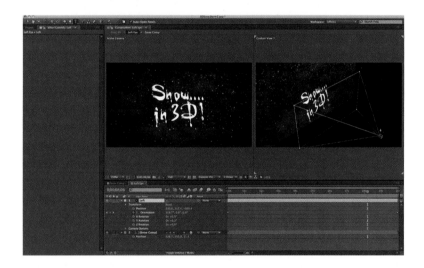

**Figure 10.30** Animating the Camera. Footage: Michele Yamazaki.

16. Once the camera is positioned as you like it, duplicate the Left Eye composition in the Project panel. Name the duplicate camera Right Eye. Open the Right Eye comp and rename the camera Right Camera. Add 10 pixels to the X Position. For example, the X Position value of my Left Camera is 659.9, so I set the X Position of the Right Camera to 669.9.

17. In the Project panel, select both Right Eye and Left Eye and drag them to the Create a New Composition button. Leave the settings at the default and click OK. Select the new composition and press the Enter key to allow for renaming the comp. Rename it "Final 3D".

18. In the Final 3D Comp, make sure Left Eye is on top. Apply the 3D Glasses filter to the Left Eye layer (Effect > Perspective > 3D Glasses). In the Effect Controls panel set the Left View to 1. Left Eye and the Right View to 2. Right Eye. Set the 3D View to Balanced Color: Red Blue. Put on your red and blue 3D glasses and adjust the Balance. This is how much red versus how much blue you will see. (Figure 10.31.)

## Hot Tip

If your snow doesn't look like it has much depth (or too much), adjust the Z position of the snow layers in the original Snow comp.

**Figure 10.31** 3D Glasses.
Footage: Michele Yamazaki.

19. You should see a pretty cool looking 3D snowstorm if you render it out and watch with your 3D Glasses. If the alignment seems off, adjust Convergence Offset. To saturate or desaturate the red and blue, adjust Balance.

You can go back through the comps and turn on Motion Blur for the comps and the layers to give it a bit more realism.

**Figure 10.32** The final 3D Glasses effect with added text.
Footage: Michele Yamazaki.

## Stereoscopic 3D ViewMaster with Dashwood 3D Toolbox

**Figure 10.33** Put on your red/cyan 3D glasses and have a look! Footage: Michele Yamazaki.

Dashwood 3D Toolbox works very similarly to the 3D Glasses plug-in but has many more options. This time we will use a combination of cut apart images and video placed in Z depth and rotated with the camera, in a kind of moving ViewMaster. Remember those cardboard disks with the images that you slid into the red ViewMaster and clicked the lever to go to the next scene? Remember how they never quite lined up?

I took some photos in New York City. This project consists of a helicopter, which has been cut out from the sky; the Manhattan Skyline, which has the sky removed; and a nice blue sky with a few clouds. We will place the elements in 3D space with a camera tied to a Null to give the feel of parallax. We'll them put this into a final comp with **Dashwood Stereo3D Toolbox LE** applied. If you have red/cyan 3D glasses, get them out!

*The project files are included on this book's DVD in the Dashwood 3D NYC folder (Mac).* The project file includes the NYC comp, which contains a scene in 3D space already set up for you. I will not be going through the setup of this comp, as it is the same procedure as the previous 3D Glasses tutorial. The project files also include the Left Eye and Right Eye comps, as well as a final composition with Dashwood Stereo3D Toolbox LE in the complete state. *Note*: To run Dashwood 3D Toolbox, you will need to install the free FxFactory engine, available at www.noiseindustries.com.

**Third-party plug-ins needed:**
- Dashwood Stereo3D Toolbox LE (Mac)
  1. Open the Dashwood 3D NYC folder and locate the NYC.aep comp. Double-click it to open it. The NYC comp contains the Manhattan skyline, a generated sky, a helicopter pre-comp and some animated text.

2. In the Effect Controls panel, drag NYC to the Create a New Composition button at the bottom of the panel. Rename the new comp Left Eye.
3. Add a Camera (Layer > New > Camera). Set the following camera settings.
   - **Type**: One-Node Camera
   - **Film Size**: 28.00 mm
   - **Focal Length**: 15.94 mm
   - **Name**: Left Camera
   - **Zoom**: 385.71 mm
   - **Angle of View**: 82.75°
   - **Enable Depth of Field**: Checked
   - **Focus Distance**: 385.71
   - **Aperture**: 2.85 mm
   - **F-Stop**: 5.6
   - **Blur**: 100.0%
4. To pan the Camera, keyframe the Orientation. (Figure 10.34.)

Figure 10.34  Left Camera.
Footage: Michele Yamazaki.

5. Once the camera move has been made and you're happy with it, duplicate the Left Eye comp. Name the duplicate Right Eye. Open the Position parameter of the Left Camera and add 10 to the X value. The X value for the Left Eye comp's camera position is 960 so for the Right Eye comp it should be 970.
6. Select both the Left Eye and the Right Eye and drag them both to the Create a New Composition. The New Composition from Selection dialog box will open. Use the default settings. Under Options, use Dimensions from Left Eye. Click OK to close the window. (Figure 10.35.)
7. Open Composition Settings (Composition > Composition Settings) and Rename the comp "Stereoscopic Final".
8. Select the Left Camera comp and apply Stereo3D Toolbox LE (Effect > Dashwood Stereo3D Toolbox LE > Stereo3D Toolbox LE).

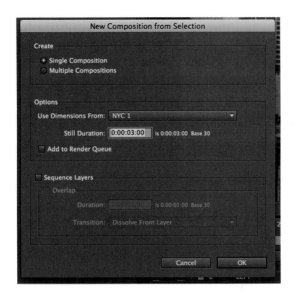

Figure 10.35 New Composition from Selection dialog box. Footage: Michele Yamazaki.

Figure 10.36 Put on your 3D glasses and have a look! Footage: Michele Yamazaki.

9. Under S3D Input Type choose Clip = Left Eye and Image Well = Right Eye. The S3D Output type should be set to Anaglyph (Red/Cyan). (Figure 10.36.)

Now this looks great as it is and you could stop here, but let's add another element to the animation—some text much closer to the camera. This can introduce a few problems with convergence that I'll show you how to fix.

10. Open the NYC1 comp. Type New York City in a nice font, in white, in the upper right side of the composition. Click the 3D Layer button to make the text layer 3D. You may need to adjust the Z position of the text to position it properly in the upper right side of the comp.

11. Open the Effects & Presets panel. Twirl open *Animation Presets > Text > 3D Text. Find the preset 3D Bouncing in Centered. Go to 1:00 in the timeline and drag the preset onto the text so the transition begins at 1:00.

12. In the timeline, twirl open Text > Animator 1. Use the Add flyout menu to the right of Animator 1 to Add > Property > Position. It will appear below Range Selector 1. Set the value of Position to −1378.0, 750.0, −1200.0. This will make the text appear that it has come in from the center of the screen, from behind the camera. (Figure 10.37.)

**Figure 10.37** Text is added so that it appears as if it is coming from behind the camera. Footage: Michele Yamazaki.

**Figure 10.38** Convergence (Pixels) adjusts the distance between red and cyan. Footage: Michele Yamazaki.

13. Once the text is set, copy the text layer. Go to NYC 2 and paste the text layer. It will be positioned exactly as it is in NYC 1.
14. Open Stereoscopic Final and go to a point where one of the letters is flying in. You should notice some major red/cyan convergence going on there. Put on your 3D glasses and have a look. If it looks ghosted and flickering, go to the Effect Controls panel for Stereo3D Toolbox LE. Adjust the value of Convergence (Pixels). I set it to –5. Moving the value to a negative will bring elements away from the camera. Using a positive value will make things appear closer to the camera. Adjust to taste and keep an eye on the rest of the shot. (Figure 10.38.)

# AUTOMATION AND KEYFRAME GENERATORS

The beauty of After Effects is that almost anything can be keyframed and be unique. Keyframing certain effects can be time-consuming and intense. Several third-party developers have included automation tools in the plug-ins. Some ship with animated presets too. This chapter looks at only the tools that either automate animation or generate keyframes for you, making your workflow faster, smoother, and all round better.

There are excellent plug-ins to animate parameters to the audio spectrum, and others to automate photomontages, the iTunes Coverflow effect, and the Ken Burns style pan and zooms. These plug-ins can save you an enormous amount of time.

## Automated Motion and Keyframes Generated from Audio

There are a few plug-ins that help synchronize music to motion graphics, either by generating keyframes from audio levels or somehow reacting to the audio. These plug-ins eliminate the tedious process of timing and tweaking keyframes, allowing you to get straight to the creative part.

Yes, it's possible to "Convert Audio to Keyframes" without a third-party plug-in. Just select your audio track, then choose Keyframe Assistant > Convert Audio to Keyframes, and follow with the Smoother keyframe assistant to smooth out the keyframes that are created. This works well for many tasks, but there are other tools that allow you to isolate certain areas of the sound file or easily map a frequency or audio clip to a parameter within the plug-in.

**Trapcode Sound Keys** ($149) was the first plug-in to emerge on the scene for generating keyframes from audio. Not long after, a lesser known but excellent plug-in, **Avidion Synchronize** ($99) was released. Synchronize has not been updated to support After Effects CS5, however. **Trapcode Form** ($199) has built-in Audio Reactors that work with parameters within the plug-in. **Boris Continuum Beat Reactor** ($99) is the newest on the market, released with **Boris Continuum Complete** 7.0 in 2010.

## Trapcode Form Audio Reactor Presets

With Trapcode Form, it's very easy to create gorgeous, complex eye candy that reacts to your audio clip. This type of animation is great for music videos and DJ or concert video support. The nice thing is that Form does not generate keyframes, so it's easy to swap out music or slide the clip along the timeline without having to deal with regenerating keyframes for each change.

There is a vast array of features in Form, with names like Base Form, Quick Maps, Layer Maps, Spherical Field, and Kaleidospace, and within those features there are dozens of other options. Form can be pretty intimidating at first and it takes some

**Figure 11.1** The tf_audio_Base-DropSurface preset in Trapcode Form. Footage: Michele Yamazaki.

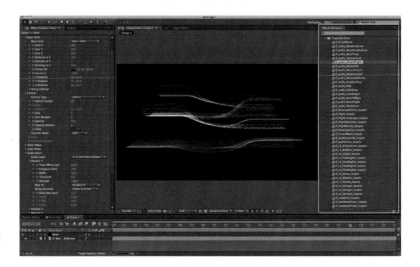

**Figure 11.2** The tf_audio_DesertFlight preset in Trapcode Form. Footage: Michele Yamazaki.

time to figure it out, but it ships with multiple audio presets. You can use them as is, or use them as jumping off points.

1. Bring your audio into a new composition.
2. Create a new solid that is the same size as your composition.
3. Open the Effects & Presets panel and twirl open *Animation Presets > Trapcode Form. Any presets that begin with tf_audio will be audio presets. Select one and drag it to the solid layer.
4. In the Effect Controls panel, under Form, twirl open Audio React. Set the Audio Layer popup to use the audio layer.
5. Adjust to taste or try other tf_audio presets.

## CAN'T SEE ANIMATION PRESETS?

If *Animation Presets isn't showing up in the Effects & Presets panel, click the flyout menu in the upper right corner of the panel. Choose Show Animation Presets from the menu. *Animation Presets will appear at the top of the menu since there is an asterisk before the name.

**Figure 11.3** To be visible, Show Animation Presets needs to be selected in the flyout menu for Effects & Presets. Footage: Michele Yamazaki.

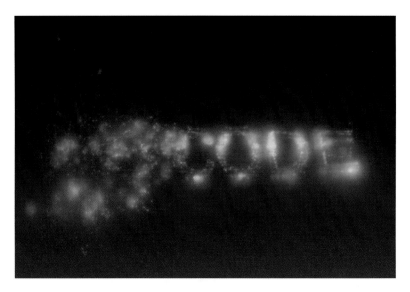

**Figure 11.4** Audio React, a function of Trapcode Form, can control the amount of glow and dispersion of particles. Footage: Michele Yamazaki.

**Web Link:**

Peder Norrby's other tracks can be found at *http://soundcloud.com/rymdenmusic.* They are free to use in any of your projects, just credit Peder Norrby/Rymden Music.

## Creating an Audio Reactor Animation from Scratch in Trapcode Form

This tutorial walks you through using the Audio React features on some text generated with the Text tool in After Effects. As beats or certain sounds in the clip occur, the text will be dispersed or moved in sync. The music included on the DVD is called "G-Star (Big End)" and was composed and performed by none other than Rymden/Peder Norrby. If the name Peder Norrby sounds familiar to you, it's because he is the developer of the Trapcode plug-ins.

The project files for this tutorial are included on this book's DVD in the Form Audio folder. Peder's music track is included.

**Third-party plug-ins needed:**
- Trapcode Form
  1. Import the music file G-Star (Big End).wav from the Form Audio folder on this book's DVD.
  2. Make a new Composition named "Form Text". I used the DVCPro HD 720 29.97 preset on this one but you can use whatever you like. Set the duration to 25:00 and the Background Color to Black. Click OK.
  3. Drag G-Star (Big End).wav into the Form Text comp. Make sure it starts at 0:00.

Use the Type tool to type the word "TRAPCODE" in large letters across the screen. Use Arial 142 pt., all caps, in red with a 1 px white outline if you want to match the look of this tutorial. Center the text in the Composition panel, and turn off the visibility for the layer.

**Figure 11.5** Trapcode in red all caps will be used to map the parameters in Audio React. Footage: Michele Yamazaki.

---

## TRAPCODE FORM TRAINING BY HARRY J. FRANK

If you'd like further training, I recommend checking out **Trapcode Form Training by Harry J. Frank** ($26), available as a download from Toolfarm.com. Harry clearly explains the Basic Fractal Shape, the Box-Strings (a Base Form), the Audio React feature, and using Layer Maps.

---

4. Create a new solid (Layer > New Solid) named "Form Layer". Click the Make Comp Size button. The color is unimportant. Apply Trapcode Form to the layer (Effect > Trapcode > Trapcode Form).

First, we'll set up the Base Form, the Layer Map with the text, then the Particle. We will map the Audio React settings to the text then adjust the colors and opacity with Quick Maps.

5. Twirl Base Form settings open. Set the following and leave the rest of the section at their defaults (Figure 11.6).
   * **Base Form**: Box-Strings
   * **Size X**: 1280 (the width of the comp)

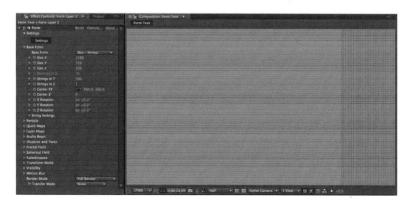

**Figure 11.6** The Base Form will look like a screen full of horizontal stripes. Footage: Michele Yamazaki.

**Figure 11.7** Setting the Layer Maps Color and Alpha to Lightness to A allows the text to be visible. Footage: Michele Yamazaki.

**Figure 11.8** The look with Disperse set to 20 and Twist set to 2. Footage: Michele Yamazaki.

- **Size Y**: 720 (the height of the comp)
- **Strings in Y**: 500
- **Strings in Z**: 1

6. Next, twirl down Layer Maps. Under Color and Alpha, set the Layer to TRAPCODE, which is the text layer. Set the Functionality to Lightness to A. This will create an alpha channel using the lightness of the layer. Set Map Over to XY. This maps the particles over the height and width only. You should now see an outline of the text. (Figure 11.7.)

7. Under Disperse and Twist, set Disperse to 20 and Twist to 2. (Figure 11.8.)

8. The glowing effects are made with Particle > Particle Type set to Glow Sphere (No DOF). Set Sphere Feather to 100. The text will now appear more solid.

9. Audio React is where the magic happens. Twirl open Audio React and set the Audio Layer to the G-Star (Big End) track.

10. Twirl open Reactor 1. First set Map To to Disperse and Delay Direction to X Left to Right. You should see some changes in the text, which will differ depending on where you are in the timeline. Set the following:
    - **Frequency**: 3000
    - **Width**: 20
    - **Strength**: 9000 (this will give the text a lot of movement on certain beats and sounds)
    - **Delay Max [sec]**: 0.3 (this causes the effect to happen slightly after the other effects, which we will set up with Reactor 2 and 3)

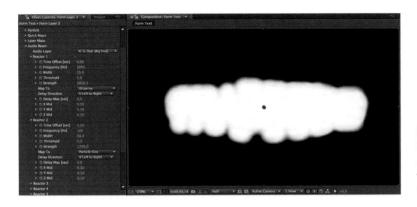

**Figure 11.9** After setting up Reactors 1 and 2, depending on your point in the timeline, the text may look like a cloud. Footage: Michele Yamazaki.

11. Twirl Reactor 2 open (Figure 11.9). Set the following:
    - **Map To**: Particle Size
    - **Delay Direction**: X Outwards
    - **Strength**: 1200
12. Twirl Reactor 3 open (Figure 11.10). Set the following:
    - **Map To**: Disperse
    - **Delay Direction**: Z Outwards
    - **Frequency**: 3000
    - **Threshold**: 86
    - **Strength**: 6160

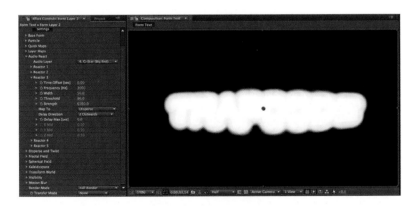

**Figure 11.10** After adjusting the values in Reactor 3, the cloud forms tighter around the text shape. Footage: Michele Yamazaki.

13. Back under Particle, we want to further refine the particles in use. Make the following changes:
    - **Size Random**: 100
    - **Opacity**: 100
    - **Opacity Random**: 100
14. Under Quick Maps is where the parameters for Color and Opacity can be changed and linked to Audio Reactions. Twirl open Quick Maps > Color Map and create a gradient. Either pick colors yourself or click the Random button.

**Figure 11.11** Quick Maps Colorize the text. Footage: Michele Yamazaki.

I found a lovely blue and tan gradient for the color map that worked very well with the animation. Set Map Opac+Color over to radial. You should now see the gradient mapped over the cloudy text.

15. Set Map #1 to Audio React 1 and Map #1 over to X. Set Map #2 to Audio React 2 and Map #2 over to Y. (Figure 11.11.)

16. We have not set up Size and Fractal Strength for the Layer Maps yet because they would not be seen in the earlier step with Layer Maps. Twirl down Layer Maps > Size. Set the Layer to TRAPCODE and Map Over to YZ.

17. Under Layer Maps > Fractal Strength, again, set Layer to TRAPCODE and Map Over to XY. (Figure 11.12.)

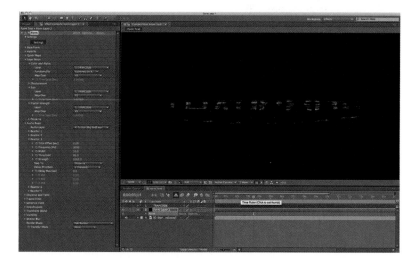

**Figure 11.12** Size and Fractal Strength are set for Layer Maps. Footage: Michele Yamazaki.

**Figure 11.13** Fractal Field settings fill in the text with color and particles. Footage: Michele Yamazaki.

18. Under Fractal Field, there are a lot of changed settings that will fill in the text with color and particles (Figure 11.13). Below are the settings I used, but make adjustments until you're happy with the look.
    * **Affect Size**: 3
    * **Flow X**: 5
    * **Flow Y**: 63
    * **Flow Z**: 10
    * **Flow Evolution**: 10
    * **Offset Evolution**: 10
    * **Gamma**: 11.8
    * **Add/Subtract**: 3.3
    * **Min**: –1.0
    * **Max**: 1.0
    * **F Scale**: 1.0
    * **Complexity**: 10
    * **Octave Multiplier**: 1.0
    * **Octave Scale**: 1.5

19. The animation and "splashes" will have different looks depending on how you trim the music. To keep the same basic look but change the splashes, open Quick Maps and change the Opacity Maps to your own custom settings.

20. To add more interest and movement, adjust the values under Transform World. I applied a Wiggle expression to X, Y, and Z Rotation.

    ```
    wiggle(0.5,20)
    ```

21. This will cause the movement to wiggle once every 2 seconds (the value of 0.5 translates to something that happens a half a time per second, so once over two seconds). The maximum amount of movement will be 20° from the start point. Option (Alt) + click the stopwatch for the parameter and type the wiggle expression to add it.

**Figure 11.14** Trapcode Sound Keys and Video Copilot Twitch join forces for some fun, beat driven visuals. Digieffects DE Visual Harmonizer was added to the background as a final touch. Footage credit: Crowd Control, clip # 00467_001_25.

## Dance Club Eye Candy with Trapcode Sound Keys and Video Copilot Twitch

For any of you DJs who like to time your video to the beat of the music, **Trapcode Sound Keys** ($149) is the perfect tool for the task (not live … it's After Effects after all, rendering is mandatory!).

First, we'll use Trapcode Sound Keys to capture the levels of a music track into keyframes. Then, we'll use a short clip of video and Time Remap it, linking the movements to the keyframed bass beats from the audio track. **Video Copilot Twitch** ($45) is then used to slide the footage to the treble frequencies.

Demonstrating movement with audio is quite difficult on the printed page, so I've uploaded a sample movie at http://bit.ly/DancePartyFX.

The track used in this tutorial "Sweet," composed by Peder Norrby/Rymden Music, is included on the DVD. The included video file is Crowd Control clip # 00467_001_25. *Project files are included on this book's DVD in a folder named SoundKeys-Twitch.*

**Third-party plug-ins needed:**
- Trapcode Sound Keys
- Video Copilot Twitch
- Digieffects Delirium DE Visual Harmonizer
    1. Import sweet_mstr.wav and kick.mov into After Effects, both found in the SoundKeys-Twitch footage folder.
    2. Make a new Composition using the HDTV 1080 29.97 preset, with a black background, and 30:00 in duration. Name the comp "Dance Party". The song is 4:14:22, but we will only use the first minute for the sake of the tutorial. Drag sweet_mstr.wav into the composition.
    3. Because the track is longer than the composition, we'll want to fade it out. Go to 25:00 in the timeline. Twirl open the

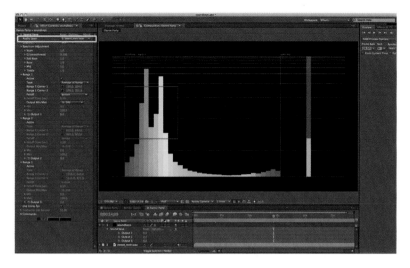

**Figure 11.15** Trapcode Sound Keys is linked to the music track, showing the audio spectrum. Footage: Michele Yamazaki.

Audio > Audio Levels for moonwalk_master.wav layer. Set a keyframe for +0.00 dB. Go to 29:29 and set the value of Audio Levels to –96.00 dB to fade the audio.

4. Create a New Solid named Sound Keys. Apply Trapcode Sound Keys to the layer (Effects > Trapcode > Sound Keys). Set the Resolution popup along the bottom of the Composition panel to Quarter resolution. Sound Keys actually looks better and is more readable at this resolution than full.

5. In the Effect Controls panel for Sound Keys, set the Audio Layer to sweet_master.wav. (Figure 11.15.)

6. Preview the clip a few times and watch the audio spectrum and levels. Twirl open Spectrum Adjustment, and set the value of Q (smoothness) to 0.500 so that the spectrum will have smoother values. Also, the Treble is a bit low and we'll be isolating the interesting sounds in the Treble area of the spectrum to tie it to the Slide value of Twitch. Increase the value of Treble to 2.0.

7. Now we need to isolate three areas of the audio spectrum: One will be tied to the kick, one to Twitch Slide, and the third to give us extra data, which can be tied to the background layer.

8. For the first few seconds the Sub Base/Base (that's bass; base is the developer's spelling) section of the spectrum is the most active, represented by reds, oranges, and yellows in the Sound Keys audio spectrum. To isolate this area, in the Effect Controls panel for Sound Keys under Range 1, click on the crosshairs for Range 1 Corner 1, and then click upper left corner of the Comp panel, just below the words Spectrum + Ranges. For Range 1 Corner 2, click on the bottom of the spectrum, near the green yellow bar. (Figure 11.16.)

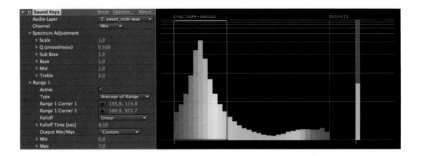

**Figure 11.16** The Base range of the spectrum is isolated.
Footage: Michele Yamazaki.

# Pro Tip

If the Treble, Mid, or Base, or Sub Base seems too low or too high, use the settings under Spectrum Adjustment to increase or decrease the levels. This will not actually change the audio levels but just how they are represented in the spectrum.

Before we go too far, a bit of explanation about the settings under Range 1, 2 and 3.

**Type:**

- **Average of Range**: Computes the average level for the sound while it is in the range
- **Peak of Range**: Uses the maximum level for the audio while it's in the range
- **On/Off Trigger**: If the sound is in the range, it is considered "on"; if it's out of range, it's "off"

**Output Min/Max**: This sets the values for the keyframes that are generated.

- **0...100**: Great for Opacity or any effect that has a range of 0–100
- **0...1**: For effects with smaller ranges or even on/off switches
- **−1...+1**: For values that can go negative or positive; if the number is higher than 1 or lower than −1, it's easy to add some simple math to an expression to multiply the value
- **0...360**: For rotation or effects that have rotational values
- **−180...180**: For rotation or other effects with this type of range
- **Custom**: your own custom value.

**Fall Off**: This will make the movement smoother, which is the prime reason that animations generated with Sound Keys look nicer than animations generated with Convert Audio to Keyframes.

- **Instant**: No gradual fall off
- **Linear**: Falls off at a constant value; the default
- **Exponential**: Quickly increases or decreases the falloff

- **None (integrate)**: The output incorporated over time to produce a continuously increasing signal
   9. When you're working on a project with Sound Keys (or any audio keyframe generator), you need to keep in mind how you would like your layers to move. The kick.mov footage will be tied to the area we just set up. The clip is of a man doing a single kick and we'll use the full duration of the clip. Since the clip is 7:00 and we'll be remapping the clip to the audio, for Range 1 set Output Min/Max to Custom, and then set Min to 0.0 and Max to 7.0.
   10. For Range 2, we'll use this same area of the spectrum as we used in Range 1, but set the Output to 0–360, which can be attached to rotational values or any parameters with a 360° phase. These values will be used for the background.
   11. For Range 3, we'll isolate the Treble hits. Twirl open Range 2 and check the Active box to activate. Set the range up a bit higher though, so that values only appear in the range during the treble hits. Go to 7:24 in the timeline for a Treble hit. Back at 5:00, the Treble values are low. Isolate the area above the blue area of the spectrum at 5:00, but encompassing the blue bars at 7:24. (Figure 11.17.)
   12. Set Type to Peak of Range, Falloff to Exponential, and the Output Min/Max to 0…100 for Range 3.
   13. Once all three ranges are set, preview the levels by RAM Previewing. Watch how the green Output bars on the right bounce.
   14. Once everything is satisfactory, at the very bottom of the Effect Controls panel, click the Apply button. It will take only a minute, but three Outputs will be keyframed on the Sound Keys layer. Select the Sound Keys layer in the timeline and

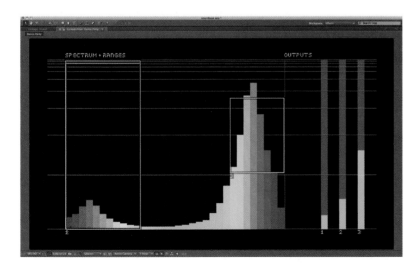

**Figure 11.17** All three Ranges are set up. Range 1 and Range 2 completely overlap. Notice the position of Range 3. Footage: Michele Yamazaki.

press the U key to see the keyframes. This is where we will be pick-whipping other parameters to.

### Setting Up the Visuals with Time Remap and Twitch

1. Now that the audio keyframes are set, we can get started on the visuals. Turn off the visibility of Sound Keys by clicking the Video (eyeball) checkbox in the timeline to hide it.
2. Drag kick.mov into the timeline and place it on top of the layer stack. Select the layer and enable Time Remap (Layer > Time > Enable Time Remap). Press the End key to jump to the last frame in the timeline. Press Option (Alt) + ] to extend kick.mov to the end of the timeline.
3. Select the Sound Keys layer and press the U key to reveal the Output keyframes. Back on the kick.mov layer, Option (Alt) + click the stopwatch next to Time Remap to add an expression. Drag the pick whip to Sound Keys Output 1. (Figure 11.18.)

**Figure 11.18** Pick-whipping Time Remap to Sound Keys Output 1. Footage: Michele Yamazaki.

4. The kick.mov footage is a bit dark, so apply Levels (Effect > Color Correction > Levels). Set Gamma to 1.25 to lighten the shot.
5. Apply **Video Copilot Twitch** to kick.mov (Effect > Video Copilot > Twitch). In the Effect Controls panel for Twitch, twirl open Enable and check Slide.
6. We're going to link Slide to the Treble section of the audio spectrum. Twirl open Operator Controls > Slide in the Timeline panel. Option (Alt) + click the Slide Amount to add an expression. Pick whip Slide Amount to Sound Keys Range 3. Set Slide Direction to $0x + 90.0°$. Go to 7:20 in the timeline to see the Slide effect. (Figure 11.19.)

**Finishing touches**: Place a background layer behind the kick .mov footage. I added a new solid and applied **After Effects 4–Color Gradient** and adjusted the colors.

On top of the gradient, I applied **Digieffects Delirium DE Visual Harmonizer** for some nice eye candy behind the man. I pick-whipped DE Visual Harmonizer's End Size to Output 1, modifying the expression with *3 to multiply the values by 3.

```
thisComp.layer("Sound Keys").effect("Sound Keys")("Output 1")*3
```

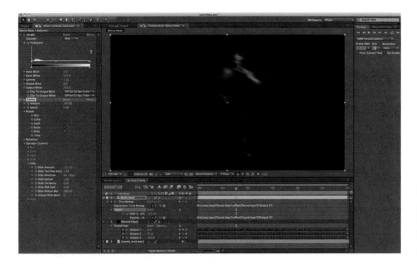

**Figure 11.19** Twitch Slide Amount is linked to the Sound Keys Output 3 keyframes. Footage credit: Crowd Control, clip # 00467_001_25.

I pick-whipped End Amplitude to Output 3, multiplying the values by 10 and adding 100 so that the value never dips below 100.

```
thisComp.layer("Sound Keys").effect("Sound Keys")
  ("Output 3")*101100
```

Lastly, I pick-whipped Start Phase to Output 2, then modified other parameters in DE Visual Harmonizer to my liking.

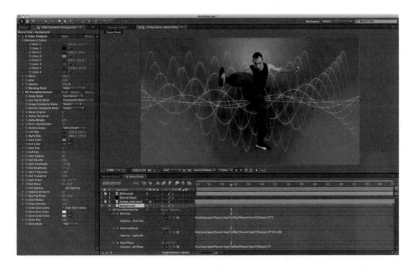

**Figure 11.20** Digieffects DE Visual Harmonizer has some parameters linked to the Sound Keys keyframe data. Footage credit: Crowd Control, clip # 00467_001_25.

Some of the gradations between colors on the background layer may look banded. If so, change the Depth in Color Settings from 8 bpc to 16 bpc. To change Project Settings, select File > Project Settings. Under Color Settings, set Depth to 16 bpc. Sound Keys is an 8-bit plug-in so you'll see a warning in the Effect Controls. In this case, you can ignore it because it's not a rendered effect but a keyframe generator.

**Figure 11.21**  If you see the little yellow yield sign next to a plug-in in the Effect Controls panel, it means that your Depth is set to 16 bpc but the plug-in only works in 8 bpc. Footage: Michele Yamazaki.

## Dancing Letters with Boris Continuum Complete Beat Reactor

Boris Continuum Complete BCC Beat Reactor does have a lot of similarities with Trapcode Sound Keys but Beat Reactor is slightly more robust in options. Beat Reactor gives the option for

**Figure 11.22**  The final result with Boris Continuum Complete Beat Reactor. Footage: Michele Yamazaki.

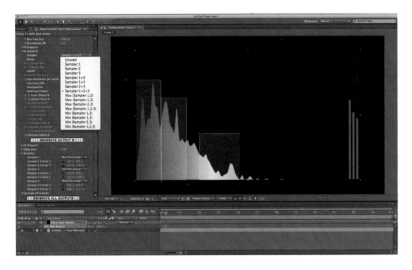

**Figure 11.23** Boris Beat Reactor and the optional Samplers. Footage: Michele Yamazaki.

up to 1028 frequency resolutions in the audio spectrum. There is also the option to set a custom range for outputting keyframes. There's an option to select multiple Samplers that are preset but can be modified.

Unlike the tutorial for Sound Keys, in which we experimented as we went along, this tutorial requires some planning. We will get the values we need for the ranges before we get started with Beat Reactor.

*The project files are included on this book's DVD in the BCC Beat Reactor Project folder.* Dr. Sassi graciously contributed the audio track "Book Drums." Thank you, Dr. Sassi!

**Third-party plug-ins needed:**

- Boris Continuum Complete

   1. Make a new Composition using the HDTV 1080 29.97 preset, 22 seconds in duration, and with a black background. Name it "Dancing Text".

   2. Drag the audio file Book_drums_drs_04.wav into the composition.

   3. Select the Type tool and type "PLUG-IN WITH AFTER EFFECTS". The font I've used for the project and for the cover of the book is named Chinese Rocks and can be downloaded for free (www.dafont.com). The font doesn't really matter for this tutorial, so choose one that you like. Make the text large and white. (Figure 11.24.)

   4. In the timeline, twirl open the text layer. Next to Text and below Switches, use the Animate flyout menu to select Per-Character 3D. (Figure 11.25).

**Figure 11.24** The text layout with the font Chinese Rocks. Footage: Michele Yamazaki.

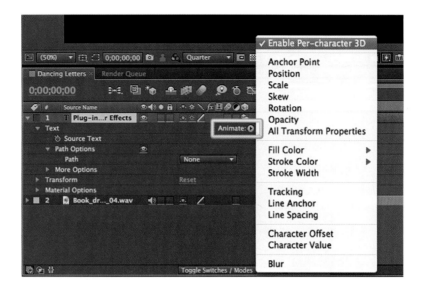

**Figure 11.25** Per-character 3D is enabled. Footage: Michele Yamazaki.

5. In the Composition panel, select "with Af" with the Type tool. This will define the Range when parameters are added. (Figure 11.26.)
6. To add Position parameters to the type, use the same Animate flyout menu and select Position. Twirl open Text > Animator 1 > Range Selector 1. This is not the Transform

**Figure 11.26** A few letters are selected. Footage: Michele Yamazaki.

**Figure 11.27** Choose Rotation in the Add Property flyout menu. Footage: Michele Yamazaki.

parameter, but Position under Text. Using the Add flyout menu for Animator 1, we'll add Rotation (Add > Property > Rotation). (Figure 11.27.)

7. Add a New Solid layer named Beat Reactor (Layer > New > Solid), and Make Comp Size. Apply **BCC Beat Reactor** to the layer (Effect > BCC Time > BCC Beat Reactor).

8. In the Effect Controls panel, set View Mode to Graph over Black and Audio Layer to Book_drums_drs_04.wav. The left and right channels of the audio are different in this track but we'll leave Channel set to Mixed. The first frame may be completely black because the audio hasn't started yet, so move to a different place in the timeline.

We'll only need two Range selectors, even though there is the option of three. For the first, FX Output A, we'll need to correlate with Position and have a minimum of 240 and a maximum of 40. The second will use FX Output B and is for Rotation, with a minimum of –20 and a maximum of 20. We'll set up custom ranges for both of these parameters.

9. In the Effect Controls panel for BCC Beat Reactor, twirl open FX Output A. RAM Preview the composition through and watch the audio spectrum to find a good place to isolate. To isolate the sample, twirl open Samplers and set Sampler:1 Corner 1 and Sampler:1 Corner 2. I'm isolating the red portion of the spectrum. Scrub the Current Time Indicator through the timeline and make sure that the red bars do not peak through the sampler area.

10. Open FX Output A and set Range Min to –40 and Range Max to 40. Twirl FX Output A closed. (Figure 11.28.)

11. Twirl open FX Output B. Set Sampler to Sampler:2 and repeat the process above, sampling the green and blue portion of the

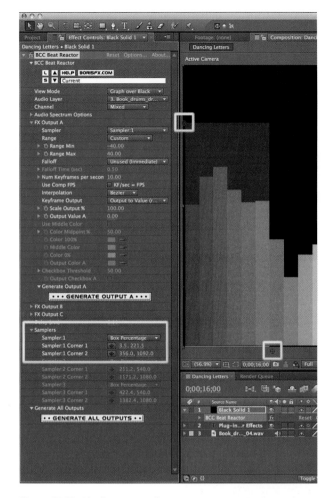

spectrum. Set Range Min to −20 and Range Max to 20. (Figure 11.29.)

12. When both samples are set to go, scroll to the bottom of the Effect Controls panel and click the Generate All Outputs button. This will generate keyframes on the Beat Reactor layer and a popup window will let you know when it's finished. Don't worry, if you make a mistake and you don't like the setup you've made, you can readjust it and recalculate the keyframes. Select the Beat Reactor layer and tap the U key to reveal only the keyframed parameters. Turn off the visibility of the Beat Reactor layer. (Figure 11.30.)

13. At the top of the Effect Controls panel, set View Mode to Hide Graph so that the text is visible and the graph is hidden.

14. On the Text layer, twirl open Text in the timeline. Find Animator 1 and Option (Alt) + click the Position stopwatch to add an expression. Drag the pick whip to Output Value A. (Figure 11.31.)

**Figure 11.28** 1 isolates a small portion of the spectrum. Footage: Michele Yamazaki.

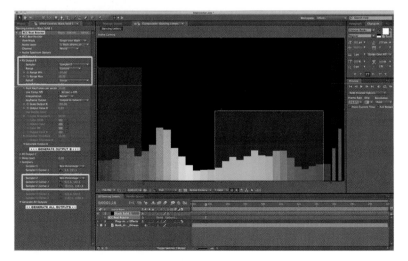

**Figure 11.29** FX Output B and Sampler:2. Footage: Michele Yamazaki.

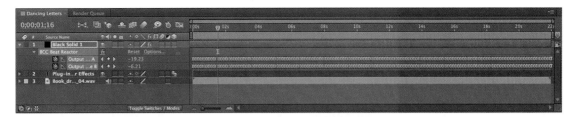

Figure 11.30  Beat Reactor generated keyframes. Footage: Michele Yamazaki.

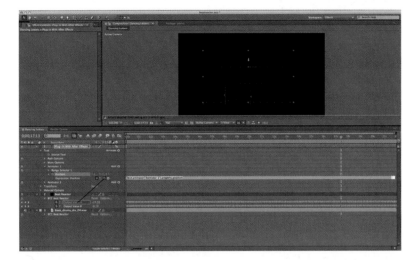

Figure 11.31  Position is being pick-whipped to Output Value A. Footage: Michele Yamazaki.

Figure 11.32  Changing the Expression will make the X and Z Positions stay in place while the effect is only driving the Y parameter. Footage: Michele Yamazaki.

15. We only want to move the Y position. We do not want to change X and Z parameters, which are the first and third "temp" inside the array brackets. Set them both to 0, as shown in the following expression. (Figure 11.32.)

```
temp = thisComp.layer("Beat Reactor").effect("BCC Beat
Reactor")("Output Value A");
[0, temp, 0]
```

16. Under Range Selector 1, for Offset we'll set up a quick Expression. Option (Alt) + click the stopwatch for Offset. Type the Expression:

```
wiggle(1,100)
```

17. This will cause the letters in the Range area to move left and right randomly.
18. Twirl open Advanced. Set Shape to Round to smooth out the animation. (Figure 11.33.)
19. Repeat this process for Animator 2 and X and Y Rotation, linking it to Output Value B. First set Animator 2 > Range Selector 1 Start to 10% and End to 40%. This will select about 30% of the area.
20. Option + click both X Rotation and Y Rotation to add Expressions. Pick whip both to Output Value B. (Figure 11.34.)

After playing this through, I'd like a bit more movement. We'll return to Beat Reactor and modify the Range and regenerate the keyframes. The new values will automatically be replaced.

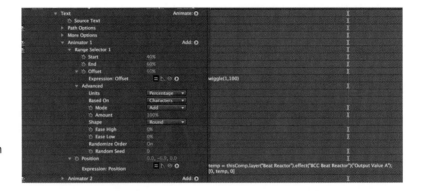

Figure 11.33 Beat Reactor with a wiggle expression. Footage: Michele Yamazaki.

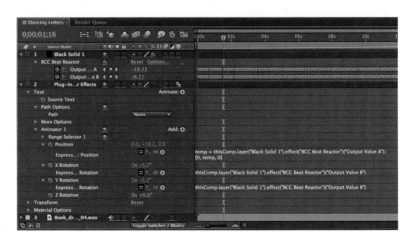

Figure 11.34 X Rotation and Y Rotation are linked to Output Value B. Footage: Michele Yamazaki.

21. Select the Beat Reactor layer and tap the E key to bring up the effect. Double-click Beat Reactor to open it in the Effect Controls panel.

22. Twirl open FX Output A and set Range Min to 280.00 and Range Max to 80.00. Twirl open FX Output B and set Range Min to −40 and Range Max to 40.

23. At the bottom of the panel, click Generate All Outputs. A popup window will tell you that it worked.

24. Watch the comp play through again. Make adjustments to taste. Add a background, a Camera, and some lights to make it more interesting.

**Figure 11.35** I added BCC Noise Map with Flow Direction linked to Output Value B, BCC LED and BCC Tritone, plus a Camera and a Spot Light. Footage: Michele Yamazaki.

## Automating Photo Montages with CoreMelt ImageFlow Fx

**Figure 11.36** CoreMelt Image-Flow Fx Carousel plug-in. Footage: Michele Yamazaki.

# Hot Tip

ImageFlow tends to run very slowly with large images, so scale your images in Photoshop to the largest size you'll want to present them onscreen first.

All of us have made photomontages for a wedding, graduation, birthday party, or other special event for family and friends. These types of animations are usually pretty easy to put together, but can be time-consuming to keyframe and organize.

**CoreMelt ImageFlow Fx** ($129) is a great way to automate this process. According to Alicia VanHeulen of Toolfarm, who demoed the CoreMelt plug-ins at NAB 2010, "ImageFlow Fx can really help you avoid the more tedious aspects of creating montages. It's also especially useful if you have a client sitting in on your edit and you want to give them something to react to instantly with as little set up as possible."

ImageFlow Fx is extremely easy to set up because it comes with a library of 30 premade animation styles, plus mattes and frames, all of which can be modified to suit your project. "Many of these presets would take hours to create from scratch and have a nice 3D look to them," Alicia said. "ImageFlow is under $150 and will more than pay for itself in your first job."

You just need to either import your images into After Effects or link a folder of images from your hard drive. This "link" feature is not something that is often seen in After Effects plug-ins, but can speed up workflow because you don't need to keep reimporting and replacing. Just add or swap images in the folder and reload them. Be sure to have only images that you want to use in the folder you are linking to.

Project files and images are not included for this tutorial.

**Third-party plug-ins needed:**

- CoreMelt ImageFlow Fx
    1. Create a new Composition using the settings of your preference (Layer > New > Composition.
    2. Add a new Solid Layer in your composition (New > Layer > Solid) and make it the same dimensions as your composition.
    3. Apply one of the CoreMelt ImageFlow Fx plug-ins to the solid. I chose Fall Forward (Effects > C2 ImageFlow – Instant Montages > Fall Forward). Placeholders for images will appear on screen, with the text "Select your Media type from the 'load' dropdown list. Then select your folder using the 'choose' button". (Figure 11.37)
    4. There is no background tool built into ImageFlow Fx, so place a Solid Layer with a Ramp applied to give the

**Figure 11.37** The default image for all ImageFlow Fx plug-ins with the instructions in the Composition panel. The Load dropdown list and Choose Folder are highlighted on the left in the Effect Controls panel. Footage: Michele Yamazaki.

**Figure 11.38** ImageFlow Fx Fall Forward with images linked and parameters modified. Footage: Michele Yamazaki.

background some interest at this point. It also helps images in the background or with low opacity pop a bit more because they may be blending into the background color if it's dark

5. RAM Preview the comp and adjust the parameters, which will be different for each ImageFlow Fx plug-in. (Figure 11.38.)

**Mask Options:** To apply a mask to the edges of the images, in the Effect Controls for ImageFlow Fx, check the Use Mask box. A new section will appear in the Effect Controls panel. Double-click the black and white image of the mask to bring up the mask presets. Choose one that you like. There are other options that are self explanatory: Blur Mask, Blur Strength, Mask Pos (position), Mask Scale, Mask Aspect, and Mask Rotation. There is also an option to use your own images as masks by setting Type to Image

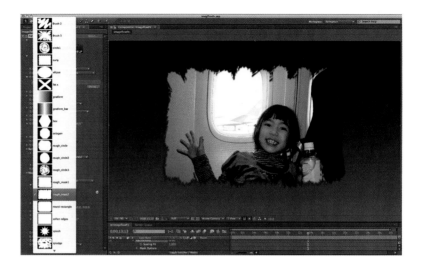

**Figure 11.39** ImageFlow Fx Masks applied to the photos. Footage: Michele Yamazaki.

Well. There is a full explanation of this aspect in the ImageFlow Fx manual.

**Picture Frame**: To apply a picture frame, check the User Frame box, and then choose a preset from the Choose Frame menu. There is an option to scale the frame and to use your own frame. Instructions for using your own frame are in the ImageFlow Fx manual.

**Figure 11.40** An ImageFlow Fx Picture Frame is applied to the image. Footage: Michele Yamazaki.

## Pro Tip

If you need to have the images in a certain order for ImageFlow Fx, make sure they are numbered first. It works best to number them in this format 01, 02, 03, and so on. If you have more than 100 photos, start with 001. This way they stay in order. If your images can be random, don't worry about naming them in any consistent manner.

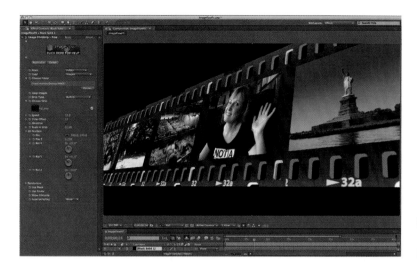

**Figure 11.41** CoreMelt Image-Flow Fx FilmStrip is free. Footage: Michele Yamazaki.

The plug-in supports background transparency so the user can use custom background images.

## Cover Flow Effects

Both Aquafadas and idustrial revolution, "fourth-party" developers of FxFactory, have recreated the cover flow effect from Apple's iTunes where album covers scroll by. The plug-ins link to an external folder on the user's hard drive to link the images for the animation, and it's completely automated. No keyframes need to be set at all, unless you want to.

Reflections are built in as well as text generators, so it's easy as can be. This will make that video that you promised for your cousin's wedding happen very quickly and it will look slick!

**Figure 11.42** Aquafadas PulpFx Abstract Coverflow, which uses the FxFactory Engine, is a fast way to create a slide-show effect. Footage: Michele Yamazaki.

**Figure 11.43** idustrial revolution CoverFlux, which also uses the FxFactory engine, is another Cover Flow effect. Footage: Michele Yamazaki.

### Ken Burns Style Effect with Boris Continuum Complete BCC Pan and Zoom

If you do any documentary editing or even photo montages for weddings, the Ken Burns effect will be something you'll certainly use to make still images more interesting. Ken Burns, if you don't know the name, is a documentary filmmaker. He is known for working with old photos and slowly panning and zooming into a small area of the shot.

You don't need a third-party plug-in to achieve this effect as it is easy enough to do with After Effects by animating the Anchor Point and Scale, or by making the image layer 3D and animating a Camera in 3D space. If you're new to After Effects, **Boris Continuum Complete BCC Pan and Zoom** ($199, or as part of

**Figure 11.44** Boris Continuum Complete BCC Pan and Zoom's Preview mode. Footage: Michele Yamazaki.

Boris Complete, $999) makes it incredibly easy to visualize and time the movement. The plug-in autoanimates but can also be keyframed. We'll use the Auto-Animation Workflow.

*Project files for this tutorial are located on the DVD in the BCC Pan and Zoom folder.* The photo I've included is one that I shot in Chinatown in Vancouver. It's included with the project files on the DVD. A nice feature of this plug-in is that it is not necessary to import the footage into After Effects as the files can just be linked externally to an image file. This is useful if you're working with a group of people and photos are still being edited. As long as the file name and path stays the same the photos will automatically update.

**Third-party plug-ins needed:**
- Boris Continuum Complete BCC Pan and Zoom
  1. Make a new Composition named "Chinatown" using the HDTV 1080 29.97 preset, 10 seconds in duration.
  2. Create a new Solid layer, the same size as the comp named Pan and Zoom. Apply BCC Pan and Zoom (Effects > BCC Distortion Perspective > BCC Pan and Zoom).

     In the Effect Controls panel for BCC Pan and Zoom, under Source, choose External File. You'll see a message appear in the Comp panel telling you to link to an external file. Under Source > External File, click the L button and navigate to the file. The file is named chinatown.JPG. (Figure 11.45.)
  3. This image is a larger format than the video screen but BCC Pan and Zoom will set it so it perfectly fits in the Composition. This setting is under Transforms > Adjust Scale: Fit at 100 Percent. It will maintain the aspect ratio of the image. This can be set to Off or Letterbox as well. Leave it at the default settings.

**Figure 11.45** When Pan and Zoom is applied to a layer, this message appears, asking you to link to an external file. The Source section to link an External File is highlighted. Footage: Michele Yamazaki.

**Figure 11.46** Preview mode with BCC Pan and Zoom. Footage: Michele Yamazaki.

4. Click the checkbox for Preview Mode to bring up the interface. The window in the upper right corner shows the output. The main part of the screen is for setting up the movement. (Figure 11.46.)

5. We'll be going from a wide shot to a zoom on the statues. We'll leave Setup A, or the beginning point of the shot, as is. To position the image in Setup B, set Preview Target to Setup B. A target will appear onscreen with double square boxes and a circle. The square is for position and the circle is for rotation. The inner square is Action Safe. Drag the square so that it frames the statue and building. (Figure 11.47.)

**Figure 11.47** Setup B. Footage: Michele Yamazaki.

6. If you run a RAM Preview while in Preview mode you'll see a very fast preview of the move that was just set up.

7. Uncheck Preview Mode and preview the animation. It looks pretty good but the animation can be tweaked. Twirl open Animation. These settings are in frames, so a 5.00 Hold Start is a five-frame pause before the zoom.
8. Click the checkbox for Preview Ease Curve and then adjust the values of Ease In and Ease Out. You'll see a visual representation of the curve. Set both Ease In and Ease Out higher, to about 50.
9. Clicking the checkbox at the bottom of the Effect Controls panel can enable motion blur.

# KEYING AND COMPOSITING GREENSCREEN FOOTAGE

Greenscreen (or bluescreen) and keying adds versatility and endless options to a production. Some effects-heavy Hollywood films, such as *Star Wars: Episode II—Attack of the Clones,* are shot almost entirely on greenscreen or bluescreen. It's a great way to put your actors in a scene that would be perilous in real life, like the earth falling apart in *2012,* or in a world that doesn't exist, like *Tron.* Greenscreen can help make your characters look like they're flying, like *Superman* or *Harry Potter* on a broomstick. You could even use green clothing to make areas of your actor disappear like in *The Invisible Man.*

"Pulling a key," a term referring to removing green or blue from a greenscreen or bluescreen shot, is a technique that is imperative for all compositors to know well. There are lots of tools out there to help pull a key but the technique is generally the same for greenscreen or bluescreen. It seems easy, like a shortcut to rotoscoping (cutting out elements frame by frame with the masking tools) for the uninitiated, but in reality, keying and compositing greenscreen can be time-consuming and takes a great deal of skill and patience. You will only get better with practice and by learning the techniques of the pros.

In this chapter, I've chosen to not just explain how to use some of the keyers, but to dive into some of the best-practice techniques that can be used with any of the keyers. I'll introduce you to **Red Giant Primatte Keyer**, **Boris Continuum Chroma Key**, **Digital Film Tools zMatte**, and **The Foundry Keylight**. **Ultimatte AdvantEdge** is another well-known keyer for After Effects but will not be updated for 64-bit, so is not covered in this book.

## Preprocessing Greenscreen Footage

There are a few preprocess steps—steps you have to take before you begin to key—that can help you obtain the best key possible, depending on your footage, of course (garbage in, garbage out!). These steps can help speed up your workflow and render time.

- **Degrain your footage if it is noisy**. Degraining footage can be render intensive so if your footage is low quality or dark, you may need to take this step. Pay special attention to the

**Figure 12.1** With greenscreen footage shot on DV, your green channel will often be the cleanest and blue channels will usually be the noisiest. Footage: Michigan Film Reel.

blue channel since lower quality formats tend to be noisy in the blue channel (hence, greenscreen is preferred over bluescreen). (Figure 12.1.) See the section on Noise and Grain in Chapter 14 for more information.

- **Separate fields**. If you have interlaced footage, make sure you have separated fields properly and removed pulldown. You do not want to key redundant frames if you don't have to, and interlaced footage can make keying challenging. To separate fields, go to File > Interpret Footage > File and separate on a clip-by-clip basis.

## FURTHER READING

For more on separating fields and pulldown, and in-depth information on deinterlacing, check out *Creating Motion Graphics with After Effects*, 5th Edition by Chris and Trish Meyer (http://amzn.to/jgGSJk). The Meyers also extensively cover this topic in their Lynda.com training module.

- **Deartifact blocky edges**. If your edges are in need of deartifacting (they are jaggy) try to smooth them out with a deartifacting plug-in. **Digital Film Tools zMatte, Red Giant Primatte Keyer** and **Red Giant Key Correct** ($399) come with built-in deartifacters. If you don't have those tools, try using a channel blur set very, very low on the blue channel, and try blurring horizontal only.

## Pro Tip: Shoot Progressive when Keying

If you have any control over the shoot, it's highly advised to avoid interlacing altogether when you plan to key.

# Pro Tip: What Causes Jaggy Edges?

Steppiness and blockiness are often seen when in-camera sharpening is used. If you haven't shot your footage yet, turn off in-camera sharpening and set your camera to the default settings. The problems are also caused by the compression introduced by codec (such as DV) and the video format (such as 4:1:1).

- **Even out your greenscreen**. If your footage is not evenly lit, a recommended tool to smooth out the greenscreen is **Red Giant Key Correct Smooth Screen** or **Digital Film Tools zMatte Screen Smoother**. You can sometimes just bump up the green channel but that will often add more spill, the green reflected on your actor. This step can often be skipped because of your garbage matte, explained in the next step. Only bother evening out the greenscreen if it's widely varied in brightness close to your actor. (Figure 12.2.)

Figure 12.2 *Left*: The untouched greenscreen shot. *Right*: The greenscreen is smoothed with Red Giant Key Correct Smooth Screen. Footage: Michigan Film Reel.

- **Add a garbage matte**. This step should not be skipped. A garbage matte, a.k.a. junk matte, is a loose articulated mask around your main subject, isolating it and removing unneeded stuff—extra greenscreen, equipment, shadows, tracking dots, and so on. The less your keyer has to calculate, the better your final result.
  1. Mask your clip and place keyframes to follow your subject's movement, using the "bisecting the timeline" method. This method involves placing your matte around your object on frame 1, setting a keyframe for the mask, jumping ahead in the timeline to the end of your clip, and moving the mask points around your subject again. Remember to make the mask loose.
  2. Find the midway point between these keyframes and move the mask again if necessary.
  3. Repeat this method through the duration of the footage that you need to key. After Effects will do the in-betweens for you, so it speeds up workflow dramatically as opposed to adjusting frame by frame.

**Figure 12.3** A garbage matte is a loose matte that is keyframed to isolate the foreground image. Footage: Michigan Film Reel.

4. Check your clip frame-by-frame and adjust mask points if the mask is clipping your actor. (Figure 12.3.)

## Keyers and Tools

Now that you've preprocessed your footage, you can move on to the main task at hand, the key itself. **The Foundry's Keylight**, an industry-leading keyer for After Effects, ships with and is installed with the nondemo version of After Effects. Keylight is a robust keyer that, simply put, does a better job than the other keyers that ship with After Effects.

Why would you need a keyer besides Keylight? Depending on your footage—the quality, the lighting, and the noise—one keyer may work better than another. Some keyers come with compositing tools such as edge tools, light wraps, color matchers, and more. I recommend owning at least one other third-party keyer in addition to Keylight. A plug-in with compositing tools will help your workflow. If you have a tough keying job, try some demos and see what works for that particular job.

### The Foundry Keylight

The Academy Award-winning Keylight ships with After Effects so it's a natural choice for a keyer. It's easy to use and powerful and a great tool for keying those tough-to-key areas like hair, fuzz, semitransparent areas, and reflections. It has built-in spill suppression, which removes reflected green on your subject, and also gives several options on viewing the key and matte.

**Web Link: Need Practice Greenscreen Footage?**

Hollywood Camera Work has lots of great shots to practice keying, and they're free. There are lots of challenging shots to improve your skills with spill, sheer fabrics, smoke, glasses, wispy hair, motion blur, and more. *www. hollywoodcamerawork.us/ greenscreenplates.html.*

**Web Link**

The Keylight User Guide can be downloaded here: www. thefoundry.co.uk/products/ keylight/user-guides/.

**Figure 12.4** The man with the gun was shot on greenscreen and is keyed and composited with Keylight. Footage: Michigan Film Reel. Otter photo: Michele Yamazaki.

If you're new to keying, this is the quick-start method of using Keylight. *Project files are on this book's DVD in the Keylight Project folder.* The project file contains two versions of the Comp, the Basic Keylight Key, used in this tutorial, and Angie Mistretta's Method, highlighted in the next section of the chapter.

**Third-party plug-ins needed:**
- The Foundry Keylight (ships with After Effects)
  1. Import the footage shooting.mp4, supplied on this book's DVD in the Keylight folder. Drag it to the Create a New Composition button at the bottom of the Project panel. Open the Composition Settings (Composition > Composition Settings) to rename the project Basic Keylight Key. Also in Composition Settings, set the Background Color to a color that completely contrasts with the greenscreen, such as bright purple, orange, or pink, so that it's easy to see your edges and areas of greenscreen that might otherwise be missed.
  2. Apply a garbage matte to your footage, following the process detailed earlier in this chapter.
  3. Apply Keylight to your greenscreen (or bluescreen) footage (Effects > Keying > Keylight). In the Effect Controls panel, click on the Screen Colour eyedropper to select it, then click on an area with a prominent shade of green near your actor. This should remove most of the greenscreen in the shot. I chose near the left of the actor's head. (Figure 12.5.)
  4. On the View pulldown menu for Keylight, change it to Screen Matte. This will show you the black and white matte.
     Twirl down Screen Matte controls and adjust Clip White and Clip Black. The idea is to make the background as black and the foreground as white as possible with a bit of gray

**Figure 12.5** Use the eyedropper to grab Screen Colour. Footage: Michigan Film Reel.

**Figure 12.6** With View set to Screen Matte, the black and white matte can be seen. With the example on the left, Clip Black and Clip White are adjusted minimally, and Screen Despot Black and Screen Despot White are used to clean up any specks. The image on the right has Clip Black and Clip White adjusted too much so the edges are jaggy. Footage: Michigan Film Reel.

around softer edges, like hair and fur. If the matte is too sharp, edge detail is lost. The idea is to push/pull Clip White and Clip Black values until you have clean edges with a minimal loss of detail, so use it as sparingly as possible.

5. If your matte has specks or small holes, adjust Screen Despot Black and Screen Despot White. (Figure 12.6.)

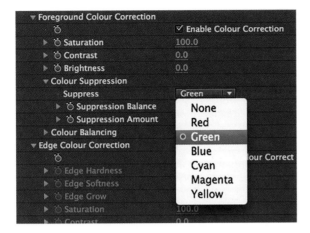

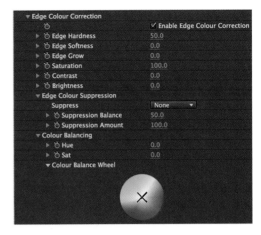

**Figure 12.7** Foreground Colour Correction settings in Keylight. Screenshot: Michele Yamazaki.

**Figure 12.8** Edge Colour Correction settings in Keylight. Screenshot: Michele Yamazaki.

6. There is only a small spot on the gun with green spill, or reflected color from the greenscreen. For spill removal, enable Colour Suppression under Foreground Colour Correction. If you have spill, or perhaps the lighting guy was overzealous with the magenta gels, the controls are under Colour Suppression. Just choose Green for greenscreen footage and adjust Suppression Balance and Suppression Amount until the green is removed. (Figure 12.7.)

7. For added control, Edge Color Correction adjusts the color that will be replaced around the edges. This is very useful if green fringe is a problem on hair and softer edges and the spill suppressor is not enough. This works especially well if areas of the subject are keyed separately—the hair, clothing, and skin isolated from each other. (Figure 12.8.)

## Pro Tip

Because there is no split-screen option in Keylight like you have in Primatte Keyer, it is more difficult to view both the key and the matte at the same time. There is a workaround. Make sure the View in Keylight is set to Final Result. In the tab at the top of the Comp panel, choose New Comp Viewer. Drag the second window to the right so that you have two instances of your composition. In the second comp panel, in the Show Color and Channel Management pulldown (the RGB icon at the bottom of the Composition panel), choose Alpha.

# Pro-Tip: Angie Mistretta's Preferred Method for Professional Keying—Isolate and Conquer

This is an excellent method of keying taught to me by Angie Mistretta of Pixar, which she learned at the Academy of Art from instructors who had worked on blockbusters such as *Star Wars: Episode II—Attack of the Clones*. The technique involves taking the garbage matted footage into a new comp and then building secondary garbage masks, keying isolated areas of the subject one at a time. For example, isolate the hair, the skin, the clothing, and any other parts that have different colors, textures, hairiness, or even motion blur. The matte choke, or tightening the alpha matte pixel by pixel, and spill suppression on these areas will often require different settings or adjustments.

1. Garbage matte your footage in its own comp. Name that comp "Garbage Matte". Also, go through the preprocess steps, especially degraining the footage.

2. Bring your Garbage Matte comp into a new comp, and name it "Final Key". Rename the Garbage Matte layer "Core". This is the Core of the key that will be used to fill in the middle of the key when the edges are isolated.

3. Apply Keylight just as you normally would but don't worry about making the edges too clean. Under Screen Matte, use Screen Shrink/Grow set to a negative value to shrink the matte so that you thin your subject by 10%. Note that there will probably be a strip of missing footage around the bottom or other edge of the screen if the subject goes offscreen. This is normal. (Figure 12.9.)

4. Drag the Garbage Matte comp into your Final Key comp again. Turn off the Core layer so that this new layer can be seen without any interference. Use the Pen tool to isolate an area of your actor such as the hair. Rename the layer accordingly (e.g., "Hair", "Arm", "Right Shoulder").

5. Keyframe the mask using the bisection method to follow this isolated area of the actor through the shot. Feather the mask and make sure you overlap other areas such as the skin so that the areas will blend. (Figure 12.10.)

6. Apply Keylight to this layer. Despill and adjust Clip Black and Clip White as necessary but do not color correct. Color correction will be done later when all areas are keyed. While keying this area, just focus on the area inside the mask.

**Figure 12.9** *Left:* The original shot with a garbage matte. *Right:* The Core Matte is shrunk with Screen Shrink/Grow in Keylight. Footage: Michigan Film Reel.

7. Repeat with each area of the footage until all edges are keyed. Remember to focus on the edges, ignoring interior holes. The Core Matte will fill in the center. Turn on the Core Matte layer and make sure that it is the top layer in your timeline. Make sure all masks are feathered and adjust any masks if there needs to be more overlap. (Figure 12.11.)

8. If your comp has a strip of missing footage at the bottom or edge of the screen, drag the Garbage Matte into the main comp. This will happen if you're isolating edges on the left and right side and the Core Matte in the center doesn't reach the bottom edge, leaving a hole. Add another instance of the Core Matte and use the Rectangle Mask tool to isolate the missing area, giving it some overlap. Feather the mask so that there are no hard edges.

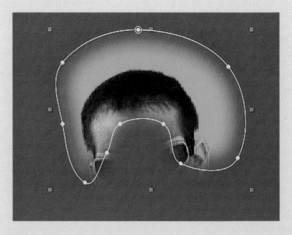

Figure 12.10  Isolating the hair with a matte before keying.

9. Once the key is complete and clean around every edge, drag the Final Key comp into the Create a New Composition button at the bottom of the Project panel, or create a new composition and drag the Final Key footage in. Name the composition "Composite".

10. Drag your background into the Composite comp. Any color correction, light wraps, and other foreground compositing processes should be done at this point.

Figure 12.11  The Hair layer is selected with the hair isolated. The Core Matte is on top. The flowchart on the right shows how the elements are organized.

**Web Link**

For more on the multiple mask method, check out *Toolfarm Expert Series Professional Training for Keylight* by Angie Mistretta, available at *www.toolfarm.com*. It is a great resource for keying, even if you're using a different keying plug-in.

## Red Giant Primatte Keyer

**Red Giant Primatte Keyer** ($499) is created for designers, with more of a visual interface than just the usual sliders and dials. Unlike other keying effects, the user clicks and drags over the footage to select the matte foreground and background. The first time I tried it, I was a little thrown. Not typically a manual reader, I couldn't figure out how to use Primatte Keyer. I had to open the manual! Once I realized how it worked, it became my go-to plug-in for keying. It is easy to use, very fast, and has numerous extras like a Deartifacter, Spill Killer, Color Matcher, and Light Wrap.

Here is a basic "jump into Primatte tutorial" that will get you going. *Footage and project files are included on this book's DVD in the Primatte Project folder.*

**Third-party plug-ins needed**

- Red Giant Primatte Keyer

1. Bring the clip JasonMSGS.mp4, included on this book's DVD in the Primatte Project folder, into After Effects. Drag it to the Create a New Composition button at the bottom of the Project panel. Place the background image, the image of the otter, behind the greenscreen footage.

2. Take care of the preprocess tasks, such as garbage matting footage. Apply Primatte Keyer to the footage. Set the mode under Deartifacting to DV/HDV, which is the source of the video. This can help with jaggy edges. (Figure 12.13.)

3. Under Keying > Selection, click the Select BG button. In the Comp panel, click and drag on the green (or blue for blue-screen) background close to your subject. Take small samples, or "bites." It will keep removing areas of green as you sample. Only worry about areas inside your garbage matte. (Figure 12.14.)

**Figure 12.12** A greenscreen shot of Jason in front of an image from an aquarium in Tokyo. The footage was keyed with Red Giant Primatte Keyer Pro. Footage: Michigan Film Reel. Image: Michele Yamazaki.

**Figure 12.13** Deartifacting is set to DV/HDV to match the format of the footage.

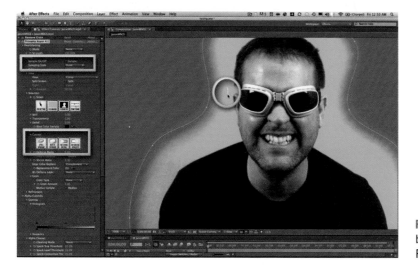

**Figure 12.14** Selecting the background for removal with Primatte Keyer.

4. Once you have most of the green selected, under Keying > View, change the View to Matte. Under Selection again, click the Clean FG button. Click and drag on any gray, semitransparent areas inside your subject. Once it's fairly clean, click the Clean BG and do the same on the background. Remember to do it in small increments. Don't worry if you have specks at this point, especially outside of the garbage matte, which won't matter anyway. (Figure 12.15.)

5. When you have a nice black and white matte, under the Alpha Controls and under Gamma, adjust the Histogram. This works just like Levels.

6. To clean up any specks or holes, adjust the Alpha Cleaner. There are other refinement adjustments that can

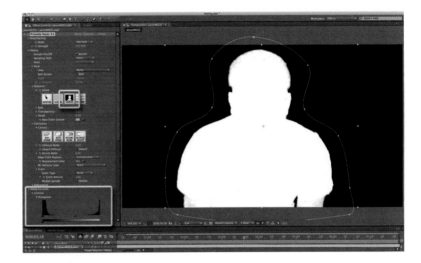

**Figure 12.15** Cleaning up the foreground matte in Primatte Keyers. The histogram, mentioned in Step 6 is at the bottom of the Effect Controls panel.

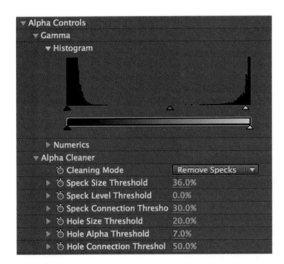

**Figure 12.16** Alpha Controls and the Alpha Cleaner help remove specks and holes.

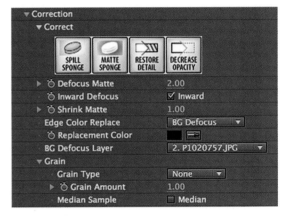

**Figure 12.17** Edge Color Replace with the background layer chosen will help blend the edges.

be tweaked. Don't be afraid to check the manual if you get stuck. (Figure 12.16.)

Set View back to Comp.

7. To soften the edges of the matte go to Keying > Correction > Defocus Matte. There are also options to Inward Defocus and Shrink Matte if you're seeing a green fringe around your footage. I have had good results setting Edge Color Replace to BG Defocus and then choosing my background image in the BG Defocus Layer pulldown menu. (Figure 12.17.)

8. Primatte Keyer has compositing tools built into the plug-in under the Composite Controls section, which uses the color information in your background layer for Spill Killer, Color Matcher, and Light Wrap. Choose the Background Layer in the pulldown menu.

9. To remove green spill, click Enable next to Enable Spill Killer. Choose Green for Color Mode to remove any green spill. Adjust the Range, Tolerance, and Strength as needed.

10. To bring more blue into the foreground from the background click Enable for Enable Color Matcher (under Color Matcher). The Strength and Levels in the Highlights, Midtones, and Shadows are adjustable.

11. Lastly, under Composite Controls is Light Wrap. Light Wrap brings some of the background colors and luminance levels onto the edges of the foreground footage to help the composite look natural. To use this feature, click Enable under Enable Light Wrap. Adjust the Operation, Blur, Comp Mode, Width, and Brightness until it looks natural. (Figure 12.18.)

Figure 12.18  Composite Controls help to blend the foreground footage into the background naturally. The Light Wrap is exaggerated so that it is easily visible.

# Pro Tip: Dealing with Motion Blur on Greenscreen Footage

If your footage has a lot of motion blur, you will need to use a keying plug-in that can handle partial transparency and "unmultiply" the background color from the blurred areas. Motion blur is extremely difficult to cleanly key, but it's relatively easy to add motion blur in postproduction with RE:Vision Effects ReelSmart Motion Blur (more on ReelSmart Motion Blur in Chapter 3). If you have control over the video shoot, using a high shutter speed will lessen motion blur, but will result in less a filmic look when shooting on video.

## Digital Film Tools zMatte

**Digital Film Tools** promotes **zMatte** ($395) as a tool with a proprietary matte extraction technology, but I like it as a fantastic keying tool! Just apply zMatte, choose green or blue and the key already looks pretty darn good, even with low-quality footage.

zMatte is a full compositing suite solution and ships with the following plug-ins: **Color Suppress, DeArtifact, Edge Composite, Frame Averager, Holdout Composite, Keyer, Light Wrap, Matte Generator, Matte Repair, Matte Wrap**, and **Screen Smoother**.

Here is the quick-start method for keying with zMatte. The plug-ins, once installed, show up under DFT zMatte. *Greenscreen footage and project files are included on this book's DVD in the zMatte folder.*

**Figure 12.19** Greenscreen footage of the man with a gun is keyed with zMatte and placed in front of the Ghibli Museum in Mitaka, Japan. Footage: Michigan Film Reel. Image: Michele Yamazaki.

**Third-party plug-ins needed:**

- Digital Film Tools zMatte
    1. Bring the footage shooting3.mp4, included on this book's DVD in the zMatte folder, into After Effects. Drag it to the Create a New Composition button at the bottom of the Project panel.
    2. Take care of the preprocess tasks, such as garbage matting footage.
    3. Before we start keying, let's even out the greenscreen to make keying easier. Apply zMatte Screen Smoother to the footage (Effect > DFT zMatte > zMatte Screen Smoother). In the Effect Controls, twirl open Matte and set Extract On to Green. Under Color Correct, increase Green until the greenscreen is smoother and less noisy. Also try adjusting Gamma, Saturation, and other settings.
    4. Apply zMatte Keyer to the footage (Effect > DFT zMatte > zMatte Keyer). Under Primary Matte, choose Greenscreen or Bluescreen. The key should already look pretty decent. (Figure 12.20.)

**Figure 12.20** The default settings for zMatte's Primary Matte set to Extract on Green Screen.

5. Switch the View of zMatte from Output to Primary Matte and you will see that the matte needs cleaning up. As with other keyers, the object is to make the matte as black and white as possible without losing any edge detail. Adjust the Background and Foreground values, as well as the Black Clip and White Clip values, until the matte is clean. The Background and Foreground values and Black and White Clip values work very similarly, however the Background and Foreground values work only when Extract On is set to Blue Screen or Green Screen. Black Clip and White Clip will work with any option under Extract On. (Figure 12.21.)

6. Still under Primary Matte, add a bit of Horizontal Blur to soften any jagged edges. "Gang Blur" is a term used in

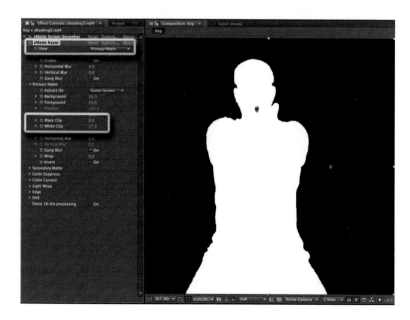

**Figure 12.21** Primary matte adjustments.

Digital Film Tools plug-ins that means linking the Horizontal and Vertical Blurs together.

7. To remove the green spill, twirl open Color Suppress. Either use Auto color or uncheck Auto color and select another shade of green. Adjust the Range just until the green is removed, without changing the other colors in the shot.

8. Place the background layer behind the footage and Scale and Position it appropriately.

9. Back on the shooting3.mp4 layer, in the Effect Controls for zMatte, twirl open Light Wrap. Choose the background layer in the pulldown menu for Background. Adjust the Light and Wrap settings until it looks natural.

10. If you're noticing some green fringe around the edges, twirl open Edge. Set the Size of the edge. Lower the Saturation and lower the levels of Green until the fringe color no longer appears. (Figure 12.22.)

11. You may notice a hole in the matte where the gun is reflecting green from the greenscreen. One way to fix this is to place another layer of shooting3.mp4 behind of the keyed footage with a mask isolating the spot that is being keyed out. To remove the green, apply Spill Killer (Effects > DFT zMatte > Spill Killer) and adjust the Tolerance until the green is removed. (Figure 12.23.)

12. Color correct the shot as needed.

**Figure 12.22** Light Wrap and Edge settings.

**Figure 12.23** Another instance of the greenscreen footage is placed over the keyed footage with the area with the hole masked. Spill Killer removes the green spill.

**Figure 12.24** The Before and After versions of fixing the hole with a duplicate masked layer.

## WHAT IS THE SECONDARY MATTE USED FOR IN ZMATTE?

There is also a Secondary Matte available in zMatte. If you're wondering, the zMatte User Guide explains: "We like to use an inner/outer keying method that involves creating a Primary Matte which has gray values in the foreground's edge. This will give a nice, smooth edge in the final composite. Next, the trick is to use the Secondary Matte to fill in any gray areas of the Primary Matte while retaining the gray values in the edge. You can do this by adjusting the Blur, Shrink/Grow, and/or Wrap parameters of the Secondary Matte to retain the Primary Matte's edge values."

## Pro Tip: Built-in DeArtifact Tool versus Separate DeArtifact Plug-in

The zMatte Keyer includes a DeArtifact tool but it's also available as an individual plug-in. Why two options? They work the same way, but you would choose to use the individual plug-in if you need to apply another plug-in between the DeArtifact and the Keyer. If you don't, the DeArtifact within the Keyer plug-in is fine.

### Boris Continuum Chroma Key

**Boris Continuum Chroma Key ($299)** is a very fast and precise set of keying and compositing plug-ins. It used to be necessary to buy the full Boris Continuum Package but now the **BCC Chroma Key** can be purchased as a unit, which makes sense if you don't have the budget for the full package. It comes with the following plug-ins: BCC Chroma Key, **BCC Matte Choker** to tighten in on edges, **BCC Light Wrap** and **BCC Match Grain**. There are not a lot of controls as with some keying plug-ins but BCC Chroma Key is a very "smart" plug-in and picks up the keyable area quickly and cleanly.

It's very easy to get started with BCC Chroma Key. *The project files are on this book's DVD in the BCC Chroma Key folder.*

**Third-party plug-ins needed**

- Boris Continuum Complete or Boris Chroma Key Unit

1. Bring the footage TrackPhone.mp4, included on this book's DVD in the BCC Chroma Key folder, into After Effects. Drag it to the Create a New Composition button at the bottom of the Project panel. Place the background image, the image of the bokeh light blurs, behind the greenscreen footage. Click the eyeball in the Timeline panel to hide the TrackPhone.mp4 layer so that you can see the background layer to position and scale it. Click the eyeball again to unhide the video.

2. Go through the preprocess steps (garbage matte, etc.) with your greenscreen footage.

3. Apply BCC Chroma Key and select the greenscreen color near the edge of your subject with the Eyedropper tool. There is also a BCC preset for greenscreen footage called greenscreen. bcp that works pretty well as a jumping-off point. Use the preset menu within the Effect Controls panel and select it. It will automatically remove a default shade of green. (Figure 12.25.)

4. Switch Output to Show Matte to see which areas are not being keyed out and should be. Density, Balance, and Lightness adjustments will fill holes and specks. There's a Compare pull-down menu that allows the user to see the original footage plus the matte or the final output, but unfortunately does not

Figure 12.25  The greenScreen. bcp preset can be seen in the pulldown menu.

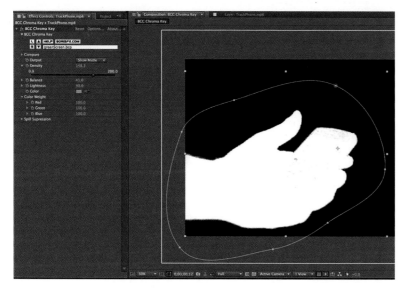

Figure 12.26  Output is set to Show Matte so that the Matte can be seen.

let the user see the matte on one side and the final output on the other. It's still useful though. (Figure 12.26.)

5. Spill Suppression is built into the BCC Chroma plug-in. It is pretty straightforward but settings will vary from footage to footage. Adjust the settings for Spill Suppression to remove any spill. (Figure 12.27.)

6. To lose the fringe, apply the BCC Matte Choker (Effects > BCC Keys Mattes > BCC Matte Choker) plug-in to choke

**Figure 12.27** Spill Suppression settings.

**Figure 12.28** The key "fringe" of dark color on the edge of the key that can be removed with BCC Matte Choker.

**Figure 12.29** The final key with Boris Continuum Chroma Key plug-ins plus some BCC DeGrain applied to the foreground footage.

in the edges and soften the edges. Try the presets first and make adjustments (or just dive in). (Figure 12.28.)

7. Add a subtle light wrap if needed with the BCC Light Wrap plug-in (Effects > BCC Keys Mattes > BCC Light Wrap). (Figure 12.29.)

## Compositing Tools and Matte Tools

The final step of creating a great key is to make a convincing composite. Basically what any compositor needs are tools for spill suppression, light wrap, color correction and matching, edge blending, wire removal, blurs and focus, adjusting light angles, and matching or adding grain. Many of these topics are covered in other chapters. Color correction is such an in-depth topic that it easily deserves its own chapter (see Chapter 2).

Several plug-ins exist solely to help the user achieve a natural-looking edge to a key and a convincing composite. A few of these have been mentioned: Red Giant Key Correct and others that are built into the plug-ins such as Digital Film Tools zMatte, Boris Chroma Keyer, and Keylight.

## Alpha Channel and Matte Cleaners

Sometimes you have a hole or some specks in your matte you just can't get rid of. Often this is a result of some reflected green on something shiny, like jewelry, glasses, or a prop, or often something in the shot is just too close of a color to the greenscreen. Duplicating the foreground layer without the keyer and masking and feathering the area around the hole will help a lot.

Sometimes it's not that easy. It may be a lot of small specks that are causing the edges of the matte to become jaggy as the keyers' values are increased. If that's the case, there are alpha and matte cleaners to help.

Red Giant Primatte Keyer and Key Correct have a very nice Alpha Cleaner plug-in that cleans up holes, specks, or both. Just be aware that when you use plug-ins like this your edges can become jaggy, so you'll want to use these tools with a light hand and soften the edges with an edge blur of some sort.

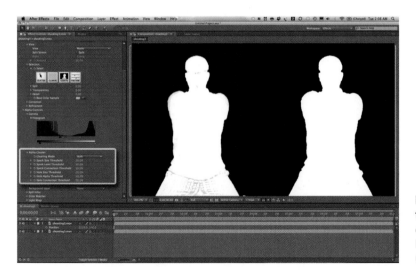

**Figure 12.30** The example on the left has holes. The instance on the right is cleaned up with Red Giant Primatte Keyer Alpha Cleaner.

**Boris Continuum BCC Matte Cleanup** is another option and works well for fixing a hole in the matte. It allows the user to isolate the hole with position crosshairs for the Region of Interest Top-Left and the Region of Interest Bottom-Right. The Blend, Choke, Black and White levels, Spread, and Gain can be adjusted to fill in the hole. Most plug-ins that fill holes in mattes will adjust the choke or alpha levels for the entire matte. This one is nice because it will isolate the hole.

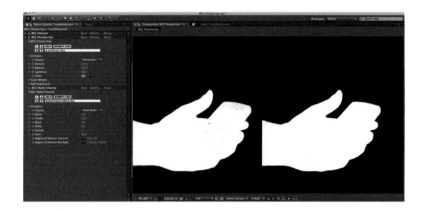

**Figure 12.31** Boris Continuum BCC Matte Cleanup.

## Spill Suppression Comparison

Spill is green reflected from your greenscreen onto your actor or props. It tends to show up around the edges of wispy hair and on white or reflective objects. It's often fairly easy to remove. Many keyers have built-in spill suppression, but if your keyer does not, here are a few to try.

# Pro Tip

Despill before you do any excessive choking.

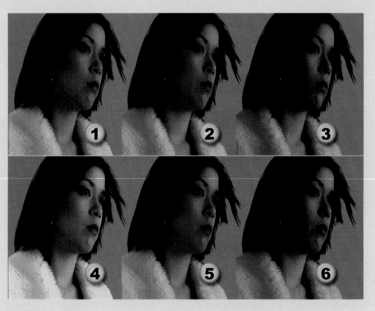

**Figure 12.32** Spill suppression comparison. Footage: Hollywood Camera Work
*www.hollywoodcamerawork.us/greenscreenplates.html*

All samples were adjusted to remove as much green as possible without tinting or desaturating the rest of the footage (as much as possible).

1. Original shot with no spill suppression.
2. **After Effects Spill Suppression** is an anemic plug-in for spill suppression. The options are Color to Suppress, Color Accuracy (Better or Faster), and Suppression, which allows the user to dial in the amount of suppression. It's difficult to control and will tint footage.
3. **Red Giant Key Correct Spill Killer** is very basic with just a Color Mode for selecting red, green, or blue; a Range; and a Tolerance. There is also an option to Blend with Original. This plug-in works fantastically well and will remove the green spill without throwing off the other colors in the shot. *Note*: This is the same Spill Killer technology that is built into Primatte Keyer.
4. **CoreMelt C2 Gadget Spill Suppression** is very fast, but I had trouble on certain shots because it's difficult to select the right shade to despill with. The user selects a shade of green with the eyedropper and adjusts the Color Alpha, Chroma Range, Softness, and Blur Key.

## Pro Tip: Remove Spill with Hue/Saturation

You can also remove some spill by applying Hue/Saturation (Effects > Color Correction > Hue/Saturation) and taking down the green levels. To isolate the greens so you don't get a lot of shifting hues, choose Green in Channel Control. Lower the Green Saturation and shift the Green Hue more toward the yellows (this will depend on your footage). Adjust the Channel Range to isolate the green. I have had better luck with this method than the After Effects Spill Suppression plug-in!

Figure 12.33 Hue/Saturation can be used to remove spill.

5. **PHYX Keyer Despill** plug-in is also very simple with a choice between only green or blue and an adjustable Despill amount, but it seems to work pretty well. This tool will change the color of the foreground plate slightly, so we have found that it works best to keep the value of the despill amount low. PHYX Keyer requires the free FxFactory installed to run, which can be downloaded at *www.noiseindustries.com*.

6. **Digital Film Tools zMatte Color Suppress** is set up like most of the other despill plug-ins with a pulldown menu for the color to suppress, Amount, Range, and Edge. I got decent results by pushing and pulling the Amount and Range.

## Edge Blending

The edges of your keyed footage should not be too sharp and clean nor tattered and jaggy. Edges need an ever so slight blur to them to help them look like they are organically part of the scene and not something just cut out and put over the top of your background.

**Red Giant Composite Wizard Edge Blur** filter and a Super Compound Blur filter, works on the R, G, B, or alpha channel. The set also comes with a Matte Feather plug-in that will soften harsh edges.

**Red Giant Key Correct Matte Feather** works similarly for softening mattes, with a choice of Edge Mode of Raster or Vector. There are Edge Pre-Blur and Post-Blur options for edge refinement.

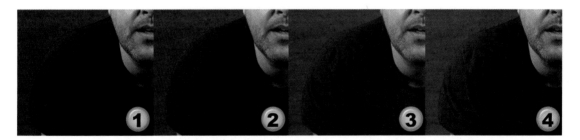

Figure 12.34 Edge blending comparisons. Sample 1 has no edge blur. Sample 2 uses Digital Film Tools Edge Composite. Sample 3 shows Red Giant Key Correct Matte Feather. Sample 4 uses GenArts Sapphire S_MatteOps.

**Digital Film Tools Composite Suite Pro** has a tool called **Edge Composite**, which is another option for isolating and adjusting the edges of an alpha matte. The user can choose the size of the edge, then adjust color correction or horizontally or vertically blur just the edges. This edge color correction is extremely useful for any green fringe around keyed hair or fur. Just tint the edges to match the hair.

**GenArts Sapphire S_MatteOps** gives several options for matte softening and manipulation. There are settings for Shrink–Grow+, Edge Softness, Post Blur, and the method of blurring (Box, Triangle, Gauss). S_MatteOps also has Noise tools, to adjust Noise Amplitude, Frequency, and other parameters.

*Creating an Edge Outline with Red Giant Key Correct Edge Finder*

**Figure 12.35** An outline around the edge of keyed footage is a quick effect with Red Giant Key Correct Edge Finder.

**Red Giant Key Correct Edge Finder** can be used for edge smoothing, and for isolating the edges of a matte. This can be extremely useful in lightening and softening edges, not only on keyed footage, but also on hard-edged 3D-animated footage with an alpha channel. It can also be used for creating an outline around your keyed actor, for special effects often seen on television promos.

1. Apply Red Giant Key Correct Edge Finder directly to the keyed layer.
2. Set the Channel to Alpha, Level to 100%, Edge Smoothing to 0.0, and Outline Hardness to 100%. Adjust the Edge Width to your liking.
3. This tool has its pros and cons. One of the pros is it can be set to Vector or Raster for a slightly different look and the Fit Tolerance can be adjusted. This plug-in will let you use the outline only, so some interesting outlined people effects can be easily created. The big downside to this plug-in is that it generates the outline from the center of the alpha edge, so if a thick outline is needed, it will eat into your image. It's not possible to place the alpha outline behind the video or along the outside of the actor without applying it to a duplicate key layer and placing an instance of the key layer without the Edge Finder above the outlined layer. Another con (well, depending on the use, it could be a pro) is that any holes, specks, or defects in the matte will be outlined.

This outline effect can also be created any third-party plug-ins by using **Minimax** and **Fill**. (Figure 12.36.)

1. Duplicate the keyed layer.
2. Turn off the visibility of the top instance of the key by clicking the eyeball in the timeline.
3. Rename the bottom instance "Outline" and apply Minimax to the Outline layer (Effect > Channel > Minimax). Set the

**Figure 12.36** The outline was created using the Minimax Method. The background was created with Noise Industries FxFactory Stripes plug-in applied to a solid, then SUGARfx HUD Target (FxFactory) generator.

Operation to Maximum, the Radius to 6, the Channel to Alpha, and the Direction to Horizontal and Vertical.

4. Fill the layer with white (Effect > Generate > Fill).

## Color Matching Plates

Although this book contains a chapter specifically about Color Correction (Chapter 2), there are a few color-related plug-ins made specifically for compositing greenscreen elements and backgrounds. These color-matching plug-ins either pull directly from the background color scheme when applied to the foreground, or the user can select colors from the scene.

**Boris Continuum Complete BCC Color Match** falls into the latter category. The user chooses a Highlight Source color and a Highlight Target color, Midtone Source and Target, then a Shadow Source and Target. There's a Compare setting that allows users to see before-and-after results side-by-side as well.

**Red Giant Primatte Keyer Color Matcher** and **Key Correct Color Matcher** are basically the same tool. Apply the plug-in, select the Target or Background layer, and adjust the strength.

**Figure 12.37** Boris Continuum BCC Color Match with the before on the left and the matched color on the right. Notice how the hand on the right matches the background.

**Figure 12.38** Red Giant Key Correct Color Matcher with the before on the left and the matched color on the right.

There is no messing with eyedroppers and selecting colors. It's extremely easy and the results are excellent.

## Light Wraps

Briefly discussed earlier in this chapter, a light wrap will help the foreground image blend more naturally with the background by bringing some lighting and color from the background into the edges of the foreground. There are tutorials online about building your own light wrap, which is not all that difficult, but there is an abundance of light wrap plug-ins available and many are not expensive. Why bother futzing around with building your own when it's a one click process with a plug-in?

Some Light Wrap plug-ins on the market include:

- **Boris Continuum Chroma Keyer BCC Light Wrap** (sold as a unit or as part of Boris Continuum Complete)
- **CoreMelt C2 Luminous Glows and Blurs Light Wrap**
- **Digital Film Tools Composite Suite Light Wrap** and **zMatte Light Wrap** (same tool)
- **Red Giant Key Correct Light Wrap** and **Primatte Keyer Light Wrap** (same tool)
- **PHYX Keyer LightWrap**
- **Digieffects Light Wrap** (sold à la carte, or as part of Digieffects Delirium)

Don't forget all of the keying plug-ins that have built-in light wraps.

**Figure 12.39** Light wrap comparison with similar settings. 1. No light wrap; 2. Red Giant Key Correct Light Wrap; 3. Digital Film Tools zMatte Light Wrap; 4. PHYX Keyer Light-Wrap; 5. Boris Continuum BCC Light Wrap.

**Figure 12.40** An exaggerated light wrap with the composite on the left and the wrap only on the right.

Which is the best choice? I like BCC Light Wrap, Red Giant Key Correct Light Wrap, and Digital Film Tools Light Wraps because they're easy to use and modify.

A light wrap always looks better when applied subtly. Light wraps should not be noticeable by the viewer but should help the foreground look like it belongs with the background. Depending on the shot, it may not be needed, but if a background plate has perceived backlighting, a little light wrap can sell a composite.

## Special Effect Lighting for a Natural Composite: Digital Film Tools Composite Suite Gobos

Adjusting the angle of light isn't typically something that you want to do when compositing. Hopefully the person who shot the footage matched the light angle on the foreground and background elements. However, there are times compositors will be challenged to "fix it in post." It may be possible to flip either the foreground or background plates.

We're not talking about fixing footage, but enhancing it with special lighting effects with **Digital Film Tools Composite Suite Pro Gobo** or **Tiffen Dfx Gobos** (both products are the same but are sold with different packages from different companies).

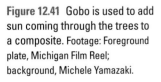

**Figure 12.41** Gobo is used to add sun coming through the trees to a composite. Footage: Foreground plate, Michigan Film Reel; background, Michele Yamazaki.

**Figure 12.42**  The Gobo interface.

**Figure 12.43**  Composited footage of a man in front of a doorway generated light through blinds. The sample on the right has Gobo applied to both the foreground image and the background image. Footage: Crowd Control, clip # 00434_002_156; background, Michele Yamazaki.

Gobos are useful to unify the scene by adding dappled light to both the foreground and background.

Shadows and lights can be added to give footage the look that it was shot in front of a window, under trees, under clouds, and hundreds of other options. Just choose the type of Gobo from several categories, and then adjust the Light, Shadow, and Matte. Under the Light settings, there are around 100 custom gels that can be used to throw color on your subject. There are DVE options for the gobo too, for positioning the gobo just perfectly and for moving shadows and lights.

# TRACKING, MATCHMOVING, MOTION STABILIZATION, AND ROTOSCOPING

Some shots are impossible to acquire with the use of a tripod or other stabilization methods, and require the use of hand-held cameras. In these instances, it's often desirable to stabilize the footage in postproduction. In this chapter, I'll show you how to use several plug-ins to stabilize as well as track elements to footage.

When adding elements through compositing into your video projects, it's important to add a realistic effect of movement as it relates to other layers in your composite. For example, in the blockbuster movie *District 9*, the space creatures had to match the shaky camera footage in order to seem like they were a part of the background layer.

In other cases, you might have to remove elements in your layers to maintain a certain effect, such as someone flying through the air. Rotoscoping and painting on your footage to remove safety wires can help create this illusion. There are numerous examples of this in modern movies and commercials such as *Crouching Tiger, Hidden Dragon*, *The Matrix*, or basically any action films that require any amount of stunt work!

## Motion Tracking

This section focuses on tracking. After Effects ships with a basic 2D point tracker, which, in my opinion, is not the best tool out there. It's a good thing that there are other options.

Imagineer mocha for After Effects CS4 blew me away the first time I saw it demoed. Not technically a plug-in but more of a standalone software, Imagineer mocha AE is a planar tracker. It exports position, rotation, scale, and corner pin data into a text document, which is then copied and pasted into After Effects parameters.

## Pro Tip: Planar Tracker versus Point Tracker

A **point tracker**, like the **After Effects Tracker**, allows the user to track user-defined points on footage. The track point is set up to follow a point using the feature region, an attach point, and a search region. After Effects' tracker is slow and tends to jump off the track easily.

A **planar tracker**, such as **Imagineer mocha** and **Silhouette FX**, uses planes to tracks an object's position, rotation, and scaling data, based on the area defined by the user.

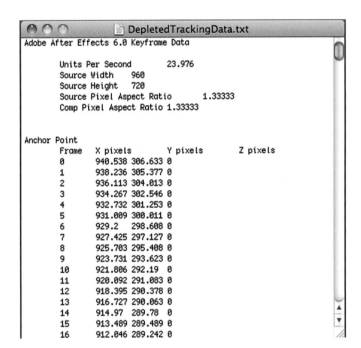

**Figure 13.1** A sample of tracking data exported from Imagineer mocha AE.

### TERMINOLOGY: MATCHMOVING

Often referred to as camera tracking, matchmoving is the process of tracking camera movement in a shot so the move can be duplicated with a virtual camera within After Effects or other software. This allows for other elements to be composited and matched perfectly into the shot.

A **2D Track** is a track of $x$- and $y$-axis for position, scale, and rotation. This type of track is great for blurring out faces or logos and replacing imagery on a billboard. A 2D Track is also useful for a perspective corner pin.

A **3D Track** is a track of three-dimensional data from two-dimensional footage. 3D trackers can use the data to mimic the real-world camera. This type of track is often used to put digital 3D objects into live-action footage, such as in the *Pirates of the Caribbean* films where digital skeletons are composited into live-action footage.

A well-liked point tracker is **SynthEyes 3D Camera Tracker** ($350), which can analyze 2D footage and create a 3D camera track, even tracking camera zooms. **Vicon boujou** ($10,000) is a matchmover that is extremely fast and easy to use (two clicks, they claim). **The Foundry CameraTracker** ($250) is not quite a two-click process but is powerful and much less expensive than boujou. CameraTracker is a plug-in integrated into After Effects, unlike other trackers mentioned which just import the data into After Effects. **The Pixel Farm PFhoe Pro** ($199) is yet another easy to use and inexpensive matchmoving tool. Because there are so many motion trackers out there, I won't cover them all. If you're interested in trying any of these tools out, look online for free trials or demos, and check their websites for more information.

## *Depleted*: Tracking with Imagineer mocha AE

Jeremy Hanke, editor of *MicroFilmmaker Magazine* and my co-author on *Greenscreen Made Easy*, contacted me a few months ago about a project that he's directing, an action-adventure sci-fi project called *Depleted: Day 419*. *Depleted* is a series of short films that take place in a post-apocalyptic future.

**Figure 13.2** A scene from *Depleted* with a tracked and replaced generator. Footage: *Depleted: Day 419*, directed by Jeremy Hanke, *http://worldofdepleted.com*.

Jeremy asked me to track a shot of an electrical box and replace it with a post-apocalyptic looking generator that vibrates. I came up with a creation of a steampunk-style composite of generators and cables.

We'll track the original electrical box in Imagineer mocha AE, which ships with After Effects CS4 and higher, then bring the tracking data into After Effects. I've created a layer to hide the original electrical box and put the new steampunk generator on the ground near where the electrical box used to be. The new generator shakes a bit and has some internal movement, and sputters out some smoke, generated with Trapcode Particular. *The project files are included on this book's DVD in the Depleted Tracking folder.*

If you don't have time to go through the entire project, the project is prebuilt on the DVD. You can use the comp titled Warehouse and skip the setup stages in steps 5 through 8. The project was created in After Effects CS5 with Imagineer mocha for After Effects CS5.

## MOCHA AE VERSION HISTORY

Ross Shain, chief marketing officer of Imagineer Systems, explained the naming convention of mocha AE over the past few versions:

- After Effects CS4 shipped with **mocha for After Effects CS4**
- After Effects CS5 shipped with **mocha for After Effects CS5** (and includes free mocha shape)
- After Effects CS5.5 ships with **mocha AE CS5.5** (and **mocha shape**). mocha AE CS5.5 includes the new interface to align the product with mocha Pro and full mocha.

**Figure 13.3** mocha for After Effects resides within the After Effects folder on your hard drive.

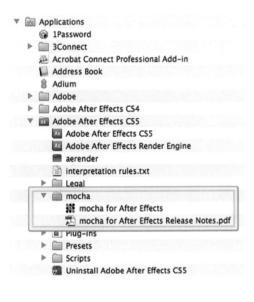

### Third-party plug-ins needed:

- Imagineer mocha for After Effects

    1. Launch Imagineer mocha for After Effects or mocha AE. If this is the first time you've launched mocha, it is within the After Effects folder in your Applications/Programs folder, in the mocha folder. Double-click "mocha for After Effects" (CS5) or "mocha AE" (CS5.5) to launch it. You can dismiss the registration dialog for now. (Figure 13.3.)

    2. Click the Create a New Project icon in the upper left corner. The New Project panel will open asking to choose a clip to import. Click the Choose button and select WarehouseIntro.mp4. The default settings are fine since we'll be tracking the full length of the clip. Click OK. (Figure 13.4.)

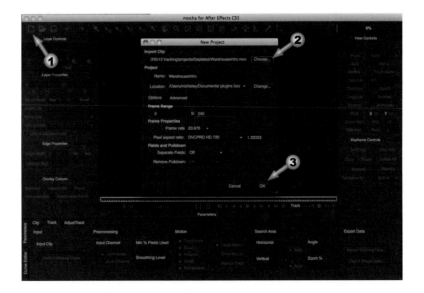

**Figure 13.4** The mocha New Project dialog box. 1. Create a New Project button. 2. Click the Choose button to choose your clip. 3. Click OK to import the clip.

Figure 13.5 The X-Spline Layer tool.

3. Play the clip or drag the indicator down the timeline and find a spot where the electric box is fully on the screen. Use the last frame. If you can't see the full width of the video, drag the mocha window wider by clicking and dragging the bottom right corner of the window. (Figure 13.5.)

4. Click the X-Spline Layer tool and click to place spline points around the electrical box. When you are finished placing spline points, Control (Alt) + click or right-click to place the final point. Use the Pick tool to click and drag points to place them. (Figure 13.6.)

5. Make sure you have the Track tab selected. Since this shot does not zoom or rotate, check only Translation in the Motion box. Since you're at the last frame, click Track Backwards to get the track started. Pay attention to the track as it runs to make sure it stays on target. When the track finishes there will be a blue bar along the timeline. Play the track to make sure it's right on. If not, adjust the X-Splines and retrack. (Figure 13.7.)

Figure 13.6 Spline points around the electrical box.

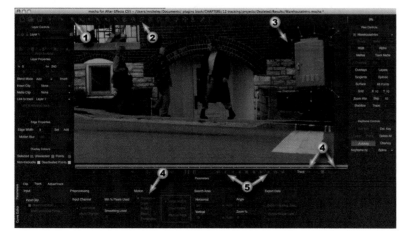

Figure 13.7 The mocha AE interface. 1. The Pick tool. 2. X-Spline Layer tool. 3. X-Splines surrounding the object to track. 4. Track Backward and Forward. 5. Play Backward and Forward. 6. The Motion Box.

## Pro Tip

If you're tracking footage that moves offscreen, mocha AE will continue to track the footage. After Effects will not.

## Pro Tip

If you're corner pinning, you need to define the Surface in mocha. To do this, place your points and track the footage. Then, click Surface.

### Further Training

For downloadable in-depth video training on tracking in mocha for After Effects, I highly recommend *Rock Steady: Successful Motion Tracking in Imagineer Systems mocha & Adobe After Effects* from Curious Turtle. *www.curiousturtle .com*.

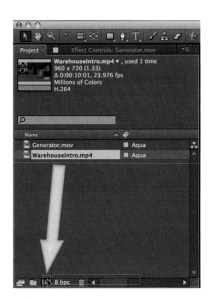

**Figure 13.8** Drag the footage to the Create a New Composition button to create a new comp.

6. Go to File > Export Tracking Data to export the tracking data. Click the Save button. Save the project (File > Save Project As) as DepletedTrackingData.txt. Close mocha AE. (*Note*: It is quicker to copy the tracking data to your clipboard and paste them into After Effects, but saving a copy of the data to your hard drive is helpful if you make a mistake and need to go back).

7. Launch After Effects and import the WarehouseIntro.mp4, Generator.mov, and generator-cover.tif files, included on this book's DVD (File > Import and shift + click to import multiple files).

8. Drag WarehouseIntro.mp4 down to the Create a New Composition button at the bottom of the Project panel. A new composition will open with the Warehouse footage that is the exact size and duration of the clip just tracked in mocha. (Figure 13.8.)

9. We'll need to cover the old electrical box before placing the new generator into the shot. The generator-cover.tif file has already been prepared by exporting the final frame and painting over it in Photoshop. Drag it into the comp and position it to cover the electrical box at the first frame. (Figure 13.9.)

10. Drag the Generator.mov into the Warehouse comp and position it on the curb on the right side of the frame.

11. On your hard drive, locate the DepletedTrackingData .txt file and open it in a text editor such as BBEdit, Text Edit, or Notepad. Select all of the text and copy it to your clipboard by using Command (Ctrl) + C.

12. Make sure you're at the first frame in the Timeline panel, which is the same first frame you tracked in mocha. This is *very* important. Select the generator-cover.tif layer and paste the tracking data

Figure 13.9 The right side of the original shot is on the left. The shot with the covered electrical box is on the right.

to the layer from your clipboard (Command/Ctrl + V). This will paste data for Anchor Point, Position, Scale, and Rotation.

13. Press A to bring up the Anchor Point parameter, and then click the stopwatch to remove the keyframes. Click the A key to reveal the Anchor Point parameter. Scrub the Anchor Point parameter until it covers the electrical box just perfectly. Play the comp through a few times to make sure the cover is lined up properly. (Figure 13.11.)

14. Drag the Generator comp into the Warehouse comp and position it on the right side of the screen on the sidewalk. Paste the data from DepletedTrackingData.txt, which should still be on your clipboard. Follow the same instructions as above for the generator-cover.tif file. Click the A key to reveal the Anchor Point parameter. Click the stopwatch to

Figure 13.10 The Generator Cover.

Figure 13.11 Line up the cover to hide the electrical box.

**Figure 13.12** Pasted tracking data for Generator.mov and generator-cover.tif.

remove all Anchor Point keyframes. Scrub the Anchor Point parameter until the generator is positioned on the sidewalk in the right place. Watch it through and make sure it's lined up properly. If it slides just a bit, keyframe the Anchor Point so that it stays put on the curb. (Figure 13.12.)

### HOW WAS THE GENERATOR COVER IMAGE CREATED?

I exported a still frame from the video at a spot that had the entire electrical box onscreen. I imported the still frame into Photoshop and added a new layer on which to create the cover. Using the Rubber Stamp tool, I sampled from the surrounding areas until the electrical box was neatly covered. The still frame was deleted and the Generator Cover saved with an alpha channel.

**Finishing touches:** If the edges of either generator-cover.tif or the Generator layers look too hard-edged, use an alpha feather tool. I applied **Red Giant Key Correct Pro Matte Feather**, which is an excellent package to own if you do any sort of compositing work, to blend the edges a bit better.

To add a bit of vibration to the Generator, add a Null Object. Add an expression by Option + clicking the Anchor Point on the Null Object and typing the following Expression:

```
wiggle(10,.5)
```

Parent the Generator to the Null Object.

**Figure 13.13** The final effects and settings for the *Depleted* project.

The final step is to color correct the shot to match the Generator to the footage and give the entire shot a look.

Use Levels or Hue/Saturation to match the Generator to the footage. Alternately, apply **Red Giant Key Correct Color Matcher** to the Generator and select the footage as the Target Layer. Set the strength to 100.0%.

Add an Adjustment Layer over the top of the other layers. Color correct using your method of choice. I applied **Red Giant Magic Bullet Looks.**

## Corner Pinning with mocha AE

If you're corner pinning, you need to define the Surface in mocha. In this sample, I'm tracking a cell phone to replace the screen content. *The project is included on the DVD in the Track Phone folder, including the footage TrackPhone.mp4, courtesy of Michigan Film Reel.* The project was done with After Effects CS5 and mocha for After Effects CS5. I only tracked the first 3 seconds for this tutorial but feel free to track the full duration of the clip.

**Third-party plug-ins needed:**
- Imagineer mocha for After Effects
    1. Bring the footage into mocha, just as you did in the previous tutorial. In mocha, define the area and track the entire phone, matching perspective as closely as possible.
    2. Click the Surface button, which will bring up a rectangle for matching the corner pin.
    3. Place the corners of the Surface rectangle on the corners of the phone screen by clicking and dragging the corners, giving it a pixel or two of overlap of the screen. Zoom in so that the corners are accurate. (Figure 13.14.)

**Figure 13.14** Match up the corner pin rectangle to the corners of the phone screen. The Surface button is highlighted.

**Figure 13.15** The mocha export dialog. The Export button is highlighted.

4. Track the clip by clicking the Track button.
5. Click the Export Tracking Data button. Choose After Effects Tracking Data (supports motion blur). Choose Copy to Clipboard. (Figure 13.15.)
6. In After Effects, paste the tracking data to the footage layer that you wish to corner pin. The footage will be corner pinned to the phone screen area using the After Effects Corner Pin plug-in. (Figure 13.16.)
7. Place the original tracked footage behind the corner pinned footage.

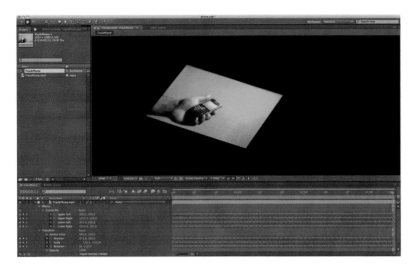

**Figure 13.16** The footage is corner pinned in After Effects.

## Pixelation of a Face with Boris Continuum Complete BCC Witness Protection

If you ever need to obscure someone's face, hide a corporate logo, and even block an obscene hand gesture, **Boris Continuum Complete BCC Witness Protection** is the perfect plug-in for the job. The built-in tracker works extremely well, once you figure out how it works.

*Project files are included on the DVD in the BCCWitnessProtection folder. The footage of Jason with the lightsaber2.mp4 is included, courtesy of Michigan Film Reel.*

**Figure 13.17** Boris Continuum Complete BCC Witness Protection is used to track and disguise the face of Jason.
Footage: Michigan Film Reel.

**Third-party plug-ins needed:**

- Boris Continuum Complete

1. Import the lightsaber2.mp4 file, which is included on this book's DVD, into After Effects. Drag the footage from the Project panel to the Create a New Composition button at the bottom of the Project panel.

2. When using any motion tracker, trim the clip to the duration that you need, in our case, 4 seconds. There is no point in tracking unneeded footage, as it takes extra time and processor power. Go to 4:00 in the timeline. Press the N key, for End Work Area, which will set the work area to the first 4 seconds. To trim the composition, go to Composition > Trim Comp to Work Area.

3. Apply BCC Witness Protection (Effects > BCC Effects > BCC Witness Protection) to the lightsaber2.mp4 layer.

4. Jump to the first frame of your clip by tapping the letter I (that's I for "in-point"). To track in Boris Continuum plug-ins, the play head always needs to be at the first frame of the clip.

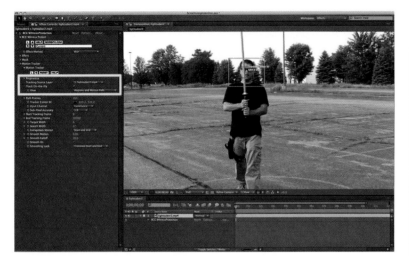

**Figure 13.18** The Tracker Center KF crosshairs are centered over Jason's face.

**Figure 13.19** The footage with the Target Width and Search Width set up.

5. Twirl down the Motion Tracker settings in the Effect Controls panel for BCC Witness Protection. First, choose the Tracking Source Layer, which in this case should be lightsaber2.mp4.

6. Check Track On-the-fly and set the view to Regions and Motion Path so that you will be able to see both the area that is being tracked as well as the path it is creating. Check Show Motion Path so you can see the path as it's drawn. Click the crosshairs for Tracker Center KF and then click on exactly the center point of the area we want to track—in this case, the center of Jason's face. (Figure 13.18.)

7. Adjust the Target Width and the Search Width. The center box is the Target Width, the area that will be tracked, and is Jason's head in this case. The Search Width, the outer box, is the area in which his head moves. The corners of the Target Width and Search Width boxes will turn green when they can be pulled and dragged to size. Scrub through the duration of the timeline to and adjust the Search Width so that Jason's head stays within the outer box. (Figure 13.19.)

8. For this footage, we'll set Input Channel to Red since the skin tones contain red.

9. At this point, you should be ready to track. Press the spacebar to play the comp or click the play button in the Preview panel. Because Track On-the-fly was checked, the tracker will track each frame as it plays. Keep an eye on it as it plays to make sure it doesn't make any incorrect jumps out of the track. (Figure 13.20.)

**Figure 13.20** BCC Witness Protection tracking the face of Jason.

**Figure 13.21** The final composite with the actor's face pixelated. The comp is magnified to 200%.

10. After the track plays through the end of the clip, uncheck the Track On-the-Fly and Show Motion Path boxes to see the effect.

11. In the Effect Method pulldown menu, choose Mosaic" Twirl open Effect and adjust the Contrast/Scramble to taste. To make smaller mosaic squares, lower the value of Amount/Brightness.

12. Twirl open Mask and adjust the Region Radius and Softness until it fully covers the face, and not much more. (Figure 13.21.)

## Pro Tip

If you're working with keyed footage, I recommend applying BCC Witness Protection to an Adjustment Layer, because the mosaic will only go as far as the edge of the matte. Just be careful if you're working in a more complex comp with video edits or text overlays, to trim and stack the Adjustment Layer so that it only affects the footage you want it to effect.

## Pro Tip

Depending on the footage, adjusting Preprocess settings may be necessary. Preprocess will allow the user to boost luminance values so the tracker will have an easier time tracking the footage. The View Preprocessed Source checkbox needs to be unchecked before you select the Track On-the-Fly checkbox.

### Matchmoving Text to Live Footage with The Foundry CameraTracker

Matchmoving text to footage is often seen in commercials and music videos. One of my favorite scenes in *Fight Club* is the IKEA scene where furniture appears piece by piece in a room and text is tracked to the panning camera, mimicking the catalog.

This tutorial is a much simpler version of matchmoving to a panned shot. It takes a handheld shot of my cat Matilda in the yard, tracked with The Foundry CameraTracker, and matchmoves the word "cat" in several languages. This plug-in is very complex and this tutorial barely scratches the surface. It is just meant to introduce you to the plug-in, and I'll stick with the default settings to keep it simple. To learn more, check out The Foundry's

**Figure 13.22** The final composite of the cat video and matchmoved text with Red Giant Magic Bullet Looks applied.
Footage: Michele Yamazaki.

YouTube channel containing several CameraTracker tutorials.

*The project file is included on this book's DVD in the CameraTracker-Matilda folder.*

1. Import the cat footage into After Effects. Drag it to the Create a New Composition button at the bottom of the Project panel. The clip will open in a new comp.

2. First we need to trim the clip. Go to 6:07 and tap the B key to set the beginning of the work area. Then, hit Option (Alt) + [ to trim the clip. Go to 12:12 and set the end point of the work area by tapping the letter N. To trim the clip at this point, Option (Alt) + ]. To trim the composition to the duration of the work area, go to Composition > Trim Comp to Work Area. RAM Preview the comp through a few times by pressing the 0 key on the extended keyboard or by clicking the play button in the Preview panel to get the feel for timing. We'll be adding seven words to the animation.

3. Apply The Foundry CameraTracker to the footage (Effects > The Foundry > CameraTracker). (Figure 13.23.)

4. Click Track Features. For the best results, the comp should be at Full Resolution. If it is not, a warning dialog pops up. CameraTracker will start at the first frame and will display hundreds of orange points and lines that indicate features in the flowers and grass to track. At the end of the clip, CameraTracker will start going through the clip in reverse and rechecking points. (Figure 13.24.)

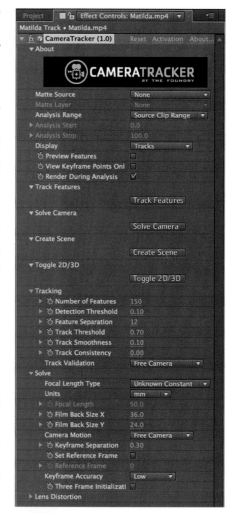

**Figure 13.23** CameraTracker Effect Controls.

**Figure 13.24** The results of Track Features.

5. After the track completes, scrub through the comp and take a look at how the track points have been applied. Points on the track will be selected in the next step and words linked to those tracks. First, though, the camera will need to be added, so click Solve Camera. (Figure 13.25.)

6. Once it finishes processing, a message will appear telling you that the track was solved with a Reference Frame number. This frame is where the Solve was started. The number of keyframes is displayed. In my case Keyframes = 26. The last bit of information is the total RMS reprojection error, which tells the quality of the track. Anything below 1.0 pixel is a decent track. My track is 0.608 pixels. Click OK to close the info box. The tracks will also turn green at this point. (Figure 13.26.)

7. If the Solve Camera data were above 1.0, you would want to go into the Solve section of the plug-in and adjust the focal length, if you know the details of your camera. If you don't have this information, CameraTracker either gets data from the Meta information or gives its best educated guess. Adjust the settings and run Solve Camera again.

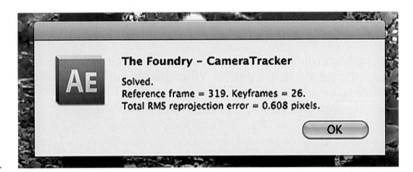

**Figure 13.25** The solve message.

**Figure 13.26** The results of Create Scene.

8. Click Create Scene to add a camera and a Null Object, which the camera is parented to. The camera will have keyframes set for Position and X, Y, and Z Rotation. This camera will match any 3D layer to the tracked movement in the video clip. If you switch the View to a Custom View and scrub through the comp, you can see the camera movement through the scene. Set View back to CameraTracker – Camera (1). (Figure 13.27.)

9. Adding the text is next. I've chosen seven words for cat in multiple languages: cat, gato, chat, kitte, pishyakan, kocka, and neko. Type each of these words onscreen in a simple font such as Arial. The font size is not all that important because the text will automatically be set to Continuously Rasterize and will be positioned in 3D space. Make each layer of type a 3D layer by checking the Check the Enable 3D box under Switches.

10. Because we will have a lot of layers, hide all of the text layers except "cat" by clicking the Shy layer checkbox under Switches and clicking the Shy button along the top of the timeline. Use the Rotation tool to position cat on an angle. (Figure 13.28.)

11. Go to the first frame in the comp. On the video track, select CameraTracker so that the track points can be seen in the Comp panel. Use the Selection tool to grab the xs on the track points of 7 or 8 track lines. Choose the long tracks and select tracks across the screen from left to right so that you have full coverage across the screen. (Figure 13.29.)

12. In the lower left of the Comp panel is the CameraTracker Menu. Go to Create > Null Object. A new Null will be added to the comp. Rename it "cat".

Figure 13.27 Keyframes on the camera position, generated by CameraTracker.

Figure 13.28 Position the word "cat" in the grass.

Figure 13.29 Individual track lines turn yellow when selected.

13. If the Parent column is not visible in the Timeline panel, open it by pressing Shift + F4, or right-clicking on any column header. Parent the cat Text layer to the cat Null layer.

14. The text has most likely moved somewhere off screen. Select the cat text layer and tap the P key to bring up Position parameters. Zero out the X, Y, and Z Position values so that it will move back onscreen where you can see it, then drag the position of the text somewhere toward the middle of the screen. Preview the movie and notice how the word "cat" now follows the movement of the pan.

15. Deselect Shy along the top of the timeline to reveal all of the layers. Make the cat text and Null layers shy and click to disable the Shy box for the text layers gato and chat. Click Shy again along the top of the timeline to hide items in the timeline. You should now only see the footage layer, gato, and chat.

16. Jump about one second ahead. Repeat steps 7, 8, and 9 with the remaining text layers, adjusting the position so that they are staggered. Here are the basic steps, condensed:
    * Move to a point in the timeline.
    * Select 7–10 points on the track.
    * From the CameraTracker menu at the bottom of the Comp panel, select Create > Null Object.
    * Select the Null and press Return to rename it to match the name of the text layer, and then press Return again to accept the new name.
    * Parent the text layer to the appropriate Null.
    * Zero out the Position parameters of the text layer and reposition the text layer.
    * Continue to Shy and unShy layers as you need them. (Figure 13.30.)

**Figure 13.30** The procedure is repeated for all text layers. When you are finished, your timeline should look like this when all layers are visible.

**17.** Watch the comp through and reposition any text layers that
need to be modified. Place some in front of the cat near her
feet and some over the tail only.

For some tracking jobs you'll need to make tracked elements
appear to move behind areas of footage. To do so, you'll need
to duplicate the footage and carefully rotoscope the areas that
will appear over the tracked element. For example, we'll be using
the Roto Brush tool to mask out the tail on a duplicated layer
in a future step, so that it looks like the words are moving behind
the tail.

### Using Roto Brush to Complete the Illusion

**1.** Once you are happy with the text position, duplicate the video
layer and move it to the top of the stack. Move to a point in
the timeline where you wish the tail to appear over the text.
Double-click this duplicate layer to open its Layer panel. Select
the Roto Brush tool and paint over the tail only, using a brush
that is not as wide as the tail. The stroke should go down the
center of the tail. It is not necessary to paint along the edges of
the tail. The Roto Brush span expires after 20 frames, so make
sure you keep making new strokes to extend the span, represented by the gray line with the green lines and yellow dots.
(Figure 13.31.)

**Figure 13.31** The Layer panel on the right shows the tail being cut out by the
Roto Brush.

**2.** To remove areas that should not be selected, hold down the
Option (Alt) key and paint over the areas that need to be dese-
lected. Move along the timeline and fix any areas that were not

rotoscoped correctly. Toggle the Transparency Grid to see the results.

3. Once the tail is cut out properly, play the video through to make sure the video looks right over the tail. (Figure 13.32.)

**Finishing touches:** When you are finished, color correct the video by placing an Adjustment Layer on top of all layers and apply **Red Giant Magic Bullet Looks, Magic Bullet Colorista,** or another color correction tool. I also added a Tilt-Shift effect with Red Giant Magic Bullet Looks to miniaturize the cat.

**Figure 13.32** The final shot with the tail rotoscoped with the Roto Brush.

**Figure 13.33** The final project, with the Roto Brush shown in the Effect Controls.

## Motion Stabilization

I've been to concerts, botanical gardens, and amusement parks where they just don't let tripods in the door, and with my caffeine habit, my footage always comes out shaky. Maybe you have a steady hand but have you ever shot on a boat or in a car? Even on a calm day and a smooth road, you will get some movement.

Motion stabilization is most often used to smooth and remove camera shake from handheld footage. It's a godsend in that situation, and will help your audience from getting motion sickness.

## Motion Stabilization with Boris Continuum Complete BCC Optical Stabilizer

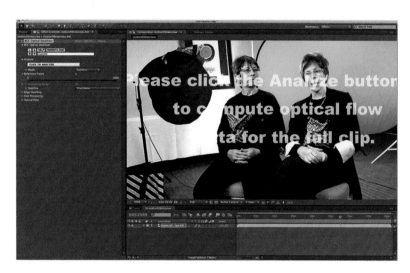

**Figure 13.34** Boris Continuum Complete BCC Optical Stabilizer is used to stabilize interview footage of Becky Padilla and Elaine Montoya, founders and producers of the annual motion event in New Mexico and motion.tv.

Demonstrating motion stabilization is very difficult in a book, but **Boris Continuum Complete BCC Optical Stabilizer** ($99) is extremely fast and easy to use and did a great job with the interview of Becky Padilla and Elaine Montoya at the Motion Conference in 2009, which was handheld.

BCC Optical Stabilizer uses Optical Flow technology, which estimates the motion between frames of video and stabilizes or smoothes to counteract shakiness. Stabilizing will remove pretty much all movement without the need to track first. If you have handheld footage that pans or zooms, smoothing is the best option. For footage that is locked on a single spot and is shaky, stabilization is key. I recommend checking the online help files on BorisFX.com for complete information on the filter, as what follows is a very basic introduction to the plug-in. Footage files are not included, so use some of your own handheld footage, or use another shot on this DVD.

1. Apply BCC Optical Stabilizer to the footage you need to stabilize (Effect > BCC Time > BCC Optical Stabilizer). A message will come up onscreen over your footage: "Click

### Web Link

Optical Flow technology is used in time-based effects like faux motion blur and time stretching. For a very technical explanation of Optical Flow technology, complete with diagrams, visit *http://en.wikipedia.org/wiki/Optical_flow*.

the Analyze button to compute optical flow data for the full clip."

Note that it says "for the full clip." If you set a work area, it doesn't make a difference. It will process the entire clip. If you do not want to process the entire clip, trim the clip instead of just marking a work area.

2. Choose a Reference Frame, which is framed to your liking. This will be used as a reference for BCC Optical Stabilizer as the basis for stabilization of all other frames.

3. There are options for smoothing and stabilization. The interview shot from the Motion Conference is handheld but does not zoom. To remove all of the shakiness I set Mode to Stabilize. (Figure 13.35.)

**Figure 13.35** BCC Optical Stabilizer analyzing motion in the shot.

4. Under Stabilize there are three options. I chose Translation + Rotation.
   - Translation stabilizes the X and Y-axis only.
   - Translation + Rotation stabilizes X and Y, plus rotation (good for footage like the interview in this example).
   - Translation + Rotation + Scale stabilizes X and Y, plus rotation and scale (good for footage where the camera pans or zooms).

5. Click Analyze and BCC Optical Stabilizer will run. After it finishes, RAM Preview the clip. If you're seeing black edges, it's because the position of the footage is being moved from the exact center of the Comp panel to smooth it, positioned based on your Reference Frame. You have a few options under Edge Handling. You can clip the top, left, bottom, or right. Under Edge Handling, choose one of the following options:
   - **Color:** Any color you choose will appear around the edge. Use the Edge Color color picker to choose the color.

- **Reflect:** Mirrors the edges. This is a great way to hide edges; they will often just blend into the corners and your viewer will have no idea.
- **Transparent:** Nothing will appear outside the edges, but anything below the layer will appear around the edges.
- **Repeat:** Repeats the colors in the last pixel on the edge, giving the look of stripes.
- **Tile:** Tiles the footage, using content adjacent to the edge.

## AN INTERVIEW WITH JEREMY HANKE ON BORIS CONTINUUM COMPLETE OPTICAL STABILIZER

Jeremy Hanke is the editor-in-chief of *MicroFilmmaker Magazine*, the online magazine for low-budget and no-budget filmmakers. In addition to his editorial duties at MFM, he is currently spearheading the *World of Depleted*, an international science fiction franchise, which permits creative contributors to help sculpt a post-apocalyptic world and share in the profits generated therein. For more, you can check out *www.microfilmmaker.com* and *www.worldofdepleted.com*.

**Michele Yamazaki: We've chatted about tracking and stabilization in the past and you've mentioned BCC Optical Stabilizer. Why do you like it?**

**Jeremy Hanke:** I've been very impressed with **Boris Continuum Complete BCC Optical Stabilizer** for a number of years. I think I became most attached to it during postproduction on a film that I did special effects for called, *The Guardian* (written and directed by Nick Denney). We used a handmade crane rig that was pretty stable, until we had to use it for an elaborate swoop in shot in the midst of extremely powerful wind gusts. Despite our extremely brawny crane grips, we just weren't able to get the shot without a couple of shudders. When I brought it into the editing suite, I was concerned that the plug-in would be useless as it tried to differentiate intended movement from unintended movement. However, it worked like a champ and created a beautiful shot. When it came time to work on *Depleted: Day 419*, it was a natural weapon in my arsenal.

**Michele: Did BCC Optical Stabilizer work as well as expected in postproduction?**

**Jeremy:** Originally, I wasn't expecting much optical stabilizer work in *Depleted: Day 419* at all. However, a few things ended up changing my expectations. We had a number of driving shots that we had to get for *Day 419*, but we expected them to all be outside the picture vehicle as our protagonists head from one location to the next. However, we ran into a slew of vehicle breakdowns and problems throughout the only day we could shoot these scenes. An hour and a half before we lost light, and having captured only 2 of 12 shot setups, my DP Nate Eckelbarger and I decided to go totally guerilla and ride the picture truck with the camera on a tripod. We captured the actual driving footage we needed in the bed of the truck and then, from time to time, would find a place to disembark and have the truck drive by so we could get the passing shots we wanted.

In the end, this created a style that I was pleased with, but it resulted in a lot of bumpy footage from the bed of the truck. When I dumped it into

# Pro Tip Jeremy Hanke Explains the 180° Rule

The 180° rule simply states that there is a line of action that exists between your main character and other actors or points of interest in a scene. As long as you keep your camera on the correct side of this line, you can cut between shots and have the visual layout of the scene make sense to your audience. Most people break this rule, either because they're unaware of it or because it was a rushed shoot and the line shifted when new participants in a dialog showed up. You will not be able to edit shots from both sides of the line together without confusing your audience, since left will become right and right will become left whenever you cut from one shot to another.

Boris Continuum Complete BCC Optical Stabilizer, I was very impressed by how much it looked like we had been using an actual steady rig of some sort! We used Smooth motion rather than Stabilize, as smoothing is designed to create a more fluid, Steadicam-style shot, whereas Stabilize actually tries to create a locked-down, tripod-style shot.

Another time that it came in to save my bacon occurred during the tense scene leading up to the main action sequence. While we had done a great job of getting most of the shots we needed, I realized that we had not actually gotten one last shot of our nemesis. Without the shot to bookend two disparate shots of our protagonists, we'd break the 180° rule. To fix this problem, I took a shot of our villain before we had called action. The shot had some shake to it, so it would've been unusable without the stabilizer. With it, however, it looked like a believable handheld shot.

**Michele:** Did you learn any good tricks or workflow techniques with BCC Optical Stabilizer?

**Jeremy:** I did. The big thing you have to be aware of is that BCC Optical Stabilizers and some others (not including the After Effects stabilizer) perform their function by zooming in on the footage itself. By and large, you'll lose at least 7% to 15% of your overall frame due to this zoom, depending on how much shake there is in your footage. If your focus is rock solid, you can zoom in as much as 15% without noticeable softening of edges. As such, if you're going to be in a situation where stabilization might become important, it's good to try to have as deep a field of view as possible. (Counter-intuitively, this is achieved by adjusting the f-stop of your lens to let in as little light as you can and still properly expose your image.) As a number of the scenes I've needed to do this for (the truck shot from *Day 419*, the crane shot from *The Guardian*) were shot outdoors, we had enough light to do this easily.

## Stabilizing Shaky Footage with CoreMelt Lock & Load X

**CoreMelt Lock & Load X** ($149) is a very fast plug-in for stabilizing footage and dealing with rolling shutter. It works in After Effects, Final Cut Pro, and Motion. Lock & Load X compensates for the wobbly distortion of rolling shutter, also known as "Jell-O-vision" often seen in CMOS video. (For more on rolling shutter, see

**Figure 13.36** CoreMelt Lock & Load X was used to stabilize a handheld shot of a walk through a forest. CoreMelt Glows & Blurs plug-ins are used to finish off the shot and give it ambience. Footage: Harriet Titan.

Chapter 14 "Fixing Video Problems." This is a well-documented issue with the Canon 5D Mark II and 7D, among others.

## Rotoscoping Tools in After Effects

Rotoscoping, where elements are cut out frame by frame, is often a very tedious process. The first rotoscoping job I did involved cutting out four people walking through a park for an infomercial. I used an early version of After Effects and went frame by frame and it took days to process just a few seconds of footage. If only I had the tools available today to speed up the process and save my nerves!

Using the Pen tool to create layer masks in After Effects can still be fine for some rotoscoping jobs, but there is also the Roto Brush tool introduced in After Effects CS5. The Roto Brush tool is demonstrated earlier in this chapter in the section, "Matchmoving Text to Live Footage with The Foundry CameraTracker." There are easier ways to rotoscope for certain effects such as colorization, and also a few tools to make the (often) tedious task of rotoscoping just a bit easier.

In this section, I'll go over some other plug-ins to help in rotoscoping. First, I'll go through the basics of **Imagineer mocha shape**, which ships with After Effects CS4 and higher. Then, there is a tutorial using **Digital Film Tools Power Stroke** to selectively color footage. Lastly, I'll talk about **RE:Vision Effects PV Feather**.

### Imagineer mocha shape

**mocha shape**, bundled free with mocha products, lets you import shapes into After Effects without rendering by exporting rotoscoping data. Unlike After Effects Masks, mocha shape supports

**Further Reading**

For in depth information on rotoscoping, check out the book *Rotoscoping: Techniques and Tools for the Aspiring Artist* by Benjamin Bratt.

**Figure 13.37** The lenses of the glasses have been rotoscoped with Imagineer mocha shape. idustrial revolution Volumetrix is applied to create light rays from the eyes. Foreground footage: Crowd Control, Clip # 00087_004_25; background footage: Michele Yamazaki.

**Figure 13.38** Another sample of the rotoscoped glasses with Imagineer mocha shape and idustrial revolution Volumetrix.

variable per-point edge feathering, meaning each point in the mask can have different feather values. In this example, I am using mocha AE CS5. There are no project files included with this tutorial.

**Third-party plug-ins needed:**
- Imagineer mocha AE CS5+
  1. As in the tutorial for mocha, define your roto shape by clicking on the area with the Create X-Spline Layer tool. Drag points with the Pick tool so that the points hug the edges of the shape you want to isolate. Magnify the footage so you can see the edges closely. (Figure 13.39.)
  2. Click Track Forwards below the lower right of the footage panel. Watch the X-Spline Layer as it tracks. If it jumps off track, simply stop the track, readjust the points and continue to Track Forwards or Track Backwards, to fix any areas that were off track. (Figure 13.40.)

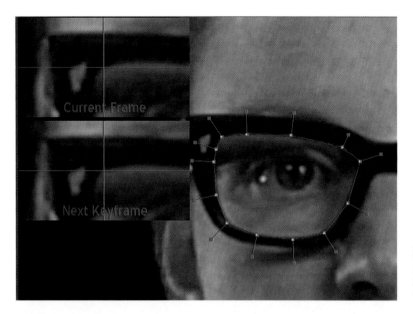

Figure 13.39 Drag the roto points so that they cleanly match the edges of the object you want to cut out.

Figure 13.40 Track Forward button below the lower right of the footage panel.

3. To export the shape data from mocha shape, select the layer you want to export, and then click the Export Shape button. The Export Shape Data... dialog box will pop up. There are three options: Selected layer, All visible layers, and All layers. In my example I have two shape layers, one for each lens in her glasses, so I'll choose All layers. All visible layers would also work. (Figure 13.41.)

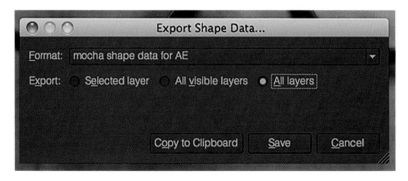

Figure 13.41 Export Shape Data dialog box.

4. Like mocha, the data can be saved to a clipboard to copy and paste to After Effects, or saved as a text document and imported into AE. This time I'm going to click Copy to Clipboard. Click OK.

5. Save your mocha AE project, in case you need to come back. It's safe to close mocha AE now.

6. Open After Effects and import the clip you just tracked. Drag the clip to the Make a New Composition button at the bottom of the Project panel.

7. In the Composition panel, select the footage layer. At the first frame, paste Command (Ctrl) + V. The rotoscoped areas should now be cut out onscreen. If you press the U key, you should now see several keyframed parameters. (Figure 13.42.)

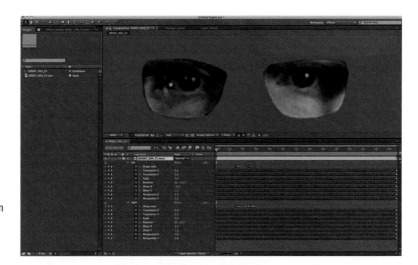

**Figure 13.42** The roto data from mocha is pasted into the footage in After Effects. The Comp is zoomed to 400%.

**Figure 13.43** idustrial revolution Volumetrix is animated to give light rays coming from the actor's eyes, which is an effect that you might see on *Doctor Who*.

8. Drag another instance of the footage behind the rotoscoped layer. You may need to reposition the rotoscoped layer. If so, select the rotod layer, press the A key to bring up Anchor Point settings, and if there are any keyframes there, click the stopwatch to remove them. Scrub the values for Anchor Point until your footage lines up perfectly.

**Finishing touches**: For this example, I used **idustrial revolution Volumetrix** to add light rays from her eyes. Other things I could have done are tinting the lenses, adding other footage inside the lenses, and using night vision or static effects in the lenses. I finished off the shot by adding **Red Giant Magic Bullet Looks** to the background footage layer.

## Colorization Effects with Digital Film Tools Power Stroke

There are a few methods of isolating or colorizing a single area of footage as seen in *Sin City* and other films. These methods include the Roto Brush, Imagineer mocha and mocha shape, and the numerous leave/change color effects third-party plug-ins, as well as those built into After Effects. **Digital Film Tools Power Stroke** uses keyframable masks and color, and in this tutorial I'll walk you through the process of tinting a portion of a still image. A friend asked me to tint the light pink flower on her new baby's head to red so that she could use it on her Christmas cards.

**Figure 13.44** *Left*: Before the color effect; *Right*: after the color effect. Footage: Christina Heyboer, closertotheheartphoto graphy.com.

# Hot Tip

The process in this tutorial can be done with video, but you will need to keyframe the mask, which can be mighty tedious. A much faster method is to bring the footage into **Imagineer mocha** and track it. In the mocha Export Shape Data dialog box choose Copy to Clipboard. In After Effects, select the layer in your timeline then go to Edit > Paste mocha mask. The mocha shapes are pasted as masks, which can be used with Digital Film Tools Power Stroke.

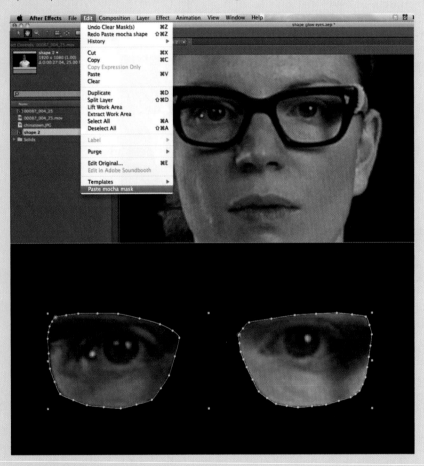

**Figure 13.45** On top, the Paste mocha mask command in the Edit menu. On the bottom is the final result.

A great feature of **Digital Film Tools Power Stroke** ($195) is that several masks can be used inside each other so you can be very detailed on which areas are colorized. With this plug-in, it is not necessary to get in extremely tight around a subject as you would with traditional rotoscoping. Power Stroke will be able to determine the edges of an element using luminance and other values in the footage.

*The project files are included on this book's DVD in the DFT PowerStroke folder.*

In this project, we will end up with three masks on the footage layer.

- **Mask 1:** An outer mask that surrounds flower, the area to be desaturated.
- **Mask 2:** The main mask, which will have the main red colorization.
- **Mask 3:** The center of the flower with the gem.
  Third-party plug-ins needed:
- Digital Film Tools Power Stroke
    1. Import Nora.jpg into After Effects and drag it to the Make New Composition button at the bottom of the Project panel. Use the Pen tool to create the main mask around the flower. (Figure 13.46.)

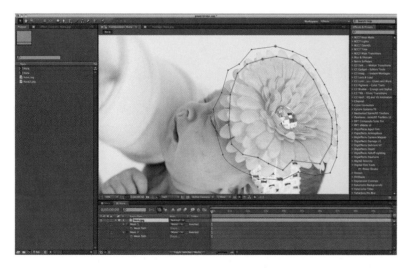

**Figure 13.46** Mask 1 is in blue and Mask 2 is in forest green. Mask 3 will be created in Step 5.

2. When you're drawing the masks, set the Mask Mode to None. If you are using video, do not keyframe the mask yet, just a single frame. Wait until after the effect is applied and set up. You will not know how close the masks need to be until you set up the color effect. (Figure 13.47.)
3. Apply Digital Film Tools Power Stroke (Effects > Digital Film Tools > Power Stroke) to the footage.
4. Under Adjust 1, under Mask, select Mask 1. This is the area that will be desaturated. Set Saturation to –100. (Figure 13.48.)
5. Adjust mask points until you are satisfied with the selection and the flower still remains pink while the rest of the image is black and white.

**Figure 13.47** Set Mask Mode to None so that the image will not be hidden. Click the colored boxes to the left of Mask to change the mask color.

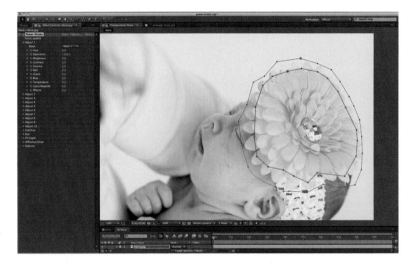

**Figure 13.48** An inner and outer mask surround the flower.

6. Under Adjust 2, choose Mask 2 for Mask. Adjust Hue, Saturation, Brightness, Contrast, and all other settings under Adjust.

7. To achieve the bright red color we'll need more than can be obtained by making these adjustments. Twirl open Colorize. Under Mask 2 I selected Mask 2 and set the color to bright red. Readjust the settings for Adjust 2 to tone them down. (Figure 13.49.)

8. Because the red color is very strong and much more saturated than the original pink, be very careful about not losing detail by over-saturating or making the color too dark.

9. The color is starting to look really flat. To reintroduce the gemstone in the center of the flower, draw a new mask, Mask 3, on the gemstone. Under Adjust 3, choose Mask 3 and set Contrast to 35.0. (Figure 13.50.)

**Figure 13.49** Adjust 2 settings are used in conjunction with colorizes to achieve the right color.

**Figure 13.50** Mask 3 once again reveals the original colors of the gemstone in the center of the flower.

# Hot Tip

A trick for working with multiple masks is to colorize them so that it's easy to keep track of which is which. To change the mask color, go to the timeline and click the colored box next to Mask 1, Mask 2, and so on. Use the color picker to select a color. Make sure you choose a color that is easy to see over your footage.

## Feathering Individual Mask Vertices with RE:Vision Effects PV Feather

One drawback about the built-in masking tools in After Effects is that there is no way to feather individual mask points with different values on the same mask. A workaround is to apply multiple overlapping masks, but this can get complicated if there are many masks. A simpler option is mocha + mocha shape, mentioned previously in this chapter. The downside of mocha is that you need to leave After Effects and import the data.

**RE:Vision Effects PV Feather** ($69) can help with this situation, if you'd like to stay within After Effects. PV is an abbreviation for "Per Vertex" and it uses an inner and an outer mask. The inner mask is a fill mask, filling the area with the content from the footage, and the outer mask is the feathering control.

**Figure 13.51** PV Feather applied to duplicate video layers with the same settings. The sample on the left shows the mask and vertices. The sample on the right shows the results. Footage: Michigan Film Reel.

# Removing Unwanted Elements from a Shot

There are many times when something will need to be removed from a shot. If you're shooting in a public street, for example, you may need to remove a car driving through the shot or a stray pedestrian that wandered onto the set. You may have a crew member accidently come into the camera's field of view. You may need to remove safety wires from an actor or stunt person, or maybe you're shooting the next epic *Star Wars* fan film and need to remove the wires from a Tie Fighter.

Object removal can be time-consuming and laborious, with rotoscoping or painting or cloning frame by frame. But, there are tools to make the job faster and easier. In this section, I'll show you **Boris Continuum Motion Key** plus some plug-ins for wire removal.

## Removing an Element with Boris Continuum Motion Key

At NAB 2008 I worked at the Boris Booth and demoed plug-ins in their little theater. One plug-in that always excited the audience was **Boris Continuum Motion Key** ($199), which uses Optical Flow technology to remove unwanted foreground objects like an extra car in the shot or crew that accidently walked on set. Why were they so excited? There is no rotoscoping involved!

The sample I showed at NAB had a car driving through an intersection of a busy street. The object is to remove the car and keep everything else intact without rotoscoping, painting, or using any sort of clone tool. How does it work? Amazingly well!

Here are a few tips to get the best results with Motion Key:

- The footage should be locked down or shot with a tripod and the object moving with the scene. Preprocessing with a stabilizer can be helpful.

Figure 13.52 The original shot with the actor walking toward the car. Footage: Michigan Film Reel.

Figure 13.53 The final result, after Boris Continuum Motion Key has removed the actor. Footage: Michigan Film Reel.

- The footage should be well-lit.
- It's easiest with a single moving element to remove in a shot.
- Watch out for shadows and reflections. If they are not fully removed, it can be a dead giveaway that something has been removed.

Here are the basic steps to remove an object from a shot.

1. Import your video footage into After Effects. Drag the clip to the Make New Project button at the bottom of the Project panel.
2. Apply BCC Motion Key to the video layer (Effects > BCC Keys Matte > BCC Motion Key).

3. With the Mode in Setup Region, change the default Oval to a Rectangle for Area Selection if it fits the shot better, as it does in my example. (Figure 13.54.)

**Figure 13.54** The Setup Region is positioned over the actor that is being removed from the shot.

4. Find the point in the shot where the entire object is in the shot. Position the Area Position/Offset over the object to remove. Adjust the Aspect Ratio, Area Scale, and Area Angle so that the rectangle surrounds the object completely. (Figure 13.55.)

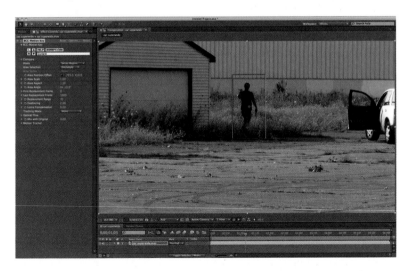

**Figure 13.55** The BCC Motion Key Setup Region.

5. Keyframe the Area Position/Offset parameter to follow the object to be removed. Move through the timeline and reposition the rectangle so that it is always surrounding the object.
6. Change the Mode from Setup Region to Remove Area and preview the comp to see the result. Adjust the Feathering to hide any sharp edges.

## Wire/Rig Removal

Wires are used in films to move elements that can't be moved on their own. They're also used for the safety of the actor as they're performing stunts. The basic idea here is to remove the wire and fill in that space with the elements behind it. Cloning is a great way to achieve this task, but going frame by frame can take time and sometimes the results can look splotchy or bubbly.

**Figure 13.56** Fishing line was attached to the steering wheels to give the appearance they were moving without a driver, and removed with Boris Continuum Complete BCC Wire Remover.

**Figure 13.57** The original footage. Footage: Sia "I'm in here" music video. Director: David Altobelli. Producer: Suzanne Joskow. Visual effects supervisor: Noah Rappaport.

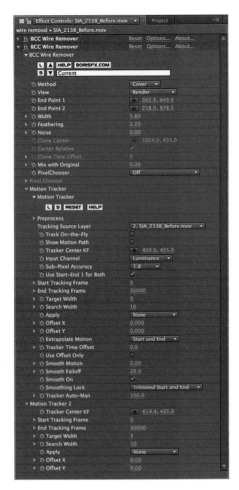

**Figure 13.58** BCC Wire Remover Effect Controls panel with dual Motion Trackers for each end of the wire.

There are a few third-party plug-ins for After Effects available to make this job easier and faster: **Boris Continuum BCC Wire Remover, Red Giant Key Correct Wire/Rig Remover**, and **Cycore FX CC Simple Wire Removal**. All wire removal plug-ins are not created equal!

With the shot at the beginning of this section, I tried all three plug-ins. I had no success with Red Giant Key Correct Wire/Rig Remover and limited success with Cycore FX CC Simple Wire Removal. Both plug-ins have points placed each end of the wire to create a line or mask, and then allow the user to clone from an offset position. Neither plug-in gave results worthy of screenshots for the book!

Boris Continuum Complete BCC Wire Remover, on the other hand, had very impressive results by cloning or blending pixels together from adjacent areas. The built-in Motion Tracker works the same as it does in with BCC Witness Protection (presented earlier in this chapter). I was able to obtain a quality track near the steering wheel but not at the other end of the line, but there is not a lot of contrast and the fishing line is thin. The end that couldn't be tracked took only a few minutes to manually keyframe. Each wire needs a separate instance of the effect on the footage layer; in this case I had four wires, so I applied BCC Wire Remover four times to the footage.

Because of the fine wire, the Width and Feathering needed to be lowered from the default for the blend to look natural.

**Figure 13.59** *Left*: The original shot. *Center*: The Preview showing red masks. *Right*: The final render.

# FIXING VIDEO PROBLEMS

Nothing is worse than coming back from a long shoot and realizing that as careful as you were, something is wrong. Or maybe you're on a tight deadline and waiting for footage from your client and when you get it, it's noisy or is in the wrong format. There are many common problems with video and you're bound to run into little snags from time to time, especially if you end up working with others who are inexperienced. The problems can range from noisy footage from shooting in poor conditions, to field issues, and rolling shutter problems. In this chapter, I'll also cover uprezzing footage from SD to HD, a common procedure when mixing footage from different sources.

Sometimes you will be unable to avoid problems, but luckily there are usually tools to fix the problems. This chapter dives into some of the more common issues and gives you some options on how to fix them.

## Noise and Grain

If you're working with footage that is underexposed, no matter how high-end of a camera you are using, you are going to see some grain and noise. The amount of noise depends on a number of factors including the lighting, compression or artifacting, and video format. Although it's best to keep your footage in the most natural state possible, sometimes denoising or degraining is needed. Denoising can add more problems to the mix—mainly softening or blurring your footage. Use a light touch when you do fix noisy footage. If the noise is not too bad, it's best not too do too much.

Angie Mistretta created some keying training for Toolfarm and currently works at Pixar. She taught me quite a bit about removing grain from greenscreen footage before keying and she is the one who originally brought the idea of degraining per channel to my attention. Angie works with the purpose of always using a light touch on video, to keep it as unaffected as possible and to only improve, not degrade footage.

When working with DV footage, generally the blue channel will be the channel with the most noise, so try and use filters that can degrain per channel. Remove grain plug-ins blur the footage.

**Figure 14.1** Trainer Angie Mistretta discusses per channel noise reduction in her Keylight Training. Footage: Angie Mistretta/Toolfarm, Professional Keying with Keylight from Toolfarm Expert Series.

By removing grain per channel, you are isolating the channel with the most noise and hopefully preserving the detail in the other channels. With greenscreen and DV footage, the green channel will usually be the least grainy, while the blue channel is usually the noisiest channel.

## Pro Tip

To view both the full RGB and a single channel at the time, use the pulldown menu at the top of the Composition panel and select New Comp Viewer. A new tab with the same video will open along the top of the Composition panel. Click to lock one of them and drag the other to the left side of the Composition panel, until the side of the window highlights. Let it go and you should see two videos side by side. Command + Option + Shift + N will split the panel in one click!

**Figure 14.2** The noise per channel is obvious when each channel is shown side by side in a quadrant. 1. RGB; 2. Red channel; 3. Green channel; 4. Blue channel. Footage: Angie Mistretta/Toolfarm, Professional Keying with Keylight from Toolfarm Expert Series.

Use the RGB pulldown window at the bottom of the Composition panel to select a different channel. As you move along the timeline you'll now see two views of your Comp. This is a great way to monitor an alpha channel or matte as well.

## Noise and Grain Comparisons

There is no shortage of tools to remove noise for After Effects and I'll talk briefly about several. What follows are descriptions of many of the plug-ins available. When comparing the plug-ins, I tried to give them a consistent treatment and very minimal noise reduction so that the detail was not lost. The numbers reference the Noise Comparison image in Figure 14.3.

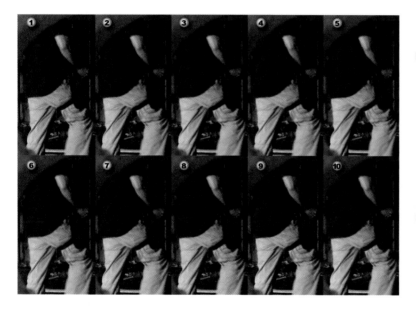

**Figure 14.3** A comparison of noise reduction plug-ins available for After Effects. 1. Original footage; 2. After Effects Remove Grain; 3. PHYX Fast Noise Reduction; 4. Noise Industries FxFactory Noise Reduction; 5. RE:Vision Effects DE:Noise; 6. GenArts Monsters GT M_RemGrain; 7. GenArts Sapphire S_GrainRemove; 8. Boris Continuum Complete BCC DeGrain; 9. CoreMelt C2 Gadget – Editors Tools Noise Limiter; 10. Red Giant Key Correct Denoiser. Footage: Michigan Film Reel.

1. **Original Footage:** The shot in the example is of a friend walking through an abandoned building; the video is shot through a peephole. Shot in HDV 1080i, there is not a lot of light and the shot is very grainy.
2. **After Effects Remove Grain:** One of my favorites is the Remove Grain plug-in that ships with After Effects, which was acquired by Adobe from Grain Surgery, along with the Add Grain and Match Grain filters. The plug-ins are very robust. They can sample areas of the video and work per channel to give you a fine level of control. (Figure 14.4.)
3. **PHYX Cleaner ($199) Fast Noise Reduction (FxFactory):** There are not a lot of options with this tool. There is no degrain per channel, but it's very fast. Options include High Frequency Noise

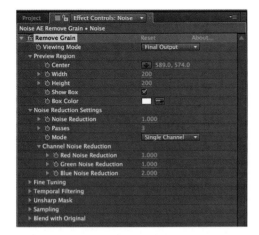

**Figure 14.4** After Effects Remove Grain Effect Controls. Screenshot: Michele Yamazaki.

**Figure 14.5** PHYX Cleaner Fast Noise Reduction Effect Controls. Screenshot: Michele Yamazaki.

**Figure 14.6** Noise Industries FxFactory Noise Reduction Effect Controls. Screenshot: Michele Yamazaki.

Removal, uma Smoothing, and Luma Sharpening Amount. The values must be kept low or the footage will "bloom." (Figure 14.5.)

4. **Noise Industries FxFactory ($399) Noise Reduction:** Again, not many options: Noise Level, Sharpness, and Color Space, which gives you a pulldown menu for Linear or Uncorrected. There is a single preset called Noisiest of All, which tends to blur the detail. The values for Noise Level have to be kept extremely low (0.05!) or details begin to blur. There is no per channel control. (Figure 14.6.)

5. **RE:Vision Effects DE:Noise ($149)** has two plug-ins, DE:Noise and DE:Noise Frame Average, which work temporally, sampling surrounding frames. DE:Noise does not work per channel but is still more robust than the previously mentioned plug-ins. De:Noise has a Pre-Process Control for adjusting the contrast, then allows you to choose the Temporal Process Mode (Median, Average, Motion weighted average, min, max, and more). The values can be adjusted for Spatial Radius and Threshold %. There are several other options, like using an ALT Track Source and Post Processing Controls. The DE:Noise Frame Average did a pretty nice job of removing the noise and keeping the detail.

With a light touch, DE:Noise did a better job at removing noise and keeping detail than most other plug-ins, but, as with any degraining plug-in, you will lose a bit of detail in the process. (Figure 14.7.)

6. **GenArts Monsters ($999 node-locked or floating) GT M_RemGrain:** M_RemGrain does allow blurring or sharpening per channel. With M_RemGrain, I had to crank the values about halfway for it to have much effect and then suddenly, the detail

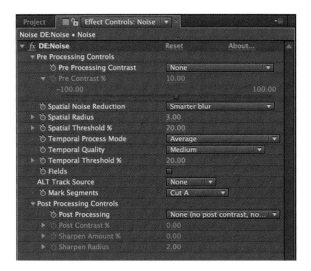

**Figure 14.7** RE:Vision Effects DE:Noise Effect Controls.
Screenshot: Michele Yamazaki.

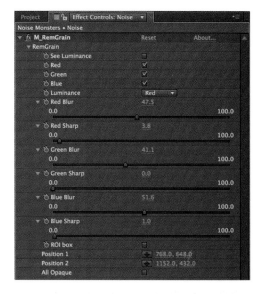

**Figure 14.8** GenArts Monsters M_RemGrain Effect Controls. Screenshot: Michele Yamazaki.

blurred. For example, there appeared to be no difference setting the Green Blur from anywhere between 1 and 39, but at 40, the footage began to blur. By combining the blur and sharpen settings, though, I was able to get a pretty decent result. The sliders seem not sensitive enough, then too sensitive. (Figure 14.8.)

7. **GenArts Sapphire ($1699 node-locked, $2499 floating) S_GrainRemove:** This one works quite differently from the Monsters M_RemGrain, with Smooth adjustments for Luma and Chroma, Edge Width, Edge Scale, and Edge Threshold, and an option to Show Result or Show Edges. As with most of the remove grain plug-ins, the default is way too strong. Because the shot I was using has so much green, smoothing the chroma more than the luma gave nice results. By keeping the values of all of the settings low, I was able to blur a good bit of the noise without losing a lot of the detail. Sapphire GrainRemove is one of the better tools on the market, in my opinion. (Figure 14.9.)

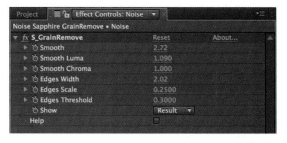

**Figure 14.9** GenArts Sapphire S_GrainRemove Effect Controls. Screenshot: Michele Yamazaki.

8. **Boris Continuum ($999) BCC DeGrain:** I am a big fan of the Boris Continuum Complete package because of the amount of control that they give the user. DeGrain is no exception. BCC DeGrain works temporally and the user can select the frame or sample layer with the noise.

What is unique about this plug-in is that it walks the user through a four-step setup to first Select the Sample; second, Blur the Grain; third, Suppress Ripples and finally, Restore

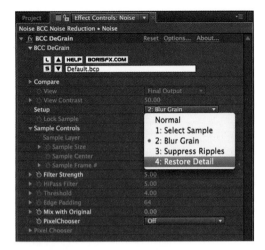

**Figure 14.10** Boris Continuum Complete BCC DeGrain Effect Controls. Screenshot: Michele Yamazaki.

**Figure 14.11** CoreMelt C2 Gadget – Editors Tools Noise Limiter Effect Controls. Screenshot: Michele Yamazaki.

Detail. On top of all of this is the Pixel Chooser, which allows the user to isolate areas of the video with a mask or matte, so a color channel can be isolated if needed.

There is a bit of a learning curve with the Pixel Chooser, but overall, the results of BCC DeGrain are very good. (Figure 14.10.)

Note: CoreMeltFREE was introduced in March of 2011. Visit http://bit.ly/CM-Free to learn more.

9. **CoreMelt C2 Gadget (free) – Editors Tools Noise Limiter:** As with all of the others, the values need to be very low to get a good result. This plug-in has about ten options: Input checkbox, Noise Level, Noise Sharpen, Median checkbox, Protect Edges, Edge Detail, Edge Intensity, Unsharp Intensity, and Unsharp Radius. There is also a checkbox for Use Mask, which opens some very robust masking options to isolate the area that you want to eliminate the noise. (Figure 14.11.)

10. **Red Giant Magic Bullet Denoiser ($99):** This plug-in has very few options but when the Time Depth is set low and the Average is set low, the plug-in samples from surrounding frames and actually does a pretty nice job of eliminating noise and keeping detail. (Figure 14.12.)

**Figure 14.12** Key Correct Denoiser Effect Controls. Screenshot: Michele Yamazaki.

Again, let me repeat, keep your footage as untouched as possible and although there are a lot of tools out there for degraining, it doesn't mean you have to use them. Often it is better to leave some grain than to blur the shot and remove detail.

---

**DID YOU KNOW?**

In video, it's noise. In film, it's grain.

---

## Matching Grain or Noise

The original purpose of adding grain is to match synthetic shots to other source footage. For a believable composite when combining computer-generated elements, photos, and live-action footage, it's important to match the grain. 8mm film, for example, will have a lot more grain than a photo, and quite often, 3D renders have absolutely no noise at all. By matching the grain size and structure, you can make a better composite. Another purpose for adding grain to a shot is to give video more of a filmic look and feel.

My favorite is the Match Grain plug-in that ships with After Effects, which is quite robust. The Effect Controls for Match Grain are similar to the Remove Grain effect. The user selects the layer to sample from and adjusts the Intensity and Color of grain.

The examples show two pieces of footage, which were never meant to be together. The background plate is from the film *Depleted: Day 419* while the skater footage is from Crowd Control. The grain on the skater footage is matched to the grain on the background. The footage is zoomed to 200%. Notice the grain is especially noticeable on her thigh.

A third-party option, which has a very similar result to AE's Match Grain, is **Boris Continuum BCC Match Grain**. BCC Match Grain also allows the user to sample another layer, and a specific frame and section of that frame. The grain size and contrast are adjustable and there is the Pixel Chooser option that lets the user isolate the area where the grain is added.

**Figure 14.13** After Effects Match Grain. On the left, the skater footage has Match Grain applied to match the background plate. The skater on the right has no Match Grain. Footage: Background plate, Depleted: Day 419, directed by Jeremy Hanke, http://worldofdepleted.com; foreground plate, Crowd Control, 00182_001_138.

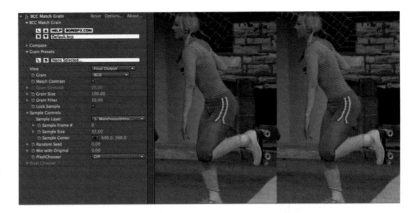

**Figure 14.14** Boris Continuum Complete BCC Match Grain. On the left, the skater footage has BCC Match Grain applied to match the background plate. The skater on the right has no Match Grain. Footage: Background plate, Depleted: Day 419 , directed by Jeremy Hanke, www.worldofdepleted.com; foreground plate, Crowd Control, 00182_001_138.

## Pro Tip

When sampling grain, choose a smooth area of an image, such as clear sky or a wall. If you choose an area with texture (the surface of water, a paved road, or wood-grain pattern), the match grain plug-in will pick up the texture and reproduce it as grain.

There are also several plug-ins to add grain on the market and included with After Effects that allow you to set the grain manually.

## Flicker, Strobing, and Lighting Shifts

In college I did an independent study in lighting for one credit. I borrowed a light kit and did comparisons of different lights with different filters. This is where I first noticed the problem with fluorescent light causing flicker on footage.

Flicker seems to be a major problem in a couple places:

1. Footage shot under LED or fluorescent lights, or on computer monitor
2. Lighting changes in stop motion animation

The issue with fluorescent, LED lighting, or computer monitors usually stems from the light source or monitor and camera running on different AC power cycles. Why does this happen? Fluorescent lights flicker at twice the electrical supply frequency. This flicker creates fluctuations with brightness and color temperature, which causes problems in video and photography.[1]

---

[1]Source: Wikipedia: Fluorescent Lamp; http://en.wikipedia.org/wiki/Fluorescent_lamp.

Other causes are DSLRs with an automatic iris or automatic exposure mode, which can cause more problems as the lens tries to compensate for the flickering light. If you can shoot without automatic settings and use a manual aperture, it may help.

With stop motion animation, shifts in lighting are the likely cause. If you haven't yet shot, white balance the camera and set the camera to manual so it won't automatically adjust exposure as the light changes.

If you have already shot, there are a few plug-ins that may help with flicker problems. After Effects has built-in Color Stabilizer and Auto Contrast, which are both worth a try. Here are a few third-party options.

- **GenArts Sapphire** ($1699 node-locked, $2499 floating) includes many flicker tools, including **FlickerRemove**, **FlickerRemoveColor**, **FlickerRemoveMatte**, and **FlickerRmMatteColor**. These are just a few plug-ins from the huge Sapphire bundle, so don't let the price scare you away.
- **Red Giant Software Film Fix** ($799) automatically eliminated flicker but has been discontinued and is only available for After Effects 7. Hopefully Red Giant will resurrect this great product.
- **Granite Bay Software GBDeflicker** ($99) is a newer and lesser known plug-in that has become very popular, especially for those working with stop motion footage. It works well and is inexpensive. It works in After Effects, Premiere Pro, and Premiere Elements.
- **CoreMelt C2 Pigment Flicker Tool** (free) is another tool to remove flicker from a shot. It can also add flicker to a clip by sampling luminance value changes in another clip.

## A Comparison of Video Upscaling Plug-ins

In the past few years there have been many new tools introduced to take SD video and scale it to HD video. If you have a large library of SD stock footage that you would like to use in HD projects, you'll need to upscale, or uprez, it. You might also need to uprez archived SD footage in a new HD production so the frame size matches. Sure you can scale video in After Effects and sharpen it but there other options that can give better quality.

In this comparison, I'm using an NTSC SD clip from Artbeats, clip DWH01-07, an aerial shot of Houston, Texas. I'm uprezzing it to HDTV 1080 frame size.

This section compares **Red Giant Magic Bullet Instant HD** ($99), **Instant HD Resizer**, and **Boris Continuum Complete BCC UpRez** ($99). One oddity I've noticed about the different upscaling tools is that none of the presets equal the same size for each

**Web Link**

For more information on shooting film and video under fluorescent lights, check out Cinematography.net: *http://bit.ly/g32kmr*.

**Figure 14.15** A comparison of upscaling plug-ins. 1. After Effects Scale; 2. Red Giant Instant HD Resizer; 3. Red Giant Instant HD; 4. Boris Continuum BCC UpRez. Footage: ArtBeats Clip # DWH01-07.

**Figure 14.16** Red Giant Instant HD has an incredibly long list of Output Size presets to choose from for upscaling video. Screenshot: Michele Yamazaki.

plug-in. I have upscaled all of the video to the same size so that it will match across the board. The After Effects shot is upscaled 293.2% to fill the frame for comparison.

With **Red Giant Magic Bullet Instant HD**, drag the footage into a comp that is the destination size, in this case, HDTV 1080. The effect is applied directly to the footage and there is a long list of Output Size presets to choose from.

Instant HD has parameters for adjusting Filter Type, Sharpness, Quality, and Antialiasing. I've had mixed results with Instant HD. Sometimes the Instant HD uprezzed footage looks a lot better and other times no better than the After Effects scaled footage. I used the Output Size preset Fill 1920 × 1080 (2133 × 1422) DV NTSC. It was very difficult to match the After Effects upscaled footage with any of the presets from Instant HD.

**Red Giant Instant HD Resizer** was acquired from Digital Anarchy and instead of scrapping it or working it into Instant HD, it is bundled as a separate plug-in with Instant HD, giving the user another option.

Resizer also comes with a few presets but has options to manually size the video. The user can set the Aspect Ratio, method of Filling the Frame, Cropping options, and Field Order. There are, of course, Quality settings as well. Under Advanced, the Smoothness settings will remove blur artifacting. With a low

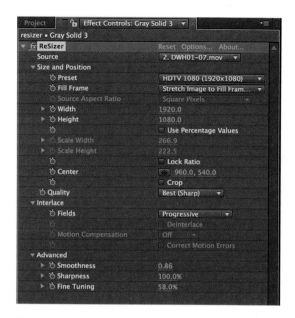

**Figure 14.17** The Red Giant Instant HD Resizer Effect Controls panel. Screenshot: Michele Yamazaki.

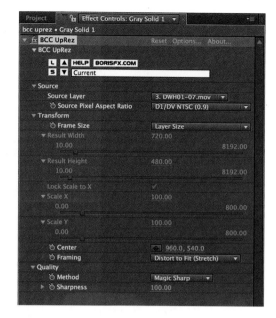

**Figure 14.18** BCC UpRez has many of the same options that other upscaling plug-ins have, but wins my vote for the best upscale plug-in for After Effects. Screenshot: Michele Yamazaki.

setting it works well but higher values blur the footage. Sharpness obviously sharpens the footage.

**Boris Continuum Complete UpRez** does a great job of upscaling video and keeping video looking sharp with its Magic Sharp and Magic Smooth settings. Instead of applying the filter to the footage, make a comp-sized Solid layer and set the Source Layer, which should be below the Solid in the timeline. Set the source Pixel Aspect Ratio, in this case, D1/DV NTSC (0.9). I chose a custom scale to match the other samples and set Quality to Magic Sharp.

Of the upscale plug-ins for After Effects, my clear choice is Boris Continuum BCC UpRez. It does the nicest job keeping footage crisp and downplaying artifacting.

With **Noise Industries FxFactory Pro Upscale**, the effect is applied directly to the source footage. Instead of it upscaling the footage to the size of the composition, it allows the user to choose a portion of the video and scale it to the size of video frame only. This works well if your footage is the same size as the final output, but closer shots are needed. Since it doesn't really serve the same purpose as the others, it was not included in the comparison. With Upscale, the Height and Width should be equal or the video will be stretched. Also if Edge Smoothing is not set low, the video will artifact.

**Figure 14.19** FxFactory Upscale asks the user to set the region to upscale. This region will fill the original video frame. Screenshot: Michele Yamazaki.

**Figure 14.20** Fields are exaggerated in this example to demonstrate how they are interlaced. The inset is enlarged by 200%. Footage credit: Daniel Evans, LifebloodSkateboards.com.

# Interlaced Video

Interlaced video comprises two separate fields that make a single frame of video. These fields are alternating lines of an image that create each frame, or each field makes up half the resolution of the frame. Fields were introduced to smooth out motion and reduce flicker that was introduced by the slow rate of the broadcast signal, because early televisions didn't handle content with a lot of movement too well. The frame rate of NTSC television is 30 frames per second (29.97, actually), making the field rate 60 interlaced fields per second (technically 59.94).

## WHAT DO THE P AND I STAND FOR?

If you see the term 1080i or 1080p, it means HDTV that is interlaced (with interlaced fields) or progressive (no interlaced fields). The i stands for interlaced and p is for progressive.

In After Effects, the process of removing interlacing is known as separating fields. Newer cameras and software will embed information into the video and After Effects will automatically separate fields for you. Most of the time, After Effects built-in Interpolation Rules do a good job of auto detecting fields by referencing at the frame size and sometimes codec.

To separate fields manually in After Effects, select your footage in the Project panel. Click the Interpret Footage button at the bottom left of the Project panel or go to File > Interpret

Footage > Main. Under Fields and Pulldown, select Lower Field First in the Separate popup if you're using for NTSC D1. To improve the look of the video, check Preserve Edges, which by default is unchecked.

**RE:Vision Effects FieldsKit** ($89) provides many more field separation and pulldown options than After Effects' built-in effects. FieldsKit comes with three plug-ins: **Deinterlacer, Reinterlacer**, and **Pulldown**. Using proprietary field reconstruction and adaptive motion techniques, FieldsKit Deinterlacer can construct nicer looking frames and better edges by using surrounding pixel information. FieldsKit Deinterlacer used in combination with RE:Vision Effects Twixtor, can mimic the look of 24 fps film with video footage.

Another way to give your interlaced footage the look of 24 fps progressive film is **Red Giant Magic Bullet Frames** ($199). Magic Bullet Frames is a fast deinterlacing filter that uses a motion-adaptive algorithm to smooth video. This 24p conversion includes a feature to make sure that clips stay the same duration when they are converted from 29.97i frames to 24 frames during the pulldown process, so no clip trimming is required. Magic Bullet Frames includes six plug-ins: **Broadcast Spec, Deartifacter, Frames, Frames Plus, Letterboxer,** and **Opticals**. The Deartifacter plug-in can remove compression from DV footage.

Another benefit of Magic Bullet Frames is that one license will work in After Effects, Final Cut Pro, Motion, or Premiere on the same machine too.

**Web Link**

To better understand working with fields and 3:2 pulldown, Chris Meyer, co-author of the *Creating Motion Graphics with After Effects* books, has online training modules on Lynda.com titled "Understanding Fields and Interlacing in After Effects" and "Working with 3:2 Pulldown in After Effects." Non-subscribers can get a free 7-day pass by going to *www.lynda.com/go/ chrisandtrish.*

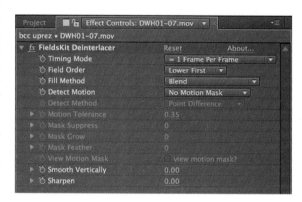

**Figure 14.21** RE:Vision Effects FieldsKit's Effect Controls set at the defaults. Screenshot: Michele Yamazaki.

# Rolling Shutter

Rolling shutter is the skew or wobble often seen when something moves quickly in front of a camera or a camera pans quickly. CMOS sensors are especially prone to rolling shutter. Rolling shutter is often seen in footage from iPhones and other cell phone cameras, Flip HD cameras, and other digital cameras. Rolling shutter happens because the CMOS sensor in the camera records from top to bottom instead of frame by frame. It will cause a car to look skewed and slanted if it moves quickly perpendicular to the camera, or a building to slant if the camera pans quickly.

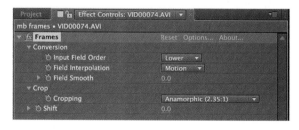

**Figure 14.22** Red Giant Magic Bullet Frames Effect Controls panel. Screenshot: Michele Yamazaki.

**Figure 14.23** This sample shows the wobble or "Jell-O-vision" type of rolling shutter caused by vibrations inside a cockpit. This wobble was so extreme that none of the rolling shutter plug-ins for After Effects could remedy the problem. Footage: Steve Kahn Edit on Hudson.

Rolling shutter issues can also be caused by vibration. Those wobbly distortions, also known as "Jello-vision" can be extremely difficult to fix.

CCD cameras do not have rolling shutter problems because they capture the entire frame at once instead of scanning from top to bottom. For an excellent explanation and a video breakdown of how rolling shutter occurs and CMOS versus CCD cameras, visit *http://dvxuser.com/jason/CMOS-CCD/*.

There are a couple of tools on the market worth checking out if you have rolling shutter problems in your footage. To address this problem, **CoreMelt Lock and Load X** ($149) includes specific shutter coefficients for several popular cameras on the market. **The Foundry RollingShutter** ($500 node-locked, $740 floating) uses Local Motion Estimation technology. **proDAD Mercalli** ($199) is a stabilization plug-in that also has a rolling shutter reduction feature.

Jack Binks, plug-ins manager for The Foundry, shared his insider knowledge on rolling shutter issues and gave some background on The Foundry RollingShutter when I visited The Foundry's office in London in January 2011:

*There are a few different methods to correct rolling shutter. There is a global solution, which essentially creates a four-corner pin, skewed to the image, to try and correct it. That's really good in some respects because it's nice and fast and everything in the image is transferred equally. The problem with it is that, if you had a foreground object moving left to right and a pan going right to the left, the rolling shutter on one object is going to be a different amount of skew to the rolling shutter on the other object. So, if you correct for the foreground object, the background object is going to get double the amount of skew. And, if you correct for the background movement, the foreground object gets double the amount of skew. That's probably 20 to 25% of cases.*

*The RollingShutter plug-in that we have is actually more aimed at correcting a few things, like camera tracking. If you introduce double the amount of skew you're really going to screw up your chances of ever pulling a decent track. So what we do, is rather than using a global solution, we use the motion estimation engine from* **Kronos** *to calculate a per-pixel amount of skew. The foreground object should be skewed by the correct amount to correct it versus the background being skewed in the right direction at its correct amount. That's why that's really powerful. The downside to doing a local correction is the same thing that you can see with something like Kronos or Twixtor or any other motion estimation engine, where you start seeing those warping artifacts coming in. Being able to do both a global and a local correction is obviously a powerful thing.*

**Figure 14.24** The image on the left has a skew caused by a fast pan inside a moving vehicle. The image on the right was straightened with The Foundry RollingShutter. Footage: Michele Yamazaki.

I have to agree with Jack. I did a rolling shutter correction test on two clips. One was a panning shot from inside a moving vehicle and the buildings had a definite slant to them. The Foundry RollingShutter fixed it by just applying the plug-in and no tweaking. I could not get a decent result from either proDAD Mercalli or CoreMelt Lock and Load X. The second clip of the cockpit shown at the beginning of this section was such an extremely wobbly shot that none of the plug-ins could fix this clip. As I said earlier, sometimes nothing will fix a shot. You're best to try a demo version of the plug-in to see which will work for you.

## Lens Distortion/Barrel Distortion

If you need to remove lens distortion or bowed footage caused by a wide-angle lens, or straighten out footage that was shot with a fisheye lens, you have a few options. One is the built-in **Optics Compensation** tool that ships with After Effects, and often does the job just fine.

Third-party options include **Tiffen Dfx Digital Filter Suite** ($599.95) with its **Lens Distortion** and **Wide Angle Lens** plug-ins to add or remove lens distortion. **Digital Film Tools Composite Suite Pro ($395) Distortion** works the same as Tiffen's Lens Distortion filter.

## User Story: Fixing the Worst-Case Scenario—Stabilizing, Uprezzing, and Deinterlacing SD Footage, by Rob Birnholz

For a recent HD multiscreen trade show exhibit, the client asked that I replace previously composited HD material with archival SD shots of semi-trucks driving on a highway. The replacement footage was provided on BetaSP, and while not completely terrible was still of dubious quality (especially compared to the 1080p shots already in place). Aside from the low resolution of 4:3 BetaSP, they were shot handheld from the back of another vehicle on a gray, overcast winter day.

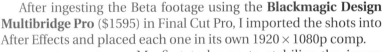

**Figure 14.25** The final shot after stabilizing, uprezzing, deinterlacing, and color correcting. Footage: Rob Birnholz, Absolute Motion Graphics.

**Figure 14.26** BetaSP footage in a 1080 HD comp. Footage: Rob Birnholz, Absolute Motion Graphics.

After ingesting the Beta footage using the **Blackmagic Design Multibridge Pro** ($1595) in Final Cut Pro, I imported the shots into After Effects and placed each one in its own 1920 × 1080p comp.

My first task was to stabilize the image and minimize as much shake and vibration as possible. I could have spent a lot of time with either the After Effects Tracker or **Imagineer mocha**, but my first choice when stabilizing footage is to try **CoreMelt Lock & Load X**. In my experience, this amazing filter results in a usable smooth shot more than 75% of the time with a single button-click. And it's fast! I'm not exaggerating when I say Lock & Load has saved me hours every time I've used it. For those instances when the default settings aren't precise enough, the plug-in has numerous controls for fine-tuning results.

Stabilizing footage usually involves a series of tradeoffs. Motion blur is often present in frames that are part of fast or extreme camera moves. Even though we can minimize or remove the apparent camera shake, the blur remains, seemingly out of place in a now steady shot. It becomes a judgment call how much of this blurring is acceptable. Also, the inherent repositioning of stabilized footage means it has to be scaled up to hide the otherwise visible frame edges that would be bouncing around (Lock & Load X does a great job of handling this dynamically, smoothly scaling shots for the least amount of image loss for any given frame).

After applying Lock & Load X and stabilizing the shot, I prerendered and reimported it to save rendering time further down the line.

Next it was time for uprezzing. I have two preferred plug-in methods for converting SD footage to HD, **Red Giant Magic Bullet Instant HD** and **Resizer**. Each is applied differently and uses special algorithms to achieve higher quality images than by simply scaling up a shot natively in After Effects. Since source quality varies wildly, I always try both methods and choose whichever one yields the best result.

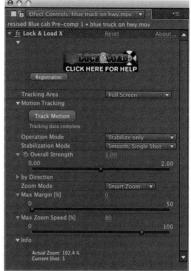

**Figure 14.27** CoreMelt Lock & Load X Control panel. Footage: Rob Birnholz, Absolute Motion Graphics.

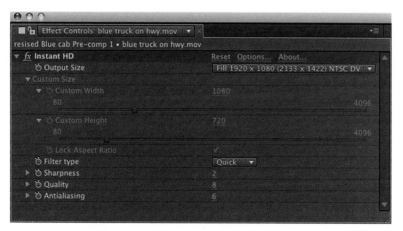

**Figure 14.28** Red Giant Instant HD control panel. Footage: Rob Birnholz, Absolute Motion Graphics.

Of the two, I usually try Instant HD first since it's applied directly to the SD clip in question. The controls are straightforward, with only a minimum of tweaking available. Once applied, the desired output size is selected from an extensive list in a pulldown menu. The amount of choices may seem like overkill, but it's easy enough to try several options until you discover the proper setting (or choose Custom and dial in your own width and height sizes).

**Figure 14.29** Red Giant Instant HD results. Footage: Rob Birnholz, Absolute Motion Graphics.

Even though the results from Instant HD look good, I still wanted to try Resizer for comparison purposes. Resizer is not applied directly to a source clip, but rather to an intermediate solid on another layer. The footage layer to be resized is then selected from a pulldown menu in Resizer's control panel. Resizer also ignores any filters applied to the source layer, so the target needs to be precomposed if you have any filters applied to your unscaled footage.

Resizer features a less extensive selection of preset aspect ratios, but also allows for custom scaling of footage. Resizer adds controls for repositioning a shot within the frame, plus features built-in deinterlacing options.

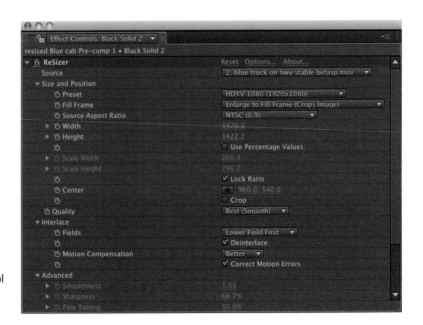

**Figure 14.30** The Resizer Control panel. Footage: Rob Birnholz, Absolute Motion Graphics.

Occasionally, upscaling with these filters produces unwanted artifacts, similar to the errors sometimes found when using Optical Flow for retiming shots. In this case the fine lines of the truck grill resulted in distortions that made glitches and popped during playback. When displayed on the large screens of a trade-show booth, these artifacts would be extremely distracting. Fortunately Resizer includes four degrees of Motion Compensation to help minimize these errors. Based on that alone, I ended up using Resizer for most of the replacement truck shots in this project.

It's also important to consider interlacing issues when upscaling. Since this project was to be rendered 1080p, deinterlacing meant I faced a double whammy: I was throwing away half my resolution even before scaling the shots from $720 \times 486$ to $1920 \times 1080$.

There are several advanced techniques for higher quality deinterlacing than you get with AE's basic built-in functionality, including plug-ins from RE:Vision Effects, GenArts Sapphire, and Boris FX. In my case I used **Sapphire's S_FieldRemove** filter (chosen because I already own it). As with most Sapphire filters, the results are extremely high quality with almost no tweaking required. (Even though Resizer has its own options for deinterlacing, I like to compare the results with other methods before settling on a final image.) Compared to AE's standard deinterlacing or Resizer's options, the Sapphire filter did a superior job, which was essential since any errors would be exaggerated after scaling up to HD.

**Figure 14.31** Artifacts on Grill (appear as tiny dots); reduced with Motion Compensation. Footage: Rob Birnholz, Absolute Motion Graphics.

**Figure 14.32** Sapphire S_Field-Remove filter: before and after. Footage: Rob Birnholz, Absolute Motion Graphics.

Being that the original footage was lacking in color and contrast, I added an Adjustment Layer to the resized comp and applied a combination of **Red Giant Magic Bullet Colorista II** ($299) and **Magic Bullet Looks** to enhance the contrast and saturation of the shot, and added some blue gradients to the sky. A touch of **Sapphire S_Vignette** further helped focus the eye on the main subject of the shot, which was the truck cab itself. The comp containing this now stabilized, upscaled, and color-graded shot was then masked off and parented to a background frame and composited over a background in my final comp.

# REFERENCE AND WORKFLOW

Not every plug-in exists to make beautiful visual effects, cool transitions, or help with compositing magic. Some exist only to help you achieve those effects. They are the behind-the-scenes tools, sort of like the guy in the restaurant who does all of the prep work, chopping the lettuce and preparing the lemon wedges for dinner service. It's a very important job that needs to be done but with none of the glamour of the executive chef.

When I started my internship at Postworks in 1995, I learned a few things the first week that I had not learned in college: how to read and set up a waveform monitor and vector scope and the importance of keeping elements in title safe and action safe areas. Although I do not create content for television anymore, it's basic knowledge that everyone who works with video should have (and if you do not, do yourself a favor and visit Wikipedia.org and learn about vectorscopes, waveform monitors, and safe area).

Something else I got very used to at Postworks was workflow between After Effects and Avid. There are many tools to assist workflow between After Effects and other software such as Apple Final Cut Pro, Maxon Cinema 4D, and 3ds Max.

This chapter takes a look at those tools that help users view video levels, see reference guides, and help workflow by linking between applications and footage types.

## Practice Safe Broadcasting: Waveform Monitor and Vectorscope

A vectorscope and waveform monitor work together to analyze the characteristics and levels of a video signal. The vectorscope is an oscilloscope that displays chrominance information, or the color information of the video. The waveform monitor shows luminance information, or brightness of the video. In broadcast, it's important to have colors in a broadcast-safe range. There are targeted areas for the video, which these tools can reveal.

Why do you need a waveform monitor and vectorscope? If your whites are too hot they will wash out surrounding colors, vibrate on screen, and even cause some TVs to buzz! If colors, especially reds, are too bright they will cause similar reactions. I once worked with a client who would always ask me to make

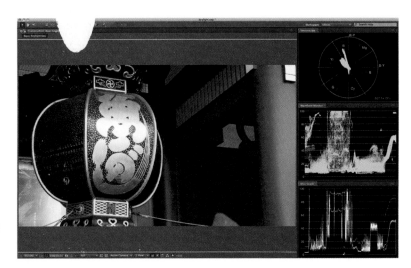

Figure 15.1 An example of a vectorscope (*top right*), waveform monitor (*middle right*), and slice graph (*bottom right*), using Synthetic Aperture Test Gear. Footage: Michele Yamazaki.

the text bigger and make it brighter red. I'd see the ads on television and hear them buzz and it would make me cringe. This was much more of a problem with analog video than digital video, but it's still a good idea to keep the video in the proper range.

The vectorscope and waveform monitor that I learned to read were hardware, but this is the digital age. Some applications such as Apple Final Cut Pro have waveform monitors and vectorscopes built in, but After Effects does not. There are a couple of tools for After Effects that fill this need, however.

Figure 15.1 contains a slice graph, which displays similar information to the waveform monitor with the information broken down into specific colors. A slice graph can reveal uneven lighting in greenscreen footage or spikes levels of red, green, or blue.

For in-depth information on the proper range for video levels, I highly recommend the book *Digital Compositing for Film and Video* by Steve Wright (2010).

Figure 15.2 Meta/DMA Scopo Gigio. Screenshot: Michele Yamazaki.

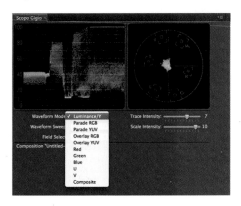

**Meta/DMA Scopo Gigio** ($125) has the same features as hardware vectorscopes and waveform monitors but shows up as a docked or floating panel that can be selected from the Window menu within After Effects. This greener option is much less expensive than purchasing hardware (and less dusting). Scopo Gigio works in NTSC and PAL, and in standard definition or high definition. It shows IRE, Volt, and RGB displays. Just view the scopes and if your levels are too high, use Levels, Hue/Saturation, or another plug-in to get them into the proper range.

**Synthetic Aperture Test Gear** ($95) has all of the testing tools you could possibly need for monitoring color, luminance, and even audio. Test Gear includes

**Figure 15.3** Synthetic Aperture Test Gear. Footage: Michigan Film Reel.

four video monitoring tools, three audio measurement tools, and two color tools.

- Waveform Monitor
- Vectorscope
- Histogram for viewing red, green, blue, and luminance levels
- Image Slice Display for viewing red, green, and blue information across the screen
- Gamut Display for legal broadcast colors
- Audio Waveform Display for checking audio levels
- Audio Phase Display for making sure 2-channel audio is set up correctly
- Audio Spectrum Display for viewing audio frequencies
- Color Picker
- Color Swatch Book

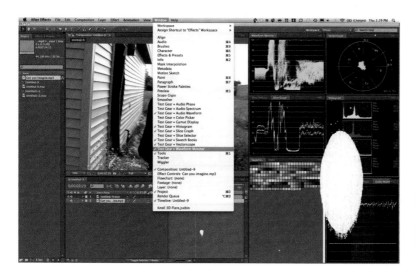

**Figure 15.4** Select only the Test Gear tools that are needed by choosing them under the Window menu. Footage: Michigan Film Reel.

Besides being a useful reference, what's great about Test Gear is that the panels can be individually selected under the Window menu so the screen won't get cluttered. The palettes can float or be docked into the After Effects interface panel or tabbed together to keep the screen tidy.

Test Gear ships with extremely useful documentation that explains how to use the scopes and monitors with your video. From the guide: "For the waveform monitor displays to be accurate, you must configure Test Gear's preferences to reflect your video system and the coding used by the image you are analyzing." The guide continues with further detailed instructions on how to set up Test Gear's preferences. There is also a section at the end of the guide titled "Understanding Waveform Monitor and Vectorscopes," useful for those who may be unfamiliar with how to read and use them or anyone who could use a refresher course.

**Figure 15.5** Synthetic Aperture Color Finesse. Screenshot: Wes Plate.

**Synthetic Aperture Color Finesse** (included with After Effects or $575 for the multihost version) also has waveform monitors and vectorscopes, and there are several reasons to choose it. First, it comes free with After Effects so you won't have to fork out any cash for it. Second, because Color Finesse is a color-correction tool, you have all of the adjustments in the interface. Note that you must apply it to a precomp or an Adjustment Layer to see the levels for the entire comp. If it's applied to a layer, the plug-in will reference only that layer. The downside to the plug-in is that you must go into the Color Finesse interface to see the monitors, whereas Scopo Gigio or Test Gear are dockable and have floating panels always available in After Effects.

**Figure 15.6** Red Giant Magic Bullet Looks with the RGB Parade open. Blue levels are high within the Crime Scene Alternative preset applied to this comp. Footage: Michele Yamazaki.

**Red Giant Magic Bullet Looks** ($399) also has tools for referencing output levels: an RGB Parade and a Slice Graph. These tools are only for use with Looks but if you apply the effect to an Adjustment Layer and open Looks you can view the levels of your current video, then use Looks to bring them into the proper range.

To turn on the graphs in Magic Bullet Looks, click the Graphs: On button in the upper right corner of the Looks interface. RGB Parade and Slice Graph are tabbed so that users can toggle between them.

## Masks and Guides

You're probably familiar with title safe and action safe, but there are many more safe zones and sizes out there and plug-ins to help make sure you stay within these parameters.

**Digital Film Tools Composite Suite Pro ($395) HDTV Masks** has guides for several aspect ratios, including 1:85 (a common aspect ratio for film), and TV Transmitted, TV Safe Action, and TV Safe Title, each of what show the "center cut" 4:3 area inside a 16:9 composition. The Masks/Reticle are customizable by color, thickness, and opacity so they can be visible over any footage. I recommend placing the masks on an Adjustment Layer over footage and toggling the visibility on and off when needed.

Composite Suite Pro Film Masks work exactly the same way as Pro HDTV Masks except with 2:40 and 1:85, which are common film sizes, and 1:66 aspect ratio, which is 15:9 and sometimes used by broadcasters.

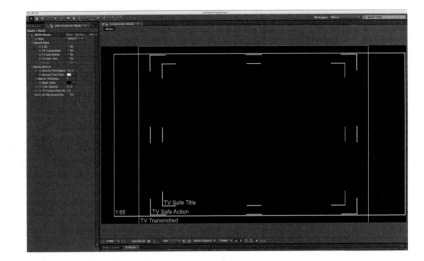

**Figure 15.7** Digital Film Tools Composite Suite Pro HDTV Masks with all Aspect Ratios enabled. Screenshot: Michele Yamazaki.

**Figure 15.8** Digital Film Tools Composite Suite Pro Film Masks with all Aspect Ratios enabled. Screenshot: Michele Yamazaki.

**Figure 15.9** Noise Industries FxFactory Frame Info. Footage: Michigan Film Reel.

## Safe Areas

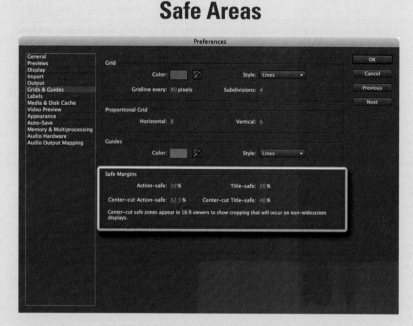

**Figure 15.10** Safe areas can be customized in After Effects Preferences, under After Effects > Preferences > Grids & Guides. Screenshot: Michele Yamazaki.

Not so much a guide as informative, **Noise Industries FxFactory ($399) Frame Info**, a plug-in in the FxFactory bundle, gives details on the frame number, fps, frame size, aspect ratio, and more. This information is available in the Project panel or by selecting Get Info, but it's most convenient to have it handy right in the Comp panel.

## Speed Up Workflow with Templates

**SUGARfx** Templates use the FxFactory engine, so they are very fast. The fact that they are templates in the form of a plug-in is sort of a rarity in After Effects. They are extremely easy to use, useful, and look beautiful. These templates are not After Effects project files but plug-ins that function as templates.

**SUGARfx Toolbox: Slate Tools Slate Master** ($49) is a plug-in that includes multiple slate layouts. The text is completely modifiable as are the fonts and colors, and can include your own images or logos, linked externally.

The SUGARfx Toolbox: Slate Tools also contains **SUGARfx Warning**, which has presets for the FBI warning in English and

**Figure 15.11** SUGARfx Slate Master. Screenshot: Michele Yamazaki.

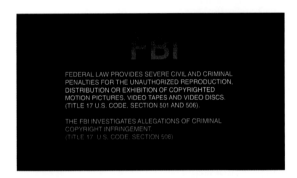

**Figure 15.12** The FBI Warning preset in SUGARfx Toolbox: Slate Tools Warning. Screenshot: Michele Yamazaki.

Spanish, DVD Usage License, Non Theatrical Licensing, Piracy Notice, and more. It saves on typing!

For more of a graphic style, SUGARfx has other templates such as **SUGARfx HUD** ($79), which contains three plug-ins: **Binoculars, OSD (On Screen Display)**, and **Target**. Each plug-in has tons of options including presets; editable colors, lines, and shapes; video effects; text options; and more. It's a lot of fun and useful if you're working on an espionage or science-fiction movie.

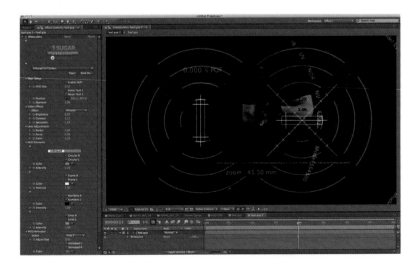

**Figure 15.13** SUGARfx HUD Binoculars. Footage: Crowd Control, clip # 00074_003_47.

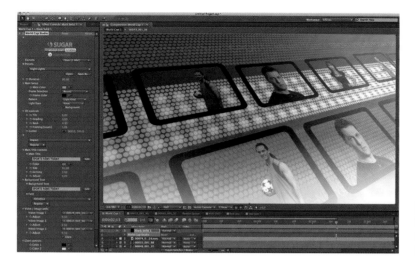

Figure 15.14 World Cup Studio interface. Footage: Crowd Control, clip # 00045_001_52, 00033_001_98 and 00074_001_24.

**SUGARfx World Cup Studio** ($119) is a sports news style template for bumpers, titles, lower thirds, backgrounds, over-the-shoulder shots, and video boxes for showcasing players. There are 3D controls for the full animation, adjustments for the frames around footage, full title settings, title controls, and color controls.

**Web Link:**

All SUGARfx Templates require the free FxFactory installed to run, which can be downloaded at *www .noiseindustries.com*.

# After Effects Integration with Other Hosts

Although After Effects works great with Premiere Pro using Dynamic Link, there is often a time when After Effects will need to work with other host applications such as **Apple Final Cut Pro**, **Avid**, **Maxon Cinema 4D**, and **Autodesk 3ds Max**. This section is about the tools that work as a bridge between these applications and After Effects, helping to speed workflow.

## Automatic Duck Pro Import AE by Wes Plate

**Automatic Duck Pro Import AE** ($495) is different from most other After Effects plug-ins. Instead of affecting an image visually or adding a visual element, Pro Import AE creates an After Effects composition by reading an AAF or OMF file from an Avid editing system or by reading an XML file from Final Cut Pro. This makes it possible to use your Avid of Final Cut Pro editing system to quickly edit your clips together and roughly build your clip layers then immediately move that timeline into After Effects to continue working.

A limitation of After Effects is that it does not lend itself well to real-time editing chores such as shot selection and trimming or synchronizing clips and edits to sound cues. Nonlinear editors such

**Figure 15.15** Take a Final Cut Pro sequence into After Effects with Automatic Duck Pro Import AE. Screenshot: Michele Yamazaki.

as Apple Final Cut Pro, Avid Media Composer, and Adobe Premiere Pro are very well-suited to the tasks of editing, however their compositing and animation capabilities are nowhere close to what After Effects offers. Ideally you might want to combine the powers of the editing system with After Effects. Premiere Pro users have long had built-in interchange with After Effects, and Automatic Duck's Pro

Import AE plug-in provides very similar functionality to Final Cut Pro and Avid users.

Pro Import AE is able to translate the basic structure of the timeline as well as many of the small details. Parameters from FCP's Motion tab such as Scale, Center, Rotation, and Opacity, mirroring similar parameters from Avid effects such as Picture-In-Picture, Superimpose, and 3D Warp, translate into a layer's Scale, Position, Rotation, and Opacity settings. Speed changes and Time Remapping similarly translate. Even parameters that are animated with keyframes in FCP's Motion tab or Avid's Effect mode have those same keyframes and values appear in After Effects. Many third-party plug-ins also translate, along with blending modes, cropping, and feathering; you even get access to your entire media file in After Effects, so you can actually adjust clip edit points without needing to revert back to your NLE.

Automatic Duck first started shipping the Pro Import AE plug-in in 2001, so the company has been doing these timeline translations for a while now and are well-known around the world for producing the industry's best options for timeline translation. At the time of this writing Pro Import AE was shipping in version 5.0 and was compatible with After Effects CS3, CS4, and CS5.

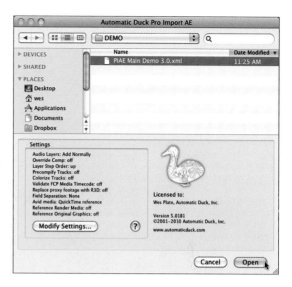

Figure 15.16 The Automatic Duck Pro Import AE Import window. Screenshot: Wes Plate.

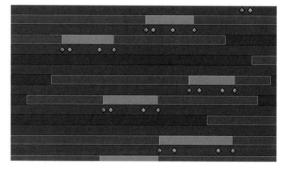

Figure 15.17 A timeline of footage brought into AE from FCP using Automatic Duck Pro Import AE. Screenshot: Wes Plate.

## Working Boris XML Transfer from Final Cut Pro to After Effects

**Boris XML Transfer** ($299) allows users to effortlessly import Final Cut Pro into After Effects, carrying over all of the Boris Continuum Complete and Final Effects Complete effects and their settings. The Final Cut Pro clips are fully editable in After Effects and it will preserve multiclips and subclips, layer/composite modes, audio settings, time effects such as freeze frames and time remapping, and comments and labels. Boris XML Transfer is Mac only.

The process of using Boris XML Transfer is simple. We will first export an XML file from Final Cut Pro and import it into After Effects.

1. In Final Cut Pro, select the sequence to export in the bin. Go to File > Export > XML. (Figure 15.18.)
2. In the Export XML… dialog window use the following settings:
   • Format: Apple XML Interchange Format

**Figure 15.18** Export XML Dialog. Screenshot: Michele Yamazaki.

- Options: Check Include Master Clips Outside Selection
- Check Save Project with latest clip metadata (recommended)

**3.** Name the XML file and choose the destination to save the file. Click OK.

**4.** Open After Effects. Go to File > Import > Final Cut XML via Boris XML Transfer. Find the XML file on your drive.

**5.** For more options, click Import Settings when selecting your file on your drive. Choose the options you need, then click OK. (Figure 15.19.)

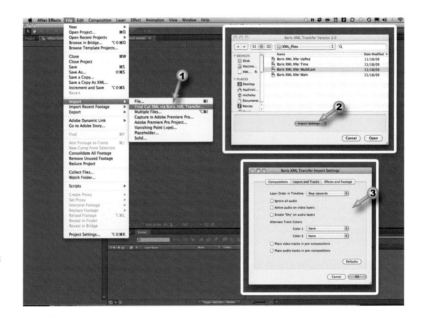

**Figure 15.19** 1. Import menu (*left*). 2. Locate the file on your drive and open Import Settings (*center*). 3. Import Settings (*right*). Screenshot: Michele Yamazaki.

**6.** When the import is complete, it will appear in the Project Panel. To open it, just click your sequence/comp. (Figure 15.20.)

If you're transferring over Boris Continuum Complete or Final Effects Complete effects from Final Cut Pro, you'll need to have them installed for both Final Cut Pro and After Effects.

One problem I've noticed with Boris XML Transfer, which is also an issue with Automatic Duck Pro Import AE, is that it does not keep the font settings from Final Cut Pro and will default to the last settings used in After Effects. You don't need to retype the text but the font face, color, and size are not retained. There are a few other small issues that are addressed in the User Guide PDF that comes with Boris XML Transfer, but they are fairly minor

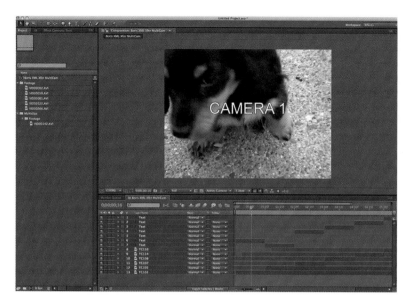

**Figure 15.20** The imported XML sequence, which was a multicam edit in Final Cut Pro. Footage: Michele Yamazaki.

issues. The plug-in will save so much time if you work between After Effects and Final Cut Pro.

## The Maxon Cinema 4D Exchange Plug-in for After Effects by Dr. Sassi

The **Maxon Cinema 4D Exchange Plug-in for Adobe After Effects CS5** is a free plug-in which enables an easy workflow from Cinema 4D to After Effects. This plug-in can safely be named an industry standard, as it has been, for years, used all over the world. It is available for free, even in 64-bit (CS5), for Windows and Macintosh. It delivers a huge amount of image and 3D data from Cinema 4D to After Effects. The most important feature of the plug-in is that it can deliver the motion information of an object, including Camera and Lights, in 3D space to After Effects, which can then be used to move the footage in After Effects accordingly.

The perspective in this tutorial is that of an After Effects artist, as you most likely are. The following tutorial represents the workflow you would use when you receive the files from a Cinema 4D artist. A complete workflow is provided on this book's accompanying DVD, as well as instructions on how to install the Maxon Cinema 4D Exchange plug-in.

Let's start with a simple example. To introduce this workflow, we'll use both a simple, as well as a more complex, scene as a base. Start with the Renderings_aec_folder, an almost empty scene. As with the more complex one, it covers the majority of the options available.

**Web Link**

Download the free **Plug-in for After Effects to Cinema 4D connection.** www. maxon.net/downloads/ updates/plugins.html. To install on the Mac, place the Cinema4DAE. plugin file in Applications > Adobe After Effects > Plug-ins on your hard drive. For Windows, put Cinema4DAE.aex in the :/Program Files/Adobe/ Adobe After Effects (CS5, CS4, etc.)/Support Files/ Plug-ins. Restart After Effects for the plug-in to work.

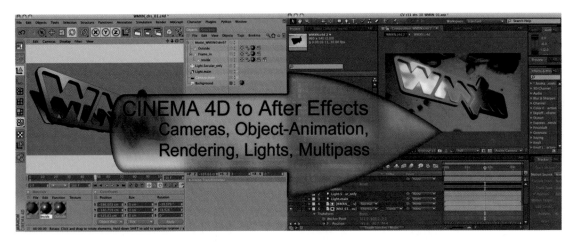

**Figure 15.21** The Maxon Cinema 4D Exchange Plug-in for After Effects. Screenshot: Dr. Sassi (V. Sassmannshausen, PhD).

*Cinema 4D project files are included on this book's DVD in a folder* named C4D to AE Simple, so that you can follow the process. There is also a more complex project in the C4D to AE Complex folder.

**Third party plug-ins needed:**
- Maxon Cinema 4D Exchange Plug-in for After Effects
  1. In After Effects, double-click in the Project panel to bring up the Import File dialog. Select the file WMXN.aec, on this book's DVD, and select open. Open the composition WMXN_drs_01.c4d. (Figure 15.22.)

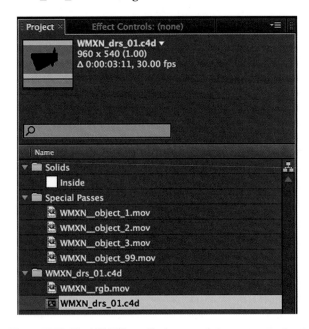

**Figure 15.22** The WMXN.aec Project panel. Screenshot: Dr. Sassi (V. Sassmannshausen, PhD).

**Figure 15.23** Click to turn off the lights. Screenshot: Dr. Sassi (V. Sassmannshausen, PhD).

2. In the timeline, click the Hide Video eyeball for the Light sources (Light.main and Light. Secular_only) to turn them off. (Figure 15.23.)

3. We're going to replace the Inside layer with the footage file named MVI_6186-MPEG-web.mov. First Import the folder Footage_water (File > Import). Three .mov files of water footage will be imported into a folder in the Project panel. In the timeline, select the Inside layer. Hold down Option (Alt) while dragging the MVI_6186-MPEG-web.mov footage onto the Inside layer. (Figure 15.24.)

4. While keeping the Inside layer selected, press the T key and set the Opacity to 100%. Then press the S key to Scale the new footage so it covers the front of the logo. (Figure 15.25.)

5. *Note*: You can adjust the timing of the new clip a bit, but don't move the keyframes.

6. To have the light and shadows available, set this MVI_6186-MPEG-web.mov layer to Overlay in the Blending Modes (for 8- or 16-bit, with this example). To move or rotate the footage, use the Anchor Point or Orientation. Do not use Position or X, Y, or Z Rotation. These are already keyframed. (Figure 15.26.)

7. Drag WMXN_object_1.mov file from the Special Passes Folder in the Project panel and place it above MVI_6186-MPEG-web.mov in the timeline. These Special Passes files are Object Buffers (the C4D term) and are used like alpha channels.

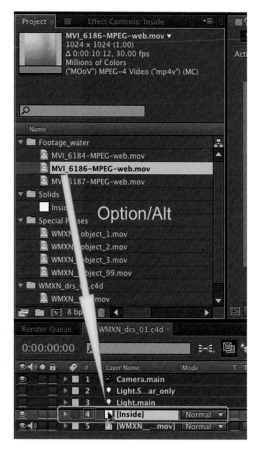

**Figure 15.24** Select the Inside layer in the timeline, and then hold down Option (Alt) while dragging the water footage into the Inside layer to replace it. Screenshot: Dr. Sassi (V. Sassmannshausen, PhD).

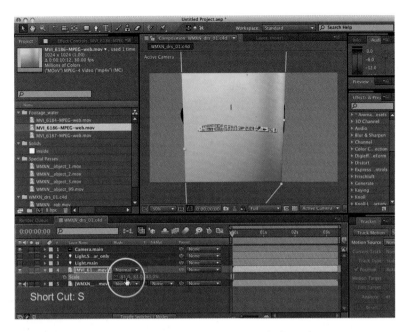

**Figure 15.25** Scale the Water Footage movie to cover the logo. Screenshot: Dr. Sassi (V. Sassmannshausen, PhD).

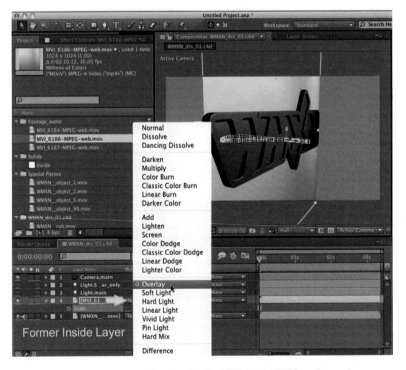

**Figure 15.26** Set the Mode to Overlay for the MVI_6186-MPEG-web.mov layer. Screenshot: Dr. Sassi (V. Sassmannshausen, PhD).

**Figure 15.27**  Use a TrkMat for compositing the Object Buffer on the logo. Screenshot: Dr. Sassi (V. Sassmannshausen, PhD).

8. In the timeline, set the TrkMat for MVI_6186-MPEG-web. mov to Luma-Matte. This utilizes the Object Buffer like an alpha channel so that it fills only a portion of the logo with the footage. (Figure 15.27.)

9. Save the project and create a RAM Preview. If you have a problem, compare this with the files in the Final folder. (Figure 15.28.)

This was a simple example, but there is also a more complex file in the folder C4D_to_Aecs5_cmplx on this book's DVD if you would like to explore further. The file contains a six-sided cube and has a bit more background (a cube cluster) and context. Each cube side has its own Object Buffer, as well as the frames, the text, and the cube itself, so you can easily set up an Adjustment Layer with those. With the more complex file you can explore your new pipeline skills more.

**Web Link**

For more on Cinema 4D, check out Cineversity at *www. cineversity.com*. Also, check the Help Content of Cinema 4D for all available and new features.

**Figure 15.28** The final WMXN logo composited with After Effects CS5. Screenshot: Dr. Sassi (V. Sassmannshausen, PhD).

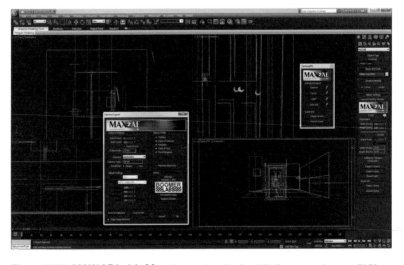

**Figure 15.29** MAX2AE in 3ds Max. Screenshot: Dr. Sassi (V. Sassmannshausen, PhD).

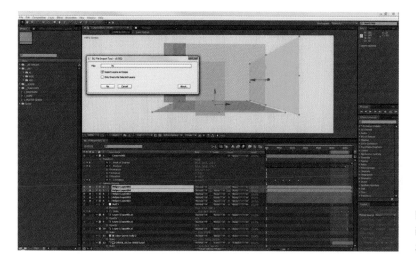

Figure 15.30 MAX2AE data importing into After Effects. Screenshot: Rhys Dippie.

## Boomer Labs MAX2AE for Autodesk 3ds Max to After Effects

**Boomer Labs MAX2AE** ($250) bridges the gap between After Effects and Autodesk 3ds Max for seamless 2D/3D integration, matching complex camera movements, lights, and objects between the two programs. It's the perfect tool for mixing 3D elements with live-action footage or 2D elements from After Effects, and, of course, allowing the use of plug-ins on 3D elements.

Here are some screenshots courtesy of Rhys Dipple of *www.assemblyltd.com*.

**Web Link**

For in-depth instruction, Alan Shisko has a great 45-minute tutorial on using MAX2AE (*http://bit.ly/max2ae*) that will get you started.

# MORE ON PLUG-INS: THE FAQ

This chapter contains information on the less scintillating but still very important topics of 64-bit plug-ins, memory allocation, and installation and deactivating plug-ins. It includes a lot of information on licenses, including floating licenses versus node-locked licenses, render-farm licenses, and how to find your Ethernet ID (commonly called a MAC address) when purchasing licenses for some plug-ins. Lastly, I've included contact information for plug-in developers. All information is subject to change, but was correct at the time of publishing. If you're in doubt, try Google.

## 64-Bit Platform in CS5 and Your Plug-ins

You've most likely heard a lot about 64-bit, but in case you haven't been paying attention, here it is in layman's terms. Adobe completely reengineered the After Effects CS5 release with native 64-bit support, which utilizes the RAM on your system for a major boost in speed and performance to the Adobe apps. Here is what you get.

1. **Longer RAM previews**: The new software architecture allows for much longer, faster RAM previews, even with full resolution and frame rate. The more RAM, the longer the previews.
2. **Larger RAM caching**: Renders will happen faster because of the improvements in caching.
3. **Speed increase**: Not only in previews and renders, but rapid switching between apps and working with Dynamic Link.
4. **Work in higher color bit depth**: If you've worked in 16-bit or 32-bit floating point color in the past, you'd have experienced very short RAM previews in After Effects. With CS5, the RAM previews can be much longer and at better resolution at higher color bit depths.

Your plug-ins will also take advantage of the reengineering in After Effects CS5. The drawback is that all plug-ins have to be updated to 64-bit native. Plug-ins that worked in CS4 won't work in CS5. Adobe realizes the importance of third-party plug-ins and made the SDK available to plug-in developers earlier than usual during the development of CS5 so that plug-ins could

Figure 16.1

**477**

be ready at the CS5 release, and many were. Toolfarm.com keeps a fantastic list of plug-ins that have been updated for Adobe After Effects CS5 and 64-bit compatibility. Many of the plug-ins are free updates, but some, like Trapcode and Red Giant, charge a nominal fee to upgrade. Some plug-ins have been around for close to a decade and that's a lot of aging code to rewrite, which takes a lot of engineering power, so it is surprising that more companies aren't charging for upgrades to CS5 compatible plug-ins.

## How Much Memory Is Allocated to After Effects?

To find out how much RAM is allocated to After Effects, look under After Effects > Memory & Multiprocessing. Although most of the time there should really be no reason to modify the memory settings, the portion of memory used by other applications can be increased, which will in turn decrease the amount for the Adobe applications. By lowering the amount of RAM allocated to After Effects, RAM previews will be shorter. This could be helpful if more memory is needed for applications such as Photoshop, Final Cut Pro, or other memory-intensive software. Note that the "RAM available for:" setting is shared among After Effects, Premiere Pro, Encore, and the Adobe Media Encoder.

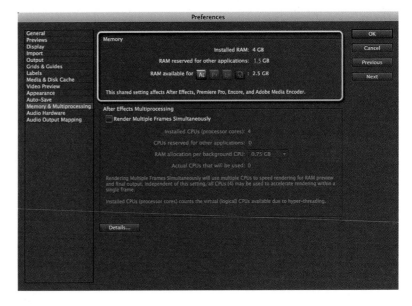

Figure 16.2 This screen shot was taken on a laptop with just 4 GB RAM installed. 2.5 GB is being reserved for the Adobe applications, even though After Effects is the only one running at the moment. 1.5 GB of RAM can be utilized by other applications on the computer. Screenshot: Michele Yamazaki.

## How to Install Plug-ins

Each plug-in will be different and some may have an installer while others may just have you drag the plug-ins to a folder on your computer. Here is some basic information about installation and troubleshooting installs that will apply to most plug-ins.

1. Before you install any plug-in, make sure After Effects is installed.
2. Make sure plug-ins are compatible with your version of After Effects. Most of the big players in the After Effects plug-ins market have updated their products for CS5, but check compatibility at the vendor's website if you are unsure. Also, check to see if your operating system is compatible with the plug-ins. Some require the most recent OS and some are Mac- or Windows-only.
3. Most plug-ins include an installer that will walk you through the process and put the plug-ins in the proper place. Many plug-ins will install inside the MediaCore folder, which allows for use of the plug-in inside either Premiere Pro or After Effects.
4. The majority of plug-in developers use unlockable trial versions or demos, so you can install a demo, and if you like it, purchase it and enter the serial number from the vendor. A few plug-ins will need a MAC address or another number that is specific to your computer. This is often the case with floating licenses, which will be explained later in this chapter.
5. Because each company's plug-ins are different, it's easier to just explain where the plug-ins end up: either in the MediaCore folder or in the After Effects Plug-ins folder. Plug-ins that are used in both After Effects and Premiere, and some that are not, are stored in the MediaCore folder. (Figures 16.3 and 16.4.)

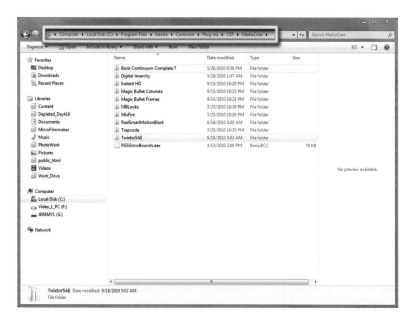

**Figure 16.3** Where plug-ins are stored on Windows: Program Files > Adobe > Common > Plug-ins > CS5 (or other version) > MediaCore.
Screenshot: Michele Yamazaki.

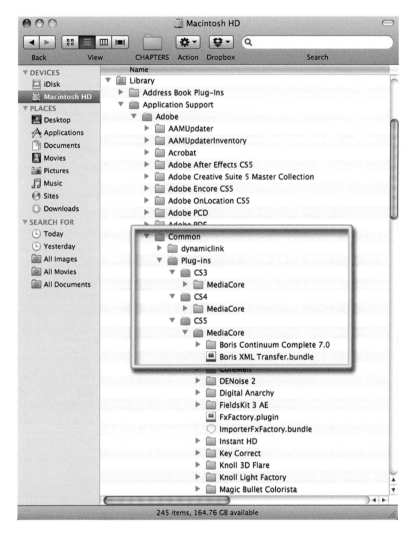

**Figure 16.4** Where plug-ins are stored on the Mac: Library > Application Support > Adobe > Common > Plug-ins > CS5 (or other version) > MediaCore or (user) > Library > Application Support > Adobe > Common > Plug-ins > (version) > MediaCore. Screenshot: Michele Yamazaki.

6.  Some plug-ins require you to drag them into the Plug-ins folder within the After Effects folder in your Applications folder. Other installers may put them there automatically. If you ever need to uninstall a plug-in and you don't see it in the MediaCore folder, check the Plug-ins folder. See the next section "Deactivating Plug-ins" for more on this.

   If you're like me and have pretty much every plug-in under the sun, and after a while the plug-ins end up being dumped in a folder called Other at the bottom of the plug-ins folder, that list of plug-ins can get very long. I use the Effects & Presets panel to find the plug-ins I need instead of the plug-ins menu because of this issue. All plug-ins will be in the proper place in the Effects & Presets panel.

## Deactivating Plug-ins

There are two ways to deactivate a plug-in without uninstalling.

1. Drag the plug-in out of the Plug-ins folder or MediaCore folder to some place else, like your desktop.
2. Find the plug-in in the MediaCore folder or the Plug-ins folder and add ¬, known as the "not character" before the name of the plug-in, for example: ¬twitch.plugin. This character is Option + L on the Mac and Alt + L on Windows. Relaunch After Effects and that plug-in will not show up in the list under the Effects menu. This is also useful when you have a conflict or plug-in that is giving you a problem.

## Node-Locked versus Floating Licenses

With a node-locked license, software can only be used on a single system.

Floating licenses, sometimes called concurrent or network licenses, allow anyone on the network to use the application, depending on the number of licenses available.

In the case of a dongle-based license, the dongle can only be used on one computer at a time, but can be moved from system to system.

## How to Move Plug-ins from After Effects CS5 to CS5.5 Without Reinstalling

If you have upgraded to After Effects CS5.5, you now have the daunting task of moving all of your plug-ins from AE CS5. Most of your plug-ins for After Effects CS5 should work just fine in After Effects CS5.5, however most do not have installers specifically for CS5.5 yet (as of this publishing). There is an easy way to work around this, a trick that will save you time because you won't need to reinstall all of your plug-ins again.

**How to Transfer CS5 Plug-ins to CS5.5 in Mac**: http://bit.ly/lg3eYB

**By How to Transfer CS5 Plug-ins to CS5.5 in Windows**, by Brandon Smith of Digieffects: http://bit.ly/kCwVJ2

## How to Transfer Licenses to a New Computer (or Uninstall Plug-ins)

Thanks to Jason Sharp and Toolfarm for help compiling this information.

*Adobe*

In the past I've had to uninstall my Adobe Suite because of a bug, but more likely you'll need to deactivate your Adobe software to reinstall it on a different computer.

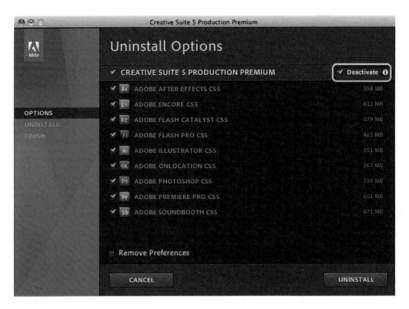

**Figure 16.5** The Adobe Application Manager for Production Premium CS5.
Screenshot: Michele Yamazaki.

1. Shut down all Adobe applications.
2. Make sure you are connected to the Internet before you deactivate.
3. In the Utilities folder, find the folder called Adobe Installers. In that folder lies the installer or uninstaller for the Adobe software. Double-click it and the Adobe Application Manager will open.
4. Check all of the applications that you want to uninstall and tick the Deactivate box in the upper right corner.
5. Also check Remove Preferences. If you're experiencing bugginess you probably want to remove them, and if you're removing the apps from the machine, you won't have use for the preferences, so it's best to just remove them.
6. Click uninstall.

*Automatic Duck*

Automatic Duck uses a Product ID that is tied to your computer's hardware, so the Product ID/activation code from your old computer will not work on your new one. Just get rid of it. You can only activate a plug-in a total of five times, with each activation occurring no less than 30 days between activations. I'm guessing the reason for this is because sneaky people may try to use one license on more than one computer by continuing to deactivate and reactivate it.

1. Install the Automatic Duck plug-in on your new system.
2. Go to my.automaticduck.com to reset your serial number. You'll need the email address that you used to register your plug-in in the first place. Click Reset.
3. Quit After Effects.
4. Throw away the key file. Where is this key file?
   **Mac OS X**:
   **Pro Import AE 5.0**: Library > Application Support > Automatic Duck > Supporting Files > AutoDuckImportAE5
   **Pro Import AE 4.0**: Library > Application Support > Automatic Duck > Supporting Files > AutoDuckImportAE4
   **Windows**:
   **Pro Import AE 5.0**: Program Files > Automatic Duck > Supporting Files > AutoDuckImportAE5
   **Pro Import AE 4.0**: Program Files > Automatic Duck > Supporting Files > AutoDuckImportAE4
5. Reactivate the plug-in on your new computer by launching After Effects and applying the plug-in to a layer. Enter all pertinent information in the registration dialog and then press the button labeled "This computer" to activate it. If you don't have Internet access and need to activate on another computer, click "Another computer."
6. Register the plug-in and you'll get a new activation code. Copy and paste the activation code into the activation dialog box.
7. Click Activate.

### Boris FX

You'll need to transfer your license to your new computer for Boris FX plug-ins.

1. Install your Boris plug-ins in After Effects and use the unlock code that you received with the download.
2. You'll need a Unique Product ID. To find it, apply a Boris filter, and press the Register button.
3. Copy and paste the Unique Product ID and mail it in a license transfer request to support@borisfx.com, or to the reseller you purchased from, and they'll send you a new permanent code. Enter it and you're good to go.

### Digieffects

Digieffects makes it very easy to move from one computer to another—just reinstall the plug-ins on the new machine. You do not need to uninstall on your previous system. The license is cross-platform so you can transfer between Mac and Windows. After transferring, delete the plug-ins from your old computer.

### The Foundry

To obtain a new license key, fill out the license transfer form at The Foundry's website thefoundry.co.uk.

### GenArts Sapphire

Sapphire licenses are cross-platform, making it easy to transfer your serial number between a Windows and Mac system. To transfer a license:

1. Uninstall Sapphire plug-ins.

    On Windows: Go to Start > Control Panel > Add or Remove Programs. Locate GenArts Sapphire Plug-ins in the list. Press the Change/Remove button.

    On Mac: Go to the Applications > GenArtsSapphireAE folder and launch the Uninstall Sapphire application by double-clicking it.

2. During the uninstall process, there is an option to register that uninstall over the web, untying it from the computer. If the uninstall is registered, you will be able to reinstall the same serial number on your other machine.

### Imagineer Systems

You must transfer the license to the new computer. Send a request to Imagineer at support@imagineersystems.com to transfer the license. Imagineer will send you instructions on how to transfer the license.

### Noise Industries FxFactory Pro

FxFactory has an uninstall function built into it. Run the FxFactory application. Under the Actions menu you will find Uninstall FxFactory. When you run the uninstaller, the FxPacks are also removed. Reinstall on the new machine.

If you wish to uninstall FxPacks you can also do this by launching the FxFactory application.

1. Turn FxPacks on or off by ticking the checkbox to the left of each FxPack.
2. Completely remove an FxPack by dragging it out of the FxFactory application and into the trash.

### Red Giant Software

Red Giant, like Digieffects, makes it very easy to move plug-ins to your new system—just reinstall. No need to uninstall on your old computer. The licenses are cross-platform so you can transfer between Mac and Windows as well. After transferring, delete the plug-ins from your old computer.

### RE:Vision Effects

You must contact RE:Vision Effects and request a license transfer. Include your serial number with the request. You'll need to remove the plug-ins off of your old machine. *Note*: Depending on the host, there may be a charge to transfer a license.

You can alternately run the ipconfig utility in DOS, which will display TCP/IP information for the network. For instructions for your operating system, go to *http://156.111.235.97/ip/ipmac.html*.

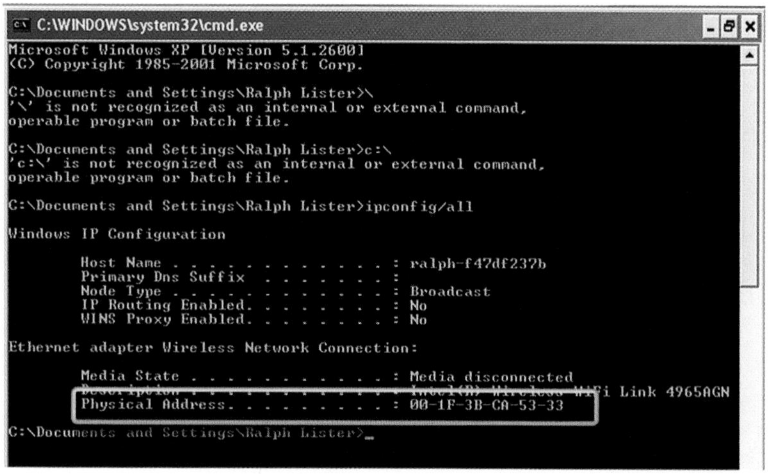

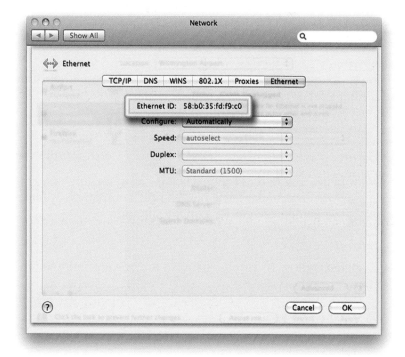

**Figure 16.6** The Ethernet ID for a Windows computer is found in the Network Connection Details info box. Screenshot: Michele Yamazaki.

**Figure 16.7** The Ethernet ID for an Apple computer is in the System Preferences > Network. Click the Advanced button. The Ethernet ID is under the Ethernet tab. Screenshot: Michele Yamazaki.

## Plug-ins in Render Farms: Specific Render Farm Policies

A render license allows a user to render on another computer without owning a full license of the plug-in. With a render-only license, no changes can be made to the effect. All added effects and changes to settings must be done on the main computer. Several company's individual policies are listed below. *Note*: Prices are correct at time of publishing but may have changed. If you do not see a plug-in listed, you likely need to buy a full license for each render node.

### ABSoft Neat Video

No render licenses. A full version must be bought for render farms. Multiuser licenses are available.

### Alien Skin

Although Alien Skin Eye Candy for After Effects has been discontinued, if you are running it on an older system you get a free install on all render-only computers.

### Boris FX

1. Boris Final Effects Complete: 5-pack of render-only licenses $895 or $199 each
2. Boris Continuum Complete: 5-pack of render-only licenses $895 or $199 each
3. Boris Native Filter Suite (Final Effects Complete and Continuum Complete): $219 per render license.

### Cycore

If you're using the CycoreFX HD version (not the one that ships with After Effects) network licenses are required.

1–9 CPUs are $79 per CPU.

A site license is $790 (unlimited CPUs).

### Digital Element

For Aurora Sky and Aurora Water, a license must be purchased for each machine in a render farm, however the company may make special arrangements depending on the situation.

### Digieffects

All Digieffects plug-ins can be installed for free on multiple render farm machines.

### Digital Anarchy

All render-only nodes are allowed a free install of Beauty Box.

### Digital Film Tools

There is no need to purchase render licences for Digital Film Tools or Tiffen plug-ins, just install the plug-ins on the render farm machine at no additional charge. Multiple licenses are only needed if the full GUI of After Effects is running.

### Frischluft

Install on all render-only nodes for Flair and Lenscare at no additional charge.

### GenArts

Render licenses for Sapphire are free, and you may install the full version on any number of render only machines.

### Pixelan

Free install on all render-only nodes.

### Red Giant/Trapcode

Red Giant has a 5-for-1 policy: For every single-user license purchased, the plug-ins can be installed on up to 5 render-only machines for free. If you need more than 5 installs for a render farm you'll need to buy another full license.

1. Magic Bullet Suite, Primatte Keyer, and Knoll Light factory do not require serial numbers for render-only machines. The render-only version is a faceless render-only version.
2. Composite Wizard, Film Fix, Image Lounge, Instant HD, Key Correct Pro, and Magic Bullet Colorista may be installed on render-only machines but do require a serial number. These plug-ins use the 5-for-1 policy.
3. For Trapcode, install normally on render-only nodes.

### RE:Vision Effects

1. RE:Flex and Twixtor Pro: $119 each for render-only licenses
2. PV Feather: $13.99 each for render-only licenses
3. Shape/Shade and FieldsKit: $17.99 each for render-only licenses
4. ReelSmart Motion Blur: $29.99 each for render-only licenses
5. RE:Map: $29.95 each for render-only licenses
6. SmoothKit, Video Gogh, and RE:Fill do not have render-only licenses but RE:Vision Effects will do a custom quote on a per-case basis

### Synthetic Aperture

Synthetic Aperture offers free install on all render-only nodes for Echo Fire, Color Finesse, and Test Gear.

*Tiffen*

Get free rendering on render farms with Tiffen Dfx and Digital Film Tools plug-ins, with no need for a render license on the render farm machine. Multiple licenses are only needed if the full GUI of After Effects is running.

*Ultimatte Corporation*

A render-only version of Ultimatte is available for $49.

*Video Copilot*

Each Optical Flare license can be installed on a maximum of 5 render-only computers. Unique license files are needed. Contact Video Copilot to set it up.

*Zaxwerks*

Zaxwerks 3D Invigorator Pro allows for free installs on render-only nodes. 3D Invigorator Classic will not work on a network.

## How to Contact a Company if You Need Support

(e-mail/phone contact list courtesy of Toolfarm.com)
- Automatic Duck: duckquestions@automaticduck.com; 1-7755-Duck-75
- Boomer Labs: support@boomerlabs.com
- Boris FX: 1-888-772-6747
- Conoa: getinfo@conoa.com
- CoreMelt: sales@coremelt.com
- CycoreFX: support@cycorefx.com; +46 (0) 18-509040 (Sweden)
- Digieffects: support@digieffects.com
- Digital Anarchy: 415-830-3689
- Digital Element: customer_support@digi-element.com
- Digital Trove: support@digitaltrove.com
- The Foundry: support@thefoundry.co.uk
- Frischluft: support@frischluft.com
- GenArts: support@genarts.com
- LME: tburroughs@little-men.com
- Meta|DMA: support@metadma.com
- Noise Industries: support@noiseindustries.com
- Pixelan: Michael Feerer: michael@pixelan.com
- Red Giant Software: 1-260-918-4505
- RE:Vision Effects: techsupport@revisionfx.com

- Synthetic Aperture: support@synthetic-ap.com
- Tiffen: techsupport@tiffen.com
- Toolfarm: sales@toolfarm.com
- Trapcode: 1-260-918-4505
- Ultimatte: support@ultimatte.com
- Video Copilot: support@videocopilot.net
- Zaxwerks: 1-626-309-9102

# INDEX

Page numbers followed by *f* indicates a figure and *t* indicates a table.